S0-CVK-373

THE MODERN MIDDLE EAST

PEOPLE, CULTURE, AND EVERYDAY LIFE

Edited by **Ozan Say**

Bridgewater State University

cognella®
academic publishing

Bassim Hamadeh, CEO and Publisher
Michael Simpson, Vice President of Acquisitions
Jamie Giganti, Senior Managing Editor
Miguel Macias, Graphic Designer
John Remington, Senior Field Acquisitions Editor
Monika Dziamka, Project Editor
Brian Fahey, Licensing Specialist
Claire Yee, Interior Designer

First published in the United States of America in 2016 by Cognella, Inc.

Cover image copyright © 2013 by Depositphotos / mrfiza

Printed in the United States of America

ISBN:978-1-62661-802-2 (pbk) / 978-1-62661-803-9 (br)

www.cognella.com   800-200-3908

Contents

SECTION 6

POLITICS AND PROTEST

MIDDLE EAST: HISTORY, GEOGRAPHY, AND PERCEPTIONS

section One

A Brief Introduction to the Middle East

by OZAN SAY

WHAT'S IN A NAME?

IN THE AGE OF THE INTERNET AND RAPID TECHNOLOGICAL development in which we live now, we usually have a vague sense of the relative novelty of things that are taken for granted. For instance, although Ray Tomlinson is credited with inventing electronic mail in 1972, the widespread and commercial use of e-mail started only in the mid-1990s. E-mail "remains the most important application of the Internet and the most widely used facility it has" (Peter 2004), yet it is already being overshadowed by social media as a form of communication. Even though we are aware that it is a fairly new invention, to realize that e-mail has been a part of our lives for only two decades can still be quite surprising to us.

Associating novelty and invention with technology is perhaps not a challenging thought, but how about the geopolitical and cultural concepts and entities that we use today? Phenomena such as the "nation," "nation-state," and "nationalism," for instance, are novel creations of the last two centuries, but for many it might be difficult to conceive a world system without them,

1

even though most of human history unfolded in the absence of these concepts. Of course, there are certain processes that help conceal the fact. For instance, when we think of particular nation-states that are recently established, we usually assume them to be more ancient in origin. This is the exact process that British historians Eric Hobsbawm and Terence Ranger elaborated upon in their 1983 book, *The Invention of Tradition*, in which they analyzed how and why different traditions are invented and what purposes these traditions have and continue to serve. Hobsbawm suggested that "'Traditions' which appear or claim to be old are often quite recent in origin and sometimes invented" (Hobsbawm 2012: 1). His assertion was that invented traditions were particularly relevant to the discussion of the recent historical innovation called the "nation," as well as to its associated phenomena, such as nationalism, the nation-state, national symbols, and histories:

> All these rest on exercises in social engineering which are often deliberate and always innovative, if only because historical novelty implies innovation. Israeli and Palestinian nationalism or nations must be novel, whatever the historic continuities of Jews or Middle Eastern Muslims, since the very concept of territorial states of the currently standard type in their region was barely thought of a century ago, and hardly became a serious prospect before the end of World War I. ... We should not be misled by a curious, but understandable, paradox: modern nations and all their impedimenta generally claim to be the opposite of novel, namely rooted in the remotest antiquity, and the opposite of constructed, namely human communities so "natural" as to require no definition other than self-assertion (ibid.: 13–14).

Because of the territorial nature of the conflict between Israel and Palestine, Hobsbawm singles out these nations and nationalisms to highlight his point about the paradox between apparent novelty and dubious claims of antiquity, and discusses how constructed historical narratives are utilized to strengthen the legitimacy of a claim to a geographical region, self-autonomy, or even to solidify a sense of group identity to serve a nationalist agenda. Of course, much like the concept of territorial states, the geopolitical and cultural term "Middle East" is relatively new, considering the actual history of the region. Although the Middle East is not an invented tradition itself, Hobsbawm's constructivist framework can help us to understand that the *term* "Middle East" was invented and has a particular history. Acknowledging the constructed nature of this term would mean that we need to see it as a product of a certain socio-historical moment in time that is imbued with political, social, and cultural meanings and symbolism. Furthermore, the naming of an object, concept, place, or a whole region—as is the case here—is a cultural practice, and, as Lévi-Strauss has pointed out, it is also a mode of classification (Lévi-Strauss 1966). The question, then, is when, and in what context, was the term "Middle East" invented?

In the 1960s and '70s, there was an intensive discussion among American historians about the origins of the term "Middle East" (Davison 1960; Lewis and Holt 1962; Keddie 1973; Carleton 1975; Koppes 1976). One of the things about which all scholars agree regarding the origin of the term is that it is decisively Eurocentric and was not coined by the native inhabitants of the region. The first usage of the term is usually attributed to an American naval officer, Captain Alfred Thayer Mahan, who had been writing articles on naval affairs and strategy at the turn of the twentieth century. In a piece he authored for the September 1902 issue of the London-based magazine *National Review*, titled "The Persian Gulf and International Relations", he wrote: "The Middle East, if I may adopt a term which I have not seen, will someday need its Malta, as well as its Gibraltar" (Koppes 1976: 95). However, it was not Mahan, but Sir Ignatius Valentine Chirol, the director of the foreign department of the British daily newspaper *The Times*, who popularized the term when he began publishing a series of articles titled "The Middle Eastern Question," beginning on October 14, 1902 (only two months after Mahan's publication), in which he also credited Mahan with having "aptly christened 'the Middle East'" (Davison 1960: 667).

Although historian Clayton Koppes gives the same account as Roderic Davison (as well as Bernard Lewis and Peter Holt) regarding the coinage of the term by Mahan and its popularization by Chirol, he also reveals an earlier use of the term by a British officer, General Sir Thomas Edward Gordon, in 1900, and suggests that there is evidence to infer that the term "Middle East" may have already gained broader currency by that time (Koppes 1976). First of all, the term appears in the title of Gordon's article, "The Problem of the Middle East", which was published two and a half years before Mahan's piece. The first sentence of Gordon's article, quoted by Koppes, reads: "It may be assumed that the most sensitive part of our external policy in the Middle East is the preservation of the independence and integrity of Persia and Afghanistan." Accordingly, Koppes suggests:

The title and first sentence of the general's article, the only times he designated the area as the "Middle East" in the essay, contain the earliest uses of the term to come to light. Gordon neither claimed to be coining a new term nor felt it necessary to define the area for his readers. This suggests that Gordon himself may not have invented the term and that it may have been gaining currency, at least among persons conversant with the region (ibid.: 96).

Whether one credits Mahan, Gordon, or someone else with coining the term "Middle East," it is clear that it emerged sometime around the turn of the twentieth century, and the context around the birth of the term is decidedly European, or even more specifically, British, political and military strategy. Marshall Hodgson, a prominent historian of Islam, points out this fact as the basis of his preference of the phrase "Nile to Oxus" over the "Middle East":

> Its principal disadvantage stems from its relatively exact military usage, where it originated. It cuts the Iranian highlands in half—the western half ("Persia") being assigned to the Mediterranean command, the eastern half ("Afghanistan") to the Indian command ... Unfortunately, the military usage as to the eastern limits of coverage has become standard in a great many works using the phrase "Middle East" (Hodgson 1974: 60–61).

Although Hodgson is somewhat correct in his assertion that the British military divisions that excluded Afghanistan from the "Middle East" correspond to the area many scholars have in mind when they use the term, the limits of the region are far from clear even today, and there is virtually no decisive definition of the borders of the "Middle East." The problem regarding this lack of definition goes back to the region's origins. For instance, although Mahan might have coined the term, as Roderic Davison points out, "[he] drew no exact bounds. For him the Middle East was an indeterminate area guarding a part of the sea route from Suez to Singapore" (Davison 1960: 667). Chirol, on the other hand, had a much wider area in mind, as he included "the approaches to India, land and sea: Persia, the Gulf, Iraq, the eastern coasts of Arabia, Afghanistan, and Tibet" (ibid.). General Gordon similarly never defined the area that corresponded to the term. Based on Gordon's service in India and Persia, Koppes suggests that Gordon's "Middle East" "would include basically the approaches to India and would be less inclusive than the term has become"

(Koppes 1976: 96). It is clear that the forefathers of the term had a rather vague and emergent idea about the boundaries of the area to which they were referring in their political analysis.

ANTECEDENTS: ORIENT, LEVANT, NEAR EAST

The problem regarding the definition of the boundaries of the Middle East also has to do with the relationship between this term and its antecedents, which are still sometimes synonymously used today. These are, namely, the "Orient," the "Levant," and the "Near East".

One of the definitions of the word "Orient" in *The Oxford English Dictionary* is, "The rising of the sun; daybreak, dawn" which reflects the Latin origin of the term. However, in the last few centuries, when the term "Orient" was used, the meaning evoked was not this original one, but the first entry provided by the OED:

> That part of the world situated to the east of a particular point; eastern countries, or the eastern part of a country; the East.

> Originally used with reference to countries lying immediately to the east of the Mediterranean or Southern Europe (i.e., east of the Roman Empire); now usually understood to mean East Asia, or occasionally Europe or the Eastern hemisphere, as opposed to North America" (Orient, n. and adj. 2004).

Although "Orient" generically means "the East," notice that it is situational: its definition takes a particular region or country as the central point. The center that has defined "the East" has always been situated in Europe, whether it was the Roman Empire or the colonial empires since the age of exploration. Although the original designation of the word indicated areas in the Eastern and Southern Mediterranean that are a part of, or situated in close proximity to, our modern conception of the Middle East, the Orient kept expanding to the east to include East Asia. As such, the term actually encompasses both the "Middle East" and the "Far East," and it is possible to find usages in which "Orient" is used to mean one or the other, or both, of these regions.

The term "Levant" is also etymologically derived from the rising of the sun, but this time from French. That is why, geographically speaking, it is almost synonymous with the Orient, "The countries of the East." However, its meaning is more specific, as it is also defined, according to the OED, as: "The eastern part of the Mediterranean, with its islands and the countries adjoining" (Levant, n.1 1902). The usage of the term in English dates back to 1497 and has usually been used to refer to the very eastern corner of the Mediterranean, where the countries of Cyprus, Syria, Lebanon, Israel, Palestine, and Jordan are located today. In addition to this core area, some- times the word's meaning was expanded to include present-day Turkey, Egypt, and Iraq as well. The term was, however, rarely used to include the Arabian Peninsula or Persia, so it is much narrower than current conceptions of the Middle East.

Perhaps, among these three corollary terms, the "Near East" is the closest to, and more likely to replace, the "Middle East," whereas "Levant" and "Orient" are mostly outdated. The OED defines "Near East" as: "The region comprising the countries of the eastern Mediterranean, formerly also sometimes including those of the Balkan peninsula, southwest Asia, or North Africa. The region defined by *Near East* is impre- cise, allowing for some overlap with *Middle East*" (Near East, n. 2003). It encompasses a much broader area than the "Levant," but, as is the case with all these terms, there is not a precise definition of the corresponding region. The term "Near East" was used to refer to the Ottoman Empire, the nearest eastern neighbor of Europe, at the height of its territorial expansion in the late seventeenth and early eighteenth centuries. Eventually it came to be used in connection with the so-called "Eastern Question," when the Ottoman Empire was described by Tsar Nicholas I of Russia, right before the Crimean War (1853–1856), as the "sick man of Europe" (Anderson 1966; Fromkin 2009). Iran and Afghanistan, although they were never a part of the Ottoman Empire, were also sometimes included in the area covered by the term "Near East." Despite these kinds of expansions, though, the term was also narrowed down, especially as used in archeology. British archeologist David George Hogarth opens his 1902 book, *The Nearer East*, by roughly defining the term:

> The Nearer East is a term of current fashion for a region which our grandfathers were content to call simply The East. Its area is generally understood to coincide with those classic lands, historically the most interesting on the surface of the globe, which lie about the eastern basin of the Mediterranean Sea; but few probably could say off-hand where should be the limits and why. … Our region … will embrace all

south-eastern Europe below the long oblique water-parting of the Balkans; all the islands eastward of Corfu and Crete, which themselves are included; all of the north-eastern corner of Africa that is fit for settled human habitation and all of Asia that lies on the hither side of a truly distinctive natural boundary (Hogarth 1902: 1–3).

Hogarth's archeological "Nearer East" basically consisted of ancient Greece, Macedonia, Anatolia, the Eastern Mediterranean, Egypt, Mesopotamia, and Persia. His definition includes the Balkans or southeastern Europe, which is rarely considered a part of the "Middle East" today, but leaves out larger regions such as the Arabian Peninsula and North Africa (except for Egypt). In any case, the archeological concept of Near East still has much currency (not in its original cumbersome "Nearer" form, but simply as "Near"), whereas the geopolitical usage of the term as synonymous with the Ottoman Empire has fallen out of favor. Dr. Alford Carleton, who spent thirty years in Turkey and Syria—first as a missionary teacher for the Near East Mission and later as an ordained minister of the Congregational Church and the president of the Aleppo College in Syria—elaborates on the transition from the "Near East" to "Middle East" rather well, based on his personal experience in the region (Oberlin College Archives 2015). In his response regarding the discussion of the "whys and wherefores of the terms Near East and Middle East" that took place in the July 1973 issue of the *International Journal of Middle East Studies*, he wrote:

> I went to the *Near East* in 1924 as a teacher, working in Turkey and Syria. By the time I gave up permanent residence there, thirty years later, it was from the *Middle East* that I returned to reside in America. I happen to know the real reasons for so dramatic a change, lying deep in the politics and rivalries of the Allied Powers (Carleton 1975: 237).

As Carleton amusingly reflects based on his personal experience, the change from "Near East" to "Middle East" took place mostly during and after World War II, even though the latter term, as mentioned earlier, originated in, and was used since, the early 1900s. This shift was mostly a result of Cold War politics and the division of academic expertise into "area studies," both as an extension of American geopolitical interests and adherence to the premise that areas of expertise could neatly and sufficiently be divided and delineated from each other in order to legitimize their independent academic existence. The first attempts to create Middle East area studies programs began immediately after WWII, in 1946, "with the establishment of a training program in international administration at Columbia University, and Army Specialized Training Programs for languages at Princeton and the Universities of Indiana, Michigan and Pennsylvania. In 1947, Princeton founded the first inter-disciplinary program specializing in the modern and contemporary Middle East" (Hajjar and Niva 1997: 3).

WHERE IS THE MIDDLE EAST?

Although some of the corollary terms are still in use (especially the term "Near East" in the field of archeology), "Middle East" has become the *nom de guerre* for the region considered in this book. However, the fact remains that no one is really in agreement as to where the Middle East is. Academic, institutional, and political definitions of the region might have sound reasons for their chosen boundaries, but there is a clear lack of consensus.

For instance, in the World Fact Book, the CIA lists Armenia, Azerbaijan, Bahrain, the Gaza Strip, Georgia, Iran, Iraq, Israel, Jordan, Kuwait, Lebanon, Oman, Qatar, Saudi Arabia, Syria, Turkey, the United Arab Emirates, the West Bank, and Yemen as countries included under the term "Middle East" (CIA 2015). The CIA's "Middle East" interestingly includes the southern Caucasian countries of Armenia, Azerbaijan, and Georgia, which, despite their historical ties (especially to Iran and Turkey), are usually excluded from definitions of the Middle East due to their being a part of the former Soviet Union.

The World Bank, on the other hand, uses the term "MENA," an acronym for the "Middle East and North Africa," which has emerged recently and is used mostly in economic and business contexts as a substitute for the term "Middle East." This was partially done to ensure the inclusion of "North Africa" in the definition of the "Middle East" since this region, with the exception of Egypt, was not considered to be a part of the Middle East when the term emerged in the early twentieth century. According to the World Bank, MENA "is an economically diverse region that includes both the oil-rich economies in the Gulf and countries that are resource-scarce in relation to population, such as Egypt, Morocco, and Yemen," and, more specifically, includes Algeria, Bahrain, Djibouti, Egypt, Iran, Iraq, Israel, Jordan, Kuwait, Lebanon, Libya, Malta, Morocco, Oman, Qatar, Saudi Arabia, Syria, Tunisia, the United Arab Emirates, the West Bank and Gaza, and Yemen (The World Bank 2013). Besides the significant inclusion of North African countries on the coast of the Mediterranean, as mentioned earlier, another minor addition is that of Djibouti, which, together with Sudan and Somalia, is sometimes considered to be a part of the Middle East. Turkey, however, has left the "MENA" and joined the ranks of "Europe and Central Asia" for World Bank purposes.

The World Health Organization (WHO), however, does not use the term "Middle East" at all in its structure of regional offices in the world, but instead curiously uses the label "Eastern Mediterranean Region" by seriously extending the reaches of that coastline to include Afghanistan, Bahrain, Djibouti, Egypt, Iran, Iraq, Jordan, Kuwait, Lebanon, Libya, Morocco, Oman, Pakistan, Qatar, Saudi Arabia, Somalia, Sudan, Syria, Tunisia, the United Arab Emirates, and Yemen (WHO 2015). Curiously, the WHO's "Eastern Mediterranean" lacks Israel in its structure, and Algeria, for some reason, is the only North African country that is not included in this region. Similar to the World Bank, the WHO excludes Turkey while adding outlier countries such as Sudan, Djibouti, Somalia, Afghanistan, and Pakistan into the "Eastern Mediterranean" region.

If similar inquiries are made in order to discern which countries are included in academic programs specializing in the Middle East, or how mass media outlets such as the BBC, CNN, Al Jazeera, *The New York Times*, and others divide their world coverage into areas, one is likely to find a different list for each program, institution, or media outlet. It seems that the definition of the Middle East depends on whomever is charged with the task of defining it. However, one might ask if there is any overlap amongst these definitions. For example, most definitions of the Middle East today include the coastal countries of the Eastern Mediterranean (Syria, Lebanon, Israel, Palestine, Jordan, and Egypt), countries on the Arabian Peninsula (Bahrain, Kuwait, Oman, Saudi Arabia, Qatar, the United Arab Emirates, and Yemen), and Iraq and Iran. With minor variations, these countries are likely to be included in the definition of the region today. Beside this common list of countries, possible additions to the definition of the Middle East include Turkey, coastal North Africa, the upper Nile Valley, the southern Caucasus, and Afghanistan.

Even though Turkey has very strong ties with the Middle East—largely because it represents what remains of the Ottoman Empire, which covered most of the geography we now call the Middle East from the fifteenth to early twentieth centuries—it is nonetheless seen as an outlier country and sometimes excluded from the definition of the region (see the World Bank and WHO lists above). Geographically speaking, Turkey is at a literal crossroads, as the Bosphorus in Istanbul not only divides the city in two (into the *Anadolu* [Anatolian] and *Avrupa Yakası* [European] sides), but also forms part of the boundary between the continents of Europe and Asia. The region called *Trakya* (Thrace or Eastern Thrace) is on the European continent and forms only 3 percent of Turkey's area, whereas most of the country is in Anatolia, and hence Asia. The perception of Turkey as being part of Europe has less to do with this relatively insignificant geographical claim and more to do with the political direction of the country toward "Westernization" and secularization (which began in the late eighteenth century during the Ottoman Empire and culminated in the establishment of the Turkish Republic in 1923), as well as with the geopolitical dynamics of the Cold War, during which Turkey became a member of NATO (North Atlantic Treaty Organization) in 1952. Of course, this political movement has never been unidirectional, and Turkey has been positioned between Europe and the Middle East, both from within and from the outside. Especially since the rise of the so-called "Neo-Ottomanism" in Turkish politics in recent decades, Turkey's place at the crossroads, and its future direction, have been the subjects of much scholarly and strategic debate (Yavuz 1998; Taspinar 2008; Fisher Onar 2009). Nonetheless, regardless of past, current, or future political leanings, and despite its geographic leap into Europe, Turkey has always been an integral part of the Middle East and should be included in the definition of the region.

"North Africa," as mentioned earlier with regard to the "MENA" acronym, is usually considered to be a part of the Middle East today, but nineteenth-century definitions usually excluded this region, with the exception of Egypt. The term "North Africa" could be misleading, because within the context of the discussion of the borders of the Middle East, the referenced area corresponds to the present-day countries of Libya, Tunisia, Algeria, and Morocco, and not to the entire geographical area in the north of the African continent. As such, this definition roughly corresponds to the local term *"Maghrib,"* which emerged after the Arab Islamic conquest of the region in the seventh century. In *The Encyclopedia of Islam,* the term *"al-maghrib"* is defined as:

> the name given by Arab writers to that part of Africa which Europeans have called Barbary or Africa Minor and then North Africa, and which includes Tripolitania, Tunisia, Algeria and Morocco.
>
> The word *maghrib* means the west, the setting sun, in opposition to *mashri*, the east, the rising sun (Levant), but as Ibn Khaldūn remarks, the

general denomination was applied to a particular region. The extent of this area, moreover, varies according to different authors. Some oriental writers (e.g. al-Muḳaddasī) include in the *Maghrib* not only Northern Africa but also Sicily and Spain; the majority, however, reserve the name *Maghrib* for the first of these countries (Yver 2015).

Although there are some scholars who include Egypt in the definition of the *maghrib*, it is usually considered to be part of the *mashrik*. Similarly, there is disagreement as to whether Mauritania and the disputed territory of the Western Sahara on the northwestern coast of Africa are part of the *maghrib*; they are usually considered to be a part of this region by Arab geographers, but based on colonial divisions which considered these countries to be a part of West Africa, some scholars exclude them from their definitions (Eickelman 2002: 7).

What was formerly known as Sudan (which was the largest country in Africa and the Arab world until 2011)—or especially the northern part of that country that is now called the Republic of the Sudan—has been closely linked foremost to Egypt, but also to the wider Arab World, through language, religion, trade, ethnic ties, and geography (particularly via the Nile River). Sudan was also part of British-Egyptian colonial rule in the nineteenth century. Due to these ties, it is usually considered to be a part of the Middle East. Similarly, Afghanistan and the region known as the southern Caucasus, which mainly includes Georgia, Armenia, and Azerbaijan, are also areas that are sometimes included in the term "Middle East." Very much like Sudan, these countries have historical and cultural ties to the region, but for the purposes of this book we will exclude Mauritania, Western Sahara, the Republic of the Sudan, Azerbaijan, Georgia, Armenia, and Afghanistan from "our" definition of the Middle East.

This is more a practical exclusion than a clear demarcation of a cultural area, which rarely follows national borders anyway. One of the scholars who appropriately discussed the cultural area is anthropologist Charles Lindholm, and his demarcation comes close to the scope we will use in this book. Lindholm uses Marshall Hodgson's definition of "Nile to Oxus"—which, as mentioned before, he preferred to the term "Middle East"—as the cultural core region of Muslim society:

> The anthropological demarcation of the Middle East has generally followed Hodgson's notion of a cultural core, but moved the center to the west, excluding the Oxus region and placing it in Central Asia,

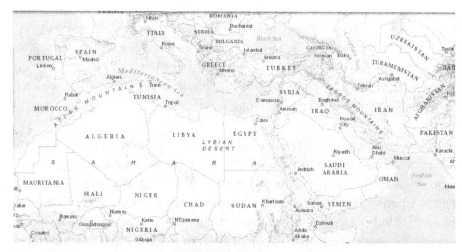

MAP 1: The wider Middle East region.

while expanding the Middle East to include North Africa (the so-called *Maghreb*, or "west"). For anthropologists, this distinction made sense because of marked differences between the two regions in terms of material culture and social practice. These differences led anthropologists to argue that the people of the Oxus belong to a different "trait complex" than the people of Maghreb, Arabia, and Persia. From this perspective it is not the pomp of the court, but local knowledge, material culture, and typical patterns of action that determine a cultural area.

If we accept the "trait complex" perspective we can delimit, albeit provisionally, the spatial range of the Middle East, which can be pictured as centered on the axis of north latitude 38, and extending from the southwest to the northeast over an expanse of approximately seven million square miles. It is bounded on the west by the Atlantic beaches of Morocco and stretches east across North Africa, into Arabia, through Iran, and finally merges into Central Asia and south Asia in northern Pakistan and southern Afghanistan. In the southwest, the region does not reach beyond the Sahara and in the southeast is halted by the Arabian Sea. In the north, the frontier is naturally set by three inland seas: the Mediterranean, the Black, and the Caspian, and then finally by the peaks of the Hindu Kush mountains (Lindholm 2002: 8).

Coming close to Lindholm's demarcation, the Middle East we will cover in this book will include: Morocco, Algeria, Tunisia, Libya, Egypt, Israel, Palestine, Jordan, Lebanon, Syria, Turkey, Iraq, Iran, Kuwait, Saudi Arabia, Bahrain, Qatar, the UAE, Oman, and Yemen.

UNDERSTANDING THE MIDDLE EAST

Now that we have tentatively defined the term "Middle East," let us look at some of the general characteristics of this region. Although we have spent some time in describing the historical, political, and cultural context that gave rise to the varying definitions of the Middle East (where there is still no clear agreement), in common usage the term seems more straightforward and self-evident. People have certain preconceived ideas about the Middle East on issues ranging from the role of religion in everyday life and politics to the general geographic features of the region. The late Palestinian-American literary scholar Edward Said's influential theory of

PHOTO 1: Camel caravan crosses the Sahara desert in Morocco. Image credit: Bachmont / CC BY 2.0. Source: http://www.sci-news.com/othersciences/paleo-climatology/science-sahara-desert-formed-7-million-years-ago-02160.html

"Orientalism," which has also led to much debate and controversy, primarily deals with the reasons for, and the process of, the production of such preconceived notions, and suggests that these are not neutral or innocent, but highly ideological (Said 1979). We will look at Said's arguments in the following chapters, but for now it is sufficient to mention that misrepresentations and stereotypical notions about the Middle East are widespread. Even though similar misconceptions exist about other regions or specific countries in the world, one cannot simply ignore this reality, especially given the fact that there is a certain asymmetry of power when it comes to representation. In addition, the stakes are much higher when we consider the consequences of these stereotypes and the effects that they have on the lives of Middle Easterners today. Having said that, though, we also need to be careful not to reinforce binaries between the so-called "East" and "West," in the sense that these preconceived notions are not simply held by "Westerners," but do exist even within the Middle East itself. That being the case, what are some of the ideas that we have when we think about the Middle East? What comes to mind when we hear the term "Middle East," regardless of the definition of its exact boundaries? Some of the common answers to these questions, in no particular order, fall under the general categories of geography, religion, ethnicity and language, gender, economy, and politics.

GEOGRAPHY

One of the most common images related to the Middle East is the desert, usually accessorized by a marching camel caravan with either the setting or rising sun in the background. The Middle East is an enormous region (approximately 4.65 million square miles), and has a very diverse physical geography. No doubt the region is home to some vast deserts, such as the Sahara Desert running across North Africa; the Arabian Desert, which almost entirely covers the Arabian Peninsula and is as big as a quarter of the US; the Syrian Desert in the Eastern Mediterranean that crosscuts Syria, Jordan, Iraq, and Turkey; and the Great Salt Desert (Dasht-e Kavir) and the Lut Desert (Dasht-e Lut) in Iran, which have a combined area of fifty thousand square miles. However, this region, which was home to some of the earliest civilizations, also contains high mountain ranges, inland seas and lakes, and significant river valleys (most notably the Nile River and the Fertile Crescent, formed between the Tigris and Euphrates Rivers).

This desert image is usually coupled with the assumption of a very hot and dry climate in the Middle East. Of course, in the desert areas the rainfall is very low and temperatures show great extremes, but as a result of a more diversified physical geography, the Middle East region as a whole is semi-arid: that is to say, the region receives precipitation below the level of potential evaporation. Furthermore, there are many areas in the region with diverse climate systems and microclimates with more than average rainfall or snow.

Another important aspect of the desert image has to do not with physical, but with human geography, e.g., the camel caravans that dot the landscape. Camel caravans usually connote a nomadic lifestyle, which has undoubtedly captured the romantic imagination of Euro-Americans. Camel nomads played an important role in trade for centuries, especially in areas with harsh terrain, and there are groups of people in the Middle East today who earn their living based on this geographic and economic lifestyle. Yet one must be careful with this image, given the fact that pastoral nomads have always been a small minority in this region, and the dominant form of nomadism has been transhumant pastoralism or seminomadism, a form of life more similar to seasonal migrants (Eickelman 2002: 11). Secondly, nomadism in general has been in decline in the region as a whole since the emergence of modern states and for political, economic, social, geological, and technological

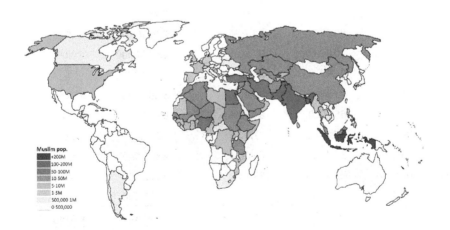

MAP 2: A map of Muslim populations by numbers (Pew Research Center 2009). Source: http://en.wikipedia.org/wiki/List_of_religious_populations#/media/File:Muslim_population_map.png

reasons. Today only a very small portion of Middle Eastern people are engaged in any form of nomadism.

Ranking of countries according to estimated 2010 and projected 2030 population that is Muslim. Compiled from Pew Research Center's Forum on Religious and Public Life (Pew Research Center 2011). *Source: Pew Research Center.*

RANK	COUNTRY	ESTIMATED 2010 MUSLIM POPULATION	PERCENTAGE OF 2010 POPULATION THAT IS MUSLIM	PROJECTED 2030 MUSLIM POPULATION	PROJECTED PERCENTAGE OF 2030 POPULATION THAT IS MUSLIM
1	Morocco	32,381,000	99.90%	39,259,000	99.90%
3	Tunisia	10,349,000	99.80%	12,097,000	99.80%
4	Iran	74,819,000	99.70%	89,626,000	99.70%
8	Yemen	24,023,000	99.00%	38,973,000	99.00%
9	Iraq	31,108,000	98.90%	48,350,000	98.90%
10	Jordan	6,397,000	98.80%	8,516,000	98.80%
13	Turkey	74,660,000	98.60%	89,127,000	98.60%
18	Algeria	34,780,000	98.20%	43,915,000	98.20%
19	Palestine	4,298,000	97.50%	7,136,000	97.50%
20	Saudi Arabia	25,493,000	97.10%	35,497,000	97.10%
22	Libya	6,325,000	96.60%	8,232,000	96.60%
27	Egypt	80,024,000	94.70%	105,065,000	94.70%
29	Syria	20,895,000	92.80%	28,374,000	92.80%
35	Oman	2,547,000	87.70%	3,549,000	87.70%
36	Kuwait	2,636,000	86.40%	3,692,000	86.40%
39	Bahrain	655,000	81.20%	881,000	81.20%
40	Qatar	1,168,000	77.50%	1,511,000	77.50%
41	UAE	3,577,000	76.00%	4,981,000	76.00%
45	Lebanon	2,542,000	59.70%	2,902,000	59.70%
63	Israel	1,287,000	17.70%	2,135,000	23.20%
		Total 2010	**Average %**	**Total 2030**	**Average %**
		439,964,000	87.89%	573,818,000	88.17%

RELIGION

It has become commonplace to see "the Middle East" and "Islam" as coterminous and to assume that the region is entirely inhabited by Muslims. It is true that the majority of the population of the Middle East consists of Muslims, and it is also true that, in terms of the percentage of Muslims within each country's population, Middle Eastern countries top the rankings. However, the assumption that the Middle East is the heartland of Islam in terms of the number of Muslims living in the world could not be further from the truth. According to *The Global Religious Landscape* report from the Pew Research Center's Forum on Religion and Public Life, based on 2010 figures:

> Although many people, especially in the United States, may associate Islam with countries in the Middle East or North Africa, nearly two-thirds (62%) of Muslims live in the Asia-Pacific region, according to the Pew Research analysis. In fact, more Muslims live in India and Pakistan (344 million combined) than in the entire Middle East-North Africa region (317 million).

> However, the Middle East-North Africa region has the highest concentration of Muslims of any region of the world: 93% of its approximately 341 million inhabitants are Muslim, compared with 30% in sub-Saharan Africa and 24% in the Asia-Pacific region (Desilver 2013).

The distribution of Muslims in the world can be seen in Map 2, where darker brown indicates a greater concentration of Muslims. It is clear from this map that Southeast Asia has the highest number of Muslims in the world. However, as Desilver states, in terms of the percentage of the population, most of the countries in the Middle East are more than 80 percent Muslim. Desilver puts the average percentage for the MENA region at 93 percent, but the Pew Research Center's definition of MENA includes Western Sahara and Sudan and excludes Turkey and Iran. If we use our own definition of the Middle East, the number of Muslims will be significantly higher than the above figures, and the percentage of Muslims will be slightly lower: in 2010, an estimated number of nearly 440 million Muslims, who constitute approximately 88 percent of the Middle Eastern population (see Table 1).

Although the region is predominantly Muslim, we must remember that the Middle East is also the birthplace of the two other Abrahamic religions which predate Islam: namely, Judaism and Christianity. Many of the holy sites and locations (such as the Sinai Peninsula and Desert, the Red Sea, Galilee, Judea, Babylon, Jerusalem, Alexandria, Cyrene, Antioch, Asia Minor, and Cappadocia) that are integral to the emergence and spread of these two religions are located in the region. Various sects of Jewish and Christian communities have called the Middle East their home for centuries. Jews make up the majority of the population in Israel: 5,855,200 people at about 75.4 percent of the total population, according to 2011 figures (Central Bureau of Statistics 2012). The most notable Christian communities in the Middle East are the Coptic, Maronite, Armenian, Greek Orthodox, and Assyrian, but there are also other smaller Orthodox, Catholic, and Protestant congregations throughout the region. Although the exact number of Christians in each country is hard to obtain due to lack of, or at best partial, census data, there is an estimated number of twelve to fifteen million Christians in the Middle East. The country with the highest number of Christians (approximately nine to ten million) is Egypt, but it is in Lebanon that Christians constitute the highest percentage of the total population at about 40 percent. Other countries with significant Christian minorities are Syria, Iraq, Iran, Jordan, Israel, Palestine, and Turkey. In addition to Judaism and Christianity, there are also Baha'i, Druze, Zoroastrian, Yazidi, Buddhist, and other lesser-known belief communities in the Middle East.

One must take care, however, in interpreting these numbers and percentages. As anywhere else in the world, declaration of religious affiliation does not necessarily indicate the level of an individual's engagement with religious practice and discourse. Very much like the vernacular phrase "Christmas/Easter Christians" in America and Europe, there are people in the Middle East who might identify as a Muslim, Jew, or Christian, but consider themselves "agnostic," "secular," "indifferent," "non-practicing," or some other label, suggesting a more complex relationship with religion. "Secular" is a highly problematic term and, in the context of the Middle East, the meaning of it is not restricted to personal belief, but includes hints of public and political identity. However, if we leave those aside and treat the term in its common-sense meaning, we can say that a significant segment of the Middle Eastern population is secular.

ETHNICITY AND LANGUAGE

The misconception of Middle Eastern people as being entirely Muslim usually follows from the identification of Middle Eastern populations as Arab and Arabic-speaking. First of all, the coupling of ethnicity and language regarding Arabs is not only not surprising but even appropriate since, despite difficulties in defining Arab ethnicity, Arabs comprise an ethnic group mostly based on linguistic commonality (Shoup 2011). Indeed, Arabs are the largest ethnic group in the Middle East, and Arabic, in its various forms, is the most commonly spoken language. Furthermore, except for in Turkey and Iran, Arabs constitute the dominant ethnic group in all of the remaining eighteen countries that we included in our definition of the Middle East. However, as a region that is located at the intersection of Asia, Europe, and Africa on major historical trade routes, and that has been the home to so many world civilizations from antiquity to today, the Middle East is bound to host a great diversity of ethnic groups and languages. Other than Arabs, there are significant numbers of Turkic, Indo-European, and other Semitic peoples living in the region today. All of these categories, including Arabs, cover numerous ethnic groups within them. For instance, Berbers can be classified as an Arab group since they predomi-nantly speak Arabic and share strong historical, social, and cultural ties with Arabs, but in certain cases they are also seen as a different ethnic group (Goodman 2005). We cannot fully cover the enormous range of ethnic groups with their similarities, differences, and overlaps here. Besides Arabs, in terms of numbers of people, the other major ethnic or ethno-religious groups are Persians, Turks, Kurds, Copts, and Jews. Other significant ethnic or ethno-religious minorities in the region include Assyrians, Armenians, Greeks, Maronites, Yazidis, Turkmens, Baluch, Circassians, Azeris, and Romanis (Pacini 1998; Nisan 2002; McKiernan 2006; Acikyildiz 2010; Chatty 2010; Longva and Roald 2012; Castellino and Cavanaugh 2013).

MORE MISCONCEPTIONS

Thus far we have touched upon some of the most common misconceptions, half-truths, and stereotypes about the Middle East regarding geography, religion, eth-nicity, and language. However, the list does not stop there, and it is common to hear stereotypical statements about many areas of Middle Eastern life: the status and role of women—mainly the suggestion that Middle Eastern women are oppressed, especially regarding the issue of veiling; the role of oil wealth (not its nature, production, or use) vis-à-vis political power and authoritarianism; or, especially in the post-9/11 climate, the "inclination" of Middle Easterners/Muslims/Arabs (used interchangeably and synonymously) toward terrorism and fundamentalism.

Both local and foreign anthropologists have tried to untangle these assumptions by pointing to the misconceptions and missing elements, and they attempt to historicize and contextualize each of these issues in order to provide a more complex picture of reality regarding each statement (among others, see Abu-Lughod 2002 and Keddie and Baron 2008 on the role of women in the Middle East; Al-Rasheed 2007 and Mitchell 2013 on oil, political power, and authoritarianism; and Mamdani 2005, Varisco 2005, and Soares and Osella 2009 on Islam, politics, and fundamentalism). In the following chapters we will look at some of these issues more closely, but let me already mention that the general rule about stereotypes applies to the Middle East as well. That is, stereotypes always stem from a form of truth or reality, and as such one can always find a situation or case that fulfills the prophesy. However, as usual, those truths or examples are partial at best or distorted at worst. Sensational and catchy though they may be, stereotypes are bound to be superficial. If one truly wishes to understand a group of people or a particular region, one needs to abandon the laziness of stereotypes and representations and start engaging with the complex, contradictory, and messy nature of reality.

BIBLIOGRAPHY

Abu-Lughod, Lila. 2002. Do Muslim Women Really Need Saving? Anthropological Reflections on Cultural Relativism and Its Others. *American Anthropologist* 104(3). New Series: 783–790.

Acikyildiz, Birgül. 2010. *The Yezidis: The History of a Community, Culture and Religion.* London; New York: New York: I. B. Tauris.

Anderson, Matthew Smith. 1966. *The Eastern Question, 1774–1923: A Study in International Relations.* Macmillan.

Carleton, Alford. 1975. "Near East" Versus "Middle East." *International Journal of Middle East Studies* 6(02): 237–238.

Castellino, Joshua, and Kathleen A. Cavanaugh. 2013. *Minority Rights in the Middle East.* First Edition. Oxford, UK: Oxford University Press.

Central Bureau of Statistics. 2012. "Population, by Religion". *Statistical Abstract of Israel.* http://www.cbs.gov.il/reader/shnaton/templ_shnaton_e.html?num_tab=st02 _02&CYear=2012, accessed May 12, 2015.

Chatty, Daw. 2010. *Displacement and Dispossession in the Modern Middle East. Contemporary Middle East*; 5. New York: Cambridge University Press.

CIA. 2015. *The World Factbook: Middle East.* https://www.cia.gov/library/publications /the-world-factbook/wfbExt/region_mde.html, accessed May 14, 2015.

Davison, Roderic H. 1960. Where Is the Middle East? *Foreign Affairs,* July: 665–675.

Desilver, Drew. 2013. *World's Muslim Population More Widespread Than You Might Think.* Pew Research Center. http://www.pewresearch.org/fact-tank/2013/06/07 /worlds-muslim-population-more-widespread-than-you-might-think/, accessed May 22, 2015.

Eickelman, Dale F. 2002. *The Middle East and Central Asia: An Anthropological Approach.* 4th edition. Upper Saddle River, N.J.: Prentice Hall.

Fisher Onar, Nora. 2009. *Neo Ottomanism, Historical Legacies and Turkish Foreign Policy. Centre for Economics and Foreign Policy Studies* (EDAM) Discussion Paper Series—2009/03.   http://trends.gmfus.org/doc/Discussion%20Paper%20 Series_Fisher.pdf, accessed May 18, 2015.

Fromkin, David. 2009. *A Peace to End All Peace: The Fall of the Ottoman Empire and the Creation of the Modern Middle East.* 20th Anniversary Edition. New York: Holt Paperbacks.

Goodman, Jane E. 2005. *Berber Culture on the World Stage: From Village to Video.* Bloomington; Indianapolis: Indiana University Press.

Hajjar, Lisa, and Steve Niva. 1997. (Re)Made in the USA: Middle East Studies in the Global Era. Middle East Report Middle East Studies Networks: The Politics of a Field (205): 2–9.

Hobsbawm, Eric. 2012. Introduction: Inventing Traditions. In *The Invention of Tradition.* Terence Ranger and Eric Hobsbawm, eds. Pp. 1–14. Cambridge University Press.

Hodgson, Marshall G. S. 1974. *The Venture of Islam: Conscience and History in a World Civilization.* Chicago: University of Chicago Press.

Hogarth, David George. 1902. *The Nearer East. Regions of the World.* London: W. Heinemann.

Keddie, Nikki R. 1973. Is There a Middle East? *International Journal of Middle East Studies* 4(3): 255–271.

Keddie, Nikki R., and Beth Baron, eds. 2008. *Women in Middle Eastern History: Shifting Boundaries in Sex and Gender.* Yale University Press.

Koppes, Clayton R. 1976. Captain Mahan, General Gordon, and the Origins of the Term "Middle East." *Middle Eastern Studies* 12(1): 95–98.

Levant, n.1. 1902. OED Online. Oxford University Press. http://www.oed.com .revproxy.brown.edu/view/Entry/107624, accessed May 14, 2015.

Lévi-Strauss, Claude. 1966. *The Savage Mind. The Nature of Human Society Series.* Chicago: University of Chicago Press.

Lewis, Bernard, and Peter Malcolm Holt, eds. 1962. *Historians of the Middle East. Historical Writings of the Peoples of Asia.* London: Oxford University Press.

Lindholm, Charles. 2002. *The Islamic Middle East: Tradition and Change.* Revised Edition. Malden, MA: Blackwell Pub.

Longva, Anh Nga, and Anne Sofie Roald, eds. 2012. Religious Minorities in the Middle East: Domination, Self-Empowerment, Accommodation. Social, Economic, and Political Studies of the Middle East and Asia, v. 108. Leiden ; Boston: Brill.

Mamdani, Mahmood. 2005. *Good Muslim, Bad Muslim: America, the Cold War, and the Roots of Terror.* Three Leaves Press.

McKiernan, Kevin. 2006. *The Kurds: A People in Search of Their Homeland.* First Edition. New York: St. Martin's Press.

Mitchell, Timothy. 2013. *Carbon Democracy: Political Power in the Age of Oil.* First Edition. London: Verso.

Near East, N. 2003. OED Online. Oxford University Press. http://www.oed.com .revproxy.brown.edu/view/Entry/125551, accessed May 14, 2015.

Nisan, Mordechai. 2002. *Minorities in the Middle East: A History of Struggle and Self-Expression.* Second Edition. Jefferson, N.C: McFarland & Co.

Oberlin College Archives. 2015. RG 30/385—Carleton Family Papers 1808–1853 (1973–1985), Biography/Administrative History. http://www.oberlin.edu/archive /holdings/finding/RG30/SG385/biography.html, accessed May 14, 2015.

Orient, N. and Adj. 2004. OED Online. Oxford University Press. http://www.oed.com .revproxy.brown.edu/view/Entry/132525, accessed May 14, 2015.

Pacini, Andrea, ed. 1998. *Christian Communities in the Arab Middle East: The Challenge of the Future.* Oxford: New York: Clarendon Press; Oxford University Press.

Peter, Ian. 2004. The History of Email. Ian Peter's History of the Internet. http://www .nethistory.info/History%20of%20the%20Internet/email.html, accessed May 11, 2015.

Pew Research Center. 2011. Table: *Muslim Population by Country*. Pew Research Center's Religion & Public Life Project. http://www.pewforum.org/2011/01/27/table-muslim-population-by-country/, accessed May 22, 2015.

Pew Research Center, 1615 L. 2009. *Mapping the Global Muslim Population. Pew Research Center's Religion & Public Life Project.* http://www.pewforum.org/2009/10/07/mapping-the-global-muslim-population/, accessed May 22, 2015.

Al-Rasheed, Madawi. 2007. *Contesting the Saudi State: Islamic Voices from a New Generation*. Cambridge, UK: Cambridge University Press.

Said, Edward W. 1979. *Orientalism*. 1st Vintage Books ed. New York: Vintage Books.

Shoup, John A. 2011. *Ethnic Groups of Africa and the Middle East: An Encyclopedia*. Santa Barbara, California: ABC-CLIO.

Soares, Benjamin, and Filippo Osella. 2009. Islam, Politics, Anthropology. *Journal of the Royal Anthropological Institute* 15: S1–S23.

Taspinar, Omer. 2008. Turkey's Middle East Policies: Between Neo-Ottomanism and Kemalism. *Carnegie Papers* (10): 1–29.

The World Bank. 2013. Middle East and North Africa—Countries. http://go.worldbank.org/G7ZOW4EVH0, accessed May 14, 2015.

Varisco, Daniel. 2005. *Islam Obscured: The Rhetoric of Anthropological Representation*. Palgrave Macmillan.

World Health Organization. 2015. Regional Office for the Eastern Mediterranean. WHO. http://www.who.int/about/regions/emro/en/, accessed May 14, 2015.

Yavuz, M. Hakan. 1998. Turkish Identity and Foreign Policy in Flux: The Rise of Neo-Ottomanism. *Critique: Critical Middle Eastern Studies* 7(12): 19–41.

Yver, Georges. 2015. Al-Maghrib. Peri Bearman, Thomas Bianquis, Clifford Edmund Bosworth, E. J. van Donzel, and Wolfhart P. Heinrichs, eds. *Encyclopedia of Islam*. Brill Online. http://referenceworks.brillonline.com/entries/encyclopaedia-of-islam-2/al-maghrib-SIM_4766, accessed May 8, 2015.

Orientalism

by BILL ASHCROFT AND PAL AHULWALIA

EDWARD SAID'S PUBLICATION OF *ORIENTALISM* MADE SUCH AN impact on thinking about colonial discourse that for three decades it has continued to be the site of controversy, adulation and criticism. Said's intervention is designed to illustrate the manner in which the representation of Europe's 'others' has been institutionalised since at least the eighteenth century as a feature of its cultural dominance. Orientalism describes the various disciplines, institutions, processes of investigation and styles of thought by which Europeans came to 'know' the 'Orient' over several centuries, and which reached their height during the rise and consolidation of nineteenth-century imperialism. The key to Said's interest in this way of knowing Europe's others is that it effectively demonstrates the link between knowledge and power, for it 'constructs' and dominates Orientals in the process of knowing them. The very term 'Oriental' shows how the process works, for the word identifies and homogenises at the same time, implying a range of knowledge and an intellectual mastery over that which is named. Since Said's analysis, Orientalism has revealed itself as a model for the many ways in which Europe's strategies for knowing the colonised world became, at the same time, strategies for dominating that world.

THE ORIGINS OF ORIENTALISM

In 1786, William Jones, a Justice of the High Court of Bengal and student of Sanskrit, gave an address to the Bengal Asiatic Society in which he made a statement that was to change the face of European intellectual life:

> The Sanskrit language, whatever its antiquity, is of a wonderful structure, more perfect than the Greek, more copious than the Latin, and more exquisitely refined than either, yet bearing to both of them a stronger affinity, both in the roots of verbs, and in the forms of grammar, than could possibly have been produced by accident; so strong, indeed, that no philologer could examine them all three, without believing them to have sprung from some common source, which, perhaps, no longer exists. (*Asiatic Researches* 1788, cited in Poliakov 1974: 190)

Jones's pronouncement initiated a kind of 'Indomania' throughout Europe as scholars looked to Sanskrit for an origin to European languages that went even deeper than Latin and Greek. What remained in the aftermath of Indomania was the entrenchment of Orientalism and the vast expansion of language study. For the next century, European ethnologists, philologers and historians were to be obsessed with the Orient and the Indo-European group of languages because these seemed to offer an explanation of the roots of European civilisation itself.

Jones's statement was revolutionary because existing conceptions of linguistic history supposed that language development had taken place within 6,000 years since creation, with Hebrew as the source language and other languages emerging by a process of degeneration. Jones's declaration ushered in a new conception of linguistic history, but because language was so deeply implicated in concerns about national and cultural identity, 'the authentic and useful science of linguistics became absorbed in the crazy doctrine of "racial anthropology"' (ibid.: 193). The link between language and identity, particularly the link between the diversity of languages and the diversity of racial identity, gave rise to the discipline of ethnology, the precursor of modern anthropology.

Orientalism, in Said's formulation, is principally a way of defining and 'locating' Europe's others. But as a group of related disciplines Orientalism was, in important ways, about Europe itself, and hinged on arguments that circulated around the issue of national distinctiveness, and racial and linguistic origins. Thus the elaborate and detailed examinations of Oriental languages, histories and cultures were carried out in a context in which the supremacy and importance of European civilisation was unquestioned. Such was the vigour of the discourse that myth, opinion, hearsay and prejudice generated by influential scholars quickly assumed the status of received truth. For instance, the influential French philologist and historian Ernest Renan (1823–92) could declare confidently that 'Every person, however slightly he may be acquainted with the affairs of our time, sees clearly the actual inferiority of Mohammedan countries' (1896: 85). We can be in no doubt about Renan's audience, nor the nature of the cultural assumptions they shared:

> All those who have been in the East, or in Africa are struck by the way in which the mind of the true believer is fatally limited, by the species of iron circle that surrounds his head, rendering it absolutely closed to knowledge. (ibid.: 85)

The confidence of such assertions is partly an indication of the self-confidence engendered by the huge popularity of writers like Renan and philologer and race theorist Count Arthur Gobineau (1816–82). But they are, at a deeper level, the product of the unquestioned cultural dominance of Europe, maintained economically and militarily over most of the rest of the world. Through such statements as Renan's, the 'production' of Orientalist knowledge became a continual and uncritical 'reproduction' of various assumptions and beliefs. Thus, Lord Cromer, who relied a great deal on writers like Renan, could write in 1908 that, while the European's 'trained intelligence works like a piece of mechanism', the mind of the Oriental, 'like his picturesque streets, is eminently wanting in symmetry' (Said 1978a: 38). The superior 'order', 'rationality' and 'symmetry' of Europe, and the inferior 'disorder', 'irrationality' and 'primitivism' of non-Europe were the self-confirming parameters in which the various Orientalist disciplines circulated. But what gave these disciplines their dynamism and urgency, at least in the beginning, was the need to explain the apparent historical connections between Europe and its Oriental forebears. The 'Orient' meant roughly what we now term the 'Middle East', including the 'Semitic' languages and societies, and those of South Asia, for these societies were most relevant to the development and spread of the Indo-European languages, although, as Said suggests, they tended to divide between a 'good' Orient in classical India, and a 'bad' Orient in present-day Asia and North Africa (ibid.: 99).

The identification of the Indo-European group of languages was to have incalculable consequences in world history. Not only did it disrupt conventional notions of linguistic history, and give rise to a century of philological debate, but it quickly generated theories about racial origin and development, as language and race became conflated. The Indo-European group of languages, at different times called the 'Japhetic' languages (after Noah's son Japheth, distinguished from the 'Semitic' and 'Hamitic' languages that derived from his other sons Shem and Ham), or 'Indo-German', began to be called 'Arian' from their supposed origin round Lake Aries in Asia. The term 'Aryan' gained widespread authority in 1819 from the efforts of German philosopher Friedrich Schlegel (1772–1829) (Poliakov 1974: 193). This term came to symbolise an idea close to the hearts of European states—that a separate language indicated a separate racial/national origin. Schlegel's rhetoric in galvanising German youth with the myth of an Aryan race, early in the nineteenth century, began a process that led eventually to the Holocaust of the Second World War. Thus, the concept that had the potential to unite peoples of wide cultural disparity—the Indo-European community of languages—peoples as diverse as Indians, Persians, Teutons and Anglo-Saxons—became the source of the most strident racial polarisation as it fed deeply ingrained European racial pretensions.

It is tempting to see Orientalism as simply a product of the growth of modern imperialism in the nineteenth century, as European control of the Orient required an intellectual rationale for its cultural and economic dominance. But the discourse was what we might call 'overdetermined': that is, many different factors all contributed to the development of this particular ideological construction at this time in history, of which the emerging imperialism of European states was but one (albeit a significant one). These tributaries of influence also varied from country to country: for example, the industrial dominance of Britain and the political economy of its colonial possessions; the post-revolutionary sense of national destiny in France; the centuries-old concern with the Teutonic community of blood in Germany. All these conspired to produce a passion for the study of Oriental cultures that saw the birth of entirely new disciplines of natural and human sciences, such as ethnology, anthropology, palaeontology and philology, and the transformation or formalisation of existing ones such as history and geography. Far from being a monolith, the variety of intellectual disciplines Orientalism encompassed, its 'over-determination'

from the different cultural histories of the major European states, meant that different intellectual styles of Orientalism were developed.

But despite the complexity and variety of Orientalist disciplines, the investiga-
tions of Orientalist scholars all operated within certain parameters, such as the
assumption that Western civilisation was the pinnacle of historical development.
Thus, Orientalist analysis almost universally proceeded to confirm the 'primitive',
'originary', 'exotic' and 'mysterious' nature of Oriental societies and, more often than
not, the degeneration of the 'non-European' branches of the Indo-European family of languages. In this respect, Orientalism, despite the plethora of disciplines it
fostered, could be seen to be what Michel Foucault calls a 'discourse': a coherent
and strongly bounded area of social knowledge; a system of statements by which
the world could be known.

There are certain unwritten (and sometimes unconscious) rules that define what
can and cannot be said within a discourse, and the discourse of Orientalism had
many such rules that operated within the area of convention, habit, expectation
and assumption. In any attempt to gain knowledge about the world, what is known
is overwhelmingly determined by the way it is known; the rules of a discipline
determine the kind of knowledge that can be gained from it, and the strength, and
sometimes unspoken nature, of these rules show an academic discipline to be a
prototypical form of discourse. But when these rules span a number of disciplines,
providing boundaries within which such knowledge can be produced, that intellectual habit of speaking and thinking becomes a discourse such as Orientalism. This
argument for the discursive coherence of Orientalism is the key to Said's analysis
of the phenomenon and the source of the compelling power of his argument.
European knowledge, by relentlessly constructing its subject within the discourse
of Orientalism, was able to maintain hegemonic power over it. Focusing on this one
aspect of the complex phenomenon of Orientalism has allowed Said to elaborate
it as one of the most profound examples of the machinery of cultural domination,
a metonymy of the process of imperial control and one that continues to have its
repercussions in contemporary life. *Orientalism,* then, pivots on a demonstration of
the link between knowledge and power, for the discourse of Orientalism constructs
and dominates Orientals in the process of 'knowing' them.

A 'UNIQUELY PUNISHING DESTINY': THE WORLDLINESS OF *ORIENTALISM*

Orientalism is an openly political work. Its aim is not to investigate the array of disciplines or to elaborate exhaustively the historical or cultural provenance of Orientalism, but rather to reverse the 'gaze' of the discourse, to analyse it from the point of view of an 'Oriental'—to 'inventory the traces upon … the Oriental subject, of the culture whose domination has been so powerful a fact in the life of all Orientals' (Said 1978a: 25). How Said, the celebrated US academic, can claim to be an 'Oriental' rehearses the recurrent paradox running through his work. But his experience of living in the United States, where the 'East' signifies danger and threat, is the source of the worldliness of *Orientalism*. The provenance of the book demonstrates the deep repercussions of Orientalist discourse, for it emerges directly from the 'disheartening' life of an Arab Palestinian in the West.

> The web of racism, cultural stereotypes, political imperialism, dehuman-izing ideology holding in the Arab or the Muslim is very strong indeed, and it is this web which every Palestinian has come to feel as his uniquely punishing destiny … The nexus of knowledge and power creating 'the oriental' and in a sense obliterating him as a human being is therefore not for me an exclusively academic matter. Yet it is an *intellectual* matter of some very obvious importance. (ibid.: 27)

Orientalism, as we can see, is the fruit of Said's own 'uniquely punishing destiny'. In this book, a Palestinian Arab living in America deploys the tools and techniques of his adopted professional location to discern the manner in which cultural hege-mony is maintained. His intention, he claims, was to provoke, and thus to stimulate 'a new kind of dealing with the Orient' (ibid.: 28). Indeed, if this binary between 'Orient' and 'Occident' were to disappear altogether, 'we shall have advanced a little in the process of what Welsh Marxist cultural critic Raymond Williams has called the "unlearning" of "the inherent dominative mode"' (ibid.: 28).

Said's own work of identity construction underpinned the passion behind *Orientalism*. The intellectual power of the book comes from its inspired and relent-lessly focused analysis of the way in which a variety of disciplines operated within certain coherent discursive limits, but the cultural, and perhaps even emotional, power of the book comes from its 'worldly' immediacy, its production by a writer whose identity has been constructed, in part, by this discourse, who still feels the effects of Orientalist 'knowledge'. Passion can be a confusing and unreflective element in intellectual debate, and while the passion no doubt explains a great deal about the popularity of *Orientalism,* the refusal by many critics to take the book's worldliness into account has tended to limit their perception of its significance. For instance, Basim Musallam, an Arab reviewer of the book, points out that one hostile critic, scholar Michael Rustum, 'writes as a freeman and a member of a free society; a Syrian, Arab by speech, citizen of a still independent Ottoman state' (Said 1995a: 337). Edward Said, however, 'has no generally accepted identity,' says Musallam, 'his very *people* are in dispute. It is possible that Edward Said and his generation stand on nothing more solid than the remnants of the destroyed society of Michael Rustum's Syria, and on memory.' Musallam makes the critical point that 'it is not just any "Arab" who wrote this book, but one with a particular background and experience' (Musallam, quoted in Said 1995a: 337–8).

But it would be too reductive to suggest that Said's intention was merely to vent his anger while asserting a (Palestinian) nationalism that would exorcise him and other colonised subjects from the experiences and legacies of colonisation. Such a position would be anathema to his view of the 'secular' role of the public intellectual, which is to open spaces and cross borders in an attempt to 'speak truth to power'. Taking up the unfinished project of Frantz Fanon, Said moves from a politics of blame to a politics of liberation. And yet, as he has noted, despite his protestations about what he sees his work setting out to do, to create a non-coercive, non-dominative and non-essentialist knowledge, *Orientalism* has 'more often been thought of as a kind of testimonial to subaltern status—the wretched of the earth talking back—than as a multicultural critique of power using knowledge to advance itself' (Said 1995a: 336).

Before the publication of *Orientalism,* the term 'Orientalism' itself had faded from popular usage, but in the late 1970s it took on a renewed and vigorous life. The disciplines of modern Oriental studies, despite their sophistication, are inescapably imbued with the traditional representations of the nature of the Orient (especially the Middle East) and the assumptions that underlie the discourse of Orientalism. While Said laments the sometimes indiscriminate manner in which *Orientalism* has been appropriated, there is little doubt that it has had a huge impact on social theory in general. By 1995, *Orientalism* had become a 'collective book' that had 'superseded' its author more than could have been expected (ibid.: 300). One might add that it is a continually growing book, in that the analysis of the strategies of Orientalism has been useful in detecting the specific discursive and cultural operations of imperial culture in various ways. For the analysis hinges on the ideological nature of representation and the ways in which powerful representations become the 'true' and accepted ones, despite their stereotypical and even caricatured nature.

STRUCTURE

Orientalism is divided into three main parts. In the first part, Said establishes the expansive and amorphous capacity of Orientalism. It is a discourse that has been in existence for over two centuries and one that continues into the present. The focus in this section is to look at the question of representation in order to illustrate the similarities in diverse ideas such as 'Oriental despotism, Oriental sensuality, Oriental modes of production, and Oriental splendour' (1978a: 47).

The second part of the book is an exposition of 'Orientalist structures and re-structures'. Here, Said sets out to establish how the main philological, historical and creative writers in the nineteenth century drew upon a tradition of knowledge that allowed them textually to construct and control the Orient. This construction and rendering visible of the Orient served the colonial administration that subsequently utilised this knowledge to establish a system of rule.

The third part is an examination of 'Modern Orientalism'. This section shows how the established legacies of British and French Orientalism were adopted and adapted by the United States. For Said, nowhere is this better reflected than in the manner in which these legacies are manifested in American foreign policy. The book is a complex articulation of how the absorptive capacity of Orientalism has been able to adopt influences such as positivism, Marxism and Darwinism without altering its central tenets.

The term 'Orientalism' is derived from 'Orientalist', which has been associated traditionally with those engaged in the study of the Orient. The very term 'the Orient' holds different meanings for different people. As Said points out, Americans associate it with the Far East, mainly Japan and China, while for Western Europeans, and in particular the British and the French, it conjures up different images. It is not only adjacent to Europe; 'it is also the place of Europe's greatest and richest and oldest colonies, the source of its civilizations and languages, its cultural contestant, and one of its deepest and most recurring images of the Other' (1978a: 1).

Part of the pervasive power of Orientalism is that it refers to at least three different pursuits, all of which are interdependent: an academic discipline, a style of thought and a corporate institution for dealing with the Orient. As an academic discipline, Orientalism emerged in the late eighteenth century and has since assembled an archive of knowledge that has served to perpetuate and reinforce Western representations of it. Orientalism is 'the discipline by which the Orient was (and is) approached systematically, as a topic of learning, discovery and practice' (ibid.: 73). As a style of thought it is 'based upon an ontological and epistemological distinction' (ibid.: 2) between the Orient and the Occident. This definition is more expansive and can accommodate as diverse a group of writers as classical Greek playwright Aeschylus (524–455 BC), medieval Italian poet Dante Alighieri (1265–1335), French novelist Victor Hugo (1802–85) and German social scientist and revolutionary Karl Marx (1818–83).The third definition of Orientalism as a corporate institution is demonstrative of its amorphous capacity as a structure used to dominate and authorise the Orient. Hence, Orientalism necessarily is viewed as being linked inextricably to colonialism.

The three definitions as expounded by Said illustrate how Orientalism is a complex web of representations about the Orient. The first two definitions embody the textual creation of the Orient while the third definition illustrates how Orientalism has been deployed to execute authority and domination over the Orient. The three are interrelated, particularly since the domination entailed in the third definition is reliant upon and justified by the textual establishment of the Orient that emerges out of the academic and imaginative definitions of Orientalism.

EPISTEMOLOGY

The science or philosophy of knowledge, epistimology investigates the definition, varieties, sources and limits of knowledge, experience and belief. 'What can we know and how do we know it?' are questions central to epistemology. Thus, it examines the relationship or distinction between knowledge and belief, and the relative function of reason and judgement. Abstract epistemological questions, however, miss the central idea Said adapts from Foucault, that 'knowing' and power go hand in hand. Knowledge, or truth, in whatever form, belongs to that group which has power to impress its version of knowledge on others.

ONTOLOGY

The science or philosophy of being. Ontology is that branch of metaphysics which examines the existence or essence of things, producing a theory about what exists or a list of things that exist. Ontology raises certain kinds of question such as: Is being a property? Is it necessary that something should exist? What is the difference between Being in general and particular being? The character and variety of the questions asked say a lot about the culture in which the question of being is considered, and consequently, about the philosophical status of Being, and the place of the human in the world of that culture.

THE SCOPE OF ORIENTALISM

The core of Said's argument resides in the link between knowledge and power, which is amply demonstrated by Prime Minister Arthur Balfour's defence of Britain's occupation of Egypt in 1910, when he declared that: 'We know the civilization of Egypt better than we know any other country' (Said 1978a: 32). Knowledge for Balfour meant not only surveying a civilisation from its origins, but *being able to do that*. 'To have such knowledge of such a thing [as Egypt] is to dominate it, to have authority over it … since we know it and it exists, in a sense, as we know it' (ibid.: 32).

The premises of Balfour's speech demonstrate very clearly how knowledge and dominance go hand in hand:

> England knows Egypt; Egypt is what England knows; England knows that Egypt cannot have self-government; England confirms that by occupying Egypt; for the Egyptians, Egypt is what England has occupied and now governs; foreign occupation therefore becomes 'the very basis' of contemporary Egyptian civilization. (ibid.: 34)

But to see Orientalism as simply a rationalisation of colonial rule is to ignore the fact that colonialism was justified in advance by Orientalism (ibid.: 39). The division of the world into East and West had been centuries in the making and expressed the fundamental binary division on which all dealing with the Orient was based. But one side had the power to determine what the reality of both East and West might be. Knowledge of the Orient, because it was generated out of this cultural strength, 'in a sense *creates* the Orient, the Oriental and his world' (ibid.: 40). With this assertion we come right to the heart of *Orientalism,* and consequently to the source of much of the controversy it has provoked. To Said, the Orient and the Oriental are direct constructions of the various disciplines by which they are known by Europeans. This appears, on the one hand, to narrow down an extremely complex European phenomenon to a simple question of power and imperial relations, but, on the other, to provide no room for Oriental self-representations.

Said points out that the upsurge in Orientalist study coincided with the period of unparalleled European expansion: from 1815 to 1914. His emphasis on its political nature can be seen in his focus on the beginnings of modern Orientalism: not with William Jones's disruption of linguistic orthodoxy, but in the Napoleonic invasion of Egypt in 1798, 'which was in many ways the very model of a truly scientific appropriation of one culture by another, apparently stronger one' (Said 1978a: 42). But the crucial fact was that Orientalism, in all its many tributaries, began to impose limits upon thought about the Orient. Even powerful imaginative writers such as Gustave Flaubert, Gérard de Nerval or Sir Walter Scott were constrained in what they could either experience or say about the Orient. For 'Orientalism was ultimately a political vision of reality whose structure promoted the difference between the familiar (Europe, the West, "us") and the strange (Orient, the East, "them")' (ibid.: 43). It worked this way because the intellectual accomplishments of Orientalist discourse served the interests, and were managed by the vast hierarchical web, of imperial power.

Central to the emergence of the discourse is the imaginative existence of something called 'the Orient', which comes into being within what Said describes as an 'imaginative geography' because it is unlikely that we might develop a discipline called 'Occidental studies'. Quite simply, the idea of an Orient exists to define the European. '[O]ne big division, as between West and Orient, leads to other smaller ones' (ibid.: 58) and the experiences of writers, travellers, soldiers, statesmen, from Herodotus and Alexander the Great on, become 'the lenses through which the Orient is experienced, and they shape the language, perception and form of the encounter between East and West' (ibid.: 58). What holds these experiences together is the shared sense of something 'other', which is named 'the Orient'. This analysis of the binary nature of Orientalism has been the source of a great deal of criticism of the book, because it appears to suggest that there is one Europe or one West (one 'us') that constructs the Orient. But if we see this homogenisation as the way in which the *discourse* of Orientalism simplifies the world, at least by implication, rather than the way the world *is;* as the way a general attitude can link various disciplines and intellectual tributaries despite their different subject matter and modes of operation, we may begin to understand the discursive power of this pervasive habit of thinking and doing called Orientalism.

The way we come to understand that 'other' named 'the Orient' in this binary and stereotypical way can be elaborated in terms of the metaphor of theatre. Where the idea of Orientalism as a learned field suggests an enclosed space, the idea of representation is a theatrical one: the Orient is the stage on which the whole East is confined.

> On this stage will appear figures whose role it is to represent the larger whole from which they emanate. The Orient then seems to be, not an unlimited extension beyond the familiar European world, but rather a closed field, a theatrical stage affixed to Europe. (ibid.: 63)

In this way certain images represent what is otherwise an impossibly diffuse entity (ibid.: 68). They are also *characters* who conform to certain typical characteristics. Thus,

[Orientalism] shares with magic and with mythology the self-containing, self-reinforcing character of a closed system, in which objects are what they are *because* they are what they are, for once, for all time, for ontological reasons that no empirical material can either dislodge or alter. (ibid.: 70)

Imaginative geography legitimates a vocabulary, a representative discourse peculiar to the understanding of the Orient that becomes *the* way in which the Orient is known. Orientalism thus becomes a form of 'radical realism' by which an aspect of the Orient is fixed with a word or phrase 'which then is considered either to have acquired, or more simply be, reality' (ibid.: 72).

The focus of Said's analysis is provided by what he sees as the close link between the upsurge in Orientalism and the rise in European imperial dominance during the nineteenth century. The political orientation of his analysis can be seen by the importance he gives to Napoleon's invasion of Egypt in 1798. Although not the beginning of the Orientalism that swept Europe early in the nineteenth century, Napoleon's project demonstrated the most conscious marriage of academic knowledge and political ambition. Certainly the decision by Warren Hastings, Governor-General of India in the 1770s, to conduct the Indian court system on the basis of Sanskrit law paved the way for the discoveries of William Jones, who helped translate the Sanskrit. This demonstrated that knowledge of any kind is always *situated* and given force by political reality. But Napoleon's tactics—persuading the Egyptian population that he was fighting on behalf of Islam rather than against it—utilising as he did all the available knowledge of the Koran and Islamic society that could be mustered by French scholars, comprehensively demonstrated the strategic and tactical power of knowing.

Napoleon gave his deputy Kleber strict instructions after he left always to administer Egypt through the Orientalists and the religious Islamic leaders whom they could win over (ibid.: 82). According to Said, the consequences of this expedition were profound. 'Quite literally, the occupation gave birth to the entire modern experience of the Orient as interpreted from within the universe of discourse founded by Napoleon in Egypt' (ibid.: 87). After Napoleon, says Said, the very language of Orientalism changed radically. 'Its descriptive realism was upgraded and became not merely a style of representation but a language, indeed a means of *creation*' (ibid.: 87), a symbol of which was the immensely ambitious construction of the Suez Canal. Claims such as these show why Said's argument is so compelling, and why it caught the imagination of critics in the 1970s. Closer inspection would reveal that much of the most intensive Oriental scholarship was carried out in countries such as Germany, which had few colonial possessions. Wider analysis might also reveal that *various* styles of representation emerged within Orientalist fields. But Napoleon's expedition gave an unmistakable direction to the work of Orientalists that was to have a continuing legacy, not only in European and Middle Eastern history but in world history as well.

Ultimately, the power and unparalleled productive capacity of Orientalism came about because of an emphasis on textuality, a tendency to engage reality within the framework of knowledge gained from previously written texts. Orientalism was a dense palimpsest of writings which purported to engage directly with their subject but which were in fact responding to, and building upon, writings that had gone before. This textual attitude extends to the present day, so that

> if Arab Palestinians oppose Israeli settlement and occupation of their lands, then that is merely 'the return of Islam,' or, as a renowned contemporary Orientalist defines it, Islamic opposition to non-Islamic peoples, a principle of Islam enshrined in the seventh century. (ibid.: 107)

THE DISCOURSE OF ORIENTALISM

Orientalism is best viewed in Foucauldian terms as a discourse: a manifestation of power/knowledge. Without examining Orientalism as a discourse, says Said, it is not possible to understand 'the enormously systematic discipline by which European culture was able to manage—and even produce—the Orient politically, sociologically, militarily, ideologically, scientifically, and imaginatively during the post-Enlightenment period' (Said 1978a: 3).

Following on from the notion of discourse we saw earlier, colonial discourse is a system of statements that can be made about colonies and colonial peoples, about colonising powers and about the relationship between these two. It is the system of knowledge and belief about the world within which acts of colonisation take place.

Although it is generated within the society and cultures of the colonisers, it becomes that discourse within which the colonised may also come to see themselves (as, for example, when Africans adopt the imperial view of themselves as 'intuitive' and 'emotional', asserting a distinctiveness from the 'rational' and 'unemotional' Europeans). At the very least it creates a deep conflict in the consciousness of the colonised because of its clash with other knowledges about the world.

As a discourse, Orientalism is ascribed the authority of academics, institutions and governments, and such authority raises the discourse to a level of importance and prestige that guarantees its identification with 'truth'. In time, the knowledge and reality created by the Orientalist discipline produce a discourse 'whose material presence or weight, not the originality of a given author, is really responsible for the texts produced out of it' (ibid.: 94). By means of this discourse, Said argues, Western cultural institutions are responsible for the creation of those 'others', the Orientals, whose very difference from the Occident helps establish that binary opposition by which Europe's own identity can be established. The underpinning of such a de-marcation is a line between the Orient and the Occident that is 'less a fact of nature than it is a fact of human production' (Said 1985: 2). It is the geographical imagina-tion that is central to the construction of entities such as 'the Orient'. It requires the maintenance of rigid boundaries in order to differentiate between the Occident and the Orient. Hence, through this process, they are able to 'Orientalise' the region.

An integral part of Orientalism, of course, is the relationship of power between the Occident and the Orient, in which the balance is weighted heavily in favour of the former. Such power is connected intimately with the construction of knowledge about the Orient. It occurs because the knowledge of 'subject races' or 'Orientals' makes their management easy and profitable; 'knowledge gives power, more power requires more knowledge, and so on in an increasingly profitable dialectic of information and control' (Said 1978a: 36).

The knowledge of the Orient created by and embodied within the discourse of Orientalism serves to construct an image of the Orient and the Orientals as subser-vient and subject to domination by the Occident. Knowledge of the Orient, because generated out of strength, says Said, in a sense *creates* the Orient, the Oriental and his world.

> In Cromer's and Balfour's language, the Oriental is depicted as something one judges (as in a court of law), something one studies and depicts (as in a curriculum), something one disciplines (as in a school or prison), something one illustrates (as in a zoological manual). The point is that in each case the Oriental is *contained* and *represented* by dominating frameworks. (ibid.: 40)

The creation of the Orient as the 'other' is necessary so that the Occident can define itself and strengthen its own identity by invoking such a juxtaposition.

The Orientalist representation has been reinforced not only by academic disciplines such as anthropology, history and linguistics but also by the 'Darwinian theses on survival and natural selection' (ibid.: 227). Hence, from an Orientalist perspective, the study of the Orient has been always from an Occidental or Western point of view. To the Westerner, according to Said,

> the Oriental was always like some aspect of the West; to some German Romantics, for example, Indian religion was essentially an Oriental version of Germano-Christian pantheism. Yet the Orientalist makes it his work to be always converting the Orient from something into something else: he does this for himself, for the sake of his culture. (ibid.: 67)

This encoding and comparison of the Orient with the West ultimately ensure that the Oriental culture and perspective are viewed as a deviation, a perversion, and thus are accorded an inferior status.

One essential feature of the discourse of Orientalism is the objectification of both the Orient and the Oriental. They are treated as objects that can be scrutinised and understood, and this objectification is confirmed in the very term 'Orient', which covers a geographical area and a range of populations many times larger and many times more diverse than Europe. Such objectification entails the assumption that the Orient is essentially monolithic, with an unchanging history, while the Occident is dynamic, with an active history. In addition, the Orient and the Orientals are seen to be passive, non-participatory subjects of study.

This construction, however, has a distinctly political dimension in that Western knowledge inevitably entails political significance. This was nowhere better exemplified than in the rise of Oriental studies and the emergence of Western imperialism. The Englishman in India or Egypt in the late nineteenth century took an interest in those countries that was founded on their status as British colonies. This may seem quite different, suggests Said, 'from saying that all academic knowledge about India and Egypt is somehow tinged and impressed with, violated by, the gross political fact—and yet *that is what I am saying* in this study of Orientalism' (Said 1978a: 11). The reason Said can say this is because of his conviction of the worldliness of the discourse: 'no production of knowledge in the human sciences can ever ignore or disclaim its author's involvement as a human subject in his own circumstances' (ibid.: 11). The idea that academic knowledge is 'tinged', 'impressed with', or 'violated by' political and military force is not to suggest, as Dennis Porter (1983) supposes, that the hegemonic effect of Orientalist discourse does not operate by 'consent'. Rather, it is to suggest that the apparently morally neutral pursuit of knowledge is, in the colonialist context, deeply inflected with the ideological assumptions of imperialism. 'Knowledge' is always a matter of representation, and representation a process of giving concrete form to ideological concepts, of making certain signifiers stand for signifieds. The power that underlies these representations cannot be divorced from the operations of political force, even though it is a different kind of power, more subtle, more penetrating and less visible.

A power imbalance exists, then, not only in the most obvious characteristics of imperialism, in its 'brute political, economic, and military rationales' (Said 1978a: 12), but also, and most hegemonically, in cultural discourse. It is in the cultural sphere that the dominant hegemonic project of Orientalist studies, used to propagate the aims of imperialism, can be discerned. Said's methodology therefore is embedded in what he terms 'textualism', which allows him to envisage the Orient as a textual creation. In Orientalist discourse, the affiliations of the text compel it to produce the West as a site of power and a centre distinctly demarcated from the 'other' as the object of knowledge and, inevitably, subordination. This hidden political function of the Orientalist text is a feature of its worldliness and Said's project is to focus on the establishment of the Orient as a textual construct. He is not interested in analysing what lies hidden in the Orientalist text, but in showing how the Orientalist 'makes the Orient speak, describes the Orient, renders its mysteries plain for and to the West' (ibid.: 20–1).

The issue of representation is crucial to understanding discourses within which knowledge is constructed, because it is questionable, says Said, whether a true representation is ever possible (ibid.: 272). If all representations are embedded in the language, culture and institutions of the representer, 'then we must be prepared to accept the fact that a representation is *eo ipso* implicated, intertwined, embedded, inter-woven with a great many other things besides the "truth" which is itself a representation' (ibid.: 272). The belief that representations such as those we find in books correspond to the real world amounts to what Said calls a 'textual attitude'. He suggests that what French philosopher Voltaire (1694–1778) in *Candide* and Spanish novelist Cervantes (1547–1616) in *Don Quixote* satirised was the assumption that the 'swarming, unpredictable, and problematic mess in which human beings live can be understood on the basis of what books—texts—say' (Said 1978a: 93). This is precisely what occurs when the Orientalist text is held to signify, to represent the truth: the Orient is rendered silent and its reality is revealed by the Orientalist. Since the Orientalist text offers a familiarity, even intimacy, with a distant and exotic reality, the texts themselves are accorded enormous status and accrue greater importance than the objects they seek to describe. Said argues that 'such texts can create not only knowledge but also the very reality they appear to describe' (ibid.: 94). Consequently, it is the texts that create and describe the reality of the Orient, given that the Orientals themselves are prohibited from speaking.

The latest phase of Orientalism corresponds with the displacement of France and Britain on the world stage by the United States. Despite the shifting of the centre of power and the consequent change in Orientalising strategies, the *discourse* of Orientalism, in its three general modes, remains secure. In this phase, the Arab Muslim has come to occupy a central place within American popular images as well as in the social sciences. Said argues that this was to a large extent made possible by the 'transference of a popular anti-Semitic animus from a Jewish to an Arab target ... since the figure was essentially the same' (ibid.: 286). The dominance of the social sciences after the Second World War meant that the mantle of Orientalism was passed to the social sciences. These social scientists ensured that the region was 'conceptually emasculated, reduced to "attitudes", "trends", statistics: in short dehumanized' (ibid.: 291). Orientalism, then, in its different phases, is a Eurocentric discourse that constructs the 'Orient' by the accumulated knowledge of generations of scholars and writers who are secure in the power of their 'superior' wisdom.

It is Said's intention not merely to document the excesses of Orientalism (which he does very successfully) but also to stress the need for an alternative, better form of scholarship. He recognises that there are a lot of individual scholars engaged in producing such knowledge. Yet he is concerned about the 'guild tradition' of Orientalism, which has the capacity to wear down most scholars. He urges continued vigilance in fighting the dominance of Orientalism. The answer for Said is to be 'sensitive to what is involved in representation, in studying the Other, in racial thinking, in unthinking and uncritical acceptance of authority and authoritative ideas, in the sociopolitical role of intellectuals, in the great value of skeptical critical consciousness' (ibid.: 327). Here the paramount obligation of the intellectual is to resist the attractions of the 'theological' position of those implicated in the tradition of Orientalist discourse, and to emphasise a 'secular' desire to speak truth to power, to question and to oppose.

SAID, FOUCAULT AND THE QUESTION OF RESISTANCE

The accusation that, for all his dissenting analysis of Western discourse, Said has no theory of resistance (Young 1990; Ahmad 1992) has most often emerged from the view that he misappropriates Foucault. Although Said has a clear debt to Foucault, there are important points of departure. Most importantly, Said became unhappy with Foucault for what he saw as a lack of political commitment within his work and within post-structuralist discourse in general. Foucault, in particular, suggests Said, 'takes a curiously passive and sterile view not so much of the uses of power, but of how and why power is gained, used, and held onto' (Said 1983: 221). While trying to avoid the crude notion that power is 'unmediated domination', says Said, Foucault 'more or less eliminates the central dialectic of opposed forces that still underlies modern society'. The problem Said has with Foucault is a lingering sense that he is more fascinated with the way power operates than committed to trying to change power relations in society (ibid.: 221). Foucault's conception of power, as something which operates at every level of society, leaves no room for resistance. Said characterises it as a 'conception [which] has drawn a circle around itself, constituting a unique territory in which Foucault has imprisoned himself and others with him' (ibid.: 245). Said's intention, on the contrary, is not to be trapped but to articulate the potential to resist and recreate. This is implicit in Orientalism, which stresses the relationship between power and knowledge.

MICHEL FOUCAULT (1926–84)

Philosopher, born in Poitiers, France. Taught at several French universities, culminating in the prestigious position of Professor of the History of Systems of Thought at the Collège de France (1970). Foucault showed the ways in which basic ideas, normally taken to be permanent truths about human nature and society, change in the course of history. Referring to his practice as an 'archaeology', he showed how *épistemés* or discursive formations determine the manner in which the world is experienced in a given epoch. He explored the shifting patterns of power within society and the ways in which power relates to the self. Power, he says, is located in strategies which operate at

> every level: they cannot be reduced to the power of, for instance, the state or a ruling class. Rather than being simply coercive, he claimed, power is productive, and particularly productive of knowledge, being disseminated throughout the whole of society rather than simply exerted by dominant people and institutions.

For Said, the power of the Orientalists lay in their 'knowing' the Orient, which in itself constituted power and yet also was an exercise in power. Hence, for him, resistance is twofold: to know the Orient outside the discourse of Orientalism, and to represent and present this knowledge to the Orientalists—to write back to them. The reason for this is that none of the Orientalists he writes about appear to have intended an 'Oriental' as a reader. 'The discourse of Orientalism, its internal consistency and rigorous procedures, were all designed for readers and consumers in the metropolitan West' (Said 1995a: 336). He therefore finds particular pleasure in listening in to their pronouncements and making his uninvited interventions into their discussions (ibid.: 336).

However, what Said is writing back is not an 'authentic' story of the Orient that only an Oriental has the capacity to tell, but rather a revelation of the fallacy of authenticity. For there is no 'real' Orient because

> 'the Orient' is itself a constituted entity, and the notion that there are geographical spaces with indigenous, radically 'different' inhabitants who can be defined on the basis of some religion, culture or racial es-sence proper to that geographical space is equally a highly debatable idea. (Said 1978a: 322)

Hence, it is important to note that Said's non-coercive knowledge is one that runs counter to the deployment of discourse analysis within *Orientalism*. Despite his obvi-ous debt to Foucault methodologically, he maintains distance and allows for autho-rial creativity. Thus, despite accusations of his misappropriation of Foucault (Clifford 1988; Young 1990; Ahmad 1992), Said is adamant that the theoretical inconsistency of Orientalism is the way it was designed to be: 'I didn't want Foucault's method, or anybody's method to override what I was trying to put forward' (Salusinszky

1987: 137). But even more explicit than this, he arrived at a notion of non-coercive knowledge at the end of the book 'which was deliberately anti-Foucault' (ibid.: 137).

This Saidian strategy of resistance is premised upon intellectuals who exercise their critical consciousness, not simply to reject imperial discourse but to intervene critically 'within the intrinsic conditions on which knowledge is made possible' (Said 1983: 182). For Said, the location of critical consciousness lies in challenging the hegemonic nature of dominant culture as well as 'the sovereignty of the systematic method' (Said 1978b: 673). By adopting such a perspective, Said argues, it is possible for the critic to deal with a text in two ways—by describing not only what is in the text but also what is invisible. His idea of the contemporary critical consciousness is one that asserts the room for agency, for such a consciousness detaches itself from the dominant culture, adopts a responsible adversarial position and then begins to 'account for, and rationally to discover and know, the force of statements in texts' (ibid.: 713). The development of this critical consciousness is central to Said's strategy of resistance.

CRITIQUES OF *ORIENTALISM*

To maintain a view of Orientalism as a discourse is to give it a focus that opens up gaps in its coverage. Placing the beginnings of Orientalism as late as Napoleon's invasion of Egypt rather than in the eighteenth-century upsurge of interest in the Indo-European languages better suits Said's demonstration of European power in the discourse. He largely omits the German school of Orientalists and their considerable impact on the field, since Germany was not a significant colonial power in the East; and he fails to mention the strong feeling among many Orientalist scholars that in some respects Eastern cultures were superior to the West, or the widespread feeling that Orientalist scholarship might actually break down the boundaries between East and West. Furthermore, Said's use of the concept of discourse, which he readily admits is partial, emphasises dominance and power over cultural interaction.

For these and many other reasons, *Orientalism* immediately stimulated and continues to generate responses from several quarters and with varying degrees of hostility. The vigour and range of these criticisms reveal how profound the influence of the book has been. But the nature of the criticisms has invariably tended to confirm Said's claim about the constricted nature of intellectual work in the academy: its 'theological' and exclusionary specialisation, its disciplinary confinement, its tendency towards caution and its retreat from the human realities of its subject matter. For, magisterial in scope though it is, *Orientalism* is an 'amateur' work, a demonstration of that approach to intellectual endeavour Said prizes so greatly. To call it an amateur work might appear contradictory and disparaging, but this effect of the term shows us how strong that constructed link between academic specialisation and 'truth' has become. In an interview with Michael Sprinker in 1992, he responded vigorously to the charge that he was attacking all Orientalists and everything they did. 'That's a total distortion of my argument. I'm saying one of the reasons lesser Orientalists were able to do what they did in narrow political terms was partly because they had behind them, not only the resource of a tradition and a great social power, but also because the work was interesting in and of itself' (Said 2001: 151).

The book's urgent air of revealing injustice and its prodigal disregard for discipline boundaries have generated criticisms that tend to confirm the unacceptability and marginality of what Said would call a form of 'secularist analysis'. To historians, he is unhistorical; to social scientists, he conflates theories; to scholars, he is unscholarly; to literary theorists, he is unreflective and indiscriminate; to Foucauldians, he misuses Foucault; to professional Marxists, he is anti-revolutionary; to professional conservatives, he is a terrorist. Thirty years of responses to *Orientalism* have tended to reveal what lies in wait for the 'amateur' public intellectual. However, as each disciplinary attack asserts the authority of its own epistemological base, it provides yet another example of the interpenetration of truth and power: 'truth' cannot be stated until the authority of its construction—the authority of its institutional base—has been proven.

The criticisms also hinge upon the paradoxical nature of Said's identity, and, indeed, upon the nature of representation itself. For many, if not most, of the criticisms are astute and revealing, and almost all of them are valid in their own terms. But none can lay claim to an authority so absolute that it manages to undermine the work. Part of the reason for this is that the text is writing back to those very assumptions of disciplinary authority upon which many of these criticisms are based. The incontrovertible reality of the 'Oriental's' experience, and its very worldliness, are such that it continually eludes the disciplinary and epistemological assumptions of its critics. Ultimately, the worldliness of *Orientalism*—a text that expends a great deal of effort to expose the affiliations, the worldliness of Orientalist texts themselves—becomes the source of its intellectual and critical energy. The fact that the text addresses the reader not from an abstract theoretical position, but from the continuing reality of an 'orientalised' experience, explains its resilience against the persistent critical attacks it has received.

THE 'PROFESSOR OF TERROR'

Edward Alexander, writing in the right-wing journal *Commentary,* produced an example of the most hostile responses to *Orientalism,* suggesting that Said, an expert on Joseph Conrad and one who has written extensively about the novelist, is someone 'whose great insight into modern political life, as it happens, has precisely to do with the special attraction of intellectuals to terror' (Alexander 1989: 49). Alexander likens Said to a character in the Conrad novel *The Secret Agent* (1906), which describes the 'pedantic fanaticism' of a professor whose thoughts 'caressed the images of ruin and destruction'. He also analyses the longing of another (untenured) intellectual to create 'a band of men absolute in their resolve to discard all scruples in the choice of means', chief among them 'death enlisted for good and all in the service of humanity' (Alexander 1989: 49–50). Alexander's argument relies largely on misrepresentation, and is more interesting for its revelation of the level of hostility possible in the exchanges between Said and his critics than for any incisive critique of Said's position.

This caricature of *Orientalism* also represents the hostility of some of the attacks upon Said himself in US society, and is interesting for the extremity and unguarded hysteria of its reaction. Such attacks demonstrate rather acutely the claim Said makes about contemporary Orientalism: that the Arab has been invested with all the demonic terror of US racial and political xenophobia. What is interesting is how subtly such stereotypes enter into public debate in general and into academic discourse in particular. Although Alexander's attack does not represent a widespread attitude to the book itself, it provides an illuminating glimpse of the ways in which stereotypes of 'self' and 'other' tend to polarise in cultural discourse.

AREA STUDIES

The critiques mounted from within the centre, mainly from the Orientalist as well as the Area Studies domain, elicited a great deal of comment, much of it positive and instructive, a fair amount hostile and in some cases abusive (Said 1985: 1). The hostility that Said refers to was exemplified best in the works of Dennis Porter and Bernard Lewis. While Porter rejected Said's thesis on the grounds that it was both an ahistorical and an inconsistent narrative (Porter 1983), Lewis mounted one of the most vitriolic attacks on Said. This is not surprising perhaps, given Said's treatment of Lewis's work on Islam as an explicit example of contemporary Orientalism: aggressively ideological, despite his various attempts at subtlety and irony, and 'underwritten by a zealotry covered with a veneer of urbanity that has very little in common with the "science" and learning Lewis purports to be upholding' (Said 1985: 13). This should come as no surprise, says Said, to anyone familiar with the history of Orientalism: it is not surprising, he claims, that most of the criticism from specialist Orientalists 'turns out to be, like Lewis's, no more than banal description of a barony violated by a crude trespasser' (Said 1995a: 346).

Lewis, in return, described *Orientalism* as a 'false' thesis that bordered on the 'absurd'. Further, he argued that it revealed 'a disquieting lack of knowledge of what scholars do and what scholarship is all about' (Lewis 1982a, 1982b). Lewis questioned Said's professional qualifications (in terms of which degrees he possessed) and his ability to speak of Islam, his knowledge of Arab history and of Orientalist disciplines. To Lewis, as a representative of 'specialist' academic scholarship, Said's 'amateurism' is an unforgivable failure rather than a liberating strength. Critically, Lewis substantially ignored the specific criticisms levelled by Said at Orientalist practices.

Orientalist scholars like Lewis and Daniel Pipes, according to Said, continue to reproduce such representations in their attacks on him, because they 'derive from what to the nineteenth-century mind is the preposterous situation of an Oriental responding to Orientalism's asseverations'. Said reserves his greatest scorn for contemporary Orientalists such as Lewis. 'For unrestrained anti-intellectuals, unencumbered by critical self-consciousness, no one has quite achieved the sublime confidence of Bernard Lewis' (Said 1985: 6). In short, Said once again seeks to illustrate the enduring legacy of Orientalism, its contemporary manifestation and its polemical and political commitments. It needs to be emphasised that academic Oriental studies are not the whole of Orientalism. The criticisms, coming mainly from the academy, and Said's responses to them have both tended to narrow down the field of contestation unnecessarily.

THE FOUCAULT CONNECTION: METHODOLOGICAL CRITICISMS

The issue of Said's use of Foucault has been the focus of various, even very opposed, criticisms of Orientalism. Dennis Porter, for instance, argues that the employment of the notion of discourse raises overwhelming methodological problems, not the least of which is the manner in which Said deals with the questions of truth and ideology. On the one hand, says Porter, Said argues that all knowledge is tainted because the Orient, after all, is a construction. On the other, Said appears to be suggesting that there might well be a real Orient that is knowable and that there is a corresponding truth about it that can be achieved. For Porter, this ambivalence between knowledge and ideology is never resolved within Said's work. Indeed, this assumption of an implied 'real' Orient is one of the most frequent criticisms of the book, despite Said's repeated disclaimers.

If Said is correct that there is no knowable Orient, Porter argues, then 'Orientalism in one form or another is not only what we have but all we can ever have' (Porter 1983: 151). He traces the theoretical tension in *Orientalism* to the manner in which Said has attempted to bring together two differing theoretical positions in Gramsci and Foucault. Said's perceived misappropriation of Foucault can be traced to the manner in which he seeks to accommodate such diverse figures as Alexander the Great, Karl Marx and Jimmy Carter within a single discourse. Such a claim, for Porter, 'seems to make nonsense of history at the same time as it invokes it with reference to imperial power/knowledge' (ibid.: 152). On the contrary, it is claimed that Foucault did not engage in such crudities. For him, discourse was grounded historically with epistemological breaks between different time periods.

The discourse of Orientalism in this Saidian sense is unable therefore to offer alternatives to Orientalism in the past. This, combined with the manner in which Gramsci's notion of hegemony is deployed, renders the possibility of counter-hegemony impossible. It is the capacity to resist within the discourse of Orientalism itself that is nullified, and it is this that Porter finds unsatisfactory. He argues that even when Said praises individual scholars for not falling into Orientalist traps, 'he does not show how within the given dominant hegemonic formation such an alternative discourse was able to emerge' (ibid.: 153).

This contradiction, and Said's failure to view hegemony as a process that emerges by consent rather than force, lead Porter to posit three alternatives to Orientalist discourse as constructed by Said. First, Orientalist texts are heterogeneous and not homogenous. Second, there may be alternative writings within the Western tradition. Third, it would be possible to consider a textual dialogue between the Occident and the Orient that would not codify knowledge and power relations. Porter uses examples within travel literature to demonstrate that within Orientalism there exist counter-hegemonic voices that express themselves in different ways at different historical junctures. The two works that he uses to prove his thesis are those that are referred to by Said: Marco Polo's *Travels* and T.E. (Lawrence of Arabia) Lawrence's *Seven Pillars of Wisdom*. Porter's main contention is that both of these writers problematise Said's claim of a united Western tradition in the discourse of Orientalism. He sums up his case against Said as follows:

> in the end to suggest alternatives to the discourse of Orientalism is not difficult to explain. First, because he overlooks the potential contradiction between discourse theory and Gramscian hegemony, he fails to historicize adequately the texts he cites and summarizes ... Second, because he does not distinguish the literary instance from more transparently ideological textual forms he does not acknowledge the semi-autonomous and overdetermined character of aesthetic artefacts. Finally, he fails to show how literary texts may in their play establish distance from the ideologies they seem to be reproducing. (Porter 1983: 160)

Porter's critique hinges on an apparent inability to accept the premise of Said's view of the intellectual's function: to oppose. The voice of dissent, the critique (of Orientalism or any other hegemonic discourse) does not need to propose an alternative for the critique to be effective and valid. The 'alternative' offered by Said is consistently implied in his concern with the role of the intellectual and his discussion of the strategies of intellectual dissent. Indeed, what make Said's criticism compelling are the repeated examples of the ways in which prejudice and stereotyping enter into Orientalist texts that purport to be scholarly, historical and empirical. All representations may be mediated, but the simple assertions of *Orientalism* remain: that power determines which representations may be accepted as 'true', that Orientalist texts owe their alleged 'truthfulness' to their location in the discourse, and that this situation is one that emerges out of, and confirms, a global structure of imperial domination. Hegemony does not need to be monolithic. Gauri Viswanathan's analysis of the use of the discipline of English literature in India as a discourse of socio-political control (1987) shows very clearly how a hegemonic discourse can operate and be effective in *the same arena* as acts and discourses of open social resistance.

One of the most vigorous attacks on Said's alleged Foucauldian position in recent times has been mounted by Aijaz Ahmad in his book *In Theory: Classes, Nations, Literatures* (1992). Ahmad contextualises *Orientalism* with what he terms the general retreat of the Left in response to the global offensive of the Right. He is at pains to demonstrate that Said is inconsistent about whether Orientalism is a system of representations or *mis*representations. Further, Ahmad argues that Said's position is simply to suggest that 'the line between representation and misrepresentation is always very thin' (ibid.: 164). The point is to suggest that Said has adopted, through Foucault, a Nietzschean stance whereby it is not possible to make true statements, in direct contrast to the Marxist position that allows for such a possibility. Said is accused of affiliating himself with a new kind of history writing that questions the 'very facticity of facts'.

Clearly, Ahmad's problem is with the notion of discourse itself. For where does the line between representation and misrepresentation lie? All representation is, in some sense, a misrepresentation. Any 'true' representation is one that has gained cultural and political authority. This holds for the 'facticity of facts' as well. Such facts are those representations that count as facts within a particular discourse. But curiously, Ahmad is closer to Said than he realises. For Said's own problem with discourse lies in its retreat from politics. That is not to say there is a 'real' Orient somewhere outside of, or beyond, its representations, but that the material urgency of colonial experience—or to put it another way, the representations by the colonised of their own experience—must be taken into account. This tension between the materiality of experience and the constructedness of identity forms one of the most crucial issues in Said's work, as it does in political discourse of all kinds. Whereas he is criticised by Porter and others for implying a real Orient, he is criticised by Ahmad for not invoking an Orient that is real enough.

For Ahmad, this failure is untenable in a book that has been celebrated among Left cultural theorists. Yet what is particularly disturbing for him about *Orientalism* is that it appeals to extreme forms of Third Worldist nationalisms. This is a process of selective memory, where acts committed by Oriental subjects, such as the violence at the time of Partition, are overlooked in an attempt to establish the greater evil of the power of Orientalism that has made the Oriental inferior. That Said should be blamed for interpretations and uses of his book that have dismayed and irritated him seems a bit unfair. Third World nationalisms hardly need *Orientalism* to give them succour. But even more than this, what Ahmad finds ghastly as a Marxist is that Marxism itself can be reduced to being a product of Orientalism and a cohort of colonialism. This negates the role that Marxism has played as a site of resistance in the periphery.

MARXISM

Marxism in its various forms is based on the belief that all political, cultural and ideological practices and values in a society are a consequence of the socio-economic conditions of life. The ultimate cause and the great moving power of all important historic events lie in the economic development of society, the changes in the modes of production and exchange, the consequent division of society into distinct classes, and the struggles of these classes against one another. The dominant ideology of a society is perpetuated by the ruling class in its own interests, producing 'false consciousness' in the working class about the true state of economic oppression, and against which workers must struggle. Marx had little to say about societies outside Europe but Lenin argued that imperialism was a product of the economic stagnation of capitalist societies. Despite its reduction of racial, cultural and political questions to the economic, Marxism, particularly its notion of class struggle, has been a prominent feature of anti-colonial resistance throughout the world.

Ahmad sees the elevation of *Orientalism* to the status of a 'classic' as being linked inextricably to its rise to a position of prominence 'within those sectors of the university intelligentsia which either originate in the ethnic minorities or affiliate themselves ideologically with the academic sections of these minorities' (1992: 166). In this way, he is able to dismiss not only colonial discourse analysis but also post-colonial theory, which he claims has been inaugurated by Third World migrants who came from privileged classes in their own countries. For these people, an alternative to Marxism was Orientalism, in which, above all, the question of race took precedence over gender and class. This allows Ahmad to assert that 'colonialism is now held responsible not only for its own cruelties but, conveniently enough, for ours too' (ibid.: 167). In short, what Ahmad is disturbed about is the privileged locations within the West that figures such as Said, Spivak and Rushdie occupy, and the manner in which they use these locations to theorise their marginality.

Robert Young, in *White Mythologies* (1990), provides an account of the methodological problems within Said's work. He notes that a major objection to *Orientalism* has been that it offers no alternative to the phenomenon it sets out to critique. Young recognises that, because Said views the Orient as a construction, he sees no need to respond to such criticisms. However, this does not solve Said's problems of how he separates himself from the 'coercive structures of knowledge that he is describing' (ibid.: 127). This is precisely the reason that Said, it is argued, falls into the very trap he seeks to expose. Hence, for Young, 'Said's account will be no truer to Orientalism than Orientalism is to the actual Orient, assuming that there could ever be such a thing' (ibid.: 128).

To show Said's inconsistency, Young argues that the book is divided into two parts. The first part seeks to demonstrate the invention of the Orient as a construction of representation, and the second strives to show how this knowledge system and forms of representation are brought into play for the colonial powers. He points to Said's attempts to reconcile these two positions by bringing together what he terms two forms of Orientalism. One form embodied classical scholarship which constructed the Orient, while the other was the Orient articulated by travellers, pilgrims and statesmen. Although these two existed in tension, they came together in a single form with colonisation. This leads Young to argue that 'while Said wants to argue that Orientalism has a hegemonic consistency, his own representation of it becomes increasingly conflictual' (ibid.: 130).

Young argues that Said's fundamental thesis is to point out the anti-humanist nature of Orientalism. However, what is problematic for him is the manner in which Said appropriates the idea of human from within the Western humanist tradition in order to oppose the Occidental representation of the Orient. This allows Young to argue that Said's work comes perilously close to an Orientalist position, and he questions: 'How does any form of knowledge—including Orientalism—escape the terms of Orientalism's critique?'

James Clifford raises two sets of complementary questions about *Orientalism*. First, should criticism seek to provide a counter-narrative to culturally produced images such as the Orient? Second, how is the critique of Orientalism to avoid falling into the trap of 'Occidentalism'? Clifford points out the role all forms of knowledge and representation have in dealing with a group or society's others. Is it possible, he asks, to escape the manner in which Orientalism engages in the dehumanising, misrepresenting and inferiorising of other cultures? He argues that in Said's work there is no alternative to Orientalism, that his attack is firmly grounded within values derived from the 'Western anthropological human sciences' (Clifford 1988: 261). Such a stance, of humanism, of oppositional criticism, is a 'privilege invented by a totalising Western liberalism' (ibid.: 263). Clifford here raises a perennial contradiction in Said's work, which is the employment of the tools of a Western theoretical tradition to critique that tradition. Yet it might be pointed out that this process of appropriation of dominant forms and cultural discourses is a common feature of post-colonial oppositionality. One might ask if this strategy contradicts what Said reveals about the processes of Orientalism in speaking for the Orient.

Clifford is disturbed by the absence of a fully developed theory of culture in *Orientalism*. He sees Said's work on culture as being hegemonic and disciplinary, forms of high European culture which are consequently 'meaningless, since they bypass the local cultural codes that make personal experience articulate' (ibid.: 263). Clifford argues that Said misappropriates Foucault, especially through Said's humanism, which in turn means that there are major theoretical inconsistencies within *Orientalism*. Said's multiple identities, being a Palestinian who lives in the United States and one who operates as an oppositional critic deploying the very tools of the culture he seeks to rebuke, continue to raise problems for Clifford. 'From what discrete sets of cultural resources does any modern writer construct his or her discourse?' he asks (ibid.: 276). 'To what world audience (and in what language) are these discourses most generally addressed? Must the intellectual at least, in a literate global situation, construct a native land by writing like Césaire the notebook of a return?' (ibid.: 276). In one respect Clifford's questions go right to the heart of Said's work. How do any individuals construct themselves as cultural identities? How do they construct for themselves a homeland? This is precisely what makes Said so fascinating as a cultural critic. The ambivalence of his position, the many paradoxes he traverses and the tensions created in his own cultural identity reveal the very complexity of the process of constructing one's identity in the modern post-colonial world.

Michael Dutton and Peter Williams (1993) provide an extremely detailed account of the theoretical underpinnings of Said's work in *Orientalism*. Their major objection is with Said's theoretical inconsistencies. They make the oft-repeated criticism that Said makes ambivalent use of Foucault and that he fails to adhere to that methodology. They point out that Said's privileging of the author and his valorisation of literary writing and reading practices are incompatible with the way Foucault sees discourse operating. This has the effect of contracting 'both the range and scope of resistance to inequities of power and knowledge' (ibid.: 325). In short, for them, had Said been truer to Foucault, he would have been able to avoid the pitfalls that Porter, Ahmad, Young and Clifford have pointed out.

Mona Abaza and Georg Stauth (1990) have noted that, although critiques of classical Orientalism received considerable attention in the 1960s and 1970s, it was not until Said's *Orientalism* that Orientalism became a major area of inter-cultural research. They argue, however, that Said's methodology is 'reductionist' (ibid.: 210), assuming that discourse is a kind of one-way street from the powerful to the weak. This means that Said denies a 'long history of productive cultural exchange'. Furthermore, this framework is appropriated by sociologists, anthropologists and feminists to differentiate between the essence and reality of other cultures. This is a trend they term 'going native' and is similar to a type of Orientalism in reverse that has been articulated by al-Azm (1981).

Abaza and Stauth's own reductionism means that they unproblematically collapse such alternative research methodologies into a mere apology for Islamic fundamentalism (Abaza and Stauth 1990). In a similar vein, Emmanuel Sivan argues that Said's defence of Islam is seen by liberal intellectuals in the Arab world as being complicit with conservative forces that are pushing a fundamentalist agenda. He argues that Arab reviewers of *Orientalism* challenge Said 'for the manner in which he sweeps uncomfortable facts under the rug', failing either to place the historical facts in perspective or to mention them altogether (Sivan 1985: 137).

THE GENDER CRITIQUE

Lata Mani and Ruth Frankenberg argue that Said's work needs to be more nuanced and that it needs to qualify and articulate differences within the Orient. Said's general theory, they claim, is based on West Asia. Hence, they object to Said's totalising and essentialising position (Mani and Frankenberg 1985: 174–92). This represents the most frequent, and perhaps most damaging, criticism of *Orientalism* and is one to which Said has responded in the 1995 'Afterword'. The substantial point made by such criticisms is that the Occident and the Orient are constructed as monolithic entities. Said's description of power relations in such a formulation, it is suggested, fails to reflect the discursive nature of power as well as the differences, contradictions and counter-hegemonic positions evident within the discourse of Orientalism.

Zakia Pathak, Saswati Sengupta and Sharmila Purkayastha point out problems with the manner in which Said deals with the question of gender in Orientalism. Their main concern, however, is to demonstrate that Said's work is directed primarily at a Western audience. His anger and fury is to be seen from the vantage point of an expatriate. They argue that 'it is doubtful if this obsession can ever be broken out from a place in the first world' (Pathak *et al.*, 1991: 216).

Reina Lewis, in her study called *Gendering Orientalism* (1995), seeks to destabilise the 'fiction' of a homogenous Occident. This is a position that is taken up also by Joan Miller, who points out that Said fails to view women as active participants within imperial power relations (Miller 1990). Lewis sets out to show the specificity of the female subject whose gaze 'has undercut the potentially unified, and paradigmatically male, colonial subject outlined in Said's *Orientalism*' (Lewis 1995: 3). Lewis argues that women's differential gendered positions meant that this produced a gaze that was less absolute than Said's characterisation. She points out that Said refers to only a single woman writer, Gertrude Bell, and even then pays no attention to her gender position within her texts. Lewis asserts that Said 'never questions women's apparent absence as producers of Orientalist discourse or as agents within colonial power. This mirrors the traditional view that women were not involved in colonial expansion' (ibid.: 18). By omitting women, she argues, Said falls into the very trap of stereotyping which he sees as the central problem of Orientalism.

EXTENDING *ORIENTALISM*

A great number of responses to *Orientalism,* by Third World critics and like-minded theorists, have focused on the ways in which it might be extended into an understanding of the range and power of imperial representation. Homi Bhabha's discussion of how Said's pioneering work could be extended in colonial discourse analysis focuses also on the question of Foucault. Bhabha acknowledges Foucault's importance, but, like other critics, accuses Said of being too 'instrumentalist' in his use of Foucault's concept of discourse (Bhabha 1994: 72). However, Bhabha's purpose is not to expose Said's theoretical problems but to suggest a way of extending Said's analysis, which he sees as central to colonial discourse analysis. He does this by interrogating Said's project with the theoretical tools of discourse analysis, focusing on the manner in which Orientalism becomes a tool of colonial power and administration. This introduces the notion of ambivalence within the very discourse of Orientalism. For Bhabha, Said is an important figure in colonial discourse analysis because his work 'focused the need to quicken the half-light of western history with the disturbing memory of its colonial texts that bear witness to the trauma that accompanies the triumphal art of Empire' (Bhabha 1986: 149).

A special 1994 issue of *L'Esprit Créateur* devoted to 'Orientalism after *Orientalism*' seeks to go beyond what it sees as the theoretical limitations of Said's work, while recognising its formative position within colonial discourse analysis. Similar to Clifford, Ali Behdad argues that Said's attempt to characterise Orientalism as a coherent unitary system of knowledge locates his critique in the very epistemology it seeks to subvert. Said's portrayal of Orientalism leaves little opportunity for difference within the modes of representation that operate to create repressive relations between the Occident and the Orient. Behdad argues that Said construes power relations 'negatively in terms of a repressive hypothesis and constructs a totalizing interpretative framework to account for a phenomenon that in reality is discontinuous and plural in its formation' (Behdad 1994: 3). In order both to counter Said's essentialisation and to recognise Orientalism's ambivalences, a system of local criticism as an elaboration of Said's work is offered.

Mahmut Mutman also seeks to extend Said's analysis, recognising that the very debate on Orientalism is one that has been made possible by Said's book. Mutman engages in a critical dialogue with Said. He does not see himself as posing a better alternative to Orientalism; rather, his project is to illustrate the Orientalist constructions of Islam and to contextualise them within a global perspective. For Mutman, it is the local context that is subsumed in Said's account that needs to be recovered in order to understand the complexities and the intricacies of Orientalism (Mutman 1993).

In an interesting review of *Orientalism*, Amal Rassam points out how Said's work could have been extended fruitfully by including an analysis of the Maghreb. Morocco, in particular, suffered at the hands of French Orientalism, which was deployed to 'study, interpret and control' the Moroccans (Rassam 1980: 506). However, Rassam argues that Said does not deal with two important questions. These are: first, how does one really get to know another culture in its own terms? and, second, what are the alternatives to Orientalism? These concerns are echoed by Ross Chambers, who also wonders if it is possible to have a kind of humanistic knowledge that does not play a dominating role over the people it seeks to study. Is it possible that the silent can achieve a voice and represent themselves (Chambers 1980: 512)?

SUMMARY

The analysis of *Orientalism*, which Said published in 1978, has become a classic in the study of the West's relationship with its others. The depiction of Orientalism, in all its many manifestations, as a 'discourse' has raised a storm of theoretical and methodological argument, but it has given an unparalleled focus and political clarity to the complex range of activities by which Europe gained knowledge of its oriental other. *Orientalism* is a perfect demonstration of the power of 'amateurism' in intellectual work. For while it leaves itself open to various criticisms, its originality, its scope and its tenacious conviction have altered the way we think about global cultural relations. The essence of Said's argument is that to know something is to have power over it, and conversely, to have power is to be able to know the world in your own terms. When this 'something' is a whole region of the world, in which dozens of ethnicities, nationalities and languages are gathered under the spurious category 'the Orient', then the link between that knowledge and the power it confirms becomes profoundly important. The discourse of Orientalism becomes the frame within which the West knows the Orient, and this discourse determines both popular and academic representations of the Middle East even today.

REFERENCES

Abaza, M. and Stauth, G. (1990) 'Occidental reason, Orientalism Islamic fundamentalism: A critique', in Martin Albrow and Elizabeth King (eds) *Globalization, Knowledge and Society*, London: Sage.

Ahmad, A. (1992) *In Theory: Classes, Nations, Literatures*, London: Verso.

------------. (1995) 'The politics of literary postcoloniality', *Race and Class* 36: 1–20.

al-Azm, S.J. (1981) 'Orientalism and Orientalism in reverse', *Khamsin* 8: 9–10.

Alexander, E. (1989) 'Professor of Terror', *Commentary* 88(2): 49–50.

Behdad, A. (1994) 'Orientalism after *Orientalism*', *L'Esprit Créateur* 34(2): 1–11.

Bhabha, H. (1986) 'The other question: Difference, discrimination, and the discourse of colonialism', in Francis Barker, Peter Hulme and Margaret Iversen (eds) *Literature, Politics and Theory*, London: Methuen.

Chambers, R. (1980) 'Representation and authority', *Comparative Studies in Society and History* 22: 509–12.

Clifford, J. (1988) 'On Orientalism', in *The Predicament of Culture: Twentieth Century Ethnography, Literature and Art*, Cambridge, MA: Harvard University Press.

Dutton, M. and Williams, P. (1993) 'Translating theories: Edward Said on Orientalism, imperialism and alterity', *Southern Review* 26(3): 314–57.

Lewis, B. (1982) 'Orientalism: An exchange', *New York Review of Books* 29(13): 46–8.

------------. (1982a) 'The question of Orientalism', *New York Review of Books* 29(11): 49–56.

Lewis, R. (1995) *Gendering Orientalism: Race, Femininity and Representation*, New York: Routledge.

Mani, L. and Frankenberg, R. (1985) 'The challenge of *Orientalism*', *Economy and Society* 14: 174–92.

Miller, J. (1990) *Seductions: Studies in Reading and Culture*, London: Virago.

Mutman, M. (1993) 'Under the sign of Orientalism: The West vs. Islam', *Cultural Critique*, winter 1992–3: 165–97.

Pathak, Z., Sengupta, S. and Purkayastha, S. (1991) 'The prisonhouse of Orientalism', *Textual Practice* 5(2): 195–218.

Poliakov, L. (1974) *The Aryan Myth: A History of Racist and Nationalist Ideas in Europe*, trans. Edmund Howard, London: Chatto &Windus.

Rassam, A. (1980) 'Comments on *Orientalism*', *Comparative Studies in Society and History* 22: 505–12.

Renan, E. (1896) *Poetry of the Celtic Races and Other Studies*, trans. W.G. Hutchinson, London: Walter Scott.

Said, E. (1976) 'Interview', *Diacritics* 6(3): 30–47.

------------. (1978) *Orientalism*, New York: Vintage.

------------. (1978a) 'The problem of textuality: Two exemplary positions', *Critical Inquiry* 4: 673–714.

------------. (1983) *The World, the Text and the Critic*, Cambridge, MA: Harvard University Press.

------------. (1985) 'Orientalism reconsidered', *Race and Class* 27(2): 1–16.

------------. (1995) 'Afterword', in *Orientalism*, New York: Vintage.

Salusinszky, I. (ed.) (1987) 'Interview with Edward Said', *Criticism in Society*, New York: Methuen.

Sivan, E. (1985) 'Edward Said and his Arab reviewers', in *Interpretations of Islam: Past and Present*, Princeton, NJ: University of Princeton Press.

Viswanathan, G. (1987) 'The beginnings of English literary study in British India', *Oxford Literary Review* 9(1–2): 2–26.

Young, R. (1990) *White Mythologies: Writing History and the West*, London: Routledge.

Speaking Back to Orientalist Discourse

"Opium!

Submission!

Kismet!

Lattice-work, caravanserai fountains

a sultan dancing on a silver tray!

Maharajah, rajah a thousand-year-old shah!

Waving from minarets

clogs made of mother-of-pearl;

women with henna-stained noses

working their looms with their feet.

In the wind, green-turbaned imams

            calling people to prayer"

This is the Orient the French poet sees.

This

   is

      the Orient of the books

that come out from the press

at the rate of a million a minute.

But

      yesterday

         today

            or tomorrow

an Orient like this

   never existed

   and never will.[1]

THIS QUOTATION COMES FROM A MUCH LONGER POEM, TITLED

"Pierre Loti" and written by the great Turkish poet Nazım Hikmet in 1925. Hikmet's target is not so much Loti himself as European imperialism, and his angry response is charged by his Marxist worldview and his proto-Third Worldism. Nevertheless, his speaking back to Orientalist discourse follows a turn-of-the-century Ottoman intellectual tradition. To refer to two earlier literary examples, Halit Ziya's 1908 novel *Nesl-i Ahîr* (The first generation), opens with the protagonist's quarrel with a book written by a European author on the "Orient." Although a great deal more placid than the poet's penetrating voice, the sentiments of this fictional character, a well-educated Ottoman man on a boat returning from Marseille, are also in revolt against Orientalist misconceptions: "Whenever he began reading a book on the East, especially on his own country, he felt inclined to leave it. As he witnessed the Western writers' accounts of a lifestyle they attempted to discover under the brightness of an Eastern sun that blinded their eyes and amidst the ambiguities of a language they did not understand, his nerves would unravel and his heart would ache [rebelling against] their idiotic opinions and their self-righteous courage that produced so many errors."[2]

Ahmed Mithad Efendi, another prominent Ottoman writer, dealt with the same theme in his 1889 Avrupa'da Bir Cevelan (A tour in Europe), focusing on (among other things) the European fantasy about the Eastern woman. He captured the Ingresque formula to indicate the epistemological status such representations had achieved:

> [This] lovable person lies negligently on a sofa. One of her slippers, embroidered with pearls, is on the floor, while the other is on the tip of her toes. Since her garments are intended to ornament rather than to conceal [her body], her legs dangling from the sofa are half naked and her belly and breasts are covered by fabrics as thin and transparent as a dream. Her disheveled hair over her nude shoulders falls down in waves. ... In her mouThis the black end of the pipe of a narghile, curving like a snake. ... A black servant fans her. ... This is the Eastern woman Europe depicted until now. ... It is assumed that this body is not the mistress of her house, the wife of her husband, and the mother of her children, but only a servant to the pleasures of the man who owns the house. What a misconception![3]

Ahmed Mithad's "correction" to the distortions he sarcastically describes has its own problems, of course. It is static; it is also based on a struggle for power; it replaces one "truth" with another; and it reclaims the hierarchy by inverting it.[4] I address these complex issues only tangentially; I limit myself, instead, to the presentation of several artistic and architectural responses to Orientalism in an attempt to contribute to the triangulation of recent critical scholarship in art history that examines the Orientalist discourse from the "Western" perspective. The study of Orientalist art owes a great deal to Edward Said's groundbreaking book, *Orientalism* (1978). Said enhanced the importance of viewing cultural products through a lens that highlights the underlining politics of domination, specifically where the "Orient" is concerned. Art and architectural history responded to Said's challenge and, not surprisingly, followed the model established by *Orientalism*, thus engaging in analyses of artworks that contributed to the construction of an "Orient." They offered innovative and critical readings of Orientalism, but focused solely on the "West." As Said himself stated, *Orientalism* was a study of the "West" alone. It was not intended as a cross-cultural examination of and did not claim to give voice to the "other" side, an issue Said addressed in his later writings.[5]

Triangulation is a technical term borrowed from engineering and adapted by sociology as a research tool. Used in land surveying to determine a position, it offers the possibility of multiple readings in history. In Janet Abu-Lughod's words, triangulation is based on the understanding that "there is no archimedian point *outside* the system from which to view historic reality."[6] My approach to Orientalism from the "other" side, the side of "Orientals," is aimed to bring another perspective to the discourse. Studied from this unconventional corner, Orientalism reveals a hitherto concealed dynamism, one that is about dialogue between cultures and about contesting the dominant norms. When the Oriental artists and intellectuals speak and begin shaping the terms of the debate, the Orient as represented by the West sheds its homogeneity, timelessness, and passivity, and becomes nuanced and complicated. It can no longer fit the frozen categories.

My first case study is the late nineteenth–early twentieth-century Ottoman painter Osman Hamdi, whose artistic career centers on speaking back to Orientalism. His response takes place within the very norms and artistic format of the school he addresses his critique to. Osman Hamdi's pursuit is deliberate and consistent. Nevertheless, there are other "corrective" messages to Orientalism in the Ottoman discourse, although not always explicit. Consider, for example, Prince Abdülmecid's Beethoven in the Palace (ca. 1900), which depicts a truly oppositional palace scene to the one we know from Orientalist paintings (Figure 1). A trio, consisting of a male cellist and two women, one playing the violin, the other the piano, performs for an audience of three women and one man, the prince himself. These men and women, dressed according to the latest European fashions, are immersed in the music as performers and listeners. The interaction between genders is established through music and the artistic communication implies mutual

FIGURE 1: Caliph Abdülmecid II, *Beethoven in the Palace*, 1915. Museum of Painting and Sculpture, Istanbul.

respect. The room is lavishly decorated with turn-of-the-century European furniture, including a pay-sage painting hanging on the wall, an equestrian statue on a pedestal, and a bust of Beethoven. In another example that contradicts European representations of Oriental women, Ömer Adil's *Women Painters' Atelier* (ca. 1920) shows a studio in the School of Fine Arts in Istanbul, where Ottoman women are engaged in a serious study of art—albeit in a segregated setting.[7]

Halil Bey, the flamboyant Ottoman ambassador to Paris in the mid-1860s and well-known at the time for his spectacular painting collection that included Ingres's *Le Bain turc* (1862), seems to have pursued another subtle way to deal with Orientalism.[8] Two years after he purchased *Le Bain turc*, Halil Bey bought Courbet's *Les Dormeuses* (1867), another painting with lesbian undertones, which he hung next to Ingres's bath scene. Admitting that it would be difficult to prove his thesis factually, art historian Francis Haskell feels tempted to speculate that perhaps Halil Bey showed the Ingres canvas to Courbet and suggested that he paint a "modern counterpart" to Ingres's "Oriental fantasy."[9] Courbet's painting is devoid of the paraphernalia that act as "signs" of the Orient and that speckle Ingres's canvas to

FIGURE 2: Osman Hamdi, Discussion in Front of the Mosque, ca. 1906. Museum of Painting and Sculpture, Istanbul.

Osman Hamdi / Copyright in the Public Domain.

make his bath unmistakably "Turkish." In this light, one is tempted to push Haskell's speculation a step further and read Halil Bey's intervention as a deliberate gesture to resituate the scene depicted in Bain turc to a European setting, thereby evacuating the bath from Ingres's Orientalist implications.

During the years that corresponded to Halil Bey's tenure as ambassador, Osman Hamdi was a student in Paris. There he was drawn to the atelier of Gustave Boulanger and possibly also to that of Jean-Léon Gérôme, and his own work matured under the technical and thematic influence of the French Orientalist school. Nevertheless, his "scenes from the Orient" provide acute and persistent critiques of mainstream Orientalist paintings. They represent a resistant voice, whose power derives from the painter's position as an Ottoman intellectual, as well as from his intimate acquaintance with the school's mental framework, techniques, and conventions. Osman Hamdi's men and women—dressed in the colorful garments in the Orientalist fashion and placed in "authentic" settings—are thinking, questioning, and acting human beings who display none of the passivity and submissiveness attributed to them by European painters.

Osman Hamdi addressed the major themes of Orientalist painters from his critical stance as an insider on the outside. In contrast to the constructions that convey fanaticism, exoticism, and even violence in Gérôme's series of paintings on Islamic worship, for example, Osman Hamdi presented Islam as a religion that encouraged intellectual curiosity, discussion, debate, even doubt.[10] In painting after painting, his men of religion, reading and discussing books, maintain their upright posture as an expression of their human dignity, against a background of meticulously articulated architectural details. To refer to a few examples, *Discussion in Front of the Mosque* (ca. 1906) depicts three "teachers," one reading aloud (commenting on?) a book, while the others listen with great attention, holding onto their own texts (Fig. 2). The same theme, but now showing only one man in the audience of a savant, is portrayed in *In the Green Mosque in Bursa* (ca. 1900). *The Theologist* (1901) focuses on yet another scholar surrounded by books, reading in a mosque.

Osman Hamdi's repertoire of women, both in public and domestic spaces, makes a statement about their status in the society. Dressed in elegant and fashionable clothes, they are shown moving freely in the city and sometimes interacting with men as they attend to business. The home scenes provide a striking alternative to the myriad familiar and titillating views of harem and bath by French painters. Several of his works, among them *The Coffee Corner* (1879) and *After the Iftar* (1886), depict a couple in a tranquil domestic environment, the seated man being served coffee by the woman. Although the hierarchical family structure is not questioned, the man of the house is not the omnipotent, amoral, sensual tyrant of European representations, enjoying his dominion over scores of women at his mercy and pleasure. Instead, a dialogue is offered that redefines the gender relationships

FIGURE 3: Osman Hamdi, Girl Reading, ca. 1893. Private collection, Izmir. From Mustafa Cezar, *Sanatta Batıya Açılış, ve Osman Hamdi*, Istanbul, 1971.

Osman Hamdi / Copyright in the Public Domain.

in Orientalist paintings. The scenes that show only women in domestic interiors may belong to the long lineage of *Les femmes dans leur appartement*, but Osman Hamdi's women try to reveal another "truth" about the activities that take place in upper-class Muslim homes than the ones suggested by Delacroix and Gérôme. He hints, for example, at domestic work by showing laundry drying in the background.

Among the themes Osman Hamdi addressed from the checklist of Orientalism is a grooming scene that speaks back to the particular European obsession with the Eastern female body. *In Girl Having Her Hair Combed* (1881), Hamdi Bey recasts both the young woman being tended to and the servant. The Ottoman painter's upper-class demoiselle has control over her own body as she watches herself attentively in the mirror, clearly supervising her coiffure. With this painting, Osman Hamdi counteracts Gérôme's *Le Bain* (1880), whose centerpiece is a young woman in a bath being washed by a black slave. The viewer does not have access to her facial expression, but only to her naked back, her posture and bent neck suggesting her helpless abandonment to her fate in the aftermath of this sensual preparation. Osman Hamdi's servant is a worker, simply doing her job; Gérôme sets a mysterious tone for what is to come by providing a contrast charged with innuendoes.

FIGURE 4: Grand Reception Hall, Dolmabahçe Palace, Istanbul. Abdülhamid II Albums, Prints and Photographs Division, Library of Congress, Washington, D.C.

Abdül Hamid II / Library of Congress.

Osman Hamdi's reaction to the cliché of the "Oriental" woman as sex object becomes even more acute when he focuses on a single woman. His response to Orientalism's innumerable reclining odalisques is Girl Reading (ca. 1893; Fig. 3). The painting shows a young woman stretched out on a sofa, totally immersed in a book. Her relaxed and casual tone implies that she is not reading a religious text, but perhaps a work of literature. The composition has the familiar collage of Orientalist details, complete with rugs, tiles, inscriptions, and "Islamic" architectural elements, but the shelves behind her are filled with books, making the statement that reading occupies an important part of her life. The "girl" is hence given back her thinking mind and intellectual life, which had been erased by Orientalist painters.

Corresponding to the time when Osman Hamdi was voicing his individual response to Orientalist representations of his country, an official venture attempted to bring a similar corrective. On the occasion of the 1893 World's Columbian Exposition, the Ottoman Sultan Abdülhamid II presented fifty-one photography albums to the "National Library" of the United States.[11] The ornately bound albums, which contained 1,819 photographs by various Istanbul photographers, drew the image of the empire according to the conceptions of its ruling elite. Now at the Library of Congress, the Abdülhamid albums cover the empire in several categories. Although historic grandeur, expressed by photographs of major monuments from the Byzantine and Turkish periods, as well as natural landscapes are given their due respect, the major theme is that of modernization. Modernizing reforms to rejuvenate the empire had been in place since the eighteenth century in response to successive military defeats experienced by the Ottoman army. In search of quick and practical remedies, the Ottoman rulers first imported technological innovations that were seen as proof of European superiority. Nevertheless, the exposure to the West soon embraced other fields and the history of the late Ottoman Empire became a history of Westernization. This significant development that affected all aspects of Ottoman life remained prominently absent from Orientalist accounts.

Modernization covered many areas, extending from military reforms to education to artistic production. It introduced, for example, a new architecture based on European models. One of the most telling statements regarding architectural modernity was made by the construction of Dolmabahçe Palace in 1856. It pointed to the official acceptance of Western models not only as fashionable novelties, but also to bring radical transformation to lifestyles. The overall organization of the palace, based on Beaux-Arts principles of symmetry, axiality, and regularity, was complemented by its ornate classical façades that evoked the contemporary French Empire style. Its main façade turned toward the Bosphorus, the impressive mass of the Dolmabahçe Palace was highly visible from various vistas and defined a new image of monumentality for the capital. The interior spaces corresponded to changing fashions in the everyday life of the palace: European furniture filled the rooms, revealing new customs that ranged from eating at elaborately set tables on high-backed chairs as opposed to the former pattern of sitting on the floor or on low couches around a tray, to substituting built-in couches for armchairs and sofas in living rooms in a redefinition of socializing habits (Fig. 4). The paraphernalia that filled the rooms—including crystal chandeliers, armoirs, sideboards, and European paintings—contributed further to the rupture with the former decorative traditions that relied, for example, on an extensive use of tiles on wall surfaces. Dolmabahçe's exterior and the interior photographs in the Abdülhamid albums hence offered a very different palace from the older Ottoman palaces. They also contradicted the palaces of the Orientalist discourse that had constructed imaginary *serails*.

FIGURE 5: Imperial Library, Istanbul. Abdülhamid II Albums, Prints and Photographs Division, Library of Congress, Washington, D.C.

Abdül Hamid II / Library of Congress.

FIGURE 6: Students of the Rushdié Girls' School in Emirghan, Istanbul. Abdülhamid II Albums, Prints and Photographs Division, Library of Congress, Washington, D.C.

Abdül Hamid II / Library of Congress.

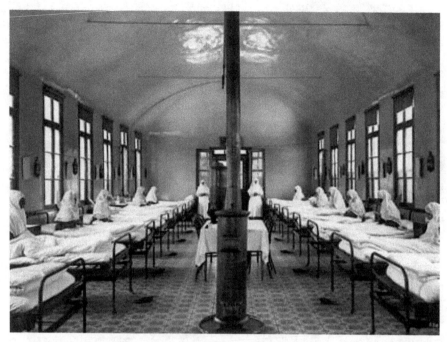

FIGURE 7: Tuberculosis Ward of the Women's Hospital in Haseki, Istanbul. Abdülhamid II Albums, Prints and Photographs Division, Library of Congress, Washington, D.C.

Abdül Hamid II / Library of Congress.

Among other aspects of modernization, industrialization was underlined by photographs of factories, docks, and arsenals. From the 1840s on, a number of state-run industries were founded on the outskirts of Istanbul. They included foundries that produced iron pipes, steel rails, swords, and knives and factories that specialized in textiles, glass, paper, chemicals, and rubber. Boats were made and maintained in modern arsenals. The products were exhibited in all major European universal exhibitions and a considerable sample was sent to the World's Columbian Exposition in Chicago in 1893.[12] The photographs of modern production facilities in the Abdülhamid albums delivered a picture of the industrial environment in the empire.

Educational reforms, conveyed through photographs of new school buildings, occupied the largest component of the exposé. To demonstrate the widespread nature of modern education, photographs of schools included the entire spectrum, from the highest institutions of learning (such as the law school) to middle and elementary levels and offered examples from diverse regions of the imperial territory. Certain institutions of great prestige were given more space. For example, an entire album was dedicated to the Imperial High School of Galatasaray, where instruction was given in Turkish and French. The photographs flaunted the building in its expansive garden, the age range of students from elementary through high school, students with their distinguished teachers, and even gym classes. Another important educational establishment was the school of medicine, shown in one photograph with its entire population. The emphasis on science and scientific research was revealed by a photograph of a group of medical students in front of a cadaver, other relevant artifacts framing the view. Respect for learning and knowledge permeated the albums in various forms, for example, by interior views from the museum of the Imperial Maritime College and the Imperial Library. A scholar of theology, as judged from his attire, reading in a well-equipped modern library in a converted historic building made a statement about the enlightened nature of Islam and its compatibility with contemporary ideas—just like Osman Hamdi's religious figures (Fig. 5).

To demystify another "misconception," the albums dedicated many photographs to women's education. Paralleling the photographs on the education of boys, many girls' schools where modern instruction was pursued were included. Groups of students carrying their books and diplomas—younger counterparts to Osman Hamdi's Girl Reading—strove to give further proof to the status of women in modern Ottoman society (Fig. 6). Women appeared in the albums in one other classification: health care. A special hospital for women received extensive coverage, including the administration building and a group of doctors. Other photos show the exteriors and interiors of individual pavilions that met high hospital standards for the turn of the century (Fig. 7). These photographs also introduced a category of working women: nurses. It is significant, however, that the distant figures of the nurses and the tuberculosis patients constituted the only mature women in the albums; the rest were schoolgirls.

The Abdülhamid II albums, then, provide an imperial image that is circumscribed in many aspects but that clearly reflects the official intention to represent the empire in a progressive light. This was a form of answering back to the European discourse that froze Ottoman culture and society in an undefined and imagined past by reductive formulas about fanatic religious practices, irrationality, ignorance, and mindless but sumptuous living. The albums attempted to transform the end-of-the-century image of the empire as the "sick man of Europe" into a rejuvenated, dynamic, and modern one.

FIGURE 8: Albert Laprade, The Habous Quarter, Casablanca. From Léandre Vaillat, *Le visage français* du Maroc, Paris, 1931.

The Ottoman Empire may have been on its way to disintegration in the face of the changing global power structure during the late nineteenth and early twentieth centuries, but it was still independent and maintained something from its past prowess. My two other case studies come from colonial contexts, where "speaking back" takes on different forms. Granted that Westernization reigned in all Ottoman social and cultural realms, the relationship between dominating and dominated cultures was far more entangled in a colonial situation. The colonial discourse that punctuated cultural differences also led to the construction of "traditions" for colonized territories. The later adoption, interpretation, and transfiguration of these traditions reveal intriguing questions about issues of authenticity in an age that desperately looks for a sense of national identity while engulfed by globalization.

Research and writing on "non-Western" architecture had already coalesced into a significant body of literature by the end of the nineteenth century in Europe. Nevertheless, in the 1920s and 1930s a major turn from monumental to residential forms occurred in the architectural discourse. North African French colonies present a particularly rich case study as their vernacular architecture was the subject of scrupulous documentation and analysis. The focus originated in part from European

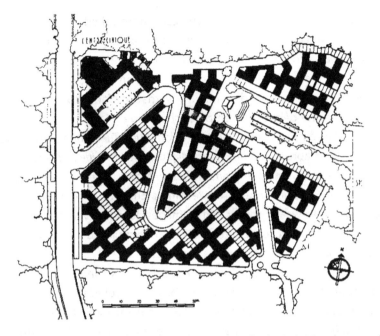

FIGURE 9: G. Glorieux and L. Glorieux-Monfred, Cité Musulmane el Omrane, site plan. From L'Architecture d'aujourd'hui, no. 20 (October 1984).

Copyright © 1984 by G. Glorieux and L. Glorieux-Monfred.

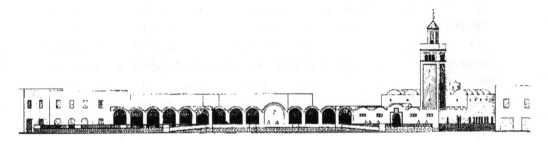

FIGURE 10: Jean-Pierre Ventre, Mosque and Market in Bizerte, elevation. From L'Architecture d'aujourd'hui, no. 20 (October 1948).

Copyright © 1948 by Jean-Pierre Ventre.

modernist sensibilities that saw in the cubical, whitewashed masses and sparse spaces of North African medinas potential sources of inspiration for a modernist vocabulary. It was also connected to the growing housing shortage in colonial cities. French architects in charge of the construction programs undertaken by the colonial administration relied on regional vernacular forms to find appropriate stylistic and spatial models for contemporary housing projects.

Popular books, such as Victor Valensi's *L'Habitation Tunisienne* (Paris, 1923), A. Mairat de la Motte-Capron's *L'Architecture indigène nord africaine* (Algiers, 1923), and Jean Galotti's *Les Jardins et les maisons arabes au Maroc* (Paris, 1926), the last with sketches by Albert Laprade, one of the leading architects working in Morocco at the time, presented a wealthy collection of images depicting vernacular buildings, often in their urban or landscape settings. These books played an important role in disseminating the image of North African vernacular architecture in the *métropole* and *outre-mer*. Le Corbusier's own interest in vernacular architecture and his recurrent incorporation of sketches and photographs in his publications to support his arguments for a modern architecture and urbanism enhanced the entry of North African "indigenous" forms into the discourse of modernism.[13] Furthermore, the creation of temporary quarters, deemed "authentic," in the world's fairs from the second half of the nineteenth century on, culminating in the extensive Tunisian section of the 1931 Paris Colonial Exhibition, played a crucial role in the dissemination of North African vernacular imagery.[14]

When French architects built housing schemes for "indigenous" people, they relied on the commentary and documentation developed by the colonial discourse on the North African vernacular. A striking example is the new medina of Casablanca (the Habous Quarter) intended to accommodate the growing Moroccan population of the city (Fig. 8). Designed by Laprade and built in the early 1920s, the scheme combined the "customs and scruples" of Moroccans with French considerations for "hygiene"[15] and highlighted the contrast between the street and the courtyards of the houses. Reinterpreting local "traditions," Laprade created "sensible, vibrant walls, charged with poetry." These walls defined cubical masses, but their irregularity gave them a "human" touch. However, the project was more than a stylistic exercise; the architect's ambition was to integrate into his design "values of ambiance" as well as a "whole way of life." The spatial and programmatic qualities adhered to these goals: there were narrow streets and courtyard houses, markets, neighborhood ovens, public baths, mosques, and Quranic schools brought together in a stylistic integrity that had "preserved everything respectable in the tradition." Laprade implied that he had improved local architecture by appropriating what was seen as valuable by modernist architectural discourse and by eliminating what was not considered "respectable."[16]

Similar projects were carried out in other North African colonies. About two decades later, the Cité Musulmane el Omrane in Tunis repeated the whitewashed houses with courtyards, but no openings to the exterior, now utilizing vaults on roofs. The architects (G. Glorieux and L. Glorieux-Monfred) organized the site plan according to a relaxed orthogonal street network that allowed for a certain flexibility in the positioning of individual units and their collective massing (Fig. 9). If Cité el Omrane formulized the principles for residential patterns, another Tunisian project dating from the same period, the mosque and market in Bizerte, articulated the essence of community center for the Muslim population (Fig. 10). Rows of vaulted small shops fronted with colonnades framed the public space, significantly named Place de la France; a mosque attached to the market structures stood out with its shifted angle oriented toward Mecca, its multiple domes, and its square minaret. The cumulative image from both projects was that of a dense settlement, composed of small and simple repetitive units woven together with some irregularity, vaults and domes further uniting the scheme on the roof level. The persistence of this pattern in the new residential projects for the indigenous people reinforced the sociocultural duality already existing and already nurtured in the colonial cities. A comparison of Cité el Omrane with its contemporary Quartier Gambetta housing project, again in Tunis but intended for Europeans, acknowledges the policy to maintain, enhance, and express cultural differences between colonizer and colonized. Quartier Gambetta was envisioned as a Corbusian grid of longitudinal apartment blocks, separated from each other by spacious gardens.[17]

During the very same years (the mid-1940s), the Egyptian architect Hassan Fathy turned to the vernacular of the Egyptian countryside in his own search for authenticity and proposed an architectural vocabulary for the "poor" that echoed the prototypes offered by French architects in their North African colonies. Fathy's pioneering drive to return to a past of purity, decontaminated from the ills of rapid change, was in reaction to the unquestioning subscription to modernity that had resulted in "cultural confusion" and loss of tradition in Egyptian cities and villages.[18] As such, it was symptomatic of "the passion with which native intellectuals defend the existence of their national culture," analyzed critically by Fanon.[19]

Fathy was a cosmopolitan architect, with strong intellectual ties to Europe and in close touch with recent developments in the profession. His designs for the village of New Gourna, then, should be historically contextualized and not read as isolated

FIGURE 11: Pablo Picasso, *Les Femmes d'Alger*, 1955. Washington University Gallery of Art, St. Louis.

experiments of a lone visionary and abstracted from French colonial architectural experiments in North Africa. Fathy's courtyards, private streets, and residential clusters, his aesthetics founded on simple forms (the square domed unit, the rectangular vaulted unit, and the alcove covered with a half dome), his public building types (markets, crafts khan, mosque, bath), and even his socially ambitious program had counterparts in the French projects. In New Gourna, Fathy attempted social reform by revitalizing the traditional way of life both in the built environment and in the patterns of production, which were founded on crafts and construction materials, specifically brick making. This approach echoed Laprade's idea of allowing for "a whole way of life" in the new medina of Casablanca. To return to Fanon's analysis of the "native intellectual," in his attempt to express national identity Fathy relied on techniques and language borrowed from European architects. Like Fanon's "native intellectual," Fathy ended up creating a "hallmark which wishes to be national, but which is strangely reminiscent of exoticism."[20]

Considering the profound impact of the colonial heritage, cultural critic Masao Miyoshi argued recently that "return to 'authenticity' ... is a closed route" and that there is no such concept as "authenticity."[21] Situating Fathy's architecture and that of the French architects building in the colonies in relation to each other shows how deeply interlaced were colonial productions and those conscientiously created in opposition to them. However, regardless of the contamination in the concepts of purity and authenticity, the meanings behind formal resemblences shift radically. The similar forms and programs of the French architects and Fathy stemmed from different agendas and carried different future implications. For Fathy, a return to vernacular forms meant endowing contemporary Egypt with a cultural image, a manifest identity in the face of the universalizing power of Western technology; it was an act of resistance. For the French colonist, in contrast, the emphasized difference of North African cultures enhanced the power of France, not only because it displayed the diversity of its possessions, but also because of its expression of tolerance toward the subjugated culture.

The intricate relationship between colonial definitions and adaptations of North African vernacular and Fathy's vocabulary has been overlooked by architectural historians and critics, who abstracted Fathy as a pioneer in a unique search for authenticity—a position that trivializes the complexity in Fathy's thinking and his worldly status among the leading architects of the twentieth century. Nevertheless, the extraordinary popularity Fathy's architecture enjoyed in a wide range of Third World (and some First World) countries makes a statement about the more discreet meanings behind the familiar forms and the significance of the search for expression of cultural identity, albeit still caught up in the exercise of "exoticism" that Fanon criticized in the late 1950s. It also points to the enduring otherness created by the colonial discourse—appropriated, twisted, and turned by the Third World architect to be endowed with an oppositional symbolism that expresses self-identity.

My last case study is Eugène Delacroix's *Les Femmes d'Alger dans leur appartement* (1834), or rather, the authority this painting carries as a reference point, as a *lieu de mémoire* during the colonial and postcolonial periods (Fig. 12). As a window into the harem of a Muslim house in the casbah of Algiers, Delacroix's painting alluded to penetrating into the most private, the most sacred part of Algerian society. An official commission charged with political meanings, it represented the conquest of Algeria by entering the Algerian home. A masterpiece, it had always been a popular

FIGURE 12: Eugène Delacroix, Les Femmes d'Alger dans leur appartement (Women of Algiers in Their Apartment), 1834. The Louvre Museum, Paris.

subject of study, but its importance as a political symbol was highlighted in about 1930, the centennial of Algeria's occupation.[22]

In her renowned book, also titled Les Femmes d'Alger dans leur appartement and published in 1979, Algerian writer Assia Djebar reads this painting in reference to Picasso's Les Femmes d'Alger (Fig. 11). One marking the beginning of French colonization, the other the end, the paintings evoke divergent interpretations for Djebar, sparked by differences in the visions of the two European artists, but more important, in the sociocultural transformations brought by the French occupation and the Algerian War. It is not Delacroix's "superficial Orient" that Djebar cares to dissect, but the subtler implications of the painting, especially the fact that the scene makes the observer conscious of his unwarranted presence in the intimacy of this room, which is enclosed upon the women frozen in an act of waiting, passive and resigned.[23]

Picasso obsessively reworked Delacroix's theme during the first months of the Algerian War, producing fifteen paintings and two lithographs from December 1954 to February 1955.[24] Djebar argues that in Picasso's work, the universe of the women of Algiers has been completely transformed from Delacroix's "tragedy" into a "new happiness" by means of a "glorious liberation of space, an awakening of body in dance, energy, free movement." Their previous hermetic situation has been preserved, she tells us, but now reversed into a condition of serenity, at peace with the past and the future. Djebar associates the "liberation" at home with the occupation of the city's public spaces by women resistance fighters taking part in the war. She establishes a metaphorical relationship between fragments of women's bodies and the explosives they carried under their clothes. She also provides a critique of women's conditions in Algeria following independence by arguing that the grenades women hid under their clothes "as if they were their own breasts" exploded against them.[25]

Djebar's reading of Delacroix's and Picasso's works to frame the dramatic change in women's lives during her country's *nuit coloniale* and its aftermath calls for continued debate and possibly disagreement, especially given Picasso's "continual struggle in the *Femmes d'Alger* series to reconcile distance with presence, possession, and watching."[26] What matters, however, is the fact that Djebar reestablishes the connection between domestic spaces and women's lives by relying on the authority of one of the most blatant symbols of French colonialism and the artistic tradition based on the reproductions and reinterpretations of this symbol, thereby accentuating the entanglements of her message. Delacroix's painting becomes a place of memory that can be turned around and recharged with new meanings. Djebar's stand does not imply "giving in" to the colonizer culture, but rather deploying it to broaden her critique.

Djebar is not alone in reloading colonial cultural formations with new meanings and providing complicated linkages between contemporary Algerian questions and the country's recent history. For example, in Kamal Dahane's 1992 documentary film, itself titled once more *Les Femmes d'Alger*, Delacroix's painting reemerges; the famous setting is recreated in the last scene, but now is emptied of women. Following the themes pursued in the film, Dahane suggests that the women have decided to leave Delacroix's symbolic realm in an act of resistance to present-day political and religious movements that attempt to ban them from public life and restrict them to the domestic realm. Novelist Leila Sebbar, whose work has been acknowledged as belonging to the "Maghrebian literature from France," takes another leap and brings Delacroix back to France, to the realities of postcoloniality in the former métropole. When she sees Delacroix's famous painting in the Louvre, the protagonist of Sebbar's Les Carnets de Shérazade associates Delacroix's women of

Algiers with the Maghrebi women imprisoned in dismal, small apartments on the outskirts of French cities.[27]

Hearing "other" voices complicates the meanings and contextual fabrics of the art objects and disrupts inherited historiographic legacies. This, in turn, helps to contest the familiar reductive formulas that explicate sociopolitical relationships and reestablish them in their social density.[28] Furthermore, as Gayatri Chakravorty Spivak observes, when the "hegemonic discourse" repositions itself so that it can "occupy the position of the other," it, too, becomes subject to a major transformation, to its own decolonization.[29]

NOTES

1. Nazım Hikmet, "Pierre Loti," in *Selected Poems of Nazım Hikmet*, ed. and trans. Taner Baybars (London: Jonathan Cape, 1967), 19–20.
2. Halid Ziya Uş ˌaklıgil, *Nesl-i Ahîr* (Istanbul: Inkilap Kitapevi, 1990), 21. This is the first printing of *Nesl-i Ahîr* as a book; it was serialized in 1908 in an Istanbul newspaper, *Sabah*. Unless otherwise noted, all translations are mine.
3. Ahmed Mithad, *Avrupa'da Bir Cevelan* (Istanbul, 1890), 164–65.
4. For further discussion on these issues, see Zeynep Çelik and Leila Kinney, "Ethnography and Exhibitionism at the Expositions Universelles," *Assemblage* 13 (December 1990): 34–59.
5. Among Said's writings dealing with this issue, see, e.g., Edward Said, "Intellectuals in the Postcolonial World," *Salmagundi*, nos. 70–71 (spring–summer 1986): 44–64; "Third World Intellectuals and Metropolitan Culture," *Raritan* 9, no. 3 (1990): 27– 50; and *Culture and Imperialism* (1993; London: Vintage, 1994). For the first article to explore Said's significance on nineteenth-century art, see Linda Nochlin, "The Imaginary Orient," *Art in America* 71, no. 5 (May 1983): 118–31, 187–91.
6. Janet Abu-Lughod, "On the Remaking of History: How to Reinvent the Past," in *Remaking History*, ed. Barbara Kruger and Phil Mariani (Seattle: Bay Press, 1989), 112.
7. Systematic art education for girls in the Ottoman Empire began with the establishment of *rüştiyes*, secondary girls' schools, in 1858. In these schools, drawing (*resim*) constituted part of the curriculum and, with calligraphy, painting, and dressmaking, complemented the academic core of grammar,

arithmetic, and geography. Painting and drawing were also part of the education of upper-class girls, taught by private instructors at home. The School
of Fine Arts (Sanayi-i Nefise Mekteb-i Alisi), based on the French model, was
established in 1881. It consisted of three departments: architecture, painting, and sculpture. Women's enrollment in the School of Fine Arts would
have to wait until the 1910s. On the education of girls in the late nineteenth-
century Ottoman Empire, see Serpil Çakır, *Osmanlı Kadın Hareketi* (Istanbul:
Metis Kadın Araştırmaları, 1994), 219–225, and Fanny Davis, *The Ottoman
Lady* (New York: Greenwood Press, 1986), 45–60. For the School of Fine Arts,
see Mustafa Cezar, *Sanatta Batıya Açılış ve Osman Hamdi* (Istanbul: İş Bankası
Yayınları, 1971).

8. Halil Bey's reputation as an art collector and a bon vivant overshadows
his career as a statesman, his commitment to progressive politics, and his
involvement in the Young Turk movement. See Zeynep Inankur, "Halil Ş̧erif
Paşa," *P* 2 (summer 1996): 72–80.

9. Francis Haskell, "A Turk and His Pictures in Nineteenth-Century Paris," *Oxford
Art Journal* 5, no. 1 (1982): 45.

10. For an astute analysis of Osman Hamdi's paintings, see Ipek Aksüğür Duben,
"Osman Hamdi ve Orientalism," *Tarih ve Toplum,* no. 41 (May 1987): 283–90.

11. For an informative article on the Abdülhamid II albums, see William Allen,
"The Abdul Hamid II Collection," *History of Photography* 8, no. 2 (April–June
1984): 119–45.

12. For a concise discussion of the industrialization efforts in the Ottoman
Empire in the nineteenth century, as well as the inherent contradictions, see
Zeynep Çelik, *The Remaking of Istanbul* (Seattle: University of California Press,
1986), 33–37.

13. The most widely disseminated of Le Corbusier's publications is *La Ville
radieuse* (Paris: Éditions Vincent, Fréal, 1933). Corbusier's interest in non-
Western vernacular architecture goes back to the 1910s, to his *Voyage en
Orient.*

14. Valensi's design mimicked an "organic" settlement, down to uses of patched
building materials and irregular plastering. In the words of a contemporary
critic, the architect had "forced himself to reconstitute something badly built,
and he succeeded perfectly." See Anthony Goissaud, "A l'exposition coloniale,
le pavillon de la Tunisie," *La Construction moderne* 18 (October 1931). For the
presentation of colonial architecture in the expositions, see Zeynep Çelik,

Displaying the Orient: Architecture of Islam at Nineteenth Century World's Fairs (Berkeley: University of California Press), 1992.

15. Léandre Vaillat, *Le Visage français du Maroc* (Paris: Horizons de France, 1931), 12.

16. Albert Laprade, "Une ville créée spécialement pour les indigènes à Casablanca," in *L'Urbanisme aux colonies et dans les pays tropicaux, La Charité-sur-Loire*, ed. Jean Royer (Paris: Delayance, 1932), 1. 94–99; Vaillat, *Le Visage français du Maroc*, 15–17.

17. For these projects, see the "Tunisie" issue of *L'Architecture d'aujourd'hui*, no. 20 (October 1948). Cité Musulmane el Omrane and Quartier Gambetta are presented next to each other in the pages of *L'Architecture d'aujourd'hui*, emphasizing the spatial and aesthetic differences between the two schemes.

18. Hassan Fathy, *Architecture for the Poor* (Chicago: University of Chicago Press, 1973), 19–20.

19. Frantz Fanon, *The Wretched of the Earth*, trans. Constance Farrington (New York: Grove Press, 1963), 209.

20. Ibid., 223.

21. Masao Miyoshi, "A Borderless World? From Colonialism to Transnationalism and the Decline of the Nation-State," *Critical Inquiry*, no. 19 (summer 1993): 747.

22. Le Corbusier's *Les Femmes de la Casbah*, painted on a wall in Eileen Gray's house in Cap Martin, known as E. 1027 and built between 1926 and 1929, dates from this period. The authority of Delacroix's painting as a cultural paradigm did not remain restricted to "high" art alone; the scene and the setting were enacted in colonial popular culture, most memorably in postcards.

23. Assia Djebar, *Les Femmes d'Alger dans leur appartement* (Paris: Des Femmes, 1979), 170–78.

24. For a comparative discussion of various versions of Picasso's *Femmes d'Alger*, see Leo Steinberg, "The Algerian Women and Picasso at Large," in *Other Criteria: Confrontations with Twentieth-Century Art* (New York: Oxford University Press, 1972), 125–234.

25. Djebar, *Femmes d'Alger*, 186–89.

26. Steinberg, *Other Criteria*, 130. Picasso's sympathy for the Algerian side in the war is expressed most blatantly in his drawing of Djamila Boupacha, whose accounts of torture had made her a cause célèbre in France and throughout the world. The portrait was published in 1962 on the cover of

Djamila Boupasha, written by Gisèle Halimi, with an introduction by Simone de Beauvoir.

27. Leila Sebbar, *Les Carnets de Shérazade* (Paris: Stock, 1985), 152. For an analysis of this novel, see Françoise Lionnet, "Narrative Strategies and Postcolonial Identity in Contemporary France: Leila Sebbar's *Les Carnets de Shérazade,*" in *Writing New Identities,* ed. Gisela Brinker-Gabler and Sidonie Smith (Minneapolis: University of Minnesota Press, 1997), 62–77.

28. Edward Said, *The World, the Text, the Critic* (Cambridge, MA: Harvard University Press, 1983), 23.

29. Gayatri Chakravorty Spivak, *The Post-Colonial Critic: Interviews, Strategies, Dialogues,* ed. Sara Harasym (New York: Routledge, 1990), 121.

PEOPLE AND PLACES

section two

Agency and Adaptation

Pastoralists of Iran

by PHILIP CARL SALZMAN

THE WORD *NOMAD* IN ITS VARIOUS FORMS DERIVES, VIA LATIN, from a Greek term meaning "to pasture"; thus, etymologically, it has the same meaning as *pastoralism*, which derives from Latin and refers to raising livestock on pasture (according to the *Oxford English Dictionary [OED]*). Consequently, the first meaning attributed to *nomad* in the *OED*, documented by quotes beginning in 1587, is "a person belonging to a race or tribe which moves from place to place to find pasture; hence, one who lives a roaming or wandering life."

However, many anthropologists (for example, Salzman 1971; Barfield 1993: 4; cp. Khazanov 1994: 15–16) have, over the past decades, found it convenient to disaggregate analytically the two main elements of the term *nomad*: (1) raising livestock on natural pasture, and (2) moving from place to place. The current convention is to use *pastoralism* to refer to the raising of livestock on nature pasture and *nomadism* to refer to moving from place to place (Galaty and Johnson 1990; Fabietti and Salzman 1996).

By means of this convention, a population's type(s) of production, on the one hand, and spatial mobility, on the other hand, are logically distinguished, so that the various relationships of production and mobility can be studied and related empirically and ethnographically. In this way, an a priori, definitional conflation of production and mobility is avoided and observation of their relationships among various peoples in the world is facilitated. This, in turn, makes possible empirical generalization, that is, the abstracting of common, observable patterns of production and mobility; it also makes possible theoretical generalization, that is, the relating of variables of production and mobility in a systematic fashion.

Now let us define *nomadism,* or *nomadic movement,* a little more precisely. What is implied in "a roaming or wandering life," as the *OED* put it, is more than wandering from the bar to the piazza and to the cantina; what is implied is the movement of the home and the household or, put another way, the spatial displacement of the home base and living establishment. Even more, the reference in the *OED* definition to "a race or tribe" (admittedly outmoded terminology) clearly points to nomadism as, in some sense, a collective activity, participated in by a community larger than the individual household. Finally, nomadism refers not to the rare or occasional displacement of people from one location to another, as in moving to a new house or migrating to a new community or country; rather, it refers to the regular, repeated, and frequent displacement of household and home base and community.

To recapitulate, I would define *nomadism* as the regular and frequent movement of the home base and household. An empirical index of this is the nature of physical structures for shelter, which among nomads are either portable, such as the tent, or temporary, such as the lean-to or the hut made with disposable, local materials.

The first empirical association that we find with nomadism is productive activity in general, for, almost always, nomadic populations are nomadic in the course of making a living. Nomadism is thus usually tied to a productive round of activities. There are many examples of different kinds of productive activities pursued nomadically, such as—to use the crude and conventional categories (about which, more later)—nomadic hunters and gatherers (Lee and DeVore 1968; Kelly 1995), nomadic traders and service providers (Clébert 1967; Fraser 1992; Gmelch 1977; Misra 1977; Rao 1987), and nomadic pastoralists (Galaty and Johnson 1990; Barfield 1993; Fabietti and Salzman 1996).

But not all populations engaging in these kinds of activities are nomadic; there are also nonnomadic populations that pursue these activities from stable, permanent bases: sedentary hunters and gatherers (Drucker 1965; Kelly 1995: 148–152), sedentary traders and retailers (Thaiss 1973; Berland 1982), and sedentary pastoralists (Angioni 1989; Bennett 1969: chap. 6; Ingold 1980: chap. 4; Meloni 1984; Murru

Corriga 1990; Ravis-Giordani 1983; Salzman 1980). Thus, a basic question, to which I will return later, is this: Under what circumstances are productive activities pursued nomadically?

I shall begin this exploration of nomadism by narrowing the field of study to pastoral nomads and by turning to ethnographic case studies that will serve to complicate a simple vision of nomadism through illustrating variations in many important dimensions.

PASTORAL NOMADS OF IRAN

Let us briefly review four ethnographically well-documented cases of nomadic pastoralists in Iran (Persia): first, the Baluch in southeastern Iran; second, the Komachi in southern Iran; third, the Basseri of southwestern Iran and other tribes of the Zagros Mountains; and fourth, the Turkmen of northeastern Iran. In the course of this review, I will draw out various general observations about nomadism.

THE BALUCH OF THE SARHAD

Baluchistan is split between southeastern Iran, western Pakistan, and southwestern Afghanistan. Iranian Baluchistan is both a distant frontier region and an ethnically distinct tribal area. It is about as far as one can be from Tehran, the national capital, without leaving Iran, and it is far from major Persian cities, such as Isfahan, Mashed, and Shiraz, and separated from them and even the nearest city, Kerman, by the great central desert. The inhabitants are ethnically Baluch, (most) speaking the Baluchi language (a western Iranian language closely related to Kurdish) and (most) following Sunni Islam rather than the Shi'a Islam of the Persians. There are no indigenous cities in Iranian Baluchistan, the population being divided into tent-dwelling nomads (*baluch*) and oasis-dwelling cultivators (*shahri*), sometimes ruled by a small elite (*hakum*). The following description is based on my fieldwork observations during the period 1968 to 1976.

The Baluchi tribes (such as the Yarahmadzai, Gamshadzai, and Ismailzai) of the high plains (altitude 5,500 feet), the Sarhad, surrounding the volcano Daptan (in Persian *Kuh-i Taftan*), lived in camping groups of black goat-hair tents year-round and migrated from place to place throughout the year pursuing their productive activities (Salzman 2000a). These tribesmen and tribeswomen were not venturing

FIGURE 1: The Yarahmadzai Baluch camping group led by Jafar Dadolzai and shared mainly by other Dadolzai usually consists of about a dozen tents. In early evening, the smoke from fires used for preparing dinner curls around the goat-hair tents. A pregnant camel comes to the tent of her owner for supplementary feed. (P. C. Salzman, 1968)

to unknown places but were moving to known and named places within their large tribal territories. But they had no set migration cycle or route, for the availability of resources was unpredictable.

The Sarhadi Baluch were engaged in a variety of productive activities, including raising sheep, goats, and camels; cultivating grain and some vegetables and fruits; and husbanding date palms (Salzman 1971, 2000a). In the past, until 1935, they regularly raided villages and caravans outside Baluchistan; more recently, beginning in the 1940s, they temporarily left the tribal territory for trading or migrant labor (Salzman 1994). These Baluch needed to supply their sheep, goats, and camels with the pasturage suitable for each species, as well as water for the animals and themselves. Though they were drawn to areas with these needed resources, they tried to avoid disease by staying away from areas with sick animals. Pursuing these goals, they nonetheless needed to remain within traveling distance of any cultivation requiring attention.

FIGURE 2: The Dadolzai herding camp migrates to a new residential location. Adults typically walk, sometimes carrying kids, lambs, and even baby camels, while young children, pregnant women, the elderly, and the ill are carried by camel. (P. C. Salzman, 1968)

In general during the 1960s and 1970s, Baluchi herding camps remained stable during the late fall and winter; pasture was poor everywhere at that time of the year, and many men were working away from the tribal territory. Migrations began in the spring, when new grass and shrubs turned the desert green. Juggling the need for different kinds of pasturage, for water, for uncrowded areas, and for access to agricultural resources, as well as the different production and activity profiles of the households in each camp, camp members continually gathered information, deliberated, and debated when and where to migrate. Decisions were difficult, but throughout the spring, herding camps migrated, usually between a half dozen and a dozen times—first in one direction, then in another, one time a short distance (1 mile), another a longer distance (40 miles).

In high summer, when the grass had withered, the tribesmen made their annual great migration (120 miles) through the Morpish Mountains and down off the Sarhad plateau to the Mashkel drainage basin (altitude 1,500 feet). They left their flocks in the hands of a few shepherds back on the cooler, less arid Sarhad, in order

FIGURE 3: A young family of the Yarahmadzai Baluch herding camp of the Dadolzai lineage migrates with campmates. The mother and children ride the camel, as the baby camel trots alongside. (P. C. Salzman, 1968)

to devote themselves to harvesting their date groves. (The date palms drew water from underground streams tapped by their roots and so did not need irrigation or continuous attention during other parts of the year.) As date palms could not be grown in the cooler temperatures of the Sarhad and livestock could not be supported in the extremely arid environs of the date groves, the nomadic movement made it possible to incorporate both forms of production in individual household economies, just as mobility on the Sarhad during the spring made it possible to raise livestock on erratic and unpredictable natural pasture.

The environment of Baluchistan is extremely arid, and what rainfall there is is extremely variable across the land. In fact, annual rainfall rarely exceeds 5 or 6 inches and comes almost exclusively in the winter, as is the case in much of the Middle East and North Africa. The rain does not fall equally everywhere in the tribal territory, and consequently, pasture does not grow equally everywhere. All tribesmen, however, have rights of access to all natural pasture everywhere in the tribal territory and to all natural water sources. This "open pasture" policy is even extended on a conditional basis to members of other tribes, who may request permission of the chief (*sardar*) to gain access. This Baluchi adaptation to unpredictable microenvironmental variation depends upon both the legal right provided by collective land tenure and the practical means provided by nomadism.

Rainfall and thus pasturage are variable not only spatially but also temporally. Out of every five years, one year sees almost no rain at all and a second even less! Annual rainfall from 1963 through 1967 was (according to the Khash weather office) 5.6, 4.2, 1.5, 2.1, and 5.4 inches—a representative pattern. The Baluchi adaptation, with its mobility and its multiple resource production, allows the Baluch to survive the worse years and to expand their production rapidly during the good years.

The adaptation thus provides not only short-term production but also security in the long run. At the same time, this subsistence production system is labor intensive, supports only a modest level of material standard of living, and has depended upon an ongoing if limited inflow of resources, whether from the traditional predatory raiding or the recent migrant labor and trading of goods.

General Observation No. 1. Nomadism can be used, as it is by the Baluch, to gain access, through spatial movement, to resources (such as pasture and water) that are sparse in any particular location. In desert regions, such as Baluchistan, the amount of pasturage at any place is very limited almost all of the time.

General Observation No. 2. Nomadism can be used as an opportunistic "rapid response" to the sudden and temporary availability of irregular and unpredictable resources, such as pasture. The migration pattern in these circumstances is consequently irregular in timing and direction and asymmetrical in pattern.

General Observation No. 3. Nomadism, the regular displacement of the household, is unlikely to be oriented to one and only one productive activity, such as pastoralism, because few populations limit themselves to one productive activity. Rather, nomadic mobility is likely to be put to work as well in aid of other productive activities, such as cultivation, as among the Baluch, or fishing, as among the Nuer (Evans-Pritchard 1940). Nomadic mobility is not infrequently from a location of one productive activity, such as pastoralism, to another, such as arboriculture. Thus, categories and labels (such as "nomadic pastoralists") tend to oversimplify and distort the multiresource economies that most nomads have and the versatile, multipurpose nomadism that they use to the fullest.

General Observation No. 4. Nomadism is not "wandering" in the sense of purposeless or directionless movement. Nomadic movement is highly purposeful, oriented toward achieving specific production (or other) goals. Nomads continually discuss where and when to move and why, and they are constantly searching for, assessing, and reassessing relevant information from direct experience and secondary sources in order to make good decisions about migration.

General Observation No. 5. Nomadism is not "wandering" in the sense of moving off in any direction and constantly entering new lands. Most nomads move within a known and customary habitat. Some, including the Baluchi tribesmen, migrate within their own, delimited territory, which they control politically.

THE KOMACHI OF KERMAN

Several hundred miles to the west of these Baluch are found the Komachi, a small group (population 550) of Persian-speaking pastoral nomads (Bradburd 1990). They raise sheep and goats, migrating some 200 miles seasonally from lowland winter pastures on the coastal plains of southern Iran to highland summer pastures—which they deem their homeland—in mountain ranges south of Kerman city. This seasonal pattern of migration, sometimes labeled "transhumance," is an adaptation to macroenvironmental variation. The summer home of the Komachi, in a valley at an altitude of over 8,000 feet in the mountains south of Kerman city, receives up to 16 inches of rain during the winter and provides good pastures and relatively cool temperatures during the summer. The winter home of the Komachi is the warm lowlands of the coast near Bandar Abbas, a region that receives an average of around 6 inches of rain in the fall and early winter and generally provides pastures of new grass in the early spring (Bradburd 1990: 13–18).

Daniel Bradburd characterizes the Komachi as "migratory peasants [rather] than marauders; they were ... economic, rather than political, pastoralists" (1990: 5). They sold livestock products, such as goat's wool for cashmere, sheep's wool for carpets, and culled animals for meat, in urban markets and had dependent ties with merchants and moneylenders (Bradburd 1990: 34–49). They bought many of the products they consumed, including goat hair (from a type of goat they did not raise) for making tents.

Much of the Komachi's region was sparsely populated, infertile pasture areas to which they were able to gain access without great difficulty. But their access was dependent upon the goodwill of absentee landowners and, more recently, government officials and was usually forthcoming as a result of gifts, fees, or patron-client ties (Bradburd 1990: 21–24). As state order has strengthened and modern agriculture has spread in recent decades, the Komachi have been forced to shift to more distant marginal areas.

General Observation No. 6. Nomadic migration patterns, such as those among the Komachi, are more regular and are repeated, where macroenvironment features (seasons, altitude, and the like) determine the availability of needed resources.

General Observation No. 7. Nomadism is not tied in a determinative fashion with political structure. The Baluchi tribes of the Sarhad were fierce and independent (but now encapsulated), whereas the Komachi, highly integrated into Persian society and totally controlled by the Persian state, were pacific, peasant pastoralists.

General Observation No. 8. Nomadism is not tied in a determinative fashion with economic orientation. The Sarhadi Baluch had a generalized, multiresource productive regime—a richly mixed economy. They produced almost entirely for subsistence; only a very small percentage of all they produced was traded locally, and none was exported from the Sarhad. In contrast, the Komachi were highly specialized and oriented toward sale, especially in the Kerman bazaar, which was, in many cases, directed toward export (Bradburd 1994).

General Observation No. 9. Nomadism is not tied in a determinative fashion with land tenure. Although the Komachi had a customary habitat in which they migrated, they had no legal title to it, nor did they control it politically as a territory of their own. Without political or military structure, they could not defend their customary habitat against intrusion. When Persian agricultural interests expanded and encroached into their migratory habitat, they were forced to shift to a less used and more remote habitat. This lack of rights to land contrasts with the tribal territories of the Sarhadi Baluch.

THE BASSERI OF FARS

Hundreds of miles to the west of the Komachi, in Fars Province, are found the Basseri (Barth 1961), a Persian-speaking tribe of 16,000, one of five tribes of the Khamseh confederacy. The province of Fars and its legendary capital Shiraz are geographically at the southern end of the great Zagros mountain range, which reaches to the northwest of Iran, dividing the Iranian plateau to the east from the desert lowlands of Mesopotamia to the west. The Basseri (in the ethnographic present of the 1950s when Fredrik Barth did his research) practiced what might be called "grand transhumance," migrating along their *il rah* (tribal road) some 300 miles between lowland winter pastures at 2,000 feet and highland summer pastures at 13,000 feet. Rainfall of around 10 inches provided rich pastures. The migration each way passed by Shiraz, taking three months for the spring migration up to the highlands and a month or six weeks for the fall migration down to the lowlands. The migrating tribesmen and their flocks were coordinated with those of other tribes, with mediation provided between the tribesmen and village agriculturalists by the Basseri tribal chief.

Although the Basseri grand transhumance was an adaptation to the macroenvironmental variations of season and altitude, the selection of breeding stock, particularly of sheep, was very precise. As Barth describes it,

> There are several common strains of sheep in Fars, of different productivity and resistance. Of these the nomad strain tends to be larger and more productive. But its resistance to extremes of temperature, particularly to frost, is less than that of the sheep found in the mountain villages, and its tolerance to heat and parched fodder and drought is less than that of the strains found in the [the lowlands]. ... The migratory cycle is thus necessary to maintain the health of the nomads' herds, quite apart from their requirements for pastures (1961: 6).

Barth (1961: 99) estimates that the value of the annual product (including offspring, milk, and wool) of a Basseri ewe was equivalent to its on-the-hoof market value, which was a 100 percent annual return for the owner. This was remarkable productivity indeed, which gave even the moderately successful Basseri pastoralist a standard of living higher than that attained by peasant village agriculturalists in Fars or by pastoralists elsewhere, such as Baluchistan.

The Basseri, though drawing upon the products of their animals and even doing a bit of catch-as-catch-can grain cultivation, were oriented to exchange and the marketplace in their complex and developed region. They both sold animals and animal products and purchased many of the goods that they consumed, including the staple, wheat, as well as much of the supplies and equipment that they used (Barth 1961: 9–10). They had individual exchange relationships with villagers and collective relations with other tribes and the state (Barth 1961: 93–99). The Basseri were thus specialist producers in the complex regional economic and political system of Fars.

Neighbors and sometime adversaries of the Basseri were the Turkish-speaking tribes of the Qashqa'i confederacy (Beck 1986, 1991), encompassing at mid-twentieth century around 400,000 persons (Beck 1991: 10). The Basseri migrated on their north-south tribal road to the east of Shiraz, but the Qashqa'i tribes followed a grand transhumance of their own, migrating on their own north-south tribal road to the west of Shiraz. Their adaptation and economy were much like that of the Basseri, a specialized, market-oriented economy based upon a transhumant adaptation to macroenvironmental variations.

Several hundred miles to the north, the great Bakhtiari tribal federation (Garthwaite 1983; Brooks 1983), with a population of a million, followed a grand transhumance route between lowland winter pastures in the western plains and highland summer pastures to the east in the Isfahan region, the renowned city of Isfahan being a commercial and political referent. Between Fars and Isfahan and north of Isfahan into Kurdistan, people employing a nomadic strategy to adapt to their environments are found throughout the Zagros range. As David Brooks (1983) describes it,

> By no means have all the tribes of the Zagros been exclusively pastoral in orientation, although it is probably accurate to say that their economic basis has been nomadism with their wealth and livelihood dependent on animals, predominantly herds of sheep and goats ... [Transhumance] migrations ... involving thousands of tribesmen and their flocks, are found everywhere in the Zagros. Migration routes differ in length and difficulty, some being a matter of only few days' travel, ... while others ... require many weeks' travel over several hundred kilometres between summer and winter quarters. [Many people also follow] forms of semi-nomadic movement between settled villages where they farm.

Even shorter migrations can exploit macroenvironmental variations through seasonal timing and changes in altitude and by so doing remain regular and predictable. This does not, however, preclude using mobility to adjust to microenvironmental variations as well, through opportunistic changes of location to gain access to better pasture, water, fuel, or shelter or to avoid disease, predators, or conflict.

General Observation No. 10. Nomadism is found in both isolated, remote, and unpopulated regions and in more crowded and developed regions. Some nomadic populations occupy remote regions, environmentally marginal and distant from centers of civilization and power, such as Baluchistan, Nuerland in the southern Sudan (Evans-Pritchard 1940), Somaliland (Lewis 1961), and the Empty Quarter of

Arabia (Cole 1975). But other nomadic populations, such as the Basseri, Qashqa'i, and Bakhtiari, migrate through regions of agricultural settlements and pass and even stop at major cities, such as Shiraz and Isfahan—famous centers of civilization, known for their markets and homes of state agencies. The Komachi, as indicated earlier, are attached to the major urban center of Kerman.

General Observation No. 11. (This is a corollary of General Observation No. 7.) Independent or quasi-independent nomadic tribes vary considerably in political structure, from the acephalus, egalitarian, decentralized Nuer, Somali, and Maasai (Galaty 1980) to the weak chief-ships of the Baluch (Salzman 1983, 2000a, 2000b) and the Bedouin (Cole 1975; Lancaster 1997) to the more strongly hierarchical and centralized tribal and confederacy chiefships of the Zagros.

General Observation No. 12. Chiefships arise in nomadic tribes in confrontation with powerful external populations (Irons 1979). Thus, acephalus, egalitarian, decentralized, nomadic tribes are more likely to be found in remote regions far from centers of power, population, and trade, and nomadic tribal chiefdoms are more likely to be found in proximity to agricultural settlements, cities, state agencies, and major markets.

General Observation No. 13. (This is a corollary of General Observation No. 7.) Nomadic pastoralism is politically centrifugal, militating against central and hierarchical power. The mobility of nomadic individuals, households, and capital resources, especially flocks, makes avoidance, escape, and attack easier and more likely successful than among sedentary populations. Nomadic mobility, in consequence, has a dampening effect on hierarchy and centralization and on chiefly coercion and oppression. Tribal chiefs thus must be sensitive and responsible to the opinions of tribesmen (Salzman 1983, 2000b).

THE YOMUT TURKMEN OF THE GORGON

The tribes of the Yomut Turkmen (Irons 1975, 1994) make their home in the northeast of Iran, in the Gorgon region east of the Caspian Sea and north of the Elburz mountain range. The northern slopes of the mountains receive some 24 inches of rain and support a forest zone in which intensive agriculture is carried out by

FIGURE 4: Yomut Turkmen yurts of one family are located in a typical Gokchadagh Plain setting during the spring. The Turkman in the foreground is in a hunting pose. (Wm. Irons, 1996)

Persian- and Turkic-speaking sedentary villagers. The rainfall declines farther to the north in a humid steppe zone and still farther north in a steppe-desert zone.

FIGURE 5: Yomut Turkmen prepare to migrate by removing the felt from the yurt and folding it into parcels that can be transported. With the removal of the felt, the skeletal structure of the yurt can be seen. (Wm. Irons, 1966)

The Yomut occupied the steppe and steppe-desert zones, those living in the steppe specializing in dry-grain cultivation and those in the steppe-desert specializing in sheep pastoralism. Each Yomut tribe included in its territory both zones and thus both pastoralists (*charwa*) and cultivators (*chomur*). Both pastoralists and cultivators produced for their own subsistence, but they were also market oriented, selling livestock, carpets, and grain in markets where they bought staples, such as rice, and other goods.

All of the Yomut, cultivators and agriculturalists alike, were nomadic. They lived in yurts, the felt-covered, hemispheric, portable dwellings typical of Central Asia—quite distinct from the black, goat-hair tents of the Iranian plateau tribes. Though mobile, the Turkmen did not ordinarily move long distances. The chomur cultivators often migrated, in the spring, 6 miles north to the Gorgon River in order to avoid the flies and mosquitoes of the forest zone. During the wet season, the charwa pastoralists made a number of one-day migrations, usually not more than 6 miles, within their local areas. During the winter and spring dry season, many would migrate around 25 miles south to the river.

Given the modest amount of movement usually undertaken by the Turkmen, there was really no pressing economic reason for them to maintain such a high level of nomadic capacity; they could have functioned quite well economically with a semisedentary residence pattern, with the agriculturalists staying on farmsteads or in villages and the pastoralists in individual or group ranches (Irons 1974: 21, 36, 69).

The nomadic strategy of the Turkmen was fundamentally political rather than economic; nomadic mobility was an adaptation to inimical state societies, particularly the Iranian state of the Persians, who were old ethnic enemies of the Turkmen.

FIGURE 6: Yomut Turkmen migrate with their household goods, including the yurt framework and felt. (Wm. Irons, 1966)

The Turkmen advanced themselves by raiding Persian villages and caravans and even selling Persian captives as slaves.

No love was lost between the Turkmen and the Persians, and the Turkmen knew well that staying out of the clutches of the Persians was good for their health and their wealth (Irons 1974: 70). In general, of course, preindustrial states were predatory rather than nurturing, living by extracting resources from a reluctant peasantry and by looting foreign lands. The Yomut not only knew this but also had the means—nomadism—to avoid being suppressed and exploited. In the extreme case, under pressure from the full armed might of the Persian Crown, the Yomut could retreat en masse across the Kara Kum Desert and stay with their relatives the Khiva Turkmen until the idle Crown troops, uselessly eating up the Crown treasury, would be pulled back; then, the Yomut could return to the Gorgon (Irons 1974: 72–74).

This case illustrates that the ecosystem of a particular human population includes other human populations, which act as competitors or predators, and that the adaptation of any group includes strategies to avoid or limit damage from those other populations. It would not be an exaggeration to say that, in this sense, all human adaptations are adaptations to a political environment. A corollary is that changes in a population's political environment will apply pressures for change in the population's adaptation.

General Observation No. 14. Nomadism is not determinatively tied to a particular kind of physiobiotic environment. Although many nomadic pastoralists exploit desert and mountainous environments that are marginal for other uses, a great number of other nomadic pastoralists, such as the Turkmen and the Zagros tribes, occupy rich habitats that could be exploited by other means.

General Observation No. 15. In some cases, as among the Turkmen, the political use of nomadism predominates over the direct productive use. Here, nomadism can "shade off," ranging from regular movement, as the term was defined initially, to the capacity for full mobility.

General Observation No. 16. Among the Turkmen, some nomadic chomur agriculturalists and some nomadic charwa pastoralists would shift areas and take up the other occupation—the agriculturalists becoming pastoralists and the pastoralists becoming agriculturalists—while all remained nomadic. This case thus highlights the fact that these activities and labels for them are not inviolable, permanent commitments that bind people. Rather, nomadism and pastoralism are capabilities and activities that can and are taken up and set aside, sometimes temporarily and sometimes indefinitely. The processes of taking up or leaving pastoralism or taking up nomadism or leaving it to settle are both very common and very widespread.

PATTERNS OF SEDENTARIZATION AND NOMADIZATION IN IRAN

In thinking about nomadism, we are sometimes influenced, consciously or unconsciously, by an evolutionary conception of the world that assumes a unilineal, directional change that cannot be reversed any more than time can be reversed. This orientation may fly in the face of historical accounts of many populations, societies, states, religions, and cultures, not to mention being contrary to much of personal experience, but we do habitually tend to think, in a manner oriented by evolutionary assumptions, of "rise and fall" rather than regular alternation or natural cycles (Salzman 1978). Thus, it is easy to assume there is a "natural (evolutionary) development" from nomadic life to settled life. But this vision would not at all correspond to life as it has been lived in the Middle East and North Africa, where nomadization and sedentarization have been ongoing, complementary processes for millennia. Quite frequently, individuals, families, or lineages shifted from a nomadic and a sedentary life and back, depending upon circumstances. People settled when it seemed beneficial to do so and became nomadic for the same reason. An example from Palestine under the Ottomans is illustrative:

> When security prevailed, masses of bedouin tended to settle permanently on the land, in the valleys and the plains, living in villages. When conditions in the villages were bad—when taxation was heavy and the [predatory] pressure of [the nomadic] bedouin was strong—the villagers tended to become nomadic. Nomadism had many advantages. Nomads paid no taxes, were not conscripted to the army, were armed (while the peasants were prohibited from keeping arms), could amass wealth in the form of livestock without being haunted by the unscrupulous tax collectors, and could even engage in occasional agriculture. They did not have to go far to the desert in order to be nomads, because large tracts of fertile lands in the valleys and on the plains were available (Cohen 1965: 7).

This shifting between strategies of adaptation in response to changes in conditions has been very common throughout the Middle East and North Africa (Salzman, ed. 1980; *Nomadic Peoples* 1984). We must also keep in mind that "settled" and "nomadic," rather than being two types, are better thought of as opposite ends of a continuum with many gradations of stability and mobility. Of course, many if not most rural producers in the Middle East fell between the two extremes, being somewhat stable but using some mobility—a strategy that, by the way, fosters a wide range of skills and knowledge that can be brought to bear and thus makes it possible to shift to a strategy of greater stability or of greater mobility in response to changing circumstances.

In considering patterns of sedentarization and nomadization, let us once again make the round of Iranian regions, which will allow us to follow up the cases already discussed and provide an instructive range of ethnographic examples.

THE BALUCH OF THE SARHAD

The Baluch of the Sarhad reduced their nomadism somewhat during the 1960 and 1970s (Salzman 1980). Though most continued living in tents and remained in herding camps, the migratory patterns of many Yarahmadzai herding groups were more restricted than previously, and the locations of herding camps were increasingly influenced by access to town and to agricultural plots. Engagement with the extratribal job market, with the local goods market, and with local administrative services, such as mail, connected Baluch to the nearby town and administrative center, Khash, and made residing far from this town a burden. The development of some qanat- (tunnel-) and motor-irrigated agriculture in the tribal territory provided a new source of production and served as an anchor for those in herding camps who had to irrigate fields every four days.

Here and there in the Yarahmadzai tribal territory, tribesmen built small houses, watag, of unbaked brick, usually no larger than just one or two small rooms, or several families built small clusters of such houses. The Yarahmadzai chiefly family built a small village at Gorchan. Sometimes, if water was available, tribesmen would experiment with small gardens and orchards. But no tribesmen lived in their houses year-round. Owners of solitary houses did not want to live alone, and they spent most of the year in herding camps with their kin, using their houses for storage most of the year and occupying them only when their herding camp was nearby. The chiefly family did spend the winter in their houses at Gorchan, but they brought out their tents and spent the spring in the pastures and the summer at the date groves. At the distant date groves, people built ever larger mud-brick, one-room houses to keep themselves (relatively) cool during the broiling days of the summer date harvest, but the date groves were occupied only during July and August. Overall, the Baluch of the Sarhad were gradually denomadizing but were still far from settling.

General Observation No. 17. Decreasing nomadic mobility is often a voluntary choice of nomadic peoples in the face of changing conditions (Salzman, ed. 1980).

THE KOMACHI OF KERMAN

For the Komachi, their summer quarters in a mountain valley south of Kerman city was their homeland. Ethnically Persian, they felt alien (surrounded as they were by Baluch and Arabs and other suspect types) in their winter quarters on the coastal plain of Bandar Abbas. If they had had any inclination to settle, it would have been in their summer quarters. But the agricultural potential was fully exploited by the villagers engaged in irrigation cultivation. Consequently, "given the *sarhad*'s [that is, the highland's] limited resources, settling into the local agricultural sector was not and probably never had been a reasonable alternative for the region's pastoralists" (Bradburd 1990: 14). An additional factor inhibiting Komachi sedentarization was their lack of land rights; the Komachi gained access to pasture through the state or traditional landowners (Bradburd 1990: 21). Even their pastoralism was vulnerable in this respect, but unimproved pasture was more readily available than irrigation water and good agricultural land.

General Observation No. 18. Some nomads who might settle if they had access to good agricultural land continue their nomadism because they have no viable alternative.

THE BASSERI OF FARS

The Basseri knew that they could not settle and keep their livestock. Their productive strain of sheep could not tolerate extremes of climate. As Barth (1961: 6) says, "It has thus been the experience of nomads who become sedentary, and of occasional sedentary buyers of nomad livestock, that 70–80% of the animals die if they are kept throughout the year in the northern or southern areas." So the Basseri who settled did not do so as pastoralists.

According to Barth (1961: 103–111), there were two processes of sedentarization. One was a spiral of failure, which saw a pastoral family drawing increasingly on their animal capital to meet ongoing consumption costs and ultimately losing so many animals that they could not continue as pastoralists. They settled in agricultural villages to become agricultural laborers on the land of others. The other process was one of accumulation and conversion to other forms of wealth. If a pastoral family was successful and their flocks grew, they looked to convert animal wealth into a more stable form of wealth when they could no longer look after their animals themselves and when the maintenance of large numbers of animals became too risky. On a small scale, livestock was converted into portable valuables, such as carpets and gold jewelry, which also had prestige value. But the likelier destination of more substantial livestock wealth was land, in which there was an active market and secure legal rights. A well-to-do pastoralist could, by converting his animals into land, become a landowner and receive landlord's rents from the agriculturalists working the land. For the Basseri, then, these two processes brought the unfortunate and the fortunate to settled life—the former as a propertyless tenant, the latter as a landlord—leaving the moderately successful Basseri to continue following his nomadic strategy.

General Observation No. 19. Sedentarization is not always a collective event. In some cases, individuals, families, and small groups drop out of nomadic life and settle. The destinies of those who settle as landlords and those who settle as agricultural laborers are starkly different.

OTHER ZAGROS TRIBES

In the 1920s and 1930s, Reza Shah, the king of Iran, set about gaining control of the country by mounting military campaigns in the unruly tribal areas (Arfa 1964). The Qashqa'i, as one of the most powerful tribes and thus one of the main threats to government control, received Reza Shah's close attention. Immobile peasants are always less threatening to the state than mobile tribesmen, and so, in 1933, Reza Shah ordered the Qashqa'i settled. Various tribal khans were executed to remove tribal leadership. When Reza Shah was forced to abdicate in 1941, most Qashqa'i immediately resumed their seasonal migrations (Beck 1991: 90–91).

General Observation No. 20. Governments often want to settle nomads as a way of gaining greater control over them. Here, we see the reaction to the centrifugal political tendency of nomadism (see General Observation No. 13). Forcible settlement has not infrequently been attempted. Sometimes, it is successful, and at other times, it is not. But it is not irreversible, and nomads who have been forcibly settled have often returned to nomadism.

Nor were the Qashqa'i great favorites of Mohammed Reza Shah, the son of Reza Shah and the king of Iran in the post–World War II period (until the Islamic Revolution in 1977). During the 1970s, when Lois Beck (1991) was doing her initial research, the state was using many methods to pressure the Qashqa'i to settle. To migrate, one needed a permit from the army, and the army was in no rush to hand out permits. So Qashqa'i and their flocks would sit helplessly for weeks at a time, with no remaining pasturage and worsening climatic conditions. Pastures were nationalized, so access depended upon the reluctant will of government officials. Reducing the number of animals nomads could possess was the next step taken by the government, with a law requiring them to cut their flocks of sheep by half and to get rid of goats entirely. As Beck (1991: 322) points out, "This law, aimed more to force nomads to settle than [as the rationale stated] to lessen the impact of herd animals on the natural environment, did not restrict the number of animals that commercial investors in cities, towns, and villages could send onto national land."

In the face of these governmental pressures, many Qashqa'i settled. One of the cases Beck describes is that of Hajji Boa:

> [Hajji Boa] had been one of the first Qermezi [section members] ... to choose to settle permanently. Although his first year as a settler was difficult, he had now quite successfully combined agriculture with pastoralism and was steadily improving his economic condition. Viewing the option that Hajji Boa represented as viable, men in dire straits privately sought his advice (1991: 142). ...

> Hajji Boa ... had understood sooner than most Qermezi men the need to place greater reliance on settled agriculture than on nomadic pastoralism because of the transformations brought about in Iran by land reform, the nationalization of pastures, the changing balance of power between the Qashqa'i and the state, and economic change (1991: 335).

Similar developments took place farther north in the Zagros, in Luristan, among the Bakhtiari, and in Kurdistan (Brooks 1983: 343), under both Reza Shah and Mohammad Reza Shah. The cycle of forced settlement followed by nomadization continued to be repeated, according to postrevolution reports of settled tribes returning to nomadism (Beck 1991: 343).

THE YOMUT TURKMEN OF THE GORGON

The Yomut Turkmen, too, had been forcibly settled, and their land was taken as Crown land (Irons 1974: 28). When Reza Shah abdicated, the Turkmen not only returned to nomadism, they also tore down the houses in which they had been forced to live. By contrast, Yomut charwa who were having difficulty in the northern pastoral sector would move to the southern agricultural sector, stake out some land, and try to rebuild household income. Similarly, some chomur agriculturalists who did well and built up capital bought livestock and moved north to take up the pastoral life. So Yomut were not loath to take initiative and to pursue apparently beneficial courses. When the opportunity came during the postwar period, Yomut expanded grain agriculture by mechanizing, and in doing so, they reduced pastoralism in areas with agricultural potential.

CONCLUSION

The nomadic strategy is one means by which people adapt to thinly spread resources and to the variability of resources across space and over time. It is also a strategy for avoiding other deleterious environmental conditions, such as extreme heat or cold, disease, and predators. Furthermore, as human predators are always a risk, every adaptation is political, relating populations through power. Above all, the nomadic strategy is a means of maximizing, given local circumstances, culturally defined objectives, such as production (as in Zagros herds), survival (as in Baluchi multiresource production), and independence (as in Turkmen mobility).

The nomadic strategy is put to use in a variety of ways, but it often involves various production activities, even if the pastoral production of livestock is for some populations the predominant (or most dramatic) one. In general, people using the nomadic strategy produce for their own consumption, even if they are heavily market oriented, and subsistence is supported by a variety of products. Productive diversification, often made possible or facilitated by nomadic mobility, is an insurance mechanism, guaranteeing survival in the face of failure in one productive sector—such as the loss of a flock from disease or predation or the loss of crops due to drought—as well as a base upon which to build. Diversification within pastoralism has the same benefit, with small stock (sheep and goats), for example, providing a fallback and a basis for rebuilding after the loss of large stock (cattle or camels).

People following a nomadic strategy usually do so within a customary habitat. Many, such as the Sarhadi Baluch and the Yomut Turkmen, have traditionally controlled territories—large expanses of land—that are their homes as they move around within them. Others, such as the Zagros tribes that make long nomadic treks annually, conceive of their territory as rights of time-space occupation, allowing them passage at a particular time on a particular route, as well as access to customary summer and winter quarters. Furthermore, even where people control territories, land tenure is almost always collective and relatively open. Natural pasture and water sources are thought of as given by God for everyone. Arrangements usually exist for the admission to the territory of outsiders, along with reciprocal arrangements for access to outside territories. However, access does not mean unbridled use, for collective social, political, and ritual mechanisms are in force to control the use of territorial resources and conserve the environment to guarantee continued availability of resources in the future.

What kind of people, we may ask, are nomads? But this is the wrong question, and it leads to false conceptions. In fact, nomads are not a kind of people but different kinds of people who use a particular strategy—that is, mobility of the household—in carrying out regular productive activities and in defending themselves. We may better understand the lives of these people if we ask what they are trying to accomplish through this strategy, how they implement this strategy, why they do not choose apparent alternative strategies, and in what ways this strategy is tied to the environmental conditions in which they live. Nomads do not live to migrate; they migrate to live. People who pursue a nomadic strategy do so for quite good reasons. Nomadism is one of a number of strategies that a population uses in pursuing a living, and its consequences and implications are only one set among many of the conditions and circumstances in which and with which the population lives and copes. Perhaps, given a better opportunity or a change in circumstances, people who now pursue a nomadic strategy would choose a nonnomadic strategy. Thus, it is more precise and more useful to think not of nomadic peoples but of nomadic strategies.

By so doing, one can avoid the reductionism or essentialism of identifying one characteristic of a population—nomadism—as the key or basic one. The people I have called "nomads" in this chapter could, depending upon particular cases, be labeled under many names: "tribesmen" or "peasants," "Muslims" or "pagans," "Persian" or "Turkic" or "Baluch" or "Arab," "fierce warriors" or "pacific civilians." There are many aspects and dimensions to peoples' lives and to a people's culture. To select and emphasize one aspect as paramount would be a distortion of the always complex human reality. And such an essentialism and reductionism would be a distortion of nomadism, for truly to understand nomadism, we must grasp its dependence on human objectives and on multiple social, cultural, and environmental circumstances. Only then can we appreciate its variability, its malleability, and its impermanence.

REFERENCES

Angioni, Giulio. (1989) *I pascoli erranti: Antropologia del pastore in Sardegna* (Wandering pastures: The anthropology of shepherds in Sardinia). Naples, Italy: Liguori.

Arfa, Gen. Hassan. (1964) *Under Five Shahs.* London: John Murray.

Barfield, Thomas J. (1993) *The Nomadic Alternative.* Englewood Cliffs, N.J.: Prentice-Hall.

Barth, Fredrik. (1961) *Nomads of South Persia.* Oslo: Oslo University Press.

Beck, Lois. (1986) *The Qashqa'i of Iran.* New Haven: Yale University Press.

------------. (1991) *Nomad: A Year in the Life of a Qashqa'i Tribesman in Iran.* Berkeley: University of California Press.

Bennett, John W. (1969) *Northern Plainsmen: Adaptive Strategy and Agrarian Life.* Arlington Heights, Ill.: AHM Publishing.

Berland, Joseph C. (1982) *No Five Fingers Are Alike.* Cambridge, Mass.: Harvard University Press.

Bradburd, Daniel. (1990) *Ambiguous Relations: Kin, Class, and Conflict Among Komachi Pastoralists.* Washington, D.C.: Smithsonian Institution Press.

------------. (1994) "Historical Bases of the Political Economy of Kermani Pastoralists: Tribe and World Markets in the Nineteenth and Early Twentieth Centuries," *Pastoralists at the Periphery: Herders in a Capitalist World,* Claudia Chang and Harold A. Koster, eds. Tucson: University of Arizona Press.

Brooks, David. (1983) "The Enemy Within: Limitations on Leadership in the Bakhtiari," *The Conflict of Tribe and State in Iran and Afghanistan,* Richard Tapper, ed. London: Croom Helm.

Clébert, Jean-Paul. (1967) *The Gypsies.* Harmondsworth, England: Penguin.

Cohen, Abner. (1965) *Arab Border-Villages in Israel.* Manchester, England: Manchester University Press.

Cole, Donald Powell. (1975) *Nomads of the Nomads: The Al Murrah Bedouin of the Empty Quarter.* Chicago: Aldine.

Drucker, Philip. *Cultures of the North Pacific Coast.* San Francisco: Chandler.

Evans-Pritchard, E. E. (1940) *The Nuer: A Description of the Modes of Livelihood and Political Institutions of a Nilotic People.* Oxford: Clarendon Press.

Fabietti, Ugo, and Philip Carl Salzman, eds. (1996) *Antropologia delle società pastorali tribali e contadine* (The anthropology of tribal and peasant pastoral societies). Como, Italy: IBIS; Pavia, Italy: Collegio Ghislieri.

Fraser, Angus. (1992) *The Gypsies.* Oxford: Blackwell.

Galaty, John G. (1980) "The Maasai Group Ranch: Politics and Development in an African Pastoral Society," *When Nomads Settle,* P. C. Salzman, ed. New York: Praeger.

Galaty, John G., and Douglas L. Johnson, eds.(1990) *The World of Pastoralism.* New York: Guilford Press.

Garthwaite, Gene. (1983) "Tribes, Confederation and the State: An Historical Overview of the Bakhtiari and Iran," *The Conflict of Tribe and State in Iran and Afghanistan,* Richard Tapper, ed. London: Croom Helm.

Gmelch, George. (1977) *The Irish Tinkers: The Urbanization of an Itinerant People.* Menlo Park, Calif.: Cummings.

Ingold, Tim. (1980) *Hunters, Pastoralists and Ranchers.* Cambridge: Cambridge University Press.

Irons, William. (1974) "Nomadism as a Political Adaptation: The Case of the Yomut Turkmen." *American Ethnologist* 1:635–658.

------------. (1975) *The Yomut Turkmen: A Study of Social Organization Among a Central Asian Turkic Speaking Population. Anthropological Paper no. 58, Museum of Anthropology, University of Michigan.*

------------. (1979) "Political Stratification Among Pastoral Nomads," *Pastoral Production and Society,* L'Equipe Ecologie et Anthropologie des Société Pastorale, ed. Cambridge: Cambridge University Press.

------------. (1994) "Why Are the Yomut Not More Stratified?" In *Pastoralists at the Periphery: Herders in a Capitalist World,* C. Chang and H. A. Koster, eds. Tucson: University of Arizona Press.

Kelly, Robert L.(1995) *The Foraging Spectrum: Diversity in Hunter-Gatherer Lifeways.* Washington, D.C.: Smithsonian Institution Press.

Khazanov, Anatoly M.(1994) *Nomads and the Outside World.* 2nd ed. Madison: University of Wisconsin Press.

Lancaster, William. (1997) *The Rwala Bedouin Today.* 2nd ed. Prospect Heights, Ill.: *Waveland Press.*

Lee, Richard, and Irving DeVore, eds.(1968) *Man the Hunter.* Chicago: Aldine.

Lewis, I. M.(1961) *A Pastoral Democracy: A Study of Pastoralism and Politics Among the Northern Somali of the Horn of Africa.* London: Oxford University Press.

Meloni, Benedetto. (1984) *Famiglie di pastori: Continuità e mutamento in una co-munità della Sardegna centrale, 1950–1970* (Shepherd families: Continuity and change in a central Sardinian community). Turin, Italy: Rosenberg & Sellier.

Misra, P. K. (1977) *The Nomadic Gadulia Lohar of Eastern Rajasthan.* Anthropological Survey of India, Memoir no. 41. Calcutta: Government of India.

Murru Corriga, Giannetta. (1990) *Dalla montagna ai campidani: Famiglia e muta-mento in una communità di pastori* (From the mountain to the valley: Family and change in a shepherd community). Sassari, Italy: Editrice Democra tica Sarda.

Nomadic Peoples [Periodical]. (1984) Special issue on "Sedentarization and Nomadization," vol. 15.

Rao, Aparna, ed.(1987) *The Other Nomads: Peripatetic Minorities in Cross-Cultural Perspective.* Cologne, Germany: Bohlau Verlag.

Ravis-Giordani, Georges. (1983) *Bergers corses (Corsican shepherds).* Aix-en-Provence, France: EDISUD.

Salzman, Philip Carl. (1971) "Movement and Resource Extraction Among Pastoral Nomads: The Case of the Yarahmadzai Baluch." *Anthropological Quarterly* 44:185–197. Reprinted in *Cultural and Social Anthropology.* 2nd Ed. P.B. Hammond, ed. NY: Macmillan, 1975.

------------. (1978) "Ideology and Change in Middle East Tribal Societies," *Man* (n.s.) 13:618–637.

------------. (1980) "Processes of Sedentarization Among the Nomads of Baluchistan," *When Nomads Settle: Processes of Sedentarization as Adaptation and Response,* P. C. Salzman, ed. New York: Praeger.

------------. (1983) "Why Tribes Have Chiefs: A Case from Baluchistan," *The Conflict of Tribe and State in Iran and Afghanistan,* R. Tapper, ed. London: Croom Helm.

------------. (1994) "Baluchi Nomads in the Market," *Pastoralists at the Periphery,* C. Chang and H. A. Koster, eds. Tucson: University of Arizona Press.

------------. (2000a) *Black Tents of Baluchistan.* Washington, D.C.: Smithsonian Institution Press.

------------. (2000b) "Hierarchical Image and Reality: The Construction of a Tribal Chiefship," *Comparative Studies in Society and History* 42, no. 1:49–66.

Thaiss, Gustav. (1973) "The Drama of Husain." Ph.D. diss., Washington University.

Identity in Relationship

by LILA ABU-LUGHOD

THIS WORLD FULL OF PEOPLE WHOSE LIVES I CAME TO SHARE
was not at all what I had envisioned. Several romantic images had informed
my subconscious expectations. Knowing that Awlad 'Ali inhabited a coastal
strip along the northern edge of the Libyan Desert,[1] I had imagined tents
along a white-sand beach, the turquoise Mediterranean glimmering in the
background. In my mind glowed a vivid passage from *Justine,* the first volume
of Lawrence Durrell's "Alexandria Quartet":

> We had tea together and then, on a sudden impulse took our bathing
> things and drove out through the rusty slag-heaps of Mex towards
> the sand-beaches off Bourg El Arab, glittering in the mauve-lemon
> light of the fast-fading afternoon. Here the open sea boomed upon
> the carpets of fresh sand the colour of oxidized mercury; its deep
> melodious percussion was the background to such conversation
> as we had. We walked ankle deep in the spurge of those shallow
> dimpled pools, choked here and there with sponges torn up by the
> roots and flung ashore. We passed no one on the road I remember

save a gaunt Bedouin youth carrying on his head a wire crate full of wild
birds caught with lime-twigs. Dazed quail. (1957, 34)

I discovered, however, that despite its proximity, the sea played little part in the
Bedouins' lives, and what appreciation of natural beauty they expressed was for the
desert where, until sedentarization, their winter migrations had taken them. The
members of my community all spoke with nostalgia about the inland desert, "up
country" (fōg), although they had last migrated seven years before I arrived. They
described the flora and fauna, the grasses so delectable to the gazelle, the umbel-
lifer that whets the appetite, the herb that, boiled with tea, cures sundry maladies,
the wild hares that must be hunted at night, and the game birds that suddenly take
flight from deep within a shrub. They praised the good "dry" foods of desert life[2] and
disparaged as unhealthy the fresh vegetable stews that are now an important part
of their diet. They recalled with pleasure the milk products, so plentiful in spring-
time when rains have created desert pastures,[3] and savored memories of the taste
of milk given by ewes who have fed on aromatic wormwood (shīḥ).

And yet, despite their appreciation of the desert's natural gifts, the Bedouins
think of the territory in which they live primarily in terms of the people and groups
who inhabit it. Theirs is an intensely social world in which people's activities and
relationships are riveting, and solitude so abhorred that no one sleeps alone; those
who spend time alone are thought to be vulnerable to attack by the evil spirits
('afārīt) who thrive wherever there are no people.

I had also expected tent-dwelling pastoral nomads who lived quietly with
their herds but found instead that these same people who touted the joys of the
desert lived in houses (even if they continued to pitch their tents next to them
and spent most of their days in the tents), wore shiny wristwatches and plastic
shoes, listened to radios and cassette players, and traveled in Toyota pickup
trucks.[4] Unlike me, they did not regard these as alarming signs that they were losing their identity as a cultural group, that they were no longer Bedouins, because
they define themselves not primarily by a way of life, however much they value
pastoral nomadism and the rigors of the desert, but by some key principles of social organization; genealogy and a tribal order based on the closeness of agnates
(paternal relatives) and tied to a code of morality, that of honor and modesty.
Their social universe is ordered by these ideological principles, which define individuals' identities and the quality of their relationships to others. These principles
are gathered up in Awlad 'Ali notions of "blood" (dam), a multi-faceted concept

with dense meanings and tremendous cultural force, two aspects of which will be explored below.

ASL: THE BLOOD OF ANCESTRY

Blood both links people to the past and binds them in the present. As a link to the past, through genealogy, blood is essential to the definition of cultural identity. Nobility of origin or ancestry (*asl*) is a point of great concern to Awlad 'Ali. The clans or tribes known as Awlad 'Ali migrated into Egypt from Libya. Most accounts concur in viewing them, like the other Sa'ādi tribes of Cyrenaica, as descendants of the Beni Suleim and Beni Hilal, the Arab invaders from the Najd who swept through North Africa during the eleventh century. Some sources put their migration into Egypt at the end of the seventeenth century, although others favor the end of the eighteenth.[5] Along with the Mrābtīn, other ambiguously related tribal groups with whom they share the Western Desert, they have remained marginal to the agrarian society of the Nile Valley, the economic and demographic core of Egypt.[6] By all estimates, the Bedouins of the Western Desert constitute far less than 1 percent of the total population of Egypt, a percentage that has probably been decreasing over the past century.[7]

The fortunes of Awlad 'Ali have always been tied to more than rainfall and the state of pasture, despite the fact that their traditional economy was based primarily on herds of camels, sheep, and goats, supplemented by rain-fed cereal cultivation in the littoral and some trade. Their movements and livelihood were determined not only by internal competition with other tribal groups who shared their way of life but also by external political and economic events affecting Libya and Egypt. They have been in contact with Europeans, Libyans, and Egyptians through trade, smuggling, and invasions, both peaceful and violent. Yet, despite centuries of contact with other groups and the efforts of successive central authorities in the Nile Valley—from Mohammad 'Ali through the British to Nasser and the current regime—to control and later to assimilate them, the Awlad 'Ali Bedouins maintain a distinct cultural identity.

In the nineteenth century, the free movement of Awlad 'Ali, their control over caravan routes, and their lack of respect for the law were a bane to Mohammad 'Ali. Finally, in exchange for their help in patrolling the borders, quelling internal rebellions, and assisting in foreign campaigns, he rewarded them with usufruct rights to the land in the Western Desert and with exemption from taxation and military conscription. By the time the British governed, the Awlad 'Ali were still far from subjugated or settled, although many had been induced to take up agriculture by the high value of cash crops, and the beginnings of competition from the railroad had loosened their hold on trade and driven them to concentrate on sheep rather than camels.[8] The British, insecure about the nomads' close ties to Libya and their smuggling activities, periodically and unsuccessfully sought to revoke their privileges to carry firearms and to claim exemption from military conscription. During World War II the Bedouins suffered the loss of herds, wells, and possessions when the battles between the British and Germans were fought on their soil.[9]

Only after the revolution and Nasser's rise to power in 1952 did government goals shift from political control to assimilation. The motives underlying the government's interest in integrating the Bedouins into the Egyptian polity, economy, and national culture were both ideological and material. As the anthropologist Ahmed Abou-Zeid explained in 1959, "Rightly or wrongly, it is generally assumed in Egypt that nomadism and semi-nomadism represent a phase of deterioration which is no longer compatible with the actualities of modern life and therefore should be abolished" (1959, 553). The government initiated projects to settle the nomads: it reclaimed land for agriculture; subsidized olive, fig, and almond orchards; subsidized fodder through the cooperatives; and made laws giving individuals who built a house the right to keep the land on which it was erected. The government also worked to improve pasture and herds, to encourage local industries, and to provide medical and educational services. In concert with Bedouin initiatives, primarily in commercial ventures, these projects radically altered the basic economy and work patterns of the Awlad 'Ali and contributed to sedentarization.[10] Nevertheless, Abou-Zeid's sanguine prediction about what impact government development projects would have on Awlad 'Ali rings hollow some twenty-five years later:

> The crowning achievement of these projects will be the reduction of the cultural and social contrast which exists at present between the Western Desert, with its nomadic and semi-nomadic inhabitants, and the rest of the country. This contrast is manifested in the different patterns of social relationships, the different values and modes of thought, and the different structure prevailing in the desert and the Nile Valley. (1959, 558)

Despite many changes in Awlad 'Ali society and economy, the goal of assimilation has not been achieved. On the contrary, much of the Bedouin identity and sense of self is articulated through distinction from or in opposition to non-Bedouins, be they *flūḥ* (peasants), *masriyyīn* (Egyptians, Cairenes), or *naṣāra* (Christians).[11] There are signs of integration into the state: most Bedouin men are aware of events in the world political arena, some hold opinions on the relative merits of the super-powers, and most have some knowledge of Egypt's internal political situation as well as its international involvements. But their passions are aroused only by tribal affairs—intra-Bedouin disputes, reconciliations, alliances, and hostilities. They may hear Egyptian programs on the radio, but their excitement is reserved for one program called "Iskandariyya-Matruh" (Alexandria-Matruh). Once a week young and old, men and women, crowd around small radios and listen with rapt attention and visible enjoyment to this program, which features traditional Bedouin songs, poems, and greetings for various parties, all identified by name and tribal affiliation.

The Bedouins' sense of collective identity is crystallized in opposition to the Egyptians or peasants, who are lumped together as "the people of the Nile Valley" (*hal wādi n-nīl*). In the Bedouins' view, the differences extend beyond the linguistic and sartorial to the fundamentals of origin, defined by genealogy, social organization, modes of interpersonal interaction, and a sort of moral nature.[12] How accurate the Bedouins' characterization of the Egyptians might be is not at issue, for Awlad 'Ali, the Egyptians with whom they share a country defined by political borders they consider arbitrary constitute a vivid "other," providing a convenient foil for self-definition; by looking at how the Bedouins distinguish themselves from the Egyptians, we can isolate the nodes of Bedouin identity.

Blood, in the sense of genealogy, is the basis of Awlad 'Ali identity. No matter where or how they live, those who can link themselves genealogically to any of the tribes of the Western Desert are *'arab* (Arabs), not Egyptians.[13] Awlad 'Ali more frequently refer to themselves as *'arab* than as *badū* (Bedouins). As in many cultures, the word they use to designate themselves also connotes the general term *people*—for instance anyone returning from a visit to kin is queried, "How are your Arabs?" But the term has a more specific meaning when used to distinguish the Bedouins from their Egyptian neighbors. In that context, it implies the Bedouin claim to origins in the Arabian Peninsula and to genealogical links to the pure Arab tribes who were the first followers of the Prophet Muhammad. It also suggests their affinity to all the Arabic-speaking Muslims of the Middle East and North Africa who, because of common origin, they presume to be just like themselves.

Blood is the authenticator of origin or pedigree and as such is critical to Bedouin identity and their differentiation from Egyptians, who are said to lack roots or nobility of origin (*asl* or *mabdā*). Some Bedouins stated this idea by characterizing the Egyptians as mixed-blooded or impure; others attributed to the Egyptians Pharaonic origins, as the following story told to me by one Bedouin man suggests:

> When Moses escaped from Egypt, the Pharaoh and all of the real men, the warriors, set off after him. They left behind only the women, children, and servants/slaves [*khadama*]. These were the weak men who washed women's feet and cared for the children. When Moses crossed the Red Sea, the Pharaoh's men drowned chasing him. This left only the servants. They are the grandfathers [ancestors] of the Egyptians. That is why they are like that now. The men are women and the women are men. He carries the children and does not take a seat until he sees that she has.

The centrality of blood, in the sense of a bloodline, pedigree, or link to illustrious forebears, is apparent from these remarks. Underlying this concern is the belief that a person's nature and worth are closely tied to the worthiness of his or her stock. By crediting the Egyptians with no line to the past or, more insulting, a line to an inferior, pre-Islamic past of servitude, this man was making a statement about their present worthlessness. The ignominy of origin is a metaphor for present shortcomings.

Nobility of origin is believed to confer moral qualities and character. Bedouins, value a constellation of qualities that could he captured by the umbrella phrase "the honor code." Although the entailments of this code will be detailed elsewhere, a few of the Bedouins' criticisms of Egyptians will introduce the themes. Men variously described Egyptians as lacking in moral excellence (*fadhīla*). honor (*sharaf*), sincerity and honesty (*sadag*), and generosity (*kurama*), at the same time claiming these as Bedouin traits. One example they gave of Egyptians' lack of honor was their insistence on using contracts in transactions—for the Arab, they explained, a person's word is sufficient.

The most highly prized Arab virtue is generosity, expressed primarily through the Hospitality for which they are renowned. As one Bedouin man put it, "We like to do [our duty to guests], not have done to." To honor guests, ideally a sheep is slaughtered. If this is not feasible, a smaller animal may be substituted. Failing that, at least some food must be put out. No guest or even passerby can leave without being invited to drink tea. Of the Egyptians one man said, "It is rare for them to invite you to their homes. You are lucky if they invite you for a cup of coffee or tea, and that after you have invited them to your home, slaughtered a sheep for them, and given them everything it was in your power to give." Some Bedouins also accuse the Egyptians of being opportunistic, of not knowing the meaning of friendship.

Fearlessness and courage are qualities considered natural in Bedouin men and women as concomitants of their nobility of origin. Although the days of tribal warfare are over, Bedouin men maintain the values of warriors, carrying arms and resorting to violence if challenged or insulted. Women support these values. All describe Egyptians as easily frightened and cowardly and lacking in the belligerence that, as we shall see, is so important in the ideology of honor.

Perhaps even more indicative *of asl* are moral qualities associated with relations between men and women. The Egyptians' lax enforcement of sexual segregation and the intimacy husbands and wives display in public are interpreted as signs of Egyptian men's weakness and the women's immorality. (…) The pivotal role of sexual segregation in Awlad 'Ali definitions of their own culture was brought home to me on a visit to a settled Bedouin family living in Bhēra, an agricultural province. Genealogically Awlad 'Ali, this family of landowners lived on a large at id productive agricultural estate, they dressed in that peculiar mix of peasant and urban garb common to the rural elite, and they spoke an Egyptian rather than a Libyan dialect. When I challenged them, the women adamantly defended their Arab identity. One argued, "We are not like the peasants. Their women go out and talk to men. We never leave the house, we don't drink tea with men, and we don't greet the guests."

That the Bedouins attribute the ease of social intercourse between men and women and men's show of affection toward women to men's weakness is clear in the story of the Pharaonic origins of the Egyptians recounted above. The point was made that the servants left behind were those who "washed women's feet and cared for the children." To this day, the man who told me that story said, Egyptian men were weak and doted on their wives. The antiquity of this view of Egyptians is attested to by Lord Cromer's comment in 1908 that "the Bedouins despise the fellaheen [peasants], whom they consider an unmanly race" (1908, 198). Many Bedouin men and women echoed this man's sentiments:

> Among the Arabs the man rules the woman, not like the Egyptians whose women can come and go as they please. When an Egyptian family goes out, the man carries the baby and the wife walks in front of him. Among the Arabs, a woman must get permission to go visiting. Among the Arabs,

if there are guests in the home, a wife can come to greet them only if they are kinsmen. She does not stay in the room. If they are nonkin, she does not enter at all.

Further evidence of the reversal of proper power relations is the alleged public affection Egyptian husbands show their wives. Stories of men cooking for bedridden wives, bringing them flowers, or doing them other favors provoked strong reactions in Bedouin women and men alike. The women's disapproval was tempered by an occasional wistful comment such as "the Egyptians spoil their women—they love their wives," but bedouin men wire less equivocal. They considered such behavior simply unmanly and a testament to female rule (which is not to deny that many of them felt affection for their wives and treated them with respect).

The other side of the coin to men's weakness is women's immodesty. Once two women giving me advice about what to do when I got married earnestly confided, "You should not let the groom have sex with you on the first night." I argued that we knew for a fact that a certain bridal couple had consummated their marriage the first night. They countered, "Oh, she is a peasant. They don't care. They have no shame [*mā yithashshamūsh*]."[14] They laughed uproariously as they recalled another peasant woman who had announced to her women guests the morning after her wedding that her husband had made love to her twice, and added, "She had no shame at all!" Bedouin brides vehemently deny that sexual intercourse has taken place, even when it is obvious to all that it has. One woman put it this way:

> The Egyptians are not like us. They have no shame. Why, the So-and-So's [an Egyptian family we knew] have a photograph from their wedding hanging on the wall in their living room where everyone can see it. In it, he has his arm around her. And they sit together and call each other pet names. An Arab woman would be embarrassed/modest [*tahashsham*] in front of an older brother, her mother-in-law, people.

Many of the ideas the Bedouins have about Egyptians are based on hearsay and the imposition of their own cultural interpretations on reported behavior. Very few of those living in the desert have much opportunity to see Egyptians at home. But, as the following incident shows, when they do have such opportunities, their ideas are confirmed. During the holidays celebrating the Prophet's birthday, an Egyptian army officer, a friend and business partner of the Haj, decided to bring his family for a weekend visit to the Western Desert, and they spent a day and a night with us before going on to a beach resort. Their visit occasioned a great deal of commotion, including the purchase and preparation of special foods, a massive cleanup, and the household's rearrangement to vacate rooms for their comfortable accommodation. The visit strained everyone's nerves and energy, but it provided an intriguing close-up look at the Egyptians.

Everyone knew about the Egyptians' lax sex segregation, so they were not surprised that the women and girls ate with the men and spent time as a group in the men's guest room. However, the evening's events were unexpected. After dinner, the man, his wife, their daughters, and his wife's sister all retired to their rooms, only to emerge in nightclothes and bathrobes and go to the men's guest room, where they sat chatting with their host and his brothers. This immodesty of dress sent shock waves through the community. Next came the scandalized realization that husband and wife intended to sleep in the same room. Although Bedouin husbands and wives sleep together under normal circumstances, they would not do so when visiting; each would sleep with members of his or her own sex. In fact, it is considered rude for a host or hostess not to sleep with his or her guests. The public admission of active sexuality implied by the couple's wish to sleep together was considered the height of immodesty. Yet everyone was polite, the values of friendship and hospitality outweighing the deeply offended sense of propriety. Perhaps more important, the Bedouins excused their guests' behavior because they recognized that the Egyptians were another sort of people, whose lack of pedigree made it difficult (although not impossible) for them to behave with honor.

GARABĀ: THE BLOOD OF RELATIONSHIP

The concept of blood is central to Bedouin identity in a second sense: through its ideological primacy in the present, as a means of determining social place and the links between people. Above all, Awlad 'Ali conceive of themselves in terms of tribes, notoriously ambiguous segmented units defined by consanguinity or ties to a common patrilineal ancestor.[15]

This tribal social organization is another point on which the Awlad 'Ali proudly differentiate themselves from their Egyptian neighbors, whom they disparage as a "people" (sha'b)—meaning that the Egyptians are not organized tribally, do not know their roots, and identify with a geographic area or, worse, with a national government. The importance of blood in social identity is apparent in the identification of Bedouins by family, lineage, and tribe. One of the first questions asked a newcomer is "Where are you from?" The answer to this question is not a geographical area (that would be the response to another question, "Where is your homeland [wutn]?") but rather a tribal affiliation. Because Awlad 'Ali apply the term *tribe* (*gabīla*) to many levels of organization, people belong to numerous named tribes simultaneously.[16] The tribe a person chooses to identify with at any given moment depends largely on the rhetorical statement the speaker wishes to make about his or her relationship to the inquirer. To assert unity and closeness, a person will point to the shared level of tribal affiliation (a common ancestor), establishing himself or herself as a paternal kinsperson of the appropriate generation.

The tribal terms in which Bedouins conceive of social bonds lend a distinctive cast to their social life. Most of the anthropological literature on Bedouins has focused on how kinship provides an idiom for political relations. I am less concerned with whether the Bedouins really organize politically in terms of segmentary lineages (Peters 1967) or with how the theory of segmentary opposition, the genealogical ordering of political life, and (Peters 1960, 1965, 1980; Behnke 1980) or more even to the historical problem of uncertain political relations (Meeker 1979) than with how kinship ideology shapes individual identity and the perceptions and management of everyday social relations. This is not to deny either the importance of kinship as the language of sociopolitical organization or the dialectic between the political and interpersonal spheres, as later arguments will show. It is merely to shift the focus to kinship as the idiom for Awlad 'Ali feelings about, and actions toward, persons in their social world, in order to show how deeply this ideology penetrates everyday life and sentiment.[17]

The social world of the Awlad 'Ali is bifurcated into kin versus strangers/outsiders (*garīb* versus *gharīb*), a distinction that shapes both sentiment and behavior. Bedouin kinship ideology is based on two fundamental propositions. First, all those related by blood share a substance that identifies them, in both senses of the word: giving each person a social identity and causing individuals to identify with everyone else who shares the same blood. Agnates share blood and flesh (*dam wlham*), although the fact that a relationship through maternal ascendants is characterized as one of *drmya* (the diminutive of "blood") suggests that the Bedouins do recognize distant maternal links as a weak form of kinship. Second, because of this identification with each other, individuals who share blood feel close.

Kinsmen preparing tea in a desert camp.

The term for kinship is *garāba* from the root meaning "to be close." The Bedouin vision of social relations is dominated by this ideology of natural, positive, and unbreakable bonds of blood between consanguines, particularly agnates, including putative or distant agnates, those related through common patrilineal descent as manifested by a shared eponymous ancestor. Tribal bonds, or relations between paternal kin, are called *'asabiyya,* which one man expressively characterized as "son-of-a-bitch bonds you can never break."[18] The Bedouins look down on the Egyptians, alleging that they know no one but their immediate kin.

Agnation has indisputable ideological priority in kin reckoning. Descent, inheritance, and tribal sociopolitical organization are conceptualized as patrilineal, extending the strong relationship between father and son (and father and daughter) back in time and outside the immediate family. The significance of agnation is reflected in how rights are distributed among members of a family. For one thing, children take their fathers tribal affiliation, although their mother's affiliation affects their status (Abou-Zeid 1966, 257). In case of a divorce, the mother has no right to keep her children, although she may temporarily take unweaned children with her and she may set up a separate household with adult sons. The superior claim of agnates to children was expressed in a comment I heard one woman (a paternal first cousin of her husband) make to her co-wife in the midst of a heated argument. She asserted, "Your son is ours, and even if we decide to sacrifice him [like a sheep], you have no right to say a word." The hyperbole produced by flared passions does not invalidate the essential message—that paternal kin have jural rights to all children born to wives of agnates.

The Bedouins consider this not just a right but also a natural bond based on sentiment, as is clear from the following story I heard about a neighbor of ours. This woman was divorced by her husband after he had brought her to her natal home for a visit and never returned for her. Her young son, considered too young to part from his mother, was with her. After a year, the boy's paternal grandfather came to the house to take his grandson back. According to reports, he asked his five-year-old grandson, "Would you like to come with me?" Although the boy had never seen him before, he ran to pack a few clothes, put his hand in his grandfather's, and left with hardly a glance back. His mother was heartbroken. Men who heard the story nodded their heads and did not seem surprised; "Blood" was all they said by way of explanation. Although women, too, perceive social relations and identity primarily in terms of agnation, their experiences lead them to a slightly different position. Many of their closest relationships, to their children and to coresident women in 'their" marital communities, are not those of agnation. Most of the women who heard the story were moved and reacted differently, wondering if the grandfather had used magic (katablu) to lure the boy into abandoning his mother.

Much has been written on the close (if often troubled) relations between men, especially brothers, in patrilineal, patrilocal societies. Yet the position of women and attitudes about the bonds created by marriage give the clearest index of the ideological dominance of agnation in social identity and relationships in Bedouin society. A woman retains her tribal affiliation throughout her life and should side with her own kin in their disputes with her husband's kin; I heard many stories of women who left for their natal homes, abandoning children, under such conditions. In her marital camp people refer to her by her tribal affiliation, and she may refer to herself as an outsider even after twenty years of marriage.

The extent to which women remain a part of their own patri-group is clear from the following incident. In one camp, when a paternal aunt of the core agnates died, her nieces and nephews all agreed that it would have been better if she had come to spend her last days with them and died and been buried in her father's camp. Even after forty years of married life away from the camp, they considered it her true home. Of the five people who washed her corpse, only one was from her husband's family; the others were her sisters and her brothers' wives. Although a woman, can never be incorporated into her husband's lineage, if she has adult sons she becomes secure and comfortable in her marital community. Once her husband dies and she becomes head of the household, her close association with her sons makes her seem the core of the agnatic cluster. There are many such matriarchs.

Not only do women derive their identities from their patriline, but they also retain their ties to their kin, even after marriage, for both affective and strategic reasons. A woman remains dependent on the moral, legal, and often economic support of her father, brothers, or other kinsmen. Only they can guarantee her marital rights. A woman cut off from her family is vulnerable to abuse from her husband and society (Mohsen 1967, 157), but a married woman with the backing of her kin is well protected. When mistreated or wronged, she argues that she need not put up with such treatment because "behind me are men."When angry, she packs a few of her possessions in a bundle and heads off toward her family's camp. And in case of divorce, she can return home, where she is entitled to support. But because she is identified with her kin, her behavior affects their honor and reputation, just as theirs affects hers. Her kin, not her husband, are ultimately responsible for her and are entitled to sanction all her wrongdoings, including adultery.

Although strategically useful, these kin ties are conceived of as based on sentiment. The sense of closeness, identification, common interests, and loyalty is expressed in the way women talk about their kin and in their attitudes toward visits home and even toward visits by their kin. Women are preoccupied with news of their kin. They rush home (if their husbands permit) whenever an event is celebrated or mourned: if they hear of an illness, a wedding, a circumcision, a return from the pilgrimage, a release from prison, or a funeral, they visit, and they are dejected and frustrated if for some reason they cannot. When a young wife left our camp "angry" without any apparent reason, some of the men suspected magic, but the women thought it more plausible that she just missed her relatives and wished to see her brother, who had just been released from prison. Her husband had been too busy to take her home for a visit, and she had been crying for days.

Visits home are anticipated with excitement, suffused with warmth, and remembered nostalgically. Women always return from such visits reporting how happy, pampered, and well fed they were. They bring back gifts, dresses, jewelry, soap, perfume, and candies. Their hair is freshly braided and hennaed, smelling sweetly of expensive cloves—kinswomen's grooming favors. And when a brother or other kinsman visits a woman's marital home, although sexual segregation may sometimes prevent her from sitting with him, she will certainly offer the choicest provisions and devote herself to the preparations personally, rather than delegating her responsibilities to grown daughters or younger co-wives. The tone of their greetings, however brief, invariably betrays affection.

Marriage presents serious problems for the consistency of an ideological system in which agnation is given priority over any other basis for affiliation. The Awlad 'Ali commitment to this system is expressed in their contempt for the perceived Egyptian propensity to reside in nuclear family units, a shameful sign of the valuation of marital ties over agnatic ones. One man said, "Arabs say that mother, father, and brother are the most dear. Even if an Arab loves his wife more than anything, he cannot let anyone know this. He tries never to let this show."

The way to resolve this problem of marriage is to fuse it with identity and closeness of shared blood. Patrilateral parallel-cousin marriage may be preferred because it is the only type consistent with Bedouin ideas about the importance of agnation. As in other parts of the Middle East, this type of marriage is the cultural ideal, although it is only one of many types of marriage practiced. Because of the prevalence of multiple kinship ties between individuals (Peters 1980, 133–34) and because the term *paternal cousin* extends to all members of a tribe (however widely defined), a range of marriages can be interpreted as conforming to this preferential type and will be justified in terms of this preference even when arranged for other reasons. Thus, even if cousins are more directly related through some maternal link, their relationship will be described in terms of the paternal one.[19] The actual frequency of cousin marriages varies depending on a number of circumstances that are too complex to explore here but that have been much debated in the theoretical literature (see Bourdieu 1977, 32–33). The actual incidence in any particular community is, however, less important than the ideological preference. In the community in which I did my fieldwork, the incidence happened to be quite high. Four of the five core household heads had married their paternal first cousins (FBD); of those who took second wives, three married more distant cousins, women from another section of their tribe. In this generation, the eldest daughter and eldest son of two brothers had married, and the brothers planned to marry other sons and daughters to each other in the near future.

What differentiates marriage to paternal kin from other types of marriage, and how are the differences evaluated? For most, the advantages do not have to do with sexual excitement. Indeed, some older men complained that the "marital" (sexual) side of such marriages, was limited. As one polygynously married man put it, "My other wives are better with me personally," although he went on to explain that he nevertheless preferred his cousin-wife, for reasons to be enumerated below. Certain young men complained that the trouble with marrying a cousin was that she was like a sister.[20] An unmarried man mused, "You won't feel like talking and flirting. And she knows everything about you, where you go, who you see." He implied that she would therefore not be in awe of her husband, reducing the power differential. Girls occasionally voiced a wish to see something new by marrying an outsider, since then they would leave the camp. They did not talk (at least to me) about the sexual aspect of marriage.

The advantages of such marriages are that they presumably build on the prior bonds of paternal kinship to take on the closeness, trust, identification, and loyalty appropriate to such bonds. In polygynous unions, the wife who is a paternal kinswoman is usually better treated than her co-wives. The young man who complained that there was no mystery with a cousin-wife also claimed that he would not beat her as much as he would an outsider. And the older man who confessed the lack of sexual excitement with his cousin-wife considered this wife to be first in his affections and in charge of his household. His other wives had tried in vain to displace his cousin in his affections, something he claimed was impossible because, after all, she is my father's brother's daughter. I know that if I am gone, she will take care of the house, entertain my guests graciously, and protect my property and all of my children. Haven't you noticed how even though she loves her own children more, she cares for the children of my other wives, even protecting them from their mothers' harshness? After all, the children are closer to her, they are her kin, her tribe. Also, if something is on my mind, it will be on her mind too. Outsiders don't care. They don't care who might enter the house while I am gone, what gets spilled, ruined, or stolen. They don't care about your name or reputation. But a father's brother's daughter cares about you and your things because they are hers.

Another man, even though he was no longer sleeping with his postmenopausal wife, treated her as head of the domestic household, entrusted her with all his money and valuables, and took only her with him on important visits. He explained, "I take my father's brother's daughter with me when I go to visit outsiders because I trust her." Nearly all the young children born to his other wives slept with her, ate with her, and spent more time with her than with their own mothers. They called her *ḥannī*, or grandmother, the person for whom children feel the deepest affection.

Women see innumerable advantages in this marriage arrangement. As wives, they are more secure and powerful if they marry paternal kin because they remain among those whose duty it is to protect them. They are not as dependent on husbands, since their right to support derives from their claim to the common patrimony. They also feel comfortable in the community, living among kinfolk with whom they share interests, loved ones, and often a lifetime of experience. Even if the match does not work out, they need not leave their children. Marriages between coresident cousins are often more affectionate because they build on childhood experiences of closeness, in a society in which relations between unrelated members of the opposite sex are highly circumscribed and often either distant or hostile.

In contrast, wives who are not patrikin to their husbands are often treated differently from wives who are paternal cousins or, even more, mothers and sisters of the core agnates. In the camp in which I lived, the men tended to overlook or skimp on gifts to these outside women at festive occasions such as weddings when men buy clothing and jewelry for the camp's women. In defense, the outsider wives tended to form alliances with one another, but this process was not haphazard either: agnation created special bonds even between in-marrying wives. Two women from the same tribe who had married men in my camp spent a great deal of time together, helped each other with work, and supported each other in arguments. If one was angry with a certain person or family, the other would also refuse to speak to them. Thus, whatever the material consequences,[21] marrying agnates protects women from having to be vulnerable to people who do not have their interests at heart and keeps them close to sources of support, and it saves men from having to bring into their households women whose primary loyalties and interests lie elsewhere.

As we have seen, consanguinity provides the only culturally approved basis for forming close social relationships in Awlad 'Ali society. However, agnation, although primary, is not the only factor informing social identity and social relationships. Awlad 'Ali individuals unite on a variety of other bases, usually trying to couch these in the idiom of kinship.

MATERNAL TIES AND A COMMON LIFE

Besides agnation, the two most important bonds between individuals are maternal kinship and coresidence ('ishra). On the surface, these two bases for forming relationships might seem to lie outside the dominant principle of agnation, but the Bedouins do not perceive them so. Using different conceptual means, they reconcile each with the ideology of lineage organization, subordinating both to the principle of paternal kinship.

Their task with regard to maternal bonds is made simpler by the fact that the distinction between maternal and paternal kin is not always clear-cut. Patrilateral parallel-cousin marriage fuses maternal and paternal ties. As Peters (1967, 272) also points out, the density of overlapping ties created by intermarriage within the lineage and by continual exchanges of women between the same two lineages over several generations also clouds the question of whether behavior and sentiment conform to the jural rules. But at least in conversation, and when applying kin terms, the Bedouins tend to give priority to the ties between agnates in case where multiple connections can be drawn. Thus, in the camp I lived in, the children of the two brothers who had married two sisters who were their paternal first cousins always called their uncles and aunts by the term for paternal, not maternal, uncle and aunt (sīd, 'anima, not khāl, khāla).

In general, individuals and their maternal kin share bonds of great fondness and a sense of closeness, but maternal descent hardly defines social identity, because

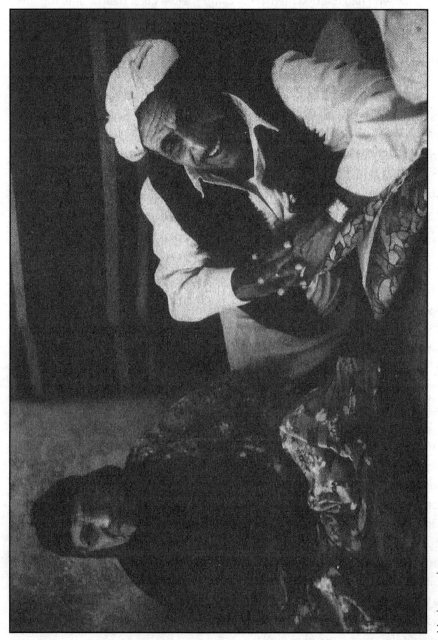

Mother and son.

it cannot be carried further than one generation, and it does not provide a strong sense of identification with others. The only hints of belief in shared substance are proverbs proclaiming the children's resemblance to their maternal uncles. The honor of the matriline can touch a woman's children in refining their status vis-à-vis the children of her co-wives. The factors that reinforce social relationships based on agnation, such as shared jural responsibility, common property, or coresidence, rarely support maternal bonds. But the tie symbolized in the word *dmāya* (the diminutive of "blood") carries with it sentiments of loyalty and amity and obligations of reciprocal attendance and gift giving at ritual occasions.

This closeness to maternal kin docs not conflict with the principle of agnation. In fact, a careful look at the relationship between a woman's kin and her children will reveal that the maternal bond derives indirectly from agnation itself. First; because adults, not children, initiate relationships, the bond to a woman's child is an extension of the bond between the woman herself and her paternal kinfolk. As one man explained, "A woman is always part of her tribe, even when she marries outside of it," so her kin care about her children because they care about her. They certainly shower affection on both when they come for visits. Indirect evidence of the way Bedouins conceive of such relationships can be found in the kinship terms for nephew and niece, which are built on siblingship: all nephews and nieces, however distant and whatever generation, are called "sister's son" or "brother's son" (*ibnakhiyyi* or *ibnakhītī*). From the point of view of those who initiate relationships, the bonds to nephews and nieces are consistent with the bonds of agnation, since these are merely the children of paternal kin.

In Bedouin society, relationships between mothers and children are, with few exceptions, extremely close and affectionate throughout life. Based on initial dependency and later concern, the mother-child bond is taken for granted, and it presents the only undisputed and undisguised exception to the rule equating closeness with agnation. Once children are older, after having lived with and come to identify with paternal kin, they feel affection or some sort of link to maternal kin as an extension of their affection for their mothers. If they love their mother, they will love those with whom she identifies and is identified. Thus, from the child's perspective, maternal kin are neither confused with nor in competition with paternal kin; they are merely thought of as the mother's agnates. If anything, the competition is between mother and father, as highlighted in the playful questioning of one father who, as his wife sat nearby, tickled his two-year-old daughter and asked over and over, "Whose daughter are you? Are you your father's daughter or your mother's?"

The other type of close relationship in Bedouin society is that between nonkin who live together, or, as one man described it, *garāba min l-galb* (kinship from the heart). By a logical reversal, Awlad 'Ali justify the development of close bonds between individuals who are neither maternal kin nor from the same tribe or who, although from the same tribe, are genealogically distant. Since close genealogical kin ideally live near each other, coresidence and paternal kinship are strongly associated. By a subtle shift, those who live together develop relationships similar to those between paternal kin. In talking about such relationships, Awlad 'Ali tend to stress the link of paternal kinship, however distant—if it exists at all. Where there is no genealogical link, the nature of the relationship is downplayed, and kinlike bonds are created through actions.

The bond of living together or sharing a life is called *'ishra*. Although marked by impermanence,[22] it suggests the kinlike bonds of enduring sentiments of closeness, as well as a more or less temporary identification and the concomitant obligations of support and unity. The bond is symbolized by the notion of sharing food, which in Bedouin culture (like many others) signifies the absence of enmity. The expression used to describe a relationship based on proximity or a shared life, *'ēsh wmliḥ* (cereal and salt), applies to husbands and wives, past and present neighbors, and patron and client families alike.

With sedentarization, the variety and permanence of neighbors has changed. Within the settled hamlets, neighbors become quasikin: they visit and assist each other at feasts marking circumcisions, weddings, and funerals and at births and illnesses, and they respect the mourning periods of neighboring families. They stand together politically in confrontations with other groups, especially those living nearby. They also spend a good deal of time together.

Many camps and hamlets, especially the wealthier ones, include a number of families or individuals who have attached themselves to the group, or to particular men, as clients. In the camp I lived in there were five such households, all so closely tied to the core families that I initially mistook them for kin. Some were indeed distant kin, a status that was stressed, but most were not, and their tribal identity was played down except in crisis situations. Yet, like kin, most had spent their whole lives in the community. For example, one family consisted of a young man, his wife and two children, and his old blind father. The old man had been a shepherd to the fathers of the core agnates, as had his father before him. The women and children called the old man by the kinship term for close paternal uncle (*sīd*), since older people in the community are rarely referred to without a kinship term. The young man was a constant visitor in the core households, entertaining guests when the patrons were absent or assisting in serving meals when they were present, helping with work, and so forth. He played a social role similar to that of the core agnates' nephews, to whom he was in fact very close.

Another client family had lived with the group for over thirty years. The head of the household had initially joined the camp as a shepherd, and he eventually entered into a partnership with one of his patrons. While I was there, his patron's brother decided to marry the old man's attractive young daughter. It was interesting to see how her attitude and those of the other camp women differed from that of a bride who married into the camp from outside at the same time. The outsider bride was uneasy, and people were tense around her. This was not true of the client's daughter—the bonds of *'ishra* already tied her to all the others in the camp. When I remarked on the difference, people explained, "She was born in the camp. There is no strangeness [*ghurba*]. Everyone is relaxed."

Merely living together confers rights and obligations comparable to those of kinship, as is evident in the following two examples. A woman who was both sister to the men in the core community and a neighbor (having married a man of a different lineage who lived nearby) was indignant at not having been invited to accompany her kinsmen to her brother's engagement feast (*siyāg*) or to the bride's ritual visit home after the wedding (*zawra*), where meat is plentiful and the groom's kinswomen need not work. As part of her appeal for justice, she argued, "I'm their sister! Why, even as a neighbor I should have gone!" Another woman, scolding someone for not assisting her pregnant kinswoman, told of a woman whose neighbor—"not even a relative!"—had baked her bread, brought her water from the well, and even washed her clothes for her.

It is not enough to argue simply that because kin usually live together, those who live together are conceived of as kin. The question is, why docs living together create such strong bonds? Because the relationships that develop are upheld not by jural responsibilities but by strong sentiment, I think the key lies in Bedouin attitudes toward "familiarity." The term *mwaliif 'ale* (to be used to or familiar with) is most often used to describe a child's feelings of extreme attachment to caretakers other than its mother (usually a grandmother, older sister, or father's wife), as evidenced by the child's violent protest when forced to part from the caretaker, miserable crying, and refusal to eat or be comforted. The term was also used in conjunction with the idea of a homeland; people explained that they felt uneasy and "didn't know how to sit or stay" in territories they were not used to. Thus the idea of attachment to the familiar emerges. Living together makes strangers familiar and hence more like kin, who are automatically familiar by virtue of being family.

IDENTIFICATION AND SHARING

Shared blood signifies close social relations only because it, in the Awlad 'Ali conception, identifies kin with one another. Kin share concerns and honor; ideally they also share residence,. property, and livelihood.[23] They express this sense of commonality through visiting, ritual exchanges, and sharing work, emotional responses, and secrets. In times of trouble their fierce loyalty sometimes leads them to take up arms together and, in the case of homicides, is institutionalized in the corporate responsibility for blood indemnity (*diyya*).

This strong identification with patrikin manifests itself in several ways. First, in many contexts individuals act as if what touches their kin touches them; an insult to one person is interpreted as an insult to the whole kinship group, just as an insult to a kinsperson is interpreted as an affront to the self. A woman, threatening to leave her husband for slurring her father's name in the heat of a marital dispute, appealed to anyone who would listen, "Would you stay if anyone said that about your father?" Likewise, one family member's shameful acts bring dishonor on the rest of the family, just as everyone benefits from the glories of a prominent agnate or patrilineal ancestor. The rationale for both vengeance for homicides and honor killings (in practice extremely rare) is that an affront to one individual or a shameful act by one person affects the whole group, not just the individual.[24]

Second, people are perceived, at least by outsiders, as nearly interchangeable representatives of their kin groups. When a host honors a guest, the assumption is that he honors the person's whole kin group, which explains why sheep are sometimes slaughtered for women guests or individuals who are not especially important personally. Members of my adopted family eagerly asked how I was treated whenever I visited people outside our camp, because they took it as an index of the esteem in which *they* were held. Only one member of an agnatic cluster need actually attend ceremonies of outside groups to fulfill the obligation of the whole group. In arranging marriages, the individuals are less important than the kin groups involved. Men would arrive at our camp and request "one of your girls" in marriage, apparently caring little which one, since they had chosen the family to *nāsib* (create an affinal relationship with). Some of these men were refused because of grudges against their kin groups. Even close personal ties with the men of our camp, in one case due to maternal kinship, were overshadowed by the suitors' tribal affiliations and the state of intertribal relations.

People often describe the existence of bonds between people, whether based on paternal or maternal kinship or just a common life, by using the phrase "we go to them and they come to us" (*nimshūlhum wyjūnā*). This expression conveys nicely the way bonds between individuals are expressed and maintained. "Coming and going" refers to reciprocity in both everyday visiting and ritualized visiting on particular occasions (*munāsabāt*), usually those marking life crises or transitions. Since these occasions are unofficially ranked in order of importance, failure to attend some is interpreted as a sign that the relationship has been terminated and the bond broken.

The impetus for such visits is identification (the sense that what happens to kin is happening to the self) and the desire to be with those who share one's feelings. Visits also provide occasions for strengthening identification between those who already have bonds. This is most obvious in the least ritualized visits, those undertaken in times of trouble or illness. During my first two months in the field, my host was mysteriously absent for a stretch. Guests kept appearing at our household, and many stayed. At the time, I did not know enough to realize that this constant flow of visitors was unusual; I merely thought that the Bedouins were indeed very sociable people. When my host returned, there was a celebration, sheep were slaughtered, and guests were plentiful and lively. I later understood that he had been detained for questioning by government authorities; everyone had been worried that he had been arrested, and they had gathered out of concern, to be with those closest to him and thus most affected. After his safe return, well-wishers came by to share their relief. Visits to the ill follow a similar protocol. Failure to visit a person who is ill is taken as an insult and a breach in relations precisely because it is a departure from what would be a "natural" concern for the well-being of those you love.

The worst form of trouble, of course, is death. Not to go to a camp in which a person has died, if you have any link either to that person or to his or her relatives or coresidents, is to sever the tie. (…) A brief look at one aspect of women's mourning behavior will clarify the participatory quality of ritual visits. Women who come to deliver condolences (*y'azzun*) approach the house or camp wailing (*y'aytun*), and then each squats before those family members to whom they are closest and "cries"

Women going to pay a visit.

(*yatabākun*) with them. This ritualized crying is more than simple weeping; it is a heart- rending chant bemoaning the woman's own loss of her closest deceased family member, usually a father, When I asked about this unusual behavior, one woman explained, "Do you think you cry over the dead person? No, you cry for yourself, for those who have died in your life." The woman closest to the person whose death is being mourned then answers with a chant in which she bemoans her loss. Women speak of going to "cry with" somebody, suggesting that they perceive it as sharing an experience. What they share is grief, not just by sympathizing, but also by actually reexperiencing, in the company of the person currently grieving, their own grief over the death of a loved one. Not only may such shared emotional experiences enhance the sense of identification that underpins social bonds, but participation in rituals that express sentiments might also generate feelings like those the person directly affected is experiencing, thus creating an identification between people where it did not spontaneously exist. The same process might apply to happy occasions celebrating weddings, circumcisions, return from the pilgrimage to Mecca, or release from prison.

Going and coming is accompanied by the exchange of gifts, animals for slaughter, money, and services.[25] I would argue that these exchanges are considered not debts, as Peters (1951, 166–67) maintains, but acknowledgments, in a material idiom, of the existence of bonds. Although gifts and countergifts are essential to social relationships, they do not establish relationships; rather, they reflect their existence and signify their continuation. If gift giving occasionally takes on a burdensome quality, it is because individual experience and contingencies of personality and history can never be fully determined by the cultural ideals of social organization.

Sharing is the common theme that runs through these ways of expressing and maintaining bonds. Visits are prompted by the sense of identification felt with individuals to whom one is close, and they provide occasions for participating in emotionally charged events that increase the basis of what is shared. By giving gifts of both material goods and services people share what they have. As we shall explore in the second half of this book, sharing thoughts and feelings, especially ones that do not conform to the ideals of honor and modesty, is also a significant index of social closeness.

IDENTITY IN A CHANGING WORLD

The profound changes that currently affect the Awlad 'Ali interact in complex ways with the ideology of blood outlined above. Kinship is still the dominant ideological principle of social organization, and despite the different look of the land, settlement patterns are marked by continuity. Although clusters of houses and tents (…) are today more common than the traditional scattered encampments of between two and ten tents, both are called by the same name (*naji*, pl. *nawāji'*) and are seen as similar. The dwellings may be permanent, but the communities, which take the name of the group's dominant lineage or family, remain socially rather than territorially defined units.

The new economic situation created by the Bedouin involvement in a cash economy—through smuggling, legitimate business, land sales, and agriculture—has radically altered both the volume and distribution of wealth. Because an economy based on herds and simple cereal cultivation depends on rainfall, assets are precarious in a region that averages two to four inches of rain per year and has drought periods every seven years or so. Herds can be wiped out in a season. Rain might or might not fall on a sown plot. Although there have always been rich and poor among the Bedouins, fortunes often reversed unpredictably, and a concentration of wealth in the hands of any one person or family was never secure. Now social stratification has become more marked and fixed: the wealthy have the capital to invest in lucrative ventures and the poor do not.

Perhaps even more important for consolidating social and political power has been the gradual expansion of the types of resources that can be privately owned, which has enabled some people to make others dependent and thus to control them. Whereas formerly, economic, political, and social status were not tied—as status and leadership were based largely on genealogy and achieved reputation, and dependency implied less economic helplessness—today they are becoming increasingly coterminous.

However, disintegration of the tribal system is hardly imminent. Kinship ties still crosscut wealth differentials, and the vertical links of tribal organization overshadow the horizontal links of incipient class formation. Although individual ownership and private control of resources are beginning to undermine the economic bases of the tribal system, the tribe remains ideologically compelling. Ironically, the cooperative societies the government introduced to break down the lineage system instead served to strengthen lineage loyalties, because the new resources made available were distributed following lineage lines by the traditional lineage heads who had assumed leadership in the new system (Bujra 1973, 156).

The new levels of wealth have even allowed the realization of traditional ideals of lineage solidarity unattainable in the traditional economy. For instance, greater access to wealth and opportunity has reduced some of the pressure on lineages to fission, enabling extended families to remain coresident units. Stein notes that in the new situation "the individual members of the extended families have each specialized to certain sources of income which in aggregate guarantees the sub- sistence and provides social security for the extended family as a whole" (1981, 42). This division of labor has revitalized the ideal of lineage solidarity and the extended family. It may also have lessened pressures to keep up alliances with lineages in other territories, thus involuting the orientation toward agnation. Another ideal that can be more readily realized with the new wealth is large family size—wealthy men marry more wives and can support more children.

The ideals of manly autonomy and tribal independence persist in resistance to government attempts to impose restrictions and curtail the Bedouins' freedom to live their own lives and run their own affairs. Although after military rule ended in the late 1950s administration of the Western Desert province was outwardly like that of any other, with a few modifications to accommodate tribal organization (Mohsen 1975, 74), in practice the province simply cannot be run the same way. For example, Bedouins vote on the basis of tribal affiliations in electing their repre- sentatives to the national parliament. And young men still try to avoid conscription into the Egyptian army by escaping to Libya or into the desert with the herds. Most disputes are settled by customary law. In the case of serious crimes such as homicides, which cannot be kept from the authorities, the judgments of the state courts are not considered valid. Furthermore, since the Bedouins look to achieve a culprit's quick release so they can settle matters according to customary law, they are often uncooperative in the courts. Wittingly or unwittingly, most people live outside the law, smuggling, crossing closed borders, carrying unlicensed firearms, avoiding conscription, not registering births, not having identity papers, evading taxes, and taking justice into their own hands. Arrests and jailings carry no stigma for the Bedouins; rather, they occasion self-righteous curses of the government agents responsible.

Nevertheless, more subtle processes linked to the persistence of old ideals and values in new circumstances have begun to transform the Bedouins' everyday existence. Women have been particularly affected. In the camp and household, the worlds of men and women have become more separate. Although sexual segregation seems always to have characterized Bedouin social life to some extent, it has ossified with the move from tents to houses. In the tents, a blanket suspended in the middle of the tent separated male and female domains when men other than close kin were present. The blankets—unlike walls—were both temporary and permeable, allowing the flow of conversation and information. Now, with each room housing one woman and her children, it has become customary to build a separate men's room (*marbū'a* or *manẓara*) for receiving guests.

The shift from subsistence to market reliance has altered the extent to which men's traditional control over productive resources allows them to control women. Women may never have owned or even controlled resources, but women were needed to extract a livelihood from them, and men and women contributed complementary skills to the subsistence economy. This balance has been undermined. In the traditional division of labor, men cared for the sheep, sowed and harvested the grain, and engaged in limited trade, Women were responsible for the household, which involved not just cooking and childcare but also grinding grain, milking and processing milk, getting water (often from distant wells), gathering brush for the cooking fires (arduous because of the primitive adze the women use and the long distance they must travel with heavy loads), and weaving tents and blankets. Peters (1965, 137–38) makes much of the interdependence of the men's and women's spheres and the rights conferred on women by control over their special tasks in the traditional economy of the Cyrenaican Bedouins. However, as women's work has become peripheralized, these rights may have diminished. Housing and furnishings are now bought with cash, food requires less processing, water is close by, and much cooking is done with kerosene, available through purchase. Women's work is confined to an increasingly separate and economically devalued domestic sphere. Women have also become profoundly dependent on men, as subsistence is now based on cash rather than on the exploitation of herds and fields, which required the labor of men and women and entitled both to a livelihood.

The code of modesty and rules of veiling have a long history, but in the new context of permanent, settled communities they determine to a much greater extent what women do. The likelihood that neighbors will be nonkin or strangers and that they will live in close proximity is greater than it was in the isolated desert camps, where members were usually tied by kinship bonds of one sort or another. In addition, the settlements often have visitors from the wider range of contacts the men develop outside the kin group in the course of their travels and commercial

Herd owners bring supplies in their truck to hired camel-herders.

ventures. Because the sexual codes require that women avoid male nonkin and strangers, they must now be more vigilant in keeping out of sight, spending more time veiled and confined to the women's section. This has curbed their freedom of movement.

With sedentarization and new economic options, these codes have restricted women's social networks and widened the gap between men's and women's experiences. Women rarely venture far from their camps except to visit natal kin. Their contacts are limited to kin, husband's kin, and neighbors. In the past, seasonal migrations brought new neighbors; in settled communities, the set of neighbors tends to become fixed, and opportunities to meet new people and make new friends diminish. In contrast, men have become more oriented to the world outside the camp. Mechanized transport has only increased men's mobility, and although men still conduct much of their business with kinsmen whom the women also know, they have more contact with outsiders whom the women do not meet. Thus, men and women from the same community live in different social worlds. A household's men and women now spend less time together, know fewer people in common, and have divergent experiences in daily life. This gap will widen as education becomes more universal, since boys are increasingly enrolled in school but old values keep girls at home.[26] Soon men will be literate and women not.

The changes in the relations between men and women and in their relative status and opportunities are neither the result of disaffection with the old system nor an emulation of the mores of imported cultures. They are certainly not the result of government policy. The Bedouins do not experience any jarring sense of discontinuity, although they acknowledge several ways things were different, say, forty years ago. Their sense of continuity may stem from the stability of the underlying principles of their life, which in new contexts created by sedentarization and market economics produce different configurations.

On close inspection, some of the most conspicuous changes prove superficial. Rather than heralding the demise of Bedouin culture and society, they merely demonstrate the Bedouins' openness to useful innovations and their capacity to absorb new elements into old structures. To take an example, the automobile and pickup truck now popular throughout the Western Desert are status objects in much the same way horses were in the past. Accordingly, the purchase of a new car occasions a sheep sacrifice and a trip to the holy man to get a protective amulet to hang on the rearview mirror. Men are identified by and with their cars. They want to be photographed with them. In young girls' rhyming ditties, young men are referred to not by name but by the color and make of the cars they drive, as in the following two songs:

> Welcome driver of the jeep
> I'd make you tea with milk if not shameful

> yā sawāg ij-jēb tafadhdhal
> ndīrūlak shāy biḥalīb lū mā 'ēb

> Toyotas when they first appeared
> brought life's light then disappeared

> Tayūtāt awwal mā jaddun
> jābū nūr l-'ēn wraddū

Like their animal antecedents, cars are used not just for transport but also for ritual. A bride used to be carried from her natal home to the groom's home in a litter mounted on a camel, accompanied by men and women riding on horses, donkeys, or whatever could be mustered, all singing, dancing, and firing rifles. Now, although the size of the bridal procession is equally important, its composition has changed; Toyotas, Datsuns, and Peugeots race, the men leaning out of the speeding vehicles firing rifles, the women sitting in the back seats singing traditional songs. Just as the procession used to circle the bridal tent before setting down the new bride, so now the cars careen around the new house or a nearby saint's tomb.

It is clear that the fundamental organizing principles of social and political life, the ideology and the values, have endured. If the most fashionable weddings are now celebrated with a blaring *mīkrōfūn* (loudspeaker system) and flashing lights visible for miles against the cloudless night skies, and if the bride is brought in a car with her trousseau following in a pickup truck, weddings are nevertheless held on traditionally auspicious days of the week and celebrated with traditional song and poetry, sheep sacrifices, and feasting. The defloration still takes place in the afternoon, with the proof of virginity triumphantly displayed. Marriages are still linked to the history of marriage alliances between tribal sections, arranged by families, the bride-price negotiated by kinsmen. At marriage the groom does not gain economic independence from his father but brings his wife into the extended household. If women have traded their embroidered leather boots and somber baggy gowns for pink plastic shoes and bright synthetic fabrics, they have not relinquished the black veils they use to demonstrate their modesty and recognize the distance and respect between men and women.

The most profound changes in the lives of the Awlad 'Ali are a result of new circumstances that have undermined the operation of traditional principles. This is clearest in the towns. The identification of kin with one another is based conceptually on common substance but is intensified by common property and coresidence. Studies of Bedouins who have settled in the city of Marsa Matruh show that residence patterns determined by accident and factors outside their control have significantly weakened the bonds between kin in favor of those between neighbors ('Abd al-Ḥamīd 1969, 129). The introduction of education and wage labor may eventually marginalize the pastoral way of life and loosen the hold of the family and tribe as educated Bedouins abandon the life of the desert, the politics of the tribe, and the values of honor and modesty at the center of the Bedouin world. This has not yet come to pass. Although they are becoming settled, the Awlad 'Ali Bedouins are a long way from being peasants. By no means detribalized, they strain under the yoke of political control and prefer to guard what autonomy they have by minimizing dealings with government authorities. In contact with non-Bedouins and the object of numerous government plans, they are still far from being assimilated. (…) The ideology of honor and modesty so closely associated with nobility of origin has a powerful hold on every Awlad 'Ali individual.

NOTES

1. The Libyan Desert is one name for the vast desert dissected by the Egyptian-Libyan border. For the most part, I will refer to the Egyptian side by the term the Egyptians prefer: the Western Desert.
2. The word the Bedouins use is *náwdshif*. Classified among the dry foods are cereals, dates, and milk products. Vegetables are not considered dry. It would be interesting to explore their food classification system further.
3. Although I have used the word *spring* to refer to a season, the Bedouins do not use it that way. For them, *rabī*, the word usually translated as "spring," is not a season but a state of pasture. When there has been sufficient rain in the months of October through January, shrubs and grasses thrive in the desert.

When the desert is green, they say there is "spring"; in bad years when there is little rain, the desert is not green and there is no "spring."

4. These changes, of course, are happening to Bedouins throughout the Middle East. For other cases in Jordan, Syria, and Saudi Arabia, see Abu Jaber et al. (1978); Chatty (1976, 1978); Ibrahim and Cole (1978); Katakura (1977); and Lancaster (1981).

5. Citing a report by those who landed with Napoleon in 1798 that the Awlad 'Ali were at war with the *Hanādī* tribes of Egypt near Alexandria, Obermeyer (1968, 7) takes issue with Evans-Pritchard's (1949) statement that the expulsion took place well after 1800. Most likely, certain segments were forced out of their territories in Cyrenaica through a process of "slow, continuous, and cumulative minor alterations which are even today part of the Bedouin system of territorial relations" (Behnke 1980, 162). The rest were driven out in a major battle at the end of the century in which the *Harābīs* enlisted the aid of the Turks and Arabs from Tripoli (Evans-Pritchard 1949, 50; Johnson 1973, 32; Obermeyer 1968, 5).

6. The Mrābṭīn claim no genealogical connection to the *Sa'ādi* tribes, nor any overarching genealogical links among themselves, although they are divided into groups called tribes. There are two categories of *Mrābiṭ* tribes: those who formerly paid tribute and those who were pious or holy figures (*mrābṭīn bil-brka*). Generally considered socially and politically inferior, those who have not lost their reputations for piety are held in awe. They used to serve as peacemakers and continue to be healers. There is much confusion about their origins and their social position, suggesting a need for a careful study of these groups. Peters (1977) discusses the relationship between the free tribes and clients of various sorts, but his research concerns an earlier period in Libya, where the situation seems to have been different. Behnke (1980) considers a more recent period. I consider some aspects of the relationship between the Mrābṭīn and the Sa'ādi, but there is much about their social and religious roles that I could not include here.

7. Total population estimates range between 120,000 and 170,000. These are no doubt inaccurate, since census figures for the Western Desert do not distinguish Bedouins from non-Bedouin migrants to the urban centers, Marsa Matruh in particular, and the reclaimed lands of Mariut. Moreover, figures specifically for Awlad 'Ali do not indicate whether Mrābiṭ tribes are included.

8. Sources for the history of Awlad 'Ali during this period include Baer (1969); von Dumreicher (1931); Falls (1913); Murray (1935); Obermeyer (1968); and Stein (1981).

9. In 1940 the British told the nomads to flee the Italian advance in the west and prepared refugee camps near 'Amriyya in the east for them. Axis armies marched into the Western Desert in 1940, and by 1942 Rommel had advanced his headquarters to Marsa Matruh. After the German defeat at Alamein in November 1942, the Bedouins returned to their lands to find much lost (Obermeyer 1968, 16–17; Bujra 1973, 144). The older Bedouins I spoke with remembered the war, the crowded camps, the bombing, the parachutes, the airplanes. As we passed the cemetery in Alamein, one man recalled terrible scenes after the battles, when the bodies of young men lay everywhere. One legacy of the war is the widespread presence of land mines, which explode, maiming and killing Bedouins every year.

10. For a discussion of the projects undertaken and their effects, sec Bujra (1973) and Stein (1981).

11. Christians—Europeans or Coptic Egyptians—do not constitute a vivid reference point for self-definition, since contact with them has been minimal; for most Bedouins, they are little more than a rumor. In any case, their religion, however little understood, is distasteful, and the European languages are alien. Christians are on the edge of the Bedouin world, necessary to the distinction between Muslim and non-Muslim, a radical but almost abstract distinction that is seldom relevant in daily life.

12. The Bedouin dialect is closely related to the Eastern Libyan dialect and differs from Cairene and rural Egyptian in vocabulary, pronunciation, and some elements of grammar. Awlad 'Ali clothing is also distinct from that of either urban Egyptians, whom the Bedouins describe as *lābis affandī* (dressed as effendis or bureaucrats, i.e., in Western clothing and bareheaded); peasants *(flūh)*; or Upper Egyptians *(ṣa'ayda),* who wear the flowing bell-sleeved gallabiya and some form of cap or turban, in the case of men, and the smocked, unbelted robes and either a black headcovering or kerchief, in the case of women. Bedouin dress differs in important ways and is thought of as more "modest" and thus in keeping with the decorum prescribed by the Koran. The Bedouins set great store by headcoverings, and their robes cover their arms to the wrists and their bodies to the ankles. Men wear on their heads a

ṣmāda, a headcover similar to that worn in other parts of the Arab world but here often wrapped as a turban; this has replaced the traditional small red felt cap called a *shanna*. Under the robe, called a *thōb*, with shirt-tailored collar, sleeves, and breastpocket, all men wear *sirwāl*, baggy pants that narrow at the ankles. For formal or ceremonial occasions, no man is caught without his *jard*, a large white woolen blanket knotted at the shoulder and draped like a toga. Women wear their hair in numerous small braids tied together in a topknot, which they cover with a black cloth called a *tarha* that is wrapped and knotted in such a way that it covers the hair, neck, and shoulders and can be pulled over the face to serve as a veil. Their dresses are long-sleeved, ankle-length, and gathered at the waist. No woman ever goes without a belt, the most common type being a woven red wool sash about sixteen inches wide and six feet long, which is folded in half along the width, wrapped several times around the waist, and fastened with a large safety pin. Women tuck into its folds an amazing array of small objects—bars of soap, lemons, jewelry, money, spices—whatever they wish to carry with them or keep away from others. The symbolism of the black veil and the red belt, the keys to femininity, is explored.

13. Since there is an official adoption procedure for both individuals and whole tribal segments, the genealogical links are certainly not always those of blood. This fact accounts for some of the heterogeneity of racial types among Awlad 'Ali. It is clear from the complaints of the British that this adoption procedure was widespread during the first decades of the twentieth century. For example, Jennings-Bramly, the Frontiers District Officer stationed in Burg el-Arab, proposed in a memorandum (London 1926) to the Minister of War dated September 24, 1926, to increase the number of men who could be conscripted by weeding out the peasants who had gotten themselves adopted, often through payments, into Bedouin tribes to avoid conscription. He condemned this "nefarious practice" and estimated that up to one-third of every tribe consisted of adopted peasants (certainly an exaggeration). Apropos of this topic, I was told a story, perhaps apocryphal, about Jennings-Bramly's attempt to rectify the situation. As I was being tested on the names of parts of the Bedouin tent, my teacher laughed and claimed that I was going to be a true Bedouin. He related that *"Bramlī,"* a clever man familiar with the Bedouins, had set up a test to separate the true Bedouins from the peasants claiming tribal status: he called each man into a traditional Bedouin

tent and asked him to name the parts. My teacher commented with pride that only a true Bedouin could answer correctly.

14. The meaning of the complex concept of *hasham* will be explored.

15. For a masterful elucidation of the issues involved in analyzing this model of political relations based on the segmenting genealogy, see Meeker (1979, u-15, 183–208).

16. The role of the segmentary model as an ideology in social life has again been brought into question in the recent work of Moroccanists such as Eickelman (1976) and H. Geertz (1979), who argue that the segmentary model obscures the realities of Moroccan economic, political, and social life and propose, respectively, a diffuse concept of "closeness" *(qarāba)* and a notion of shifting dyadic ties as more accurate models. I tend to agree with Combs-Schilling (1981) that this may be a false dichotomy and that both models are ideologies available to individuals and operative on different organizational levels.

17. If Awlad 'Ali use the kinship idiom to describe or organize political relations, it is because this idiom provides such a powerful metaphor for close social relationships and carries so much in the way of sentiment. It makes political alliance and order seem "natural" rather than arbitrary. Yet Peters reminds us not to assume that this model of social relationships espoused by the Bedouins is an accurate reflection of the way their society operates. He argues that the segmentary lineage system must be seen as a folk model "which enables them, without making absurd demands on their credulity, to understand their field of social relationships, and to give particular relationships their *raison d'être*," But, he continues, "it would be a serious error to mistake such a folk model for sociological analysis" (1967, 270). I would add that when the kinship idiom is taken out of the domestic or interpersonal realm and given ideological primacy in such culturally valued arenas as political and economic relations, its legitimacy is enhanced and its original power to inform interpersonal relations reinforced.

18. The term Awlad 'Ali use for bonds of agnation or common patrilineal descent is translated as "group feeling" by Rosenthal in his translation of Ibn Khaldun's *Muqaddimah* (1958) and as "social solidarity" by Issawi (1950). It is intriguing that Ibn Khaldun's fourteenth-century comments on "group feeling" strike many of the same notes my discussion of Awlad 'Ali conceptions of social life does. For example, in a section entitled, "Group feeling results

only from (blood) relationship or something corresponding to it," he argues that well-known ties of blood, combined with close contact, lead to the greatest solidarity because kinship creates natural bonds of affection and identification (for example, leading a person to experience shame when a relative is treated unjustly). The closer the kinship tie, the greater the group feeling. Ibn Khaldun adds, however, that the same sentiment can develop regarding neighbors, allies, or clients when close contact characteristic of kin ties develops among them (1958, 264–65).

19. Bourdieu describes the same process of "reading" kinship relations in different ways, depending on the social context. He notes that the official (male) reading recognizes links through men, whereas the heretical (female) reading notes the more direct links through women (1977, 41–42).

20. McCabe (1983) presents data from a Lebanese village suggesting that there is less sexual desire in marriages between close cousins, specifically paternal parallel cousins who have had intimate childhood association. She argues that this corroborates A. Wolf's (1970) argument (based on the analysis of marital histories for two types of marriage in Taiwan, adopted daughter-in-law marriage and marriage between strangers) that childhood familiarity suppresses sexual desire.

21. Early explanations of the Arab preference for patrilateral parallel-cousin marriage argued that it served to keep property within the family, a position criticized by Murphy and Kasdan (1959) and Keyser (1974). The literature on preferential patrilateral parallel-cousin marriage is vast. Bourdieu (1977, 32–33) presents a summary of the positions, and Eickelman (1981, 129–31) presents not only a summary but also a relatively complete list of articles on the subject.

22. The emotional pain caused by this relationship's impermanence is evident in a proverb my host recited regarding my stay with his family: Forbid living together because of parting (harram l-'ishra bisabab il-fargā).

23. Bourdieu recognizes the bonds forged by common property in his comment that "the genealogical relationship is never strong enough on its own to provide a complete determination of the relationship between the individuals which it unites, and it has such predictive value only when it goes with the shared interests, produced by the common possession of a material and symbolic patrimony, which entails collective vulnerability as well as collective property" (1977, 39–40). As Peters (1965, 1967) demonstrates for the

Cyrenaican camel-herding Bedouins, however, residence, common property, and kinship are not coterminous in practice. The Awlad 'Ali are no exception. At the core of the camp I lived in were the adult sons of two men and their various dependents, including wives, children, and clients. Attached to them were poor families belonging to two branches of the same tribe. Peters provides good comparative material from late-1940s Cyrenaica, where he estimates that the level of coresidence of agnates was as high as 80 percent (1967, 262), but he shows in his analysis of the links between members of a particular camp that a number of other types of bonds, especially those through women, determined the actual composition of the camp (Peters 1965). Beware of the discrepancy between Peters's diagram and his verbal description—corrections can be found in J. Davis (1977, 234–35).

24. For a fascinating comparison of the Turkish and Arab constructions of joint honor, see Meeker (1976).

25. A man or a group of brothers arrive with a sheep or a goat, unless they are too poor or distantly related, in which case they substitute ten Egyptian pounds for the sheep. For women, the money gift is essential. In addition, women may bring other sorts of things, such as candy, biscuits, or fruit beverage syrup (sharbāt), but these are optional. At circumcision celebrations, women give money to the mother and grandmother of the circumcised boy; at homecomings, they give to the wife or wives and mother of the man, and occasionally to his sisters. At weddings, the mother, grandmother, and sisters of the groom, and the bride the following morning, all receive nugūṭ (wedding gifts) from the groom's side of the family. The bride's relatives give money to her mother, grandmother, and perhaps an older sister. These money-gifts are generally quite small (ranging from ten piasters to an Egyptian pound, or approximately U.S. $1.45), but given women's minimal access to cash, even such small amounts can be difficult to come by. The amount given at any event depends on previous exchanges, just as the men's sacrifices are returns on previous gifts. (The only exception to this rule is the gift presented to the new bride by her husband's kinswomen and neighbors, which intitiates her into the exchange network of the community and marks the establishment of relationships between her and these women. Her first outing will be to return the gift at the appropriate occasion.) Women take note of the amount they receive and try to increase it slightly when they return the gift. For

practical reasons the escalation usually stops at one pound. Men generally do not increase the number of sheep, but they may try to improve on the original gift by giving a higher-quality animal.

26. The concern about sexuality is the main impediment to girls' education. Until five years ago, the only schools in the vicinity of my community were in the towns, about four kilometers away. No one would consider sending a daughter that far. When a local school was established within sight of the community, some of the girls attended, but most soon dropped out, complaining of the discipline and corporal punishment by urban teachers. They faced no opposition at home for their truancy. Only one girl in the community had continued to the fifth grade. Her father permitted her to continue over the objections of his brothers, who thought she was getting too old to be mixing freely with boys from outside the community. Women with daughters in school complained that school made the girls disobedient and lazy. The mutterings of the one girl who was in the fifth grade did hint that education may indeed have important effects on Bedouin lifestyles. In frustration at the heavy burden of chores she was expected to carry, she sometimes cursed "this rotten Bedouin way of life" and expressed a wish to marry someone educated and live a genteel life in a town or city. At the same time, however, she was fiercely prejudiced against foreigners, Christians, and even Egyptians and staunchly defended Bedouin values, particularly those of modesty and proper comportment. In the urban areas, where schools are more accessible and education more respected, attendance by girls is higher. Still, according to Stein's figures on the status of education in the Western Desert in 1976, girls constituted no more than 29 percent of the school population (1981, 39). It is not clear whether his figures include the non-Bedouin populations, especially in Marsa Matruh; if so, the figures would be inflated.

REFERENCES

'Abd al-Hamīd, 'Awāṭif. 1969. "Al-usra al-badawiyya al-mutawaṭṭina fī marsa matrūh" (The sedentarized Bedouin family in Marsa Mat ruh). Master's thesis, Alexandria University, Egypt.

Abou-Zeid, Ahmed M. 1959. "The Sedentarization of Nomads in the Western Desert of Egypt." *UNESCO International Social Science Journal* 11: 550–58.

------------. 1966. "Honour and Shame Among the Bedouins of Egypt." In *Honour and Shame,* ed. J. G. Peristiany, 243–59. Chicago: University of Chicago Press.

Abu Jaber, Kamel, Fawzi Gharaibeh, Saleh Khasawneh, and Allan Hill. 1978. *The Bedouins of Jordan: A People in Transition.* Amman, Jordan: Royal Scientific Society Press.

Baer, Gabriel. 1969. *Studies in the Social History of Modern Egypt.* Chicago: University of Chicago Press.

Behnke, Roy. 1980. *The Herders of Cyrenaica.* Urbana: University of Illinois Press.

Bourdieu, Pierre. 1977. *Outline of a Theory of Practice.* Cambridge: Cambridge University Press.

Bujra, Abdalla S. 1973. "The Social Implications of Developmental Policies: A Case Study from Egypt." In *The Desert and the Sown: Nomads in the Wider Society,* ed. by Cynthia Nelson, 143–57. Berkeley: Institute of International Studies, University of California.

Chatty, Dawn. 1976. "From Camel to Truck: A Study of Pastoral Adaptation." *Folk* 18: 114–28.

------------.1978. "Changing Sex Roles in a Bedouin Society in Syria and Lebanon." In *Women in the Muslim World,* ed. Lois Beck and Nikki Keddie, 399–415. Cambridge, Mass.: Harvard University Press.

Combs-Schilling, M. Elaine. 1981. "The Segmentary Model Versus Dyadic Ties: The False Dichotomy." *MERA Forum* 5(3); 15–18.

Cromer, Earl of. 1908. *Modern Egypt.* Vol. 2. New York: Macmillan.

Davis, John. 1977. *People of the Mediterranean: An Essay in Comparative Social Anthropology.* London: Routledge & Kegan Paul.

Dumreicher, Andre von. 1931. *Trackers and Smugglers in the Deserts of Egypt.* London: Methuen.

Durrell, Lawrence. 1957. *Justine.* New York: Dutton.

Eickelman, Dale. 1976. *Moroccan Islam: Tradition and Society in a Pilgrimage Center.* Austin: University of Texas Press.

------------.1981. *The Middle East: An Anthropological Approach.* Englewood Cliffs, N.J.: Prentice-Hall.

Evans-Pritchard, E. E. 1949. *The Sanusi of Cyrenaica.* Oxford: Clarendon Press.

Falls, J. C. Ewald. 1913. *Three Years in the Libyan Desert: Travels, Discoveries, and Excavations of the Menas Expedition.* London: T. Fisher Unwin.

Geertz, Hildred. 1979. "The Meanings of Family Ties." In *Meaning and Order in Moroccan Society*, by Clifford Geertz, Hildred Geertz, and Lawrence Rosen, 315–91. Cambridge: Cambridge University Press.

Ibn Khaldun. 1958. *The "Muqaddimah": An Introduction to History*. Vol. 1. Trans. Franz Rosenthal. London: Routledge & Kegan Paul.

Issawi, Charles. 1950. *An Arab Philosophy of History: Selections from the Prolegomena of Ibn Khaldun of Tunis (1332–1406)*. London: John Murray.

Johnson, Douglas L. 1973. *Jabal al-Akhdar, Cyrenaica: An Historical Geography of Settlement and Livelihood*. University of Chicago Department of Geography, Research Paper no. 148. Chicago: University of Chicago.

Katakura, Motoko. 1977. *Bedouin Village: A Study of a Saudi Arabian People in Transition*. Tokyo: University of Tokyo Press.

Keyser, James. 1974. "The Middle Eastern Case: Is There a Marriage Rule?" *Ethnology* 13: 293–309.

Lancaster, William. 1981. *The Rwala Bedouin Today*. Cambridge: Cambridge University Press.

London. Public Record Office. 1926. Lt. W. Jennings-Bramly to Minister of War. FO 141/514.

McCabe, Justine. 1983. "FBD Marriage: Further Support for the Westermarck Hypothesis of the Incest Taboo?" *American Anthropologist* 85: 50–69.

Meeker, Michael. 1976. "Meaning and Society in the Near East: Examples from the Black Sea Turks and the Levantine Arabs." *International Journal of Middle East Studies* 7: 243–70, 383–422.

————. 1979. *Literature and Violence in North Arabia*. Cambridge: Cambridge University Press.

Mohsen, Safia Kassem. 1967. "Legal Status of Women Among the Awlad 'Ali." *Anthropological Quarterly* 40: 153–66.

————. 1975. *Conflict and Law Among Awlad 'Ali of the Western Desert*. Cairo: National Center for Social and Criminological Research.

Murphy, Robert, and Leonard Kasdan. 1959. "The Structure of Parallel Cousin Marriage." *American Anthropologist* 61: 17–29.

Murray, George W. 1935. *Sons of Ishmael: A Study of the Egyptian Bedouin*. London: Routledge.

Obermeyer, Gerald J. 1968. "Structure and Authority in a Bedouin Tribe: The 'Aishaibat of the Western Desert of Egypt." Ph.D. diss., Indiana University.

Peters, Emrys L. 1951. "The Sociology of the Bedouin of Cyrenaica." Diss., Lincoln College, Oxford.

------------. 1960. "The Proliferation of Segments in the Lineage of the Bedouin of Cyrenaica." *Journal of the Royal Anthropological Institute of Great Britain* 90: 29–53.

------------. 1965. "Aspects of the Family Among the Bedouin of Cyrenaica." In *Comparative Family Systems,* ed. M. F. Nimkoff, 121–46. Boston: Houghton Mifflin.

------------. 1967. "Some Structural Aspects of the Feud Among the Camel-Herding Bedouin of Cyrenaica." *Africa* 37: 261–82.

------------. 1977. "Patronage in Cyrenaica." In *Patrons and Clients in Mediterranean Societies,* ed. Ernest Gellner and John Waterbury, 275–90. London: Duckworth.

------------. 1980. "Aspects of Bedouin Bridewealth Among Camel Herders in Cyrenaica." In *The Meaning of Marriage Payments,* ed. John L. Comaroff, 125–60. London: Academic Press.

Stein, Lothar. 1981. "Contradictions Arising from the Process of Sedentarization Among the Aulad Ali Bedouins of Egypt." In *Contemporary Nomadic and Pastoral Peoples: Asia and the North,* ed. Philip Carl Salzman, 33–44. Studies in Third World Societies, no. 18. Williamsburg, Va.: Department of Anthropology, College of William and Mary.

Wolf, Arthur. 1970. "Childhood Association and Sexual Attraction: A Further Test of the Westermarck Hypothesis." *American Anthropologist* 72: 503–15.

Where Have the Bedouin Gone?

The American University in Cairo

by DONALD P. COLE

The overall outlines of Arab Bedouin society are well known to anthropology, despite the lack of detailed studies.

—Robert F. Murphy and Leonard Kasdan 1959:18

TO ANSWER THE QUESTION "WHERE HAVE THE BEDOUIN gone?" requires identification of who are the Bedouin, consideration of where they have been, and understanding of their contemporary presences in wider Arab state societies and national cultures. The question is simple and straightforward; but an answer is neither easy nor clear-cut. "Bedouin" is not an occupation recorded on national identity cards or passports. The category of Bedouin (or nomad) existed and was counted in the censuses of colonial governments; but Bedouin are not enumerated as such in today's national censuses.[1] Indeed, the *Arab Human Development Report 2002* does not even mention the Bedouin in its analysis aimed at "creating opportunities for future generations" (United Nations Development Program 2002). Have the Bedouin ceased to exist? Are the Bedouin a part of the past with no present or future roles?

Educated urbanites I met during the course of fieldwork in Saudi Arabia in 1968–70 usually told me that the Bedouin were all but gone. They had become taxi drivers, traders, worked for the Arabian American Oil Company (ARAMCO), served in the National Guard, were low-level government employees, and so on. Many families were settling, boys were going to school, young and middle-aged men were putting aside old-fashioned styles of Bedouin clothing in favor of a new, more homogeneously national style. The Bedouin never came to town anymore on camelback but in red Ford pick-up trucks. Perhaps a few Bedouin—women, children, and old men—remained in the steppe with the herds, but this was a holdover from the past. Fieldwork (Cole 1971, 1975) showed that observation to not be true: a vigorous nomadic pastoral production system still existed. Yet, most urban Saudi Arabians, and some Bedouin, thought the present back then would be but a short period of transition to a future in which the urban and the national, or modernity, would replace nomad camp and tribe, or tradition.

Despite their statistical non-existence and the predominance of the urban, the national, and now the global, Bedouin persist in multiple and changing ways in all seventeen Arab states in Southwest Asia and North Africa and in Palestine/Israel. In searching for the Bedouin in this vast and differentiated terrain, three interrelated issues are addressed.[2] The first issue is the socioeconomic transformation the Bedouin have experienced—both at home on the range and in new occupations in villages, towns, and cities. The second issue is change in sociopolitical relations between and among the kin-based identities and groupings strongly associated with the Bedouin and the wider state systems within which they exist. The third issue explores a relatively newfound role of the Bedouin in the manufacture of cultural heritage consumed as a component of national identity, or authenticity, in some settings and/or by local and global tourism in others. At the end, this essay does not find the Bedouin as they used to be. Yet, an anthropologist born and raised in the Syrian steppe among Bedouin sheep herders has characterized the social life of the Bedouin today as,

> not one of simple and total transformation, but rather of an ongoing
> dialectic of continuity and change, an interplay between tradition and
> modernity. They are adjusting their material and political life to rapidly
> changing modern conditions and yet they continue to respect and ad-
> here to a range of traditions that help them define and perpetuate their
> ethnic integrity, their Bedouin-ness (Khalaf 1990: 241).

True, but concern with "ethnic identity," with "Bedouin-ness" reflects an important change. Indeed, this paper argues that the Bedouin and the meanings of "Bedouin" have changed during the past century and before and continue to change. "Bedouin" previously denoted a way of life that was specialized and revolved around steppe-based herding. Today, "Bedouin" refers less to a "way of life" than to an "identity." The way of life was grounded in ecology and economy, the identity in heritage and culture.

"Bedouin" is derived from the Arabic *badowi* (pl. *badu*), which can be glossed as "desert-dweller."[3] *Badu* is an antonym of *hadr*, "sedentary," "urban," "civilized," but the boundary between the two is not precise. Arabic distinguishes *badu al-rahalah*, "mobile Bedouin," which implies that some Bedouin are sedentary while others are nomadic. Mostly, Bedouin have been associated with the raising of livestock, principally sheep, goats, and camels, and occasionally cattle, horses, and donkeys—in the *badiyah* ("open country," "range," "steppe"). They have usually spoken Arabic dialects that differ from those of the *hadr* in their geographic regions and also from the dialects of other named Bedouin groups.[4] Other cultural markers have existed, such as tattoos, hairstyles, clothing, headdresses, and veils that have distinguished Bedouin among themselves and in contrast to settled villagers and urbanites. Other differences—from type of housing to styles of poetry and patterns of demeanor—have also existed between these two components of Arab societies.[5]

However, as Bourdieu warned, "one must be careful not to regard [the Bedouin] as radically different from the sedentary peoples" (1962: 66–67). Despite specificities, the Bedouin have participated in and been affected by local and global forces that have also contributed to change, historically and at present, among the settled rural and urban populations of the Arab World. That the Bedouin have been involved in change generally underway throughout the region is hardly a profound conclusion, except that the Bedouin have often been treated *as if* they were separate from the rest of the population and somehow outside of, or beyond, history. The Bedouin have also been essentialized as a principal representative of what Abu-Lughod calls "*homo segmentarius,*" (1989: 280–287). In her critique of Middle East anthropology's classic concern with "segmentation, segmentary lineage theory, or tribalism," Abu-Lughod raises the important question: "Why privilege this aspect of society and say it accounts for the whole?" (ibid: 284).

Through a synthesis of diverse ethnographic, historical, and geographical data from multiple sites in Saudi Arabia, Oman, Syria, Jordan, Egypt, Libya, and Algeria this paper demonstrates broad regional dimensions of change among the Bedouin.

Time-depth and global forces are also shown, as the contemporary transformation is linked back to the early nineteenth century and includes colonialism. The issue of segmentation is addressed not from a perspective that gives prominence to descent, honor, violence, and warfare[6] but from its role in the mundane everyday context of herding in the open country, mainly in the past. The existence of markets, states, and Islam is stressed; these institutions were as much a part of Arab culture, society, and political economy as were the genealogies and the segmentary lineages the Bedouin (and some, but not all, other Arabs) constructed. I specifically do not privilege segmentation; but it was one, among other ways, of organizing life in the steppe, of talking about one's community, and of keeping track of how people were related, or not, to each other. Segmentation lingers today and takes new forms, even as "Bedouin" takes on a more ethnic dimension. I strive, however, to not replace a segmentary essentialism with an ethnic one.

SOCIOECONOMIC CHANGE ON THE RANGE

The Bedouin were strongly linked to the livestock they raised and took care of and which were dependent on the Bedouin, who themselves depended on their animals for much of their own livelihood and sustenance. This inter-species co-dependency or symbiosis[7] was a central feature of the old Bedouin economy wherein the livestock constituted a person's and a family-household's capital (*ras mal*). These animals were owned individually as private property (*mulk*)—often by the senior male head of household as part of an inheritance and/or by purchase. Some were owned by women in the household who acquired them in lieu of a right to inheritance or through purchase. Sometimes, a herd was inherited and held in trust (*jumlah*) by brothers who did not wish to divide their capital. Likewise, merchants, amirs and shaikhs, or other individuals occasionally owned a herd or part of a herd looked after by Bedouin.

Many variations existed; but under "ordinary" circumstances the Bedouin family-household (*bait*)[8] was the basic production and consumption unit. A household traditionally equaled a herd, such that when a household divided, the herd was also divided. Family members of the household provided the labor required for herding and for processing animal products as members of the household. Likewise, they consumed what the household produced or acquired in exchange for its produce. Tents, kilims, blankets, saddlebags, and other items woven by household members (usually women) were the private property of those who made the items but were for the common use of the household just as the privately owned animals, or their products, were for the common use of the household. Cases where household members did not own the animals, or most of them, usually indicated indebtedness (to merchants) or contracted service (to amirs and shaikhs). In such cases, the household provided the labor for herding, consumed milk and perhaps other products, and received goods and merchandize or a portion of the animals' offspring. The owners kept their capital and also benefited from the offspring.

Beyond the household was the domain of kinship. Wells were commonly the property of lineages[9] or smaller groups descended from a common male ancestor usually held to have dug or cleaned out or otherwise improved the well. Natural vegetation on the range depends on the rain and is thus a gift of Allah and, like fire and air and water (if not developed), is available to all users.[10] However, access to the range depends on access to water, and it is thus through the control of water wells they developed, or claimed to have developed, that Bedouin typically controlled indirectly the territories (*dirat*) that carried their tribal or clan names in addition to local place names. Beyond the household and kin groups were markets, centered in towns and cities but with agents of urban merchants and independent traders operating in the open country among the dispersed and mobile camps. Markets linked the Bedouin to other specialists, including blacksmiths and other metalworkers, leatherworkers, and manufacturers and purveyors of arms. Bedouin livestock, and sometimes their products, "paid" for the armaments, herding and household equipment, cloth and clothing, at least some food items, coffee and/or tea, and incense that constituted basic and luxury needs of Bedouin in the steppe.

Also existing within this system were other specialized food producers, the settled farmers in oases, river valleys, and areas where rainfall was sufficient for crop production. Some of these shared kinship or friend-partnerships (*sadaqah*) with the range-based Bedouin; and in these situations exchange of animals and animal products for supplies of dates and grains were governed by the principles and norms of reciprocity.[11] In other instances, armed Bedouin extracted tribute (*khuwah*) in the form of foodstuffs from villagers, usually in isolated areas. However, the lion's share of exchange involving pastoral and agrarian produce was organized and carried out according to the principles of the market and through the mediation of merchants, traders, auctioneers, and other specialized market personnel. Meanwhile, Islamic law and morality prevailed, while central state authority existed in principle if not always, or even usually, in fact.

This socioeconomic system was complex and multifaceted. Aspects of the household mode of production were present, along with aspects of kin-ordered, tributary, and mercantile modes.[12] No single mode was dominant; they were all present in varying degrees in different situations. This multiplicity of modes is similar to a situation Altorki and I encountered in the case of 'Unayzah, a settled agricultural oasis and market center in Saudi Arabia with numerous villages and a city. While one expects a single mode to be dominant, the contrary obtained: what predominated was the *coexistence* of multiple modes. Each of these modes was indigenous to the local political economy and continued, in 'Unayzah, through the 1920s and into the 1950s (Altorki and Cole 1989: 30–31). This complex system, operating also among the Bedouin, began to fracture in the early nineteenth century. According to Bourdieu, "the widespread, vigorous nomadism of the period prior to 1830 has been replaced by a limited, controlled and weakened form of nomadism" (1962: 69). Arabic-speaking people, and especially the Bedouin, had predominated in Algeria's well-watered plains. This was the area that "felt most strongly the direct shock of colonialism, … [where] the weakening of the old social structure has been most severe, [and where] European colonists have taken over nearly all the best land" (ibid: 57).

The Bedouin and settled Arabs worked as hired hands for the colonists and were pushed off the better lands into more and more marginal areas. With population increase and limited land of poor quality, land degradation set in, poorer yields were obtained, and greater poverty was created. The spread of cultivation into drier areas reduced the extent of pasture, while restrictions were placed on nomadic migrations. The privatization of landownership, in the 1860s, also facilitated the sale of land to European colonists. These changes plus, later on, the introduction of modern transportation, increased monetarization of the economy, development of the oil industry with new employment opportunities and high wages, rapid population growth, and stagnation in traditional farming led, in the mid twentieth century, to a "crisis of the nomadic way of life" and "to the nomadism of the work-hungry, a nomadism which brings to the cities wretched persons who have been torn from their accustomed way of life and cut off from their now completely disintegrated community" (ibid, 69–70).

Algeria is an extreme case due to the 132 years of French colonialism it experienced from 1830 to 1962. Yet, a similar pattern of socioeconomic change affected Bedouin in other parts of the Arab World. In nineteenth century Egypt, according to Baer, "the most important factor in the disruption of the social fabric of nomads and semi-nomads was the socio-economic differentiation among the members of the tribe" (1969, 6–7). Horizontal and vertical expansion of cultivation, the privatization of landownership, introduction of cash crops, and the support of Egypt's rulers for these changes combined such that by the end of the nineteenth century Bedouin shaikhs had become "big landowners, while other members of the tribe 'were lost among the fallahin'" (ibid, 7). Similarly, the implementation of land registration policies in greater Syria and Iraq following promulgation of the Ottoman Land Code of 1858 was associated with the commoditization of land, the creation of large landed estates, and the emergence of masses of Bedouin, and peasants, with few or no rights of access to land for pasturage and/or cultivation.[13] As in the case of French Algeria, cultivation spread into areas formerly devoted to grazing and restrictions on migrations were increasingly enforced. The demarcation of state boundaries early in the twentieth century hampered movements, while military actions related to "pacification" policies were largely against the Bedouin.

A robust pastoral production had continued in the Arabian Peninsula and in Libya throughout the nineteenth century. These areas experienced considerable political change associated with the Wahhabi and the Sanusi religious movements, both of which called for and fostered settlement and the development of crop cultivation. Italian settler colonialism impacted strongly on the Bedouin in Libya during the 1920s and 1930s. However, the old Bedouin production system continued relatively intact in these areas and, despite all the changes elsewhere, the Bedouin persisted throughout the Arab World in the range-based raising of livestock. The Bedouin were, however, in the 1950s at the bottom of Arab state societies everywhere in terms of most indicators of socioeconomic status: almost 100% illiteracy; no access to modern health care; probably the region's highest rates of infant mortality; decline in market demand for camels and horses; and almost no alternative for work they had previously depended on in desert caravan transport.

Moreover, the governments of the states in which they lived did not support the continuation, much less investment in the improvement, of their nomadic pastoral production. Newly independent Arab governments and Saudi Arabia (which had not been colonized), the newly created Arab League, and various organizations of the newly created United Nations began to call for sedentarization of the Bedouin. The unquestioned, and largely un-researched, solution to the Bedouin "problem" from the 1940s through at least the 1970s was settlement and a shift from livestock to crop production. A number of state-sponsored settlement programs and projects, often supported financially and technically by international agencies, were planned and some were implemented. Success was limited at best. A few Bedouin took advantage of what was offered; but the projects were piecemeal and minimalist, and their impact overall was minor.[14]

Changes in the region's political economy gathered momentum in the 1950s. Oil became increasingly important; new infrastructure was built; new urbanization emerged; public education and health care expanded; occupational mobility emerged; rural-urban migration began to take-off; trade expanded; there was more money in the economy; and governmental institutions were expanding. Modest and unevenly distributed both between and within countries, these innovations nonetheless reached beyond cities to villages and to the steppes. Many Bedouin reacted positively and energetically to the new circumstances and enthusiastically crafted changes in their own pastoral production systems.

Vidal (1975) described aspects of this transformation as he had researched it in the 1950s in Saudi Arabia. What had been a minor "Bedouin Problem" for the Arabian American Oil Company (ARAMCO) and the Trans-Arabian Company (Tapline) "became particularly marked during the summer of 1956." Large numbers of Bedouin arrived and camped with their herds at pipeline pump stations across northern Saudi Arabia and at gas oil separator plants in the huge Ghawar oilfield area in eastern Saudi Arabia. What attracted them was "an assured water supply," but what surprised Vidal was "the extremely varied tribal allegiance and origin of the groups." Many campers in the Ghawar field were from nearby areas, but others came from all over the rest of Saudi Arabia and from Qatar, Abu Dhabi, Oman, Kuwait, and Iraq.

Twenty-five tribes had members present in the camps, while 2901 tents were observed at 47 sites in the Ghawar region in August 1956. This large influx was attributed partly to drought elsewhere in Arabia, but Vidal presciently noticed changes underway that suggested a break, at least partially, with the past. Good retail markets, wage-labor opportunities, modern health care, and a good network of roads and motor transport were attracting Bedouin and other Arabians to "ARAMCO's zone of operation." Pick-up and other light trucks were being acquired by Bedouin, which contributed to a speeding up of migrations. The trucks were also being used to haul water directly to herds in grazing areas and had the potential to transport fodder as well.[15]

Vidal emphasized the importance of the water supply and, as an ARAMCO employee, noted a potential strain on ARAMCO water facilities in case Bedouin became more dependent on that supply. He was concerned about the likely growth of shantytowns inhabited by semi-settled Bedouin, since these might lead to increased demand on ARAMCO for the provision of local services. Other "undesirable features" for ARAMCO included "crowding of operation roads, land ownership difficulties due to the establishment of prayer sites and cemeteries [and] a possible increase in the number of incidents between various groups of Bedouins over water problems ..." There were legal and technical matters to address, but Vidal felt the need for the government to go "into water development on a large scale" was essential. He also noted a weakening in "the feelings of tribal membership and tribal allegiance" and their replacement by "a growing feeling of national belongingness and solidarity." This changing identity he found in statements Bedouin made about their grazing lands being "one," i.e. open to all, or that "the entire country is the grazing land of Al Sa'ud" (Vidal 1975).[16]

Numerous examples exist of similar changes in other parts of the Arab World. In Syria, the Bedouin were all but wiped out during a severe drought from 1958 to 1961. According to Lewis (1987: 170–192), Syria lost most of its camels and half of its sheep. The range was barren; and while some Bedouin managed to take flocks to graze in Lebanon on rented pasture, many others had to sell livestock that had not already perished and were forced to seek jobs in cities. Many poorer Bedouin did not return to pastoral production after the end of the drought, while some better-off Bedouin consolidated their losses, sold off what remained of their camels, and entrusted any sheep that had survived to hired shepherds. However, some Syrian Bedouin chose to return to the steppe and entered into partnership relations with urban merchants who financed the restocking of sheep flocks. Meanwhile, the Syrian state introduced cooperative societies, subsidized the provision of fodder, supported the drilling of modern wells and the renovation of cisterns, and promulgated a ban on plowing the steppe in an effort to promote conservation of the natural range.

With good rains and with increasing demand for mutton in Syria's growing cities and especially in the rapidly developing Arabian Gulf, a vigorous livestock sector was reestablished by the mid to late 1960s. However, this was no longer the old kin-ordered pastoral production of the past, with family-households constituting the basic production and consumption units. Hired shepherds provided most labor inputs; migration became an individual affair no longer controlled by tribes or other kin groups; purchased (but subsidized) fodder increasingly replaced natural graze; and water from government wells was trucked to the flocks. The factors of production had become capitalized, while production was oriented towards sale in the market.

Metral (2000) provides a detailed case study of this new pastoral production and its integration with crop production during the 1980s. Sukhna is a town and a district in the arid heart of the Syrian steppe. After a long demise due to the decline in caravan transportation and in pastoral production, both the town and the district began to recover in the 1970s and were booming during the 1980s. The existence of complex and complementary networks are highlighted, showing dynamic interaction between town dwellers and Bedouin, between the steppe and richer agricultural areas in Syria, and between Syria and consumer markets in the Arabian Gulf. Some of the Bedouin who previously came into the area are now gone, having returned back to the Arabian Peninsula. Yet, many of these or their descendants now act as intermediaries and agents for the sale of Syrian meat and livestock in Arabia. While camels along with sheep figured in the livestock make up of the region in the past, sheep now predominate almost exclusively. Other aspects of the old system, like the payment of tribute (*khuwah*), are as much a part of the past as are camels and caravans. Tribal wells remain, but government wells provide water for all. Herders of sheep from a multiplicity of tribal backgrounds and different geographical areas, including many newcomers, congregate on the district's grazing lands during autumn and spring.

Meanwhile, intensification in the raising of sheep and increase in the size of flocks has been accompanied by large-scale expansion of barley production that encroaches on grazing lands. Yet, the two are linked: more sheep fuels the need for more fodder, and vice-versa.[17] Livestock fattening operations have become common; procurement and warehousing of fodder from the local district and other parts of Syria have been developed; trucks for international transport of livestock to the Arabian Gulf are owned and operated locally; and contracts to supply the Syrian army with meat have been established. This complex institutional development has been achieved locally in what was a moribund community and district and involves multifaceted investments and relations among town-dwelling traders, Bedouin pastoralists, state and public sector authorities, cooperative societies, and importers abroad. According to Metral, "lifestyles change but identities remain" (2000: 127). Behaviors such as "diversified investment," "calculating the risks," and "managing the risks" apply to both the traders and the Bedouin as people from both categories are concerned with markets, the organization of transport, the procurement of inputs, and similar market concerns. Risk in the past was linked strongly to the rain and thus to the conditions of the range. Market conditions and principles thus now seem to take precedence over ecological factors—at least in the short run.

Behnke (1980) describes another dimension of socioeconomic change among Bedouin in Libya. Development of the oil industry in the 1960s drew Bedouin men away from their family-household herds and barley fields into waged labor in the oil sector and into trade or government service in newly expanding villages and towns. Many of these Bedouin, who had spontaneously settled and taken on new occupations, found it convenient to liquidate their herds and thus sold-off their livestock. A few others, however, not only kept the livestock they owned but increased the size of their herds from an average of around sixty sheep to between three hundred and four hundred head. They hired shepherds, first from among Libyan Bedouin and later on, when these became too expensive, from among Egyptian Bedouin. The now absentee owners managed the herds-making decisions about where the flocks should graze, which animals should be culled, and when and where livestock should be sold. There was also the need to arrange supplies of fodder and presumably other provisions such as veterinary health care. Behnke called this new market-oriented herding "proto-ranching" and stressed that this transformation was indigenous to the Libyan Bedouin who had implemented it on their own initiative without technical advice or outside financial aid.

Recent fieldwork in Jordan by Rowe (1999) shows the importance of state intervention in the pastoral sector and provides detailed data on how the market has transformed pastoral production and many other aspects of life in the open country. However, Rowe argues for an equally if not more powerful "continuity with tradition." The Bedouin diet continues to stress milk and milk products and now, with more prosperity, meat. A household's livestock thus still contribute to subsistence. Bedouin social organization continues to be strongly "based on kinship and lineage." The preference for engaging in multiple economic activities "echoes the risk-adverse multiple resource economy practised in traditional pastoral society." Meanwhile, the Bedouin perceive that the natural graze and browse of the open country contributes to the good condition of herds and improves the flavor and quantity of milk.

Although access to the steppe in years of good grazing lowers significantly the amount of money needed for supplementary' fodder, most Bedouin depart for the range before knowing what its condition will be. The pull of social ties is strong and channels people to migrate to areas where there are others whom they know and interact with. Since the preponderance of social interaction is among kin, the "information landscape" continues to be linked with what one can learn from and impart to relatives who are likely to share similar backgrounds and attitudes. There is change; but simultaneously the practice of range-based livestock production remains a Bedouin specialization (Rowe 1999). Indeed, non-Bedouin legally have the right to set up tent and herd on the range just like the Bedouin; for any non-Bedouin outsider to do so on his or her own is unimaginable.

In Palestine/Israel, most Palestinian Arabs were peasants, although Bedouin herded in grazing areas in and among the villages and pastured herds on crop residues. The more range-based Bedouin were in the Negev. According to Abu-Rabia (1994), the Bedouin population of the Negev numbered between 65,000 and 103,000 people at the end of the British Mandate in 1948. However, "when the Israeli Army conquered the Negev at the end of 1948, the majority of the tribes were expelled" (1994:7), while others who were fearful "left of their own accord." The situation remained unstable until 1953 when about 11,000 Bedouin remained as "remnants of tribes or a few branches of tribes." These were relocated under military rule in a closed area of less than ten percent of the Negev (1994: 7–8). Migration outside of this area requires special permits. Goats are not allowed and sheep are supposed to be tagged and registered with the authorities. Generally, there has been a major movement out of pastoral production (1994: 17) and resettlement in several specially created Bedouin towns where high rates of unemployment are reported to prevail.[18]

Other examples exist and add nuance to that which has been presented above. Chatty (1996) details the impacts of the oil industry and associated wage labor on Bedouin in Oman, shows the multiple ways in which trucks have been incorporated into the Bedouin way of life and transformed many aspects of pastoral production in the steppe, calls attention to disparities that have accompanied socioeconomic change, and discusses how the new economy affects cherished cultural foundations such as generosity and hospitality. Her work is especially important because of how it situates women as "harbingers of change" and brings into focus the importance of education to women and for the Bedouin community.

Chatty also provides a unique ethnography of a development project, an inside view of communication and miscommunication among international bureaucrats, state officials, local and foreign experts, and the "target population." Such projects are increasingly part of the socioeconomic matrix involving Bedouin, and the multiple and conflicting interests of the different parties merit further comparative research. Meanwhile, as Chatty reminds one, "the desert can only carry a limited population of people and subsequently animals" (Chatty 1996: 141). Modern transportation and other communication systems facilitate movement between the desert and the sown, while population growth and the pull factors associated with urbanization have influenced many Bedouin to leave the range behind.[19]

SOCIOECONOMIC CHANGE OFF THE RANGE

A Bedouin teenager in Egypt's Western Desert told me in 1992 that, "We, the Arabs (i.e., Bedouin), are more honorable and are cleaner than the Fallahin (i.e., peasants); but the future is better for the Fallahin." He explained that Fallahin villages had schools and clinics and were connected by train and paved roads to cities. The village youth could live at home and go to school and then get good jobs in the urban economy. He, by contrast, lived in the desert—in a permanent stone house—but without a school, a clinic, electricity, television, or telephones. To do "anything" he had to leave his family and kin-based community and walk for half a day to the nearest road in hopes of catching a ride into town. He hated to leave his family, but for him the only hope for a decent future lay in leaving the desert for town or city.

Steppe-urban migration has paralleled rural-urban migration in the Arab World and, although not as well researched as the latter, identification of its main features is crucial for a search of where the Bedouin have gone. Migration and settlement almost always involves occupational change, as well. Cole and Altorki (1998: 213–214), for example, document a case from among the Awlad 'Ali in the Western Desert. Four brothers, the oldest born in 1914, grew up in tents and were primarily engaged in herding as young men. They began to settle in the 1930s and again after the end of World War II. In 1994, these elders were occupied in both dry farming and livestock production. They had 24 adult sons, all settled, of whom four (17%) engaged in farming and herding, four (17%) were merchants, seven (29%) worked in transport, and nine (38%) were employed as professionals. The old men are all literate but never attended school; twelve (50%) of their sons completed primary school, five (21%) finished secondary school, and seven (29%) university. These people are from among the Awlad 'Ali elite, but the generational mobility observed among them is not unique. The grandsons and granddaughters, the third generation, from this family are currently in school and are becoming adults; but their potential for "upward" mobility is likely to be more constrained than was the case for their parents. Constraints they increasingly face stem from socioeconomic conditions within the wider society and are not limited to relatively oil-poor countries like Egypt but also haunt the major oil-producing countries where expectations for upward mobility have been very high for both Bedouin and sedentary citizens.[20]

In Saudi Arabia and the Arabian Gulf, steppe-urban migration, settlement, and occupational change began modestly in the 1950s, gathered momentum in the 1960s and early 1970s, mushroomed from the mid 1970s to the mid 1980s, and currently faces stagnation or at least uncertain futures for many.[21] The first settlers in the 1950s included many Bedouin who were livestock poor. Young Bedouin men did manual labor for wages alongside their counterparts from among the sedentary people and lived in canvas tents in work camps. Some took their savings and returned home to the range. Others stayed on, gained technical skills, started to trade, perhaps bought a taxi, and constructed a "box" (sunduq) out of plywood, scrap tin, or other inexpensive materials. This "box" was a new home, located in a spontaneous settlement in the outskirts of a town where other Bedouin from his and other tribes were congregating. His wife joined him, their first kids were born there, he saved money, they improved their house, and the settlement expanded in terms of both population and institutions. By the end of the 1960s or so, the nuclear family had a modest but regular income, the children (at least the boys) were in school. Relatives from the range dropped by and thought how poor (miskin) the conditions of life were in these shanties; the people living there thought their relatives from the range were noble but slightly mad—tied to their camels or sheep and goats with no concern for the education, health care, or even cleanliness of their children.[22]

Such communities were not only developing in and around cities, they were also springing up around deep wells in the desert and in small previously uninhabited oases. Built without permits on land that technically belonged to the state, these settlements were at best paralegal. Gasoline, some basic supplies, a café, and a small mosque marked out on the ground were the nuclei of many a settlement that expanded rapidly in the 1970s and took on an air of greater permanency when a few school teachers arrived. Boys came in from the range to study in the schools, sometimes camping out with others in a shack to learn—from a curriculum that included not one item relevant to their life on the range.

The oil-revenue boom from 1974 to 1982 speeded up the development of these settlements and brought massive government financial sponsorship for the construction of legal permanent housing in special government sanctioned communities for people with "limited income" (*dakhl al-mahdud*), which was usually a circumlocution for Bedouin. Masses of skilled and unskilled expatriate labor poured into Saudi Arabia and the Arabian Gulf and were willing to work at what were locally low wages. The settled Bedouin were left to fend for themselves in small-scale trade, repair shops, drilling and contracting, low levels of the bureaucracy, and military service. A very few became rich, some developed new farms in the desert with interest free government loans, but many remained in the rungs of the lower income and lower-middle income brackets. Yet, with modest savings from time to time, they invested in buying some sheep and put them with a relative out on the range. This was an investment they could afford, in an economic sector they understood, and with a good chance for a high rate of return (a ewe can have two and sometimes even three lambs a year). The remittances sent back by such people to the herds are uncalculated, but they contributed greatly to keeping the pastoral economy afloat.

Finally, throughout the Arab World those who have been pulled most strongly off the range and into urban scenes are younger Bedouin men. Wives, as noted, often followed husbands to new settlements. Yet, one should not conclude that Bedouin women occupy passive positions limited to household and family life in the new environment. Many a settled Bedouin woman has actively engaged in trade, including setting up shop in markets. Increasingly, Bedouin girls are obtaining education and some actively pursue careers outside the family-household. Meanwhile, out in the open country the management of everyday herding activities is likely to be in the hands of women. Younger and middle-aged men come and go; homes on the range since the 1960s and 1970s are increasingly composed of women, children, and old men. In a sense, these are the people who have been left behind. In another sense, these women on the range have played major roles in keeping Bedouin pastoral production alive, even as their own now market-oriented weaving contributes to household income. Yet, proportionately fewer and fewer family-households remain on the range; almost all Bedouin families now reside in permanent housing, their herds and flocks visited by family members while the everyday work of herding is done for wages by hired male shepherds. Some of these shepherds are other Bedouin; some are foreigners, especially in Saudi Arabia.

SOCIOPOLITICAL CHANGE

The shift away from the domestic and kin-ordered dimensions of herding and the ending of tribute, indicated above, implies a significant weakening of lineage, clan, and tribal formations[23] associated with the Bedouin. Technological and economic changes have been at the forefront of this transformation, but political factors emanating from both colonial and national states have also been important. Wolf (1969) records, for example, that in Algeria the French introduced "a program for the dismemberment of the great tribes" in which people from the same kin group were settled in different locations (*douars*) and then granted access to land on the basis of locality rather than membership in the kin group. Thus, "lineages and tribes had been scattered, the familiar political structure dismantled" (1969: 214–217). Evans-Pritchard (1949) documented multiple impacts of Italian colonialism on the Bedouin in eastern Libya. The Italian occupation there triggered an all but universal Bedouin resistance from the 1910s through the 1930s that resulted in massive loss of life but also brought political change, including foundations for the eventual establishment of an independent state in Libya after World War II.[24]

In the case of greater Syria, Lewis (1987; 2000) records the strengthening of Ottoman armed forces and of government control in the open country during the second half of the nineteenth century. The Ottoman government favored one tribe against another, restricted movements, demanded payment for camping and grazing in certain areas, imposed taxes, and incorporated tribal shaikhs into government service along with granting them decorations and sometimes even the title of Pasha[25] (2000: 37). Velud (2000) shows the impacts of French mandate policies in the Syrian steppe during the 1920s and 1930s. Political control was seen to be a necessary first step before any attempt at economic development. Two mounted camel companies were thus created in 1921 leading to a separate military administration of the steppe where Bedouin proliferated. One aim was to keep "the nomadic populations apart from the nationalist fervour prevailing in the western region" (Velud 2000: 67), while another was to keep the Bedouin divided among themselves, to foment minor rivalries that existed among them, and, thereby, "to avoid the risk of a bedouin union being formed in Syria, or elsewhere beyond the Syrian border" (2000: 70).

Egypt's three deserts, the Western Desert, the Eastern Desert, and the Sinai, were administered independently of each other and separately from the Nile Valley and Delta from the mid-nineteenth to the mid-twentieth century. The Bedouin there were excluded from the Egyptian army, a major nationalist force and vehicle for upward social mobility in the local Egyptian society. The Bedouin were also denied Egyptian national identity cards until long after their compatriots received them. They thus existed in a kind of limbo until they were brought back into the army as Egyptian citizens in 1947 and as their areas were brought under the same administrative structure as the rest of the country at the end of the 1950s. In Saudi Arabia, the process of state formation in the early twentieth century involved religious-inspired settlement, military defeats, marital alliances between the leaders of the state movement and tribal leaders, replacement of customary law ('urf) by Islamic law (Shari'ah), and incorporation of Bedouin into what became the National Guard.

Space does not permit a more detailed presentation of the history of political change relevant to the Bedouin. Suffice it to note that, despite differences in style, the same general process of the extension of central state power into the range has occurred everywhere in the Arab World. No Arab state administers its territories on the basis of *tribal* territories but on the basis of geographically demarcated areas, or *place*. Local administrators are usually appointed by the central government and are almost always outsiders to the region, both geographically and in terms of social identity.[26] All non-demarcated land in the desert and steppe is state property; and tribal, or communal, rights to land ownership are not legally recognized. In Egypt, for example, individuals have been allowed to claim "squatter's rights" (wad' yad) to desert tracks and to be compensated for relinquishing those rights, but their legal ownership of the land is not recognized, while patrimonial claims of kin groups to certain areas are purely "social" or informal with no basis in state law.[27]

Customary law ('urf) continues to be applied informally among Bedouin dealing with internal issues among themselves. However, as Khalaf (1990) shows, important aspects of "Bedouin justice" such as extended periods of protection (dakhalah) whereby a whole kin group is granted refuge by another kin group is no longer practical. Most people are now settled and cannot easily pick up and move to another place, as was the case previously when they lived in tents and were primarily dependent on mobile herds. Moreover, he notes that people who have spent many years in school are "ill prepared to understand fully all the tribal legalities and the psycho-cultural implications of the [protection] system" (ibid, 231). Meanwhile, state police forces are increasingly present in communities where Bedouin live. Such communities also have more and more residents from differing backgrounds. Thus the application of Islamic law or state law increases. That said, many Bedouin continue to express high regard for their customary law and to praise it as more effective than state law.[28]

Fabietti (2000) writes of "detribalization" among the Bedouin. Economically, politically, and legally that is a well-founded conclusion. Socially, however, one can argue for the continued existence of tribal identities. When Bedouin who do not know each other meet, they usually ask about the other's lineage, clan, or tribe—suggesting an identity of kin. By contrast, for example, Cairenes are usually interested in knowing from what part of Cairo the other comes—an identity of place. North Americans are apt to ask the other about his/her occupation—an identity of occupation. For most Bedouin today curiosity about another's identity is little more than that; knowing his/her kin affiliation allows one to place the other in a framework that is meaningful mainly in terms of identification. As sedentarization and participation in the modern urban-centered economy has expanded, one notes a marked increase in the use of tribal names as surnames, especially in Saudi Arabia and the Arabian Gulf. Telephone books, for example, now list hundreds of subscribers under their tribal names. Previously, a lineage name was the more common identifier of a person's position and status. Today, use of the tribal name implies not only tribal descent status,[29] socially important among local people in the region, but also a (historical) Bedouin connection.

The Bedouin connection is shared across tribal lines. In Egypt, people from the Nile region know only that the local people in the Sinai or the Western Desert are 'arab (Bedouin). In Saudi Arabia, people from hadr backgrounds in cities and villages lump all those with backgrounds in range-based herding together as badu. Meanwhile, among Bedouin themselves one can see a growing sense of "Bedouin-ness," of a shared identity that includes a sense of a common history and subculture that cuts across tribal boundaries that perhaps divided people more in the past. While dialects have tended to vary along tribal lines, the various tribes have histories preserved in poetry that recall events relating to themselves and other Bedouin, and many Bedouin share a keen interest in and knowledge of genealogies that very often link them back, at least in theory, to a glorious and noble past. Thus one might argue that an emergent ethnicity is replacing tribal identities of the past. Yet, I am hesitant to overstress a new ethnicity. The Bedouin are Arabs, and within the Arab World "ethnic" suggests non-Arab. Meanwhile, even though range-based livestock production is much reduced among them, people with Bedouin identities still reside in the steppe—in scattered homesteads, villages, and towns. Their social ties to kinfolk in the same area remain strong. Within the local provincial setting they may actively support a kinsperson in local elections, and people from different kin groups but a common Bedouin background may combine to keep migrant settlers from elsewhere from winning control of local elected bodies.[30]

Bujra (1971), in his analysis of the Hadrami regional society in South Arabia, noted that Bedouin and settled townspeople were linked economically, spoke the same language, shared the same religion, and had common values. He recognized that Hadramis "have traditionally seen their society as being composed of the 'civilized' people (*hadr*) of the towns and the 'primitive' tribesmen (bedu);" but he saw this division as more of a continuum than a contrast. Indeed, Bujra stressed that the "contrast is within the society" and argued that

> whereas political action in tribal areas is still more or less within the framework of segmentary organization, in the towns stratification is the main framework for political action. Significantly, however, the segmentary framework is only operational within the tribes, the framework of stratification applies to the society as a whole" (ibid, 5–9).

There are, in my analysis, no separate Bedouin or tribal *societies*,[31] as such, in the Arab World. The existing *societies* are state systems within which some communities and some individuals self-identify as Bedouin, Fallahin, workers, royalty, or whatever and also consider themselves members of other collectivities—including their nation and religion. The de facto exercise of state authority in areas frequented by Bedouin has often been weak or ineffective. Yet, Bedouin have anciently recognized the legitimacy of the state as an institution and have historically served militarily and in other ways in state systems, even if they have preferred to take care of their own affairs without interference from the state. At present, the exercise of Arab state authority among Bedouin is increasingly strong throughout the region. Conversely, the role of Bedouin in the region's state systems has varied enormously over the centuries and from one area to another—strong, weak, or irrelevant, depending on the specific historical and political economic situation. Bedouin participation in Arab state politics today is probably at its lowest ebb ever. If that is, in fact, the case, it is due more to their socioeconomic status (or "class") within the context of the wider society than to their being Bedouin (or their "ethnicity"). Still, in some local settings low socioeconomic status sometimes coincides with Bedouin identity, a situation with a high potential for perceived deprivation and a motive for rebellion or resistance against the dominant political economy.

CULTURAL REPRESENTATION
AND HERITAGE

In a shift that is both a sign of the times and of new directions in anthropology, Wooten (1996) addresses "how Bdul Bedouin identity is reaffirmed through tourism." Bdul[32] have a long history of residing in Nabatean caves in the area of Petra in Jordan, where they also formerly raised goats and presented "a rather atypical image of a Bedouin tribe: no tents, no camels, few sheep, clothed in skins and living in caves." Recently, Bdul have been relocated out of the tourist site into a "Bedouin village," have shifted from goat-herding into new occupations associated with the tourist industry, and perceive that they have become prosperous as a result of tourism. Many Bdul consider that they are no longer "real" Bedouin. Thus, according to a Bdul youth, "I am *Bedu* yes, but not 'real' Bedu," while in the words of another: "Yes it is strange, I am Bedouin and the tourists know the Bdul are Bedouin but its true we are not living like the real Bedouin now. But even other Bedouin are not living like before" (quoted in Wooten 1996: 51–52).

Descent, or what Wooten calls "heritage/ancestry," was a key criterion Bdul considered when discussing their Bedouin identity. Way of life, "that of the Arab nomadic pastoralist," was another main criterion. Thus, "I'm not wearing the Bedouin dress, and I never took the goats, not once in my life, but I can't change who is my father, or my father's father" (quoted in Wooten 1996: 54). Meanwhile, "shifting self-perceptions" are heard in Bdul statements such as "its like we are almost fellahin," "the Bedouin are becoming more like Europe people, living in houses, with television and refrigerators," and "the Bdul are changing fast from tourism—you will see, the village will soon be like any village in Jordan or Europe" (quoted in Wooten 1996: 58–59). Yet, Wooten (1996: 59) argues that:

> a sense of Bedouin identity still remains, an identity that is constantly shifting and being re-defined ... 'Bedouin' is still the social category with which the Bdul are associated and in the presence of tourists, it is this identity which most often comes to the forefront (as opposed to a specific family lineage, tribe, nationality, etc) ... They still see themselves as "more Bedouin" than the Others involved in Petra's tourist industry ... [And this] industry currently helps to maintain and reinforce this identity for them.

Tourism has also "commoditized the image of the Bedouin," while tourists "now provide an audience" in front of whom Bdul "perform their Bedouin identity." The film *Lawrence of Arabia* and Lawrence's own *Seven Pillars of Wisdom* "influence [tourists'] preconceptions about Bedouin," as do literature and images produced by government and private tour companies about "exotic Jordan" in which Bedouin mounted on camels and in full regalia with daggers and rifles "appear to be the only people of Jordan" (Layne 1994: 102 quoted in Wooten 1996: 64). Within Petra, tourists encounter "Bedouin motifs" in decoration, "Bedouin tents" where they can drink "Bedouin tea" and smoke water pipes, and "Bedouin mensifs" or huge plates of rice topped by a whole goat or sheep. Bdul and other non-Bedouin Jordanians are inventing new "traditional" art, including sand-bottles filled with ribbons of colored sand and other items for sale. Bdul have set up black goat-hair Bedouin tents as shops for selling souvenirs and where one can "buy" some "Bedouin hospitality." Although never much involved with camels, a few Bdul have brought camels onto the scene at Petra as a kind of "revival of tradition." Although presented as "authentic" and believed to be so by tourists, most of the material items of this presentation are new acquisitions related to tourism—at least among Bdul.

Wooten also discusses how Bdul act out their Bedouin identity under the gaze or spectatorship of "an interactive tourist 'audience' to whom they may perform aspects of this identity and 'be' Bedouin." In doing so, they do not try to match the image of Bedouin created by the tourist industry. They don't wear Bedouin "costume" or perform warrior or camel pastoralist roles of "traditional" Bedouin. Rather, they stress "other elements of their Bedouin identity ... which reflect tourists' stereotypes and romantic images of 'hospitality,' 'naturalness' and/or 'primitiveness.'" They mix work and play and in the process of interacting with the tourists comment on their culture and explain aspects of their lives, always adjusting those comments and explanations to meet their own stereotypes of different kinds of tourist. Thus, a tourist comment is, "*I think we have a lot to learn from these people about how to live with nature, away from so many material things," while another is, "The Bedouin live so simple it is a shame that they are changing*" (quoted in Wooten 1996: 95).

That Bdul have televisions and other modern conveniences, are literate and increasingly have university-level education, and are becoming like "Europe people" are features that they do not show to the tourist. However, these are issues about themselves that Bdul stressed to the ethnographer. "Off-stage" Bdul proudly proclaim they are the "wealthiest bedu in the kingdom [of Jordan]." They express nostalgia for a remembered past but do not bemoan the change from "'poor' goat-herding Bedouin into wealthy entrepreneurs of international tourism."

Bedouin roles in tourism increasingly occupy new and varied niches in foreign and local tourism scenes in the Arab World.[33] A holiday in the Sinai will probably include a "Bedouin night" in which the "Bedouin hosts" are hotel employees and are more likely to be Upper Egyptian villagers than Bedouin from the Sinai. Desert safaris, increasingly popular, have "Bedouin guides" but such guides are seldom from the desert areas in which they are guiding. Economic roles of Bedouin in this new tourism are uncertain. Bdul claim to have benefited; a more common reading is that Bedouin are at best marginal beneficiaries of an expanding tourism industry along the desert coasts and in parts of the steppe that were previously "theirs."

Changing roles of culture associated with Bedouin are by no means limited to the realm of tourism. Aspects of such culture have become parts of state-sponsored construction of national heritage, as well as of scholarly and popular production of knowledge about dimensions of Arab heritage. A popular national radio program from Kuwait in the 1960s was the "Bedouin Hour," in which recitation of Bedouin poetry featured centrally. Transistor radios had spread rapidly in Bedouin tents, workers and National Guard barracks, shanty settlements, and towns and cities in eastern Arabia. The "Bedouin Hour" was the single most popular radio program among Bedouin, many of whom listened to it regularly and discussed it at length among themselves. The program was also popular among people from *hadr* backgrounds and often reminded them of their own poetry and cultural traditions. The poetry and other discourse on the "Bedouin Hour" addressed a wide range of specific historical events and issues of contemporary experience, which is worthy of study on its own; however, what struck one at the time is how Bedouin from different tribes increasingly identified with this production as something commonly shared among all Bedouin, *as Bedouin*. Meanwhile, it was not foreign to the local sedentary people.

Other relevant cultural events that began in the 1960s include the initiation of horse races and then of camel races in Riyadh and other Arabian cities, most notably in the United Arab Amirates.[34] Arabian horses historically span nomad and sedentary communities of the region, while the camel is of course famously linked to Bedouin. However, organized horse racing and camel racing were by no means regular features among either group in the past. Individual Bedouin might race each other's mounts on the spur of the moment. Yet, the organized races, especially of camels, resonated strongly in the 1960s among Bedouin and *hadr* throughout

much of Arabia. A resulting search for purebred Arabian horses contributed to res-
urrecting these breeds from almost dying out in the region and their consequent
reintroduction as an esteemed element of *Arab cultural* heritage. Search for purebred race camels, and also milk camels, led elite urban men back to Bedouin camps
and their herds in the steppe. This resulted not only in the acquisition of some very
fine creatures but also fostered elite appreciation of Bedouin as individuals and
as renowned collectivities strongly tied to an Arab past and many of its cherished
customs.

Private and public collections of Bedouin material culture have proliferated in
Saudi Arabia, the Arabian Gulf, Jordan, and to a lesser degree in other Arab countries.
A central exhibit of Saudi Arabia's national museum in Riyadh is of a fully furnished
black goat hair tent representative of a Bedouin home. Many of the material items
are of Bedouin manufacture; but many other items are the work of settled artisans
and craftspeople. Still, the latter items are a part of Bedouin culture, even the red
and white tea kettles made in China, as Bedouin were always specialists linked to
and dependent on the production of others—usually through the medium of market exchange. Bedouin, sedentary person, and foreigner view the museum exhibits
today. For older Bedouin and older sedentary folk they bring back fond memories;
for younger Bedouin and their sedentary compatriots they are almost as foreign as
they are to the foreigner.

Serious scholarly research informs the museum and many of the private
collections. Scholarship also underlies the recording, transcription, sometimes
translation, and analysis or interpretation of vast bodies of oral culture. Some of this
collection is the work of lay people. Among that of formal scholars is the pioneering
work of Sowayan (1985; 1991). Yet, the writing down, formal publication, and scholarly analysis of this *oral* culture trigger controversy. Shryock (1997) describes and
discusses this phenomenon at length for specific cases in Jordan where differing
versions of history and background take on political significance in the changing
roles and positions of different tribal communities in their wider polities. In Saudi
Arabia there has also been the challenge that the oral colloquial (*nabati*) poetry of
the Bedouin does not constitute "poetry" according to the canon of classical Arabic
language and literary scholarship. Moreover, some issues and topics addressed in
these Bedouin materials deviate from that which is considered correct according
to accepted Islamic scholarship and/or state political authorities. That said, thick
volumes of recorded materials have continued to be published,[35] private and

semi-public recitations are organized, and men from younger generations, with and without Bedouin identities, eagerly attend.

Bedouin theme parks are also springing up.[36] Khalaf (2001) reports on the establishment of Dubai Heritage Village in 1997 with scenes of old Dubai town, of mountain village houses, and of Bedouin tents. The site also incorporates Dubai's Diving Village, and there are shops, exhibition halls, and theatrical stages. The motives behind the village are concern for Dubai's "national heritage and its preservation" and also promotion of its tourism industry by stimulating travel and shopping. The village sponsors shopping festivals and is a "living museum" where United Arab Amirates history is performed by "living actors." During March 2001 the village staged 29 events, of which two were Bedouin events. One was the "Arabian Bedouin Lifestyle Festival" that continued daily throughout the month with representations of Egyptian, Yemeni, Libyan, Jordanian, Sudanese, Mauritanian, Algerian, and United Arab Amirates Bedouin "lifestyle activities." The second event consisted of nine Bedouin weddings performed by the "visiting Bedouin heritage groups." These "weddings" attracted huge crowds of local and expatriate visitors and, according to Khalaf, were the most popular of all displays.

CONCLUSION

So, where have the Bedouin gone? I contend that they have mainly settled and are to be found in dispersed communities and oases in the steppe, in villages, small towns, and provincial centers, and in scattered neighborhoods of cities. Some Bedouin continue to be mobile and are still out on the range. These Bedouin and many of those who have settled own livestock; however, the livestock are most likely herded by hired shepherds or by one or two sons rather than by a whole family household as before. The maintenance of herds is influenced by considerations of tradition and consumption, but livestock are also seen as capital (*ras mal*) and their raising is now oriented towards, and to a large degree is organized by, the market.

Bedouin are today citizens of states, carry national identity cards, vote where voting is allowed, and are no longer differentiated administratively from other citizens or nationals as previously occurred in some cases. Younger generations of Bedouin, both settled and from among those on the range, are increasingly literate with growing proportions completing secondary school and going on to universities. Occupationally, most Bedouin on the range have small- to moderate-scale enterprises. Many of those settled work in trade, contracting, or transportation, serve in military or police forces or other government service, and similar occupations that are moderately skilled. A few are professionals, a few hold high positions, and a few have become very rich. Some are very poor. Yet, educational levels and occupations place most Bedouin in the middle class—many in the lower rungs of that class but a few in the middle and upper rungs.

The changes Bedouin have experienced are in part, of course, the results of local histories: oil in Arabia and Libya, Arab socialist policies in Syria and Egypt, wars and battles fought by outside forces in North Africa and the Iraq-Kuwait-Saudi Arabia border areas, and so on. However, broad processes of regional transformation should not be obscured by local exceptionalisms. The multiple and changing roles of states and markets, of newer and older globalisms, of Arab national politics and culture cut across state and local boundaries and engage Bedouin and their compatriots from rural and urban backgrounds throughout the region. Thus, comparison of Bedouin communities, nomadic or settled, in different state settings is especially attractive. At the same time, comparison of small-scale farmers and small-scale herders promises a better understanding of both than if they are divided into two different worlds, as has often been the case in Middle Eastern anthropology. Comparison of both with large-scale agribusiness is also highly relevant.

Many scholars and development specialists, back in the twentieth century, thought that nomadic pastoralists would settle and become peasant farmers: the Bedouin would become Fallahin. Many Fallahin moved to cities, became urbanized, and still self-identify as Fallahin. The same holds for Bedouin. "*Baduwi*" is today used by Bedouin to identify specifically a person fully involved in steppebased herding. It is also used more generally to identify a wide range of others whose only connection to herding is heritage, or ancestral. Thus, concern with Bedouin heritage is an emerging field of study and of cultural production. Bedouin theme parks, camel races, museum exhibits, poetry recitals, and television talk-shows sustain continuation of Bedouin identity and honor it as a part of national heritage. A political dimension also exists to this cultural production and performance. Much of Bedouin poetry, especially that of men, recounts historical events from the perspectives of the Bedouin that differ from those of state rulers and others. Some younger and better-educated Bedouin are increasingly interested in writing their own society—their traditions, their specificities. They are not alone in this, as some from among the village and urban masses also search for their own authenticities. How and why this is done, concerns with "text" and "context," strongly beckon future research.

Characterizations of the Bedouin with exotic social phenomena such as segmentation, parallel cousin marriage, or raiding as a system of exchange distort the Bedouin and contribute to misrepresentations of the Arab World and the wider Middle East. All these "exotica" are, or have been, social practices among the Bedouin; but none of them has existed alone by itself or necessarily even as a dominant feature. Moreover, all of these phenomena cut across the Arab nomad/ sedentary "divide." For example, nomads, villagers, and urbanites all practice parallel cousin marriage, but not all marriages within any of those categories are with a parallel cousin.[37] It is within such a context that I argue for seeing the Bedouin as ordinary, everyday people. Colleagues rightly argue that I am stating the obvious, a simple truism. Yet, many Westerners express keen disappointment when I argue against the Bedouin having special powers or senses or of their having remained unchanged since "time immemorial." Many urban Arabs express disbelief when I stress similarities rather than differences between nomad and sedentary.

A 1959 statement by Murphy and Kasdan about the Bedouin being well known "despite the lack of detailed studies" provides the epigraph that starts this essay. With a dearth of ethnographic data, a considerable amount of Orientalist writings, and a strong comparative theoretical perspective, they crafted a stimulating discussion of one aspect of Middle Eastern social life. Yet, since my first fieldwork among Bedouin in 1968–70, I have felt the need for what Marcus (1998) calls multi-sited ethnography. That need back then was made obvious because the nomads were on the move—to different pastures and wells but also to markets, National Guard camps, homes of royal amirs, ministry offices, prisons, and on holy pilgrimage to Makkah. The scope of sites today is vastly expanded geographically and institutionally and demands greater flexibility and multi-sightedness. This paper has aimed to highlight the paths Bedouin have been traversing. A simple plea is that the Bedouin be neither cast aside as an exotic artifact of the past nor fashioned into a romantic representative of some Other. The more exciting and fruitful approach is to engage in those "detailed studies"—still only partially done—that promise a fuller understanding of where the Bedouin, and others in their wider societies, are.

ACKNOWLEDGMENTS

This essay draws on research since 1968 in Saudi Arabia and in Egypt (Cole 1971, 1975; Ibrahim and Cole 1978; Altorki and Cole 1989; Sherbiny, Cole and Girgis 1992;

Cole and Altorki 1998). It also benefits from more than 30 years teaching courses on Arab society and the Middle East and North Africa at The American University in Cairo. I am greatly indebted to Bedouin, especially from the Al Murrah in Saudi Arabia and the Awlad 'Ali in Egypt, to sedentary (hadr) citizens in Saudi Arabia, and to generations of students in Egypt. Earlier versions of this paper were presented at the 100th Annual Meeting of the American Anthropological Association, Washington, D.C., December 2001, and the University of Sharjah, United Arab Amirates, April 2002. I especially appreciate discussions at those presentations. I have also benefited greatly from comments by Soraya Altorki, Steven C. Caton, Robert A. Fernea, Sulayman N. Khalaf, Laura Nader, Mark Allen Peterson, Richard L. Tapper, Daniel Martin Varisco and three anonymous reviewers from Anthropological Quarterly. Special thanks are due Roy Richard Grinker for his support and editorial insight. Errors of fact and *judgment* are of course my responsibility.

NOTES

1. "Nomads" or "Bedouin" are clearly distinguished in Egypt's 1907 and 1917 censuses and appear in tables on nationality and race; however, neither appears as a separate category in later censuses. The 1974 census of Saudi Arabia classified people according to place of enumeration: amirate capitals (cities), villages, and water points. Many of those enumerated at water points are presumed to have been Bedouin but this is not necessarily so since water points included all informal settlements. Moreover, many who identify as Bedouin live in villages or cities. Abu-Lughod (1989, 284) has reckoned that "pastoral nomads or transhumants" make up about one percent of the population of the Middle East. The population of the Arab World in 2000 was 280,000,000 (United Nations Development Program 2000, 35). Some 2,800,000 *practicing* livestock raisers in the steppe seems reasonable. My guess, based on observations of selected cases, is that the absolute number of Bedouin on the range is about the same today as it was in the 1960s. If one includes recent settlers and descendants of Bedouin who have settled since the early nineteenth century and who still identity at least sometimes as Bedouin, then the numbers may explode into the tens of millions. As Eickelman (1998, 11) rightly warns, estimates of Middle Eastern nomads must be taken with great caution.

2. This essay is informed by anthropological and related literature, for better or worse in English. Monographs on the Bedouin include Abu-Lughod 1986, 1993; Abu-Rabia 1994, 2001; Ahmad 1974; Al Rasheed 1991; Asad 1970; Behnke 1980; Chatty 1986, 1996; Cole 1975; Cole and Altorki 1998; Davis 1988; Fabietti 1984; Ibrahim and Cole 1978; Ingham 1986a; Janzen 1980; Johnson 1973; Hobbs 1989, 1995; Lancaster 1981; Lavie 1990; Layne 1994; Lewis 1987; Marx 1967; Meeker 1979; Mohamed 1980; Moshen 1975; Muller-Mahn 1989; Peters 1990; Shryock 1997; and Young 1996. The author's research among the Bedouin was conducted in Arabic.

3. Some writers (e.g. Asher 1986, 1996) include non-Arab nomads under the rubric of "Bedouin." I restrict "Bedouin" in this paper to people in the Arabic-speaking world.

4. See Ingham 1986b, 1997 for professional linguistic discussion of this issue. My non-professional ear suggests that Bedouin increasingly speak the dominant colloquial Arabic of their country or region, often as a second dialect. This is especially the case for younger Bedouin who have worked in towns or cities and/or attended school.

5. As Hopkins and Ibrahim indicate, "Arab society has traditionally been viewed as a trinity of Bedouins, peasants, and urban dwellers, living together in some kind of symbiosis. Detailed studies have tended to stress the differences between these and other categories of people, differences which the social and economic politics of Arab and foreign regimes have long tended to exacerbate" (Hopkins and Ibrahim 1997, 1).

6. An excellent example of such an approach is Meeker 1979. See also Abu-Lughod 1986 and 1993 for discussion of descent and honor especially from the perspective of Bedouin women, and Dresch 1989 for presentation of the segmentary system in a non-Bedouin tribal setting in Yemen.

7. See Swidler 1973 for a discussion of the interrelationship between nomads and their livestock.

8. These households "typically" consisted of a senior man and a senior woman, their unmarried children, their married sons and daughters-in-law, and the latter's unmarried children. Other individuals were sometimes added (for example, a divorced daughter) and, of course, the composition changed due to the demographic cycles of its members.

9. Lineages were/are named collectivities that group together all male and female descendants through the patriline from an eponymous ancestor who existed

at about five generations remove from ego. Al Murrah refer to these entities as *fukhud*, "thighs;" Awlad 'Ali as '*ailat*, "families." Other terms are also used, for example, *al-khams*, "the five."

10. See Wilkinson 1983 and Altorki and Cole 1998, 123–124 for discussion of relevant concepts of "ownership."

11. See Bradburd 1997 for a comparative view of nomads and their trade partners in Iran.

12. For discussions of the household mode of production see Meillassoux 1981 and Sahlins 1972; for kin-ordered, tributary, and mercantile modes see Amin 1973 and Wolf 1982.

13. See Fernea 1970, 30–32 for a description and analysis of the political, economic, and social impacts of the implementation of this code in Iraq.

14. See Bocco 2000 for a critical assessment of the planning and implementation of settlement projects. See also Cole 1975, 144–158; Ibrahim and Cole 1978, 99–109; Cole and Altorki 1998, 97–104; and Chatty 1996, 165–166.

15. See also Cole 1973 and Chatty 1986 for descriptions of the introduction of trucks among the Bedouin.

16. One should not conclude from this statement that Bedouin conceived of the whole country as the private domain of the Al Sa'ud. The reference here is symbolic for the state and probably reflects what some Bedouin thought was the right thing to say to a person such as Vidal who was connected to ARAMCO.

17. Mundy and Mussallam 2000, 1–2 characterize this type of use, or abuse, of the Syrian steppe as "mining."

18. See Abu-Rabia 2000, Jakubowska 2000, and Marx 2000 for data and analyses on land, work, employment and unemployment, and relations with the bureaucracy among Bedouin in the Negev.

19. Before leaving the range, one should note that other entities and people increasingly dominate the open country. Military forces, public and private sector desert development schemes, new cities, desert and beachfront resorts, fenced highways, and oil pipelines occupy large swathes and have enormous impact on the ecology of the steppe. Gigantic feedlots with imported livestock dot the range. Urban hunters illegally hunt rare and endangered species. City folk use large areas of the range for recreational purposes. These new patterns of land use have negative environmental impacts on the arid habitats. Land degradation and desertification of the steppe is usually blamed on the Bedouin.

However, the new uses, or abuses, are the work of non-Bedouin. Indeed, many Bedouin are themselves victims of the misuses of others.

20. See Yamani (2000) for a detailed presentation of the hopes, fears, and frustrations of settled youth in Saudi Arabia.

21. For comparative perspectives from Egypt, see Bujra 1967, Abou-Zeid 1979, and Cole and Altorki 1998, 89–110. For Libya, see Benhke 1980, 79–84. The description with reference to Saudi Arabia and the Gulf is based on the author's research, including Cole 1971, 236–239, and observations from the 1970s to the 1990s.

22. 1n 1977, Saad Eddin Ibrahim and the author interviewed a middle-aged Bedouin man in the Wadi Dawasir in Saudi Arabia. When asked if he would consider settling so that his children would have better access to education, etc., he replied, "*Halali gabl ayyali*" ("My herd before my children").

23. A clan (*qabilah; hamulah*) is constituted of several or more lineages the members of which claim descent from a common ancestor. A tribe (*qabilah* or *qabilat; 'ashirah*) is a joining together of several or more clans as the descendants of a common ancestor. Leadership, separated to at least some degree from the everyday life of one's "ordinary" lineage or clan mates, was vested primarily at the level of a clan or clans and in some cases of the tribe.

24. See Ahmida 1994 for an analysis of colonialism and resistance in Libyan state-building.

25. See Salim 1962, 27–33; Amin 1970, 83–86 and 104–107; Fernea 1970, 105–107; and Cole and Altorki 1998, 67–74 and 210–213 for analyses of the roles of shaikhs and other leaders in tribal communities.

26. See Cole 1982 and Cole and Altorki 1998, 104–110 for descriptions of local administration and government in Saudi Arabia and Egypt, respectively.

27. See Fabietti 2000 for a critical analysis of how tribal grazing areas in Saudi Arabia were converted into state lands open to all in Saudi Arabia. Controversy about land tenure in desert Egypt is addressed in Cole and Altorki 1998, 199–204.

28. See Cole and Altorki 1998, 205–210 for an example of efforts to develop customary law to deal with problems and issues that confront Bedouin in the contemporary lives.

29. However, it is common in the Arabian Peninsula and Gulf for people of former slave status to have the names of the tribes to which they were previously

attached. Thus a tribal name by itself does not automatically mean freeborn Arab tribal (*qabili*) descent.

30. As Davis 1988, 141–143 has shown for a case in Libya, tribal people voting together in an election are not necessarily following "primitive" tribalism but have seriously studied and evaluated the political and economic issues at stake.
31. In this I follow the lead of Leeds 1977 who argued against the denomination of peasants as constituting societies. They are always components of a larger and more complex social, economic, political, legal, and cultural system. In the present Arab World, one may speak of a tribal community within a state society.
32. See also Shoup 1985 for a discussion of the impacts of tourism on Bedouin in the Petra region.
33. For descriptions of Bedouin and tourism in the Sinai see Aziz 2000, Gardner 2000, Lavie 1990, Meyer 1996, and Wickering 1991. For Bedouin involvement in holiday resorts and tourism in Egypt's north coast see Cole and Altorki 1998, 161–198.
34. See Khalaf 1999 for a detailed ethnography of camel racing in the Arabian Gulf.
35. An example is the three volumes by Kurpershoek 1994, 1995 and 1999.
36. For a critical reaction by Fawziyya Abu-Khalid, a Saudi Arabian (woman) writer, to the cultural heritage village of Janadiriyyah near Riyadh see Arebi 1994, 57–59 and 68–71.
37. See Cole 1984.

REFERENCES

Abou-Zeid, Ahmed M. 1979. "New Towns and Rural Development in Egypt." *Africa* 49(3):283–290.

Abu-Lughod, Lila. 1986. *Veiled Sentiments: Honor and Poetry in a Bedouin Society.* Berkeley: University of California Press

———. 1989. "Zones of Theory in the Anthropology of the Arab World." *Annual Review of Anthropology* 18:237–306

———. 1993. *Writing Women's Worlds: Bedouin Stories.* Berkeley: University of California Press.

Abu-Rabia, Aref. 1994. *The Negev Bedouin and Livestock Rearing: Social, Economic and Political Aspects.* Oxford/Providence: Berg.

———.2000. "Employment and Unemployment Among the Negev Bedouin."
   Nomadic Peoples 4(2):84–93.

———. 2001. *Bedouin Century: Education and Development among the Negev Tribes
   in the Twentieth Century.* New York: Berghahn.

Ahmad, Abd al-Ghaffar Muhammad. 1974. *Shaykhs and Followers: Political Struggle in
   the Rufa'a al-Hoi Nazirate in the Sudan.* Khartoum: Khartoum University Press.

Ahmida, Ali Abdullatif. 1994. *The Making of Modern Libya: State Formation,
   Colonization, and Resistance, 1830–1932.* Albany: State University of New York
   Press.

Al Rasheed, Madawi. 1991. *Politics in an Arabian Oasis: The Rashidi Tribal Dynasty.*
   London: IB. Tauris & Co.

Altorki, Soraya, and Donald P Cole. 1989. *Arabian Oasis City: The Transformation of
   'Unayzah.* Austin: University of Texas Press.

Amin, Samir. 1970. *The Maghreb in the Modern World: Algeria, Tunisia, Morocco.*
   Harmondsworth: Penguin.

———. 1973. *Le Developpement inegal.* Paris: Le Editions de Minuit.

Arebi, Saddeka. 1994. *Women and Words in Saudi Arabia: The Politics of Literary
   Discourse.* New York: Columbia University Press.

Asad, Talal. 1970. *The Kababish Arabs: Power, Authority, and Consent in a Nomadic
   Tribe.* London: C. Hurst.

Aziz, Heba. 2000. "Employment in a Bedouin Community: The Case of the Town of
   Dahab in South Sinai." *Nomadic Peoples* 4(2):28–47.

Baer, Gabriel. 1969. *Studies in the Social History of Modern Egypt.* Chicago: University
   of Chicago Press.

Behnke, Jr., Roy H. 1980. *The Herders of Cyrenaica: Ecology, Economy, and Kinship
   among the Bedouin of Eastern Libya.* Urbana: University of Illinois Press.

Bernal, Victoria. 1991. *Cultivating Workers: Peasants and Capitalism in a Sudanese
   Village.* New York: Columbia University Press.

Bocco, Ricardo 2000." International Organisations and the Settlement of Nomads
   in the Arab Middle East, 1950–1990." In *The Transformation of Nomadic Society
   in the Arab East,* eds. Martha Mundy and Basim Musallam, 197–217. Cambridge:
   Cambridge University Press.

Bourdieu, Pierre. 1962. *The Algerians. Boston:* Beacon Press.

Bradburd, Daniel. 1997. "Nomads and their Trade Partners: Historical Context
   and Trade Relations in Southwest Iran, 1840–1975." *American Ethnologist*
   24(4):895–909.

Bujra, Abdalla Said. 1967. "A Preliminary Analysis of the Bedouin Community in Marsa Matruh Town." The American University in Cairo, Social Research Center Report.

———. 1971. *The Politics of Stratification: A Study of Political Change in a South Arabian Town.* Oxford: Clarendon Press.

Chatty, Dawn. 1986 *From Camel to Truck: The Bedouin in the Modern World.* New York: Vantage Press

———. 1996. *Mobile Pastoralists: Development Planning and Social Change in Oman.* New York: Columbia University Press

Cole, Donald P. 1971. *The Social and Economic Structure of the Al Murrah: A Sa'udi Arabian Bedouin Tribe.* University of California, Berkeley, Unpublished Ph.D. dissertation.

———.1973. "Bedouin of the Oil Fields." *Natural History* 82(9):94–103.

———. 1975 *Nomads of the Nomads: The Al Murrah Bedouin of the Empty Quarter.* Chicago: Aldine.

———. 1982. "Tribal and Non-Tribal Structures among the Bedouin of Saudi Arabia." *Al-Abhath* 30:77–93.

———. 1984. "Alliance and Descent in the Middle East and the 'Problem' of Patrilateral Parallel Cousin Marriage." *In Islam in Tribal Societies: From the Atlas to the Indus,* eds. Akbar S. Ahmed and David M. Hart, 169–186. London: Routledge & Kegan Paul.

Cole, Donald P, and Soraya Altorki. 1998. *Bedouin, Settlers, and Holiday-Makers: Egypt's Changing Northwest Coast.* Cairo: The American University in Cairo Press.

Davis, John. 1988. *Libyan Politics: Tribe and Revolution; an Account of the Zuwaya and their Government.* Berkeley: University of California Press.

Eickelman, Dale F. 1998. *The Middle East and Central Asia: An Anthropological Approach.* Upper Saddle River: Prentice Hall.

Evans-Pritchard, Edward E. 1949. *The Sanusi of Cyrenaica.* Oxford: Oxford University Press.

Fabietti, Ugo. 1984. *Il popolo del deserto, Gli Shammar del Gran Nefud, Arabia Saudita.* Bari: Laterza.

———. 2000. "State Policies and Bedouin Adaptations in Saudi Arabia, 1900–1980." In *The Transformation of Nomadic Society in the Arab East,* eds. Martha Mundy and Basim Musallam, 82–89. Cambridge: Cambridge University Press.

Fernea, Robert A. 1970. *Shaykh and Effendi: Changing Patterns of Authority Among the El Shabana of Southern Iraq.* Cambridge: Harvard University Press.

Gardner, Ann. 2000. "At Home in South Sinai." *Nomadic Peoples* 4(2):48–67.

Hobbs, Joseph J. 1989. *Bedouin Life in the Egyptian Wilderness.* Austin: University of Texas Press.

———. 1995. *Mount Sinai.* Austin: University of Texas Press.

Hopkins, Nicholas S. 1993. "Small Farmer Households and Agricultural Egypt." In *Sustainable Agriculture in Egypt,* eds. Mohamed A. Faris and Mohmood Hasan Khan, 185–195. Boulder: Lynne Rienner Publishers.

Hopkins, Nicholas S., and Saad Eddin Ibrahim, eds. 1997. *Arab Society: Class, Gender, Power, and Development.* Cairo: The American University in Cairo Press.

Ibrahim, Saad Eddin and Donald P. Cole. 1978. *Saudi Arabian Bedouin: An Assessment of their Needs. Cairo: Cairo Papers in Social Science,* Vol. 1, Monograph 5.

Ingham, Bruce. 1986a. *Bedouin of Northern Arabia: Traditions of the Al-Dhafir.* London: KPI.

———. 1986b. "Notes on the Dialect of the Al Murrah of Eastern and Southern Arabia." *Bulletin of the School of Oriental and African Studies* XLIX(2):271–291.

———. 1997. *Arabian Diversions: Studies on the Dialects of Arabia.* Reading: Ithaca Press.

Jakubowska, Longina. 2000. "Finding Ways to Make a Living: Employment Among the Negev Bedouin." *Nomadic Peoples* 4(2):94–105.

Janzen, Jorg. 1980. *Nomads in the Sultanate of Oman: Tradition and Development in Dhofar,* trans. Alexander Lieven. Boulder: Westview Press.

Johnson, Douglas L. 1973. *Jabal al-Akhdar, Cyrenaica: An Historical Geography of Settlement and Livelihood.* University of Chicago, Department of Geography, Research Paper No. 148.

Khalaf, Sulayman. 1990. "Settlement of Violence in Bedouin Society." *Ethnology* 29:225–242.

———. 1999. "Camel Racing in the Gulf: Notes on the Evolution of a Traditional Cultural Sport." *Anthropos* 94:85–106.

———. 2001. "Globalization and Heritage Revival in the Gulf: An Anthropological Look at Dubai Heritage Village." Paper presented at Meeting of British Society for Middle East Studies.

Kupershoek, P Marcel. 1994. *Oral Poetry and Narratives from Central Arabia I: The Poetry of Ad-Dindan; A Bedouin Bard in Southern Najd.* Leiden: E.J. Brill.

———. 1995. *Oral Poetry and Narratives from Central Arabia II: The Story of a Desert Knight; The Legend of Slewih al-'Atawi and Other 'Utaybah Heroes*. Leiden: E.J. Brill.

———. 1999. *Oral Poetry and Narratives from Central Arabia 3: Bedouin Poets of the Dawasir Tribe; Between Nomadism & Settlement in Southern Najd*. Leiden: Brill.

Lancaster, William. 1981. *The Rwala Bedouin Today*. Cambridge: Cambridge University Press.

Lavie, Smadar. 1990. *The Poetics of Military Occupation: Mizeina Allegories of Bedouin Identity Under Israeli and Egyptian Rule*. Berkeley: University of California Press.

Layne, Linda L. 1994. *The Dialogics of Tribal and National Identities in Jordan*. Princeton: Princeton University Press.

Leeds, Anthony. 1977. "Mythos and Pathos: Some Unpleasantries on Peasantries." In *Peasant Livelihook: Studies in Economic Anthropology and Cultural Ecology*, eds. Rhoda Halperin and John Dow, 227–256. New York: St. Martin's Press.

Lewis, Norman N. 1987. *Nomads and Settlers in Syria and Jordan, 1800–1980*. Cambridge: Cambridge University Press.

———. 2000. "The Syrian Steppe During the Last Century of Ottoman Rule: Hawran and the Palmyrena." In *The Transformation of Nomadic Society in the Arab East*, eds. Martha Mundy and Basim Musallam, 33–43. Cambridge: Cambridge University Press.

Marx, Emanuel. 1967. *Bedouin of the Negev*. Manchester: Manchester University Press.

———. 2000. "Land and Work: Negev Bedouin Struggle with Israeli Bureaucracies." *Nomadic Peoples* 4(2):106–121.

Meeker, Michael E. 1979. *Literature and Violence in North Arabia*. Cambridge: Cambridge University Press.

Meillassoux, Claude. 1981. Meillassoux, Claude. 1981. *Maidens, Meal, and Money: Capitalism and the Domestic Community*. Combridge: Cambridge University Press.

Metral, Francoise. 2000. "Managing Risk: Sheep-rearing and Agriculture in the Syrian Steppe." In *The Transformation of Nomadic Society in the Arab East*, eds. Martha Mundy and Basim Musallam, 123–144. Cambridge: Cambridge University Press.

Meyer Gunther 1996. "Tourism Development in Egypt Overshadowed by Middle East Politics." *Applied Geography and Development* 48:69–84.

Mohamed, Abbas Ahmed. 1980. *White Nile Arabs: Political Leadership and Economic Change*. London: Athlone Press.

Mohsen, Safia Kassem. 1975. *Conflict and Law Among Awlad 'Ali of the Western Desert*. Cairo: National Center for Social and Criminological Research.

Muller-Mahn, Hans-Detlef. 1989. *Die Aulad 'Ali zwischen Stamm und Staat*. Berlin: Dietrich Reimer Verlag.

Mundy, Martha, and Basim Musallam, eds. 2000. *The Transformation of Nomadic Society in the Arab East*. Cambridge: Cambridge University Press.

Murphy, Robert F., and Leonard Kasdan. 1959. "The Structure of Parallel Cousin Marriage." *American Anthropologist* 61:17–29.

Peters, Emrys. 1990. *The Bedouin of Cyrenaica*, ed. J. Goody and E. Marx. Cambridge: Cambridge University Press.

Rowe, Alan G. 1999. "The Exploitation of an Arid Landscape by a Pastoral Society: The Contemporary Eastern Baadia of Jordan." *Applied Geography* 19:345–361.

Sahlins, Marshall. 1972. *Stone Age Economics*. Chicago: Aldine Publishing Company.

Salim, S.M. 1962. *Marsh Dwellers of the Euphrates Delta*. London: Athlone Press.

Sherbiny, Naiem A., Donald P. Cole, and Nadia Makary Girgis. 1994. *Investors and Workers in the Western Desert of Egypt: An Exploratory Survey*. Cairo: Cairo Papers in Social Science, Vol. 15., Monograph 3.

Shoup, John. 1985. "The Impact of Tourism on the Bedouin of Petra." *Middle East Journal* 39(2):277–291.

Shryock, Andrew. 1997. *Nationalism and the Genealogical Imagination: Oral History and Textual Authority in Tribal Jordan*. Berkeley: University of California Press.

Sowayan, Saad A. 1985. Nabati Poetry: *The Oral Poetry of Arabia*. Berkeley: University of California Press.

———. 1992. *The Arabian Oral Historical Narrative: An Ethnographic and Linguistic Analysis*. Wiesbaden: Otto Harrassowitz.

Swidler, W.W. 1973. "Adaptive Processes Regulating Nomad-Sedentary Interaction in the Middle East." *In The Desert and the Sown: Nomads in the Wider Society*, ed. Cynthia Nelson, 23–41. Berkeley: University of California, Institute of International Studies, Research Series, No. 21.

United Nations Development Program. 2002. *Arab Human Development Report: Creating Opportunities for Future Generations*. Amman: Icons Printing Services.

Velud, Christian. 2000. "French Mandate Policy in the Syrian Steppe." *In Transformation of Nomadic Society in Arab East*, eds. Martha Mundy and Basim Musallam, 63–81. Cambridge: Cambridge University Press.

Vidal, F.S. 1975. "Bedouin Migrations in the Ghawar Oil Field, Saudi Arabia." Miami: Field Research Project.

Wickering, Deborah. 1991. *Experience and Expression: Life Among Bedouin Women in South Sinai. Cairo: Cairo Papers in Social Science*, Vol. 14, Monograph 2.

Wilkinson, John C. 1983. "Traditional Concepts of Territory in South East Arabia." *The Geographical Journal* 149(3):301–315.

Wolf, Eric R. 1969. *Peasant Wars of the Twentieth Century*. New York: Harper & Row.

Wolf, Eric R. 1982. *Europe and the People Without History*. Berkeley: University of California Press.

Wooten, Cynthia Alison. 1996. "From Herds of Goats to Herds of Tourists: Negotiating Bedouin Identity Under Petra's 'Romantic Gaze.'" The American University in Cairo, Unpublished M.A. thesis.

Yamani, Mai. 2000. *Changed Identities: The Challenge of the New Generation in Saudi Arabia*. London: Royal Institute of International Affairs.

Young, William C. 1996. *The Rashaayda Bedouin: Arab Pastoralists of Eastern Sudan*. Ft. Worth: Harcourt Brace.

Urban Policy

Fez and the Muslim City

by EDMUND BURKE

THE NINETEENTH-CENTURY FRENCH QUEST FOR VIVID COLORS, pungent odors, and intense emotions that might relieve the oppressive grayness of bourgeois existence looked to the Orient (in this case, the Maghreb) to provide the necessary diversions. As enshrined in the paintings of Eugène Delacroix and the books of Pierre Loti, one city above all loomed in the French imagination as the apotheosis of all that was most captivating, most mysterious in the Orient. It was the Moroccan city of Fez, the "setting sun of Islam." That is to say, a certain image of Fez did—as for the realities, little of a systematic or reliable sort was known about the city until the beginning of the twentieth century.

The contrast between the long period of romantic misinformation about Fez and its society, and the sudden appearance of a more scientifically grounded view, corresponds to the brusque acceleration of the pace of change and the onset of the French colonial offensive in Morocco after 1900. There is no doubt that the Frenchmen whose studies of Fez did so much to transform Western understanding of the city, being good positivists, were convinced that they had accomplished therein a victory for science and rationality. That they also helped lay the foundations for the triumph of French imperialism in Morocco was an unstated source of great satisfaction to them. Today, we are less inclined to vaunt uncritically the virtues of "science" and "progress," and a study of the work of the first generation of French students of Moroccan cities, in particular their work on Fez, raises the question of whether their image of the city differed substantially in its assumptions from that presented by Loti.

This chapter takes up the ethnographic literature on the city of Fez during the period that runs roughly from 1894 until 1925, especially the precolonial period, during which the major outlines of what became the standard view were elaborated. The French ethnography of Fez serves as a kind of touchstone of the concerns of French urban ethnography in Morocco, more generally: the same categories were employed, the same assumptions made, and the same political axes were ground.[1] By studying Fez, we get a sense of the preoccupations of the first generation of French ethnographers. The line of analysis they pursued established the general outlines of French urban studies during the protectorate (1912–56), which lasted until the appearance of the studies of the Casablanca *bidonville* (shantytown) done by Robert Montagne and André Adam.[2] The route to a more adequate sociology of the Maghreb necessarily passes through a reconsideration of the colonial literature. It is not certain that the work of the earlier generation of colonial ethnographers will be diminished by such an inquiry.

AN ORIENTALIST IN FEZ

In February 1900 Auguste Mouliéras arrived in Morocco on an official mission funded by the Ministry of Public Instruction. Charged with studying "the functioning of the University of Fez and native education," he reached Fez on March 1, 1900, and set to work.[3] With his Arabic skills and rapport with Moroccans, he was a skilled field-worker. During his month-and-a-half-long stay he compiled a great deal of information on popular culture in Fez, to be included in his book *Fez*, published in 1902. One chapter of his book on the city was presented originally as a lecture to the Geographical Society of Algiers in 1901.[4] However, the consequences of proceeding straight to Fez without first obtaining the authorization of the *makhzan* soon became clear to him. Without official authorization, no member of the Fasi ulama would talk with him.[5] Eventually Mouliéras was reduced in desperation to paying money to speak with a supposed *alim* (scholar) who in the event turned out to be a fraud. Faced with the failure of his mission, Mouliéras redoubled his efforts. Although eventually he found people with whom he could to speak, none were members of the Fasi ulama. His interviewees included an aged Middle Atlas Berber, whom he encountered in the street; the British vice consul, James McIver MacLeod, about whom he had many misgivings: and representatives of the Jewish community of Fez. (Mouliéras's book contains one of two discussions of the contemporaneous Jewish society of Fez written by a non-Jewish author.)[6] But all these individuals and groups were marginal to Fasi Muslim society. While Mouliéras's *Fez* contains many remarkable flights of orientalist erudition (see, for example, his discussion of the different theories regarding the origins of the name of the city, the origins of the different Moroccan dynasties, or the origins of the *istiksa* prayer), he could have written them without leaving his study.[7] It is as an ethnographer that he falls down.

Initially, Mouliéras managed to establish a rapport with the Moroccans he encountered, but he became increasingly frustrated by his inability to find viable interlocutors among the Fasi ulama. Over the course of his stay, his militantly antireligious and anti-Islamic attitudes came to the surface, drawing him into violent arguments with Moroccans time and again.[8] Evoking the alleged homicidal cruelty of Moroccan rulers, including Abd al-Aziz, the then incumbent, he denounced them as "vampire sultans," implying thereby a genetic trait common to the dynasty, if not to Moroccans generally. Later, he bitterly deplored "the leaden cloak of Islam, bearing in its folds, wherever it exists, silence and darkness." Succeeding at one point in being invited to a performance of the celebrated young Fasi female singer Brika, once she began singing he was quickly disabused by her voice: "The marvelous larynx of the biggest star of Fez still rings in my ears a year later, and it is likely that the hoarse and cracked voice of Brika will remain in my memory as the archetype of human mooing in its ugliest explosion."[9] The last part of his book abounds in impassioned denunciations of Moroccan culture, a veritable bestiary of orientalist prejudices. By the end of his stay he could not wait to leave in what he seems to have come to regard as the fieldwork experience from hell. Thus Mouliéras's *Fez* is the record of an ethnographic and personal failure. Undone in part by his irascibility, prejudice, and impetuosity, he would never again be entrusted with a study mission to Morocco.

The brevity of Mouliéras's stay (barely six weeks) and the fact that he proceeded in defiance of Moroccan regulations calling for all researchers to apply for an official authorization no doubt helped shape the final outcome. More consequential was his orientalist obscurantism, a trait that links his work to the rest of the École d'Alger.

Although Mouliéras's work ethic and the ingenuity with which he interrogated his informants are genuinely impressive, in the end his work failed to make its knowledge accessible in a form in which it could be put to use, and thus failed to command the respect of policy planners. Neither empiricist in the manner of the Bureaux arabes (which sought to quantify numbers of tents, people, horses, rifles, etc.) nor sociological after the fashion of the Durkheimians (who sought to link "facts" to a theoretically guided interpretive scheme), from a policy planner's point of view Mouliéras's work was simply illegible. Full of literary flourishes, personal asides, *obiter dicta,* and feats of pure erudition, Mouliéras's *Fez* (and his *Le Maroc inconnu*) reflected the mentality of a French provincial *société savante* (learned society) more than that of a modern sociological inquiry. While we do not know how the Ministry of Public Instruction (which funded his research in *Fez*) responded to Mouliéras's report on his fieldwork, it is doubtful that French policymakers found it of much utility. Despite or because of its idiosyncratic aspects, Mouliéras's *Fez* thus provides us with a stick by which measure the work of other French observers.

For a number of reasons, urban studies constituted the core around which the interests of the early students of Moroccan society tended to gravitate. Fez in particular, because of its religious and commercial importance, excited a great deal of attention. Other cities studied were Tangier, Tetouan, Rabat, El Ksar el Kebir, Marrakech, and the coastal cities of Casablanca, Mazagan, Safi, Mogodor, and Oudjda. French policymakers were convinced that mastery of the cities was key to the eventual establishment of a protectorate. after 1912, this interest was carried forward in a series of volumes under the collective title Villes et Tribus du Maroc, which were prepared by the native affairs section of the protectorate administration. Cities of course were more easily studied than the perennially fractious tribal populations (which were mostly off-limits to French observers in the period 1900–1912). Finally, there was a French intellectual school of urban studies that traced its roots to Fustel de Coulanges's *La cité antique* (1864). Émile Masqueray's important thesis on Algeria, *La formation des cités chez les populations sédentaires de l'Algérie* (1886), played an important role in stimulating research on Maghrebi cities.[10]

Given these concerns, it is no surprise that the French should have been vitally interested in obtaining precise information about Fez. The city had long been regarded as one of the essential keys to Morocco, since it was the political and religious capital of the country, as well as a center of trade and commerce of national scale. Yet if Morocco in general was only dimly known in 1900, Fez itself was a riddle of great proportions, and its merchant class and intransigent ulama made it a real threat to French diplomatic strategy. Before 1902, few Europeans had visited Fez, save for diplomats on brief missions to the royal court. French consular representation at Fez was only permitted in 1892. The difficulty of communications with the coast and the fragility of government control over the nearby tribes helped to delay European penetration. From 1897 until 1902 the sultan resided in Marrakech, and there was a hiatus in French interest in Fez. Not until March 1902, when the court once again took up residence at Fez, did the city return to the spotlight.

The French ethnographic literature on Fez before 1904 (if the term *ethnographic* is not too grandiose—perhaps we should speak of proto-ethnography) was limited to a few travel accounts (including one by a French doctor[11]) and works of folklore by Georges Delphin and Auguste Mouliéras.[12] None of these works could lay claim to serious scientific status, although to this day they retain a certain musty charm. A more systematic study of the city was evidently called for. An excellent beginning was made in 1904 with the publication of a series of articles in the *Revue de Paris*. They were the work of an experienced French diplomat writing under the pseudonym of Eugène Aubin.[13] The following year saw the appearance of Henri Gaillard's *Une ville d'Islam: Fez*,[14] as well as a series of articles by Charles René-Leclerc on the economy of Fez,[15] and the first of a series of articles in *AM* devoted primarily to the role of Islam in the life of the city.[16] By 1912, the picture was all but complete: thereafter the literature largely fills in the blanks, adding detail and color rather than developing new categories of analysis. The relatively short time required for the elaboration of an ethnography of Fez (the same is true of Morocco more generally) is quite striking. So too is the development of certain topics, and the neglect of others. The only significant opening of a new topic was the emergence of studies of the artisan craft guilds of Fez, beginning with the work of Louis Massignon.[17] Seen against this background, Roger Le Tourneau's *Fès avant le protectorat*[18] stands as a fitting capstone to a tradition of urban ethnography and social history that began in 1904 with the work of Aubin.

An important aspect of the research on Morocco before 1912 is the explicitly political context in which it developed. The unleashing of the French colonial offensive coincided with the first publications on Morocco. The establishment of the Comité du Maroc and the Mission scientifique du Maroc (MSM) in 1903 signaled an upsurge of interest in Morocco in French colonial circles. French preoccupation with the Moroccan question has much to do with the questions French colonial circles asked and the categories of analysis they developed. The ethnographers of Fez thus embarked on their researches with one general purpose in mind—to further the development of French interests in Morocco, at the expense of European rivals. What this boiled down to was the search for the key to Moroccan society, the secret or secrets that, once known, would enable Frenchmen to plan policies regarding Morocco with the least possible disruption of Moroccan society, and the least expense of blood and treasure on the part of France. The utilitarian concept of ethnography had a number of important consequences for their analysis, influencing what they chose to treat and what they left out, as well as shaping the general context into which they sought to fit their picture of Fez.

Who were the ethnographers to whom we owe the very impressive list of works outlined above? One of the first things to be observed about them is that with only two exceptions, all were diplomats. That is to say, they were drawn from the ranks of French diplomatic personnel in Morocco, although not all of them continued to pursue such a career. Career diplomats like Henri Gaillard and Eugène Aubin [Coullard-Descos],[19] consular officials like Édouard Michaux-Bellaire,[20] and interpreters like Louis Martin and Léon Pérétié[21] were among the major contributors to the emerging ethnographic literature on Fez. Only Georges Salmon,[22] the young head of the MSM, and Charles René-Leclerc,[23] head of the Tangier office of the CM, can be excluded from this generalization. In the absence of French academic experts on Moroccan society, this in itself is not too surprising: where else could the necessary expertise have come from?

A second observation about the background of these men also suggests itself. None were trained ethnographers (the field was little developed in France at the time), and only a few of the authors discussed here had prior experience in an Arabic-speaking country. The ethnography of Fez (and to a large extent that of Morocco as well) in the period was the work of nonprofessional observers (some of whom had decades of in-country experience). Here one must distinguish between those who came before 1902, and those who came after. Michaux-Bellaire and Gaillard had lived in Morocco since the 1890s and had an intimate knowledge of the language and customs there. Gaillard was the French vice-consul at Fez from 1900 and had served previously in other posts in Morocco. Michaux-Bellaire had briefly served as acting vice-consul at Fez in 1895–96, otherwise living in Tangier and El Ksar for a prolonged period.

Another striking feature of the work of the ethnographers of Fez is the fact that the academics worked not as individuals, but as part of research teams. The MSM is perhaps the clearest example of this tendency. As we have seen, *Archives marocaines* published a series of articles all derived from Salmon's 1906 research trip.[24] It is the division of labor pioneered by the MSM that most resembles the operations of a contemporary social science research team. Even seemingly individual achievements such as the works of Gaillard and Aubin turn out upon examination to be based on the collaboration of a number of assistants and local informants. In Aubin's case, Kaddour Ben Ghabrit (1873–1954), the counselor on Muslim law of the French Legation at Tangier, provided vital assistance. An Algerian Muslim born in Sidi Bel Abbes and a graduate of the Médersa franco-arabe of Tlemcen, Ben Ghabrit was perfectly at home in French drawing rooms and the homes of the Fasi bourgeoisie. He was able to exploit his position to make himself an essential intermediary between the French and the Moroccan elite. At this point in his Moroccan career, Ben Ghabrit was still developing the ties that he would later exploit to such advantage.[25] Already his knowledge of Fasi society was legendary. Aubin's *Morocco Today* quickly became an essential reference for Europeans interested in Morocco.[26]

The early generation of French ethnographers was interested first in the role of Islam in the life of the city. A great deal of attention was devoted to exploring its complexities. In particular, there was considerable interest in the role of the shrine of Mawlay Idris, the founder and patron saint of Fez. In addition, the sprawling interrelated and very influential Idrisi sharifian families also excited attention. A motivating factor in this choice may well have been the influence of Fustel de Coulanges's *Cité antique*, with its discussion of ancestor cults.[27] But there were clearly other important reasons for their concern. One was the prevalent opinion that Moroccan Islam represented the greatest obstacle to the establishment of a French protectorate, representing a badge of nationality and a nucleus around which resistance might crystallize. Thus a careful understanding of Moroccan Islam, and especially the religious institutions and classes of Fez—given the importance of Fez and the Idrisi sharifs elsewhere in Morocco—was essential for French policymakers. The MSM research group took the lead in exploring these topics. Together with Aubin and Gaillard, they sought to focus attention on the role of the religious brotherhoods (Ar. pl. *turuq*) in Fez, and on the chief mosques and madrasas of the city. In particular the role of the Qarawiyin mosque university was stressed. Finally, they outlined the importance of the Fasi religious scholars and sharifs in forming public opinion in the city, and throughout Morocco. The major families of sharifs were delineated, their genealogies studied, and their present-day influence assessed. In keeping with the flavor of the times, these studies emphasized the religious intolerance of the Fasi ulama toward Europeans.

A second major subject of interest to the ethnographers of Fez were the no-tables (Ar. *a'yan*). Not really a class, not exactly a caste either, the notables were the wealthy merchants, local officials, and others who dominated the political and economic life of the city. French scholars were interested in the social composition of the *a'yan,* the distinctive traits of the Fasi bourgeois mentality, and the uneasy relationship between Old Fez (Fas al-bali) and New Fez (Fas al-jadid). Much of this illustrated the "manners and customs" variety of reportage so characteristic of early ethnography: the collection of social traits, rituals, and beliefs, rather than the analysis of the structure of kinship, or of the symbolic religious structures. Aubin, for example, presented the first convincing portrait of that complex of genteel customs, language, and dress that marked off the bourgeoisie from the artisans and workers of Fez, and distinguished the urban population from the people of the countryside. Both Aubin and Gaillard underscored the role of the *a'yan* in resisting the centralizing efforts of the *makhzan*.[28] Michaux-Bellaire, writing in 1922 with the benefit of a decade of hindsight, notes:

> Only Fez presents the particularity rather rare in Morocco of having a real bourgeoisie composed of wholesalers, merchants, and artisans. The head of the principal commercial establishments had under their sway not only the less wealthy members of their own families, but also a numerous clientele of employees, workers, and those in their debt: they were real merchant princes, who recall the patricians of Carthage, or more recently, of the Italian republics.[29]

Since the opposition of the *a'yan* could be dangerous to French plans, a major focus of French policy during the pre-protectorate period was determining how the *a'yan* might be won over to the French cause, or effectively neutralized.[30] The portrait of the Fasi notability in the pages of the French ethnographers is one of a proud, suspicious, and cultivated merchant class, not unaware of the balance of forces in the world, but imprisoned by its avarice and its fears of rural unrest.

The Fasi economy was a third major focus of French interest. Since Fez occupied a position of great importance in the economy of Morocco, and Fasi merchants con-stituted an important group of potential intermediaries, knowledge of their business methods and their situation at Fez might be useful. Potential French investors and merchants were naturally interested in knowing more about their Muslim business partners. The research of Charles René-Leclerc, head of the Tangier office of the

CM, into the economy of Fez was published in 1905 in *Renseignements coloniaux*, a monthly supplement to *Afrique française*.[31] Relying on statistical information provided by Gaillard, as well as on materials gathered locally by his network of informants, René-Leclerc was able to specify for the first time how the merchants of Fez had been able to exploit their privileged position to become the single most important group of economic middlemen in Morocco. He produced the first general portrait of the extent of Fasi trade with Europe, Africa, and the Near East, and examined in detail the circumstances of the production, pricing, and marketing of goods at Fez—all items of concern to French business interests. Finally, he provided an important glimpse into the structure and operation of the artisan craft guilds of Fez. (It might be remarked parenthetically that the economy of Fez was of little interest to the MSM group, who were far more fascinated with religious matters, and that the best study on the subject was written by the local agent of the French colonial lobby.)

A final area of concern of the early researchers on Fez was the structure, internal functioning, and composition of the Moroccan government, the *makhzan*.[32] Since the court resided at Fez more or less continuously from 1902 until 1912, and the bureaucracy was staffed by the graduates of the madrasas of Fez, no study of Fez could be complete without detailed treatment of the *makhzan*. It was Aubin who provided the most detailed and convincing description of the operations of the *makhzan*. Together with Gaillard, Aubin subjected the manners, customs, and recruitment of *makhzan* officials to scrutiny, and underscored the interpenetration of the *makhzan* elite and the notability of Fez. Gaillard and Aubin noted the traditional rivalry between the two major sections of Fez: the city of the government, Fas al-jadid, and the old city of Fez, Fas al-bali. Since the French government from 1904 onward pursued a policy of close collaboration with the *makhzan*, detailed knowledge of the habits of the bureaucracy was obviously important. If France were to be able to establish a protectorate, such information would be at a premium in the planning of policy.

The French ethnographic literature on Fez produced between 1904 and 1912 remains to this day an enormously impressive achievement. As a portrait of Fez on the eve of the protectorate, it is notable for its amplitude and detail. Without it, subsequent scholars would have had a much more difficult time. From the vantage point of the postcolonial present, however, the image of Fez as it emerges from this collection of diverse materials was based on a number of questionable assumptions, to which we now turn.

FEZ AND THE MUSLIM CITY

French ethnographers tended to assume that Morocco was somehow immune to the forces that were in the process of transforming the rest of the world. The assumption was especially tempting, since according to the tenets of the evolutionary views then in favor in anthropology, "survivals" were to be expected, and Morocco seemed a particularly clear example of such a survival.[33] If Morocco were assumed to be unchanging, then Fez could easily be viewed as a traditional Islamic city, somehow miraculously preserved into the twentieth century. The high walls that surrounded the city, its narrow winding streets and bustling *suq*-s, all reinforced the impression of archaism. Only later was it discovered how far wrong this judgment was. Research by historians such as Roger Le Tourneau (whose *Fès avant le protectorat* remains the reference point by which all else is measured) and Jean-Louis Miège has demonstrated that the colonial assumptions of an unchanging Morocco are erroneous.[34] Already well before the protectorate, Fasi society had undergone far-reaching social and economic change. Much the same is true in the cultural sphere, as the research of Évariste Lévi-Provençal and Abdullah Laroui has demonstrated.[35] Fez (and Morocco more generally) was undergoing a literary renaissance of important dimensions before 1912. Fez was thus neither unchanging nor cut off from the currents of thought that were in the process of transforming the Arab and Muslim world.

The assumption of ethnographers of Fez that the urban notables were the key to winning the city has already been touched on. If France could secure the support of key *makhzan* officials, religious leaders, and wealthy merchants, they believed, then Fez could be easily controlled. Behind this assumption of the dominance of the notables, it now seems clear, there stands an additional, more theoretical assumption—namely, that Moroccan society was an organic entity in which the various parts were integrated into one another, and that there was an identifiable "head."[36] This head, our observers theorized, was the *a'yan*. This assumption in turn, in the minds of at least some of the ethnographers, may have been connected to the Durkheimian notion of organic solidarity. While this assumption was not totally unwarranted (and in fact Lyautey was later to erect a native policy on the assumption of the primacy of the notability in Fasi politics, together with the assumption of an unchanging Morocco), it misled French ethnographers into an almost fatal misjudgment of the people of Fez's capacity for resistance.

Time and time again, French experts were taken by surprise by the outbreak of urban unrest and political resistance to French colonial aspirations. In 1904–5 a coalition of *makhzan* officials, religious scholars (ulama) and secular notables succeeded (with German support) in blocking a French protectorate. This opposition had not been foreseen. While the outcome of the Algeciras conference (1906) restored French claims to predominance in Morocco under an international mandate, Moroccan resistance had by no means ended. Indeed, it merely intensified. Again, the role of Fez was critical to the outcome. In December 1907 and January 1908, a series of violent riots and popular disturbances (also unforeseen by French observers) broke out at Fez. The ulama were compelled by the mob to depose Abd al-Aziz as sultan and name his brother, Abd al-Hafiz, to the throne on a platform of militant resistance to the French. Again in 1911 Fez occupied center stage, when a rural insurrection made common cause with popular forces in the city, and almost succeeded in overthrowing Sultan Abd al-Hafiz. Finally, in April 1912, a mutiny of Moroccan troops against their French instructors at Fez sparked a major urban revolt, which was only repressed with heavy loss of life on all sides.[37] In each of these instances, French Morocco experts had been wrong in their predictions. Given the considerable sophistication of their analysis of Fasi society, the question naturally arises, How could this have happened?

Several answers suggest themselves. One is that French Morocco experts were incorrect, or only partially correct, in their conclusions that the *a'yan* controlled Fez. The resistance to the French reform program in 1904–5 was largely the result of the political intervention of the *a'yan* and ulama of Fez. According to the prevailing theory the notables' role in the struggle might have been predicted, since it agreed with the paradigm of notable dominance. But the popular movements in 1907–8, 1911, and 1912 did not conform to this paradigm. Instead the social turmoil and resistance efforts were directed against the *a'yan* themselves, as well as against the French. In each of these instances, while some notables and ulama became involved with the movement, it was popular forces based in the city and the adjacent countryside that took a major role in determining the course of events. It is perhaps understandable that the French ethnographers of Fez should have been quite unprepared for the possibility of an initiative from below. The social origins of most of the ethnographers were impeccably bourgeois, and this gave them a natural sympathy for their Moroccan counterparts. In French society before World War I, moreover, the preponderance of notables at all levels of society was marked, and social forces were only beginning to emerge. Not for nothing was the Third

Republic popularly known as "La République des notables." Thus it was natural that French ethnographers should leave the lower classes of Fez out of their equation. Still, in the face of events that did not accord with the paradigm, one might think that their previous understanding would have been revised. It was not.

The individuals who made up the 1905 MSM research team on Fez were not unaware of the political and intellectual ferment. Their articles bear witness to their thoroughness, if not their perspicacity. But their assumption that Moroccan Islam was unchanging was so deeply rooted that they simply did not grasp the significance of the facts. Instead they sought to explain the popular unrest of 1907–8, 1911, and 1912 as the result of Moroccan anarchy and xenophobia. These traits were allegedly characteristic of Moroccan national culture and were the natural response of an archaic social organism when confronted with one of greater complexity and a higher level of development. Thus reasoned our ethnographers. In this way they managed to avoid dealing with the question of whether Moroccans were influenced by ideologies and currents of thought other than those presumed to derive from the so-called traditional character of their society. Blinded by orientalist stereotypes, the French never seem to have noticed the existence of Moroccan national sentiment. Nor did they ever focus on the political role of the Moroccan ulama in the pre-protectorate period. Yet as several recent studies have shown, the social movements of these years cannot be explained except through reference to the roles of the *a'yan* and the ulama.[38] Despite the major role in the important events at Fez in the period played by Muhammad ibn al-Kabir al-Kattani, an *alim* and leader of an important religious brotherhood at Fez with a sizable lower-class clientele (to cite just the most striking example), no serious French study of the role of his role, or that of his *tariqa*, the Kattaniya, exists.[39] Such gaps in the literature were more than mere oversights, and a recognition of the context in which French ethnographers worked can help us to understand the real significance of such omissions.

Most French experts were convinced that there was little or no connection between the city of Fez and the rural populations living in its environs. This left many unexplained lacunae in their portrait of the economic ties between Fez and the surrounding tribes. One assumption was that the tribes were autarchic. A second related assumption was that the goods manufactured in Fez were intended either for the consumption of the court or for export. Events like the tribal involvement in the popular uprisings of 1907–8 and 1911, which might have cast doubt on this belief, since they revealed the close collaboration of urban and rural insurgents, remained unexplainable anomalies. One person who grasped the significance of the connection between Fez and its hinterland was Michaux-Bellaire, and even he was not always consistent in this regard.[40] In 1922 he characterized it this way:

> The relations of the Berber tribes who supplied it with merchandise and from which it received the products required for its food and its industries made Fez the true market for Berbers of the central and eastern regions of Morocco. This resulted in a political bond based on a community of interests that oft en allowed the Fasi bourgeoisie to stand up to the *makhzan* and even to plot against it thanks to the support of the Berber tribes.[41]

More recent studies have emphasized the close connections between Fez and the surrounding countryside, the constant flow of men and goods into and out of the city from nearby areas, and the multiplicity of relationships between the two.[42] It is at this point that the wider political and intellectual context in which the studies of Fez took place becomes relevant, for, in fact, the assumptions that were made about the nature of Morocco and Moroccan society were widely shared at the time. These assumptions in turn appear connected with both the circumstances of French political involvement in Morocco, and the set of stereotypes about Morocco that accompanied it. Beginning in 1904, with the signing of the Anglo-French entente, France acquired a vested interest in Morocco, and with it in the continued existence of the *makhzan*. To cloak French colonial ambitions in a mantle of respectability, and thereby preserve the government from either international criticism or domestic political opposition, French policy emphasized close cooperation between the French government and the Moroccan government in the institution of needed reforms. This policy of peaceful penetration depended on the tacit acquiescence of the Moroccan government. In this way France could expand its influence in Morocco and eventually substitute itself for the *makhzan* without risking either a major war of conquest or the inevitable delays that it would have occasioned. The patriotic resistance of Moroccan tribes was recoded as the traditional opposition of *bled el siba* to the authority of the *makhzan*.[43] As long as France enjoyed a clear military superiority there was no need for an alternative explanation based on a reanalysis of the social setting and the roots of resistance.

The emergence of this *makhzan* policy coincided with a sudden change in the way French ethnographers depicted Moroccan society. As we have seen above, before 1904, French ethnographers emphasized the openness, flexibility, and absence of sharp cleavages in Moroccan society. But starting in 1904, when France acquired a vested interest in the *makhzan,* this nuanced and balanced portrait gave way to one based on a series of dichotomous images, including the supposed opposition between *makhzan* and *siba,* Berber and Arab, and city and country. These stereotypes dominated French ethnography right to the end of the protectorate. Thus French policy during the period of the Moroccan question, and the image of Morocco that crystallized during this period, were mutually reinforcing. By seizing on a few aspects of the society and paying less attention to others that were no less important, French ethnographers and politicians helped to generate a series of stereotypes about Morocco that lasted well beyond the lifetime of the protectorate. Such a stereotypical image of Morocco survived because it best seemed to explain the peculiarities of pre-protectorate Morocco, and at the same time provided a convincing rationale for French colonial dominance.[44]

FEZ: THE REVOLUTION AND AFTER

The occupation of Fez in June 1911 by the French caught the city's population completely offguard. The long siege of the city by the tribes had placed peoples' nerves on edge. Food supplies were low, and the possibility of a riot was never far from the minds of the upper class. At first, the merchants and notables of Fez were initially surprisingly willing to accept the French occupation. The restoration of order, they reasoned, would be good for business, and would no doubt soon lead to the improvement of communications between Fez and the coast. This also promised to work to their advantage. Unfortunately for them, what transpired in the months that intervened between the occupation and the signing of the protectorate treaty was a prolonged period of economic stagnation. The presence of the French army, in fact, tended to drive prices up, and there were constant incidents of jostling in the crowded streets of the city between townspeople and French troops. Clumsy administrative decisions by the Fez Native Affairs Bureau further aggravated the situation. The French native affairs officers, moreover, had no previous Moroccan experience. Many of them spoke no Arabic, and even those who did carried over their habits of rough treatment of natives acquired in service in Algeria and Tunisia.

By March of 1912, not only the artisans and common people but also increasingly many of the notables were feeling alienated from the French. The news of the signing of the protectorate treaty, accordingly, arrived in this political atmosphere with all of the effect of a bomb. The mutiny of *makhzan* troops against their French instructors on April 17 soon spread to the population of the city and led to several days of rioting and looting, primarily at the expense of the hapless Jewish population whose quarter of the city, the *mel-lah,* was looted and burned to the ground. The widespread unrest at Fez posed an immediate political problem for the new resident-general, Hubert Lyautey. Given the importance of Fez in the political life of the country, reassuring the notables and ulama of the city was crucial. One thing was certain: the policies adopted by Lyautey's predecessors were a complete failure. Lack of foresight, lack of experience, and a complete insensitivity to the pride and aspirations of the notables of Fez, together with lack of firm direction from above, were all in varying proportions responsible for the debacle. Under the circumstances a new analysis and a new policy were clearly needed. What had gone wrong?

French assumptions about the nature of Fez and Fasi society were entirely consonant with the stereotypes of the Moroccan gospel. The Fez revolts of 1907–8 and 1911, while offering warning signs that these understandings were defective, did not lead to a reevaluation. The mutiny of *makhzan* troops at Fez in March 1912 and the siege of the city that followed a month later soon changed French views. The suddenness and violence of the upheaval demonstrated the inadequacy of French ethnography of Morocco as well as the limitations of French power. Nothing in the Moroccan gospel prepared the French for the close alliance of rural and urban groups during the four-day siege. Nor could it explain the active participation of Fasi notables in the revolt. The 1912 popular upheaval at Fez cleared the way for a new French analysis of Fez and of Moroccan society.

Once order had been restored in and around the city, Lyautey turned to the task of setting the relations between Fez and the new protectorate government on a solid footing. He decided to try a new approach. The Fez Native Affairs Bureau, which dealt with the internal affairs of the city, was drastically overhauled, and its personnel changed. A brilliant young Arabist officer, Captain Georges Mellier, was placed in charge.[45] He organized a series of meetings between Lyautey and representative groups from different segments of the population of the city. Lyautey made an effort to put the notables at ease by assuring them that France had no intention of interfering with the religious freedom of Moroccans, and by strongly implying that it would be much more advantageous for them to cooperate with France than to oppose it. The new resident general spoke with a slightly different emphasis to each group. For example, he promised a group of students from the madrasas of the city that their annual rations (*mouna*) would regularly be paid and even increased, leaving unstated but clearly understood that the students had best stick to their books and keep their noses out of politics. Through the good offices of the British consul, James McLeod, Lyautey sought out Mawlay Idris ibn Abd al-Hadi, an influential uncle of the incumbent sultan, to reassure him as to French intentions and to seek his advice in the current situation. Such meetings and interviews went far to regain for France some degree of trust. In addition, and perhaps most importantly in the short run, Lyautey saw to it that the repressive measures instituted following the mutiny of April were withdrawn, or greatly reduced. As an act of clemency, many of the prisoners arrested following the mutiny were released, and the fines that had been imposed on the notables of Fez were canceled. Orders were given to French troops billeted outside the city to refrain from offending the city's inhabitants with such arrogant acts as riding at a gallop through the narrow, crowded streets. French officers were instructed on the potential dangers of unrestrained displays of French pride, such as elaborate victory ceremonials, flag raisings, and the like. Henceforth, French officers were to observe model decorum in their relationships with the citizens of Fez.[46]

While steps were being taken to lower the French profile in Fez, a daring new policy was in the process of being formulated and approved by the resident-general. It called for the establishment of an elective municipal council with control over the budget of the city, as well as an elected municipal government. The impetus for the project came from the French consul at Fez, Henri Gaillard, who had been engaged in working out the scheme since the French occupation of Fez in June 1911. The bitter feud between the diplomats and the military (a rivalry in which the military seemed to have the upper hand) had until then kept Gaillard's scheme in the background as an essentially Quai d'Orsay initiative. Lyautey was himself too much of a diplomat and too much of a pragmatist to allow such a dispute to interfere with policy planning for the new protectorate government. Especially in view of the dramatic failure of previous French policy toward the population of Fez, and the necessity of restoring order and regaining the political trust of the Fasi elite, the risks entailed in adopting so liberal a policy would be more than compensated for were it to be successful. If the policy were to fail, the degree of alienation of the notables of Fez could hardly be greater than it was already. Drawing on his almost twenty years of experience living in Fez, Gaillard possessed an unrivaled knowledge of the Fasi bourgeoisie. He was well aware of their sensitivities and pride and had already proven his understanding of the intricate web of patronage and genealogy that constituted the core of the political system of the city. Gaillard's knowledge of *makhzan* and palace circles rendered him all but irreplaceable in the present instance. In matters of native policy he was known as an admirer of British rule in Egypt, especially of the administration of Alexandria instituted under Lord Cromer. Lyautey was thus exercising shrewd political judgment in deciding to allow Fez to have a measure of municipal self-government.

In addition to the influence of Gaillard, Lyautey leaned heavily on the advice and experience of another old Fez hand, British consul James McIver McLeod. It was McLeod who advised him of the adverse political effects of the repressive failures instituted by Lyautey's predecessor, General Moinier. Some of the oldest and most influential Fasi merchants were British protégés, and McLeod enjoyed access to other segments of Fasi society that remained out of reach for the French. During the summer of 1912, McLeod found himself much occupied in filling the role of mediator between the new protectorate government and the Fasi notability. It was through the efforts of McLeod that the French were able to transform what had been in June a singularly embittered and suspicious Fasi elite into one willing to take part in an experiment in municipal self-government.

There were in fact several precedents for the establishment of the Fez municipality. One was the convening of a council of the leading members of the Moroccan elite, known as a *majlis al-a'yan*, to consider the 1904 French reform proposals.[47] A second was the ad hoc system of rule known as *shaykh al-rabia*, by which Fez governed itself during the civil war in 1907–8 and the 1911 siege.[48] Each quarter of the city selected by popular acclamation one or more prominent notables who would serve as guarantors of the security of their quarter. The selected notables in turn assembled in common and co-opted from among their number one or more individuals to serve as overall leaders of the city during the time of troubles. A ritual exchange of turbans and *silhams* (cloaks) among those selected, as in the case of other ad hoc alliances in Morocco, known as '*ar*, meant that the participants were constrained under threat of a spiritual kin bond to work together to maintain order.[49] An individual so selected was called a *shaykh al-rabia*. With these proto-representative institutions to build on and a strong sense of Fasi municipal pride, the French architects of a Muslim-Arab municipality for Fez were on relatively solid ground.

The *majlis al-baladi* (municipal council) was established by a decree (*dahir*) of September 2, 1912, addressed to the pasha of Fez.[50] It consisted of fifteen members, with the pasha of Fez serving as president. Seven of the members served ex officio as members of the municipal administration (the pasha and his three *khalifas* [chief assistants], the two *muhtasibs* [provosts of the market] of Old and New Fez, and the *na'ib* [deputy] of the *majlis,* serving as secretary). Eight additional elected members were selected for two-year terms from among the notables of Fez, two for each of the four voting districts of the city. Finally, two additional members of the municipal council were appointed who served in a purely advisory capacity and possessed no vote. They were the *amin al-mustafad,* formerly the treasurer of the city revenues, and the secretary-interpreter, charged with preparing the minutes of the meetings. The French chief of municipal services was an ex officio member. An alternate member was elected in each of the voting districts in the event of the illness or incapacity of one of those officially elected.[51]

Considerable pains were taken by the French to ensure that eligible notables cast their votes in the elections. Following the establishment of lists of eligible electors, discussion and amendment to the lists presented were allowed. Voting districts were created following the traditional divisions of the city, with New Fez counting as one district, and Old Fez being divided into the municipal quarters of Lemtiyine, Andalousiyine, and Adwa. A total of 374 notables were eligible to vote, and, of that number, 258 actually did so. Elections took place over the four-day period stretching from September 8 to 11, and a second ballot was held in one of the quarters because of a tie vote for the alternate. The results were an impressive testimony to the openness of the elections: of the twelve men elected, only one was a French protégé and included were five other protégés—three British, two Italian, and one German. Considering that the vote was held in the early forenoon of the first day of the Muslim month of Ramadan, the voting turnout was quite good. The ages of those elected ranged from 28 to 44, apparently on the principle that younger men, better acquainted with the ways of the West, would be more successful representatives in the new council. Several elderly merchants, who expected to win election automatically, discovered to their chagrin that they received only their own votes. In fact, since the seven ex officio members were all French appointees, the election of one French protégé was enough to tip the balance within the council to the French.[52]

Having badly misjudged the situation in Fez in the spring, the French seemed eager to atone for past errors. The elections to the *majlis al-baladi* and the appointment of Captain Mellier to head the Fez Arab Bureau persuaded the Fasi notables that Lyautey now understood that he could not take the cooperation of the Fasi ulama and the *a'yan* for granted. In the new political calculus, good relations with the Fasi *a'yan* and ulama required more than just a show of consultation. At first, the

Fez *majlis* functioned well. Elections were held biannually for staggered terms, and the number of participating notables steadily increased.[53] Soon, however, delegates to the *majlis* found themselves systematically thwarted by the Fez Arab Bureau in their ability to vote on certain issues.[54] By 1914 the experiment of municipal self-government was clearly losing its steam. The successors to Captain Mellier came from colonial Algeria and brought with them their colonial attitudes toward the natives. Although Lyautey had wanted to make the Fez *majlis* a model for the rest of Morocco, he was forced to recognize that this form of municipal administration was unlikely to work in the coastal cities that were under the influence of French settlers. Instead mixed municipal councils were created, in which the French delegates freely exerted their authority over the Moroccan representatives. A final blow was the establishment of separate European *villes nouvelles,* which led to the withdrawal of funds from the Arab medinas. By the end of Lyautey's tenure as resident-general in 1924, a social gulf separated the French and the Moroccans in all Moroccan cities (including Fez by this time).[55]

In 1922 Édouard Michaux-Bellaire, the head of the MSM, the analysis division of the Native Affairs Bureau, was commissioned to evaluate what had gone wrong. In a confidential memorandum he reviewed the history of the *majlis al-baladi.* After a good start, things had begun to go sour. The Fasi bourgeoisie were cruelly disappointed. They had expected to play the same influential role in Morocco under the protectorate as they had before 1912, and at first they had. But after the transfer of the administration of the city of Fez to civilian control (*controle civil*), it was clear to the Fasi bourgeoisie that their opinions were no longer taken into account. Instead they were informed of administrative decisions after the fact. At the same time a host of discriminatory regulations and petty municipal taxes were imposed without their input. Taken together with their unfulfilled economic hopes, the result was that French legitimacy was seriously undermined. Michaux-Bellaire contrasted the attitude of the pre-1912 *makhzan* toward the Fasi elite with that of the 1920s protectorate administration. Before the protectorate the government had "always treated Fez with understanding … [and] always *took account of* the bourgeoisie of Fez and … refrained from governing them like a Bedouin population … it didn't treat them like natives [*bicots*]."[56]

In retrospect the inauguration of the *majlis al-baladi* at Fez in September 1912 was the turning point that did not turn. Although the old orientalist paradigms had failed either to predict or to explain the April/May 1912 uprisings, and a new analysis of Morocco and of Fasi society seemed required, one might have expected a discursive shift in French understandings of Morocco. But this did not occur. Because of France's enormous military superiority, the opinions of Moroccans, even the opinions of the Fasi elite, were superfluous. The need for collaboration with the Fasi elite faded with each French victory. The discursive power of the Moroccan gospel and the entrenched institutional culture of the colonial military bureaucracy proved more than a match for the forces for change. The replacement of Arab Bureau officers by civilian *contrôleurs civils* and the division of Moroccan cities into modern (predominantly French) *ville nouvelles* and traditional (and entirely Moroccan) medinas after the war completed the reassertion of the old paradigms. Except in moments of crisis, when the *majlis al-baladi* at Fez was still useful as a kind of political thermometer, by 1919 it had become a fossilized appendage of the native affairs bureaucracy.[57] For a critical understanding of the postwar context, we turn again to Michaux-Bellaire:

> In politics, you can't do [Pierre] Loti [an author of orientalist fantasies]. The muezzin's chants, the minarets, the old mosques, and the veiled women are tourism or art or poetry, sometimes even love or at least desire, but they are not administration or even organization. The Muslims do not love us, especially not here; they can have sympathy for a few [Europeans] who love them and who defend them against us; but it is perfectly unbearable to them that we govern them.[58]

Why did the new approach to native policy and applied sociology fail to take hold? We can rephrase our understanding of what happened in the language of Pierre Bourdieu as the reassertion of the power of the political field over that of the intellectual field.[59]

NOTES

1. For a bibliography of French urban studies of Morocco, 1894–1924, see André Adam, *Bibliographie critique de sociologie, d 'ethnologie et de géographie humaine du Maroc* (Algiers: SNED, 1972). More generally, see *AM* and *AF* (in which most early urban studies first appeared).

2. Robert Montagne, *Naissance du prolétariat marocain* (Paris: Peyronnet, 1952); and André Adam, *Casablanca: Essai sur la transformation de la société marocaine au contact de l'Occident*, 2nd ed. (Paris: Éditions du Centre national de la recherche scientifique, 1972).

3. Auguste Mouliéras, *Fez* (Paris: Challamel, 1902), 80.

4. Auguste Mouliéras, "La ville de Fez," *Bulletin de la Société de géographie d'Oran* 21 (1901): 1–31.

5. Mouliéras, Fez, 158–159.

6. Ibid., chap. 32. It includes a detailed discussion of the role of the Alliance Israelite in Morocco; see pp. 231–247, 272–291.

7. Mouliéras, Fez, ii4–i20.

8. Ibid., 296–298. See especially his debate with the young *alim* Si Bou-Bekr, 391 ff.

9. Mouliéras, Fez, 350.

10. Émile Masqueray, *La formation des cités chez les populations sédentaires de lAlgérie: Kabyles du Djuradjura—Chaouias de l'Aures Beni Mzab* (Paris: E. Leroux, 1886).

11. Félix Weisgerber, "La ville de Fès," *Revue française de l'étranger* 24 (1899),: 591–596; and "Maroc, Voyage du Dr. Weisgerber," *Comptes-rendus des séances de la Société de géographie* (Paris, 1900), 259–264.

12. Gaetan Delphin, *Fas, son université et l'enseignement supérieur musulman* (Paris: E. Leroux, 1889); and Moulieras, Fez.

13. Eugène Aubin [Collard-Descos], "Fez le dernier centre de la civilisation maure," *Revue de Paris*, February 15, 1904, 851–872; March 1, 1904, 173–196; March 15, 1904, 424–448. Later published as *Le Maroc d'aujourd' hui* (Paris: A. Colin, 1904); English trans., *Morocco Today*.

14. Henri Gaillard, Une ville d'Islam: Fez; Esquisse historique et sociale (Paris: J. André, 1905).

15. Charles René-Leclerc, "Le commerce et l'industrie à Fez," *RC*, supplement to *AF*, 1905, 229–253; 295–321; 337–350.

16. Georges Salmon, "Les chorfa idrissides de Fez,"*AM* 1 (1904): 425–459.

17. Louis Massignon, "Les corps des métiers et la cité islamique," *Revue international de sociologie* 28 (1920): 473–489; and "Enquête sur les corporations musulmanes d'artisans et de commerçants au Maroc," *Revue du monde musulman* 58 (1924): 1–250.

18. Roger Le Tourneau, *Fés avant le protectorat:Étude économique et sociale d'une ville de l'Occident musulman* (Casablanca: L'Institut des hautes études marocaine, 1949).

19. Henri Gaillard (b. 1869) was a graduate of the École des langues orientales who began his Moroccan career in 1895 at Tangier, then served in Casablanca (1897–1900) and Fez (1900–1912). He became the first secretary-general of the protectorate, and finished his career as consul general in Cairo. Léon Eugène Aubin Collard-Descos (b. 1863) began his diplomatic career at Athens in 1885. He served at a variety of posts in the Middle East, China, Latin America, and Spain before being sent to Morocco in 1902.

20. See, Capt. Justinard, "E. Michaux-Bellaire," *AF*, 1930, 411–412; and R. Gerofi, "Michaux-Bellaire," *Tinga I* (1953): 79–85.

21. Antoine-Louis Martin (b. 1882), after graduating from the École des langues orientales, served as a member of the MSM from 1908 to 1910, and then held a number of diplomatic posts in Morocco. Léon-Marie-Jules-Simon Pérétié (b. 1879) had a diploma from the École des langues orientales. He served in Egypt from 1904 until 1909, when he came to Morocco, and was attached to the MSM. He later held diplomatic posts in the Middle East.

22. See the obituary by Alfred Le Chatelier, "G. Salmon, Chef de Mission," *AM* 7 (1906): 463–473. Also AF, 1906, 258.

23. Charles René-Leclerc held brevet in Arabic and Berber from the École des langues orientales. He began his Moroccan career as head of the Delegation Générale of the Comité du Maroc at Tangier in 1905, at which position he remained until 1912.

24. The following articles derived from Salmon's 1906 trip to Fez: Salmon, "Les chorfa idrissides de Fez"; Salmon, "Les chorfa filala et djilala de Fez," *AM* 3 (1905): 97–118; Salmon, "Le culte de Moulay Idris et la mosquée des chorfa à Fez," *AM* 3 (i905),:413–429; Édouard Michaux-Bellaire, "Description de la ville de Fez," *AM* 11 (1907): 1–115; Louis Martin, "Description de la ville de Fez, quartier du Keddan," *Revue du monde musulman* 9 (1909): 433–443 and 621–642; A. Pérétié, "Les méder-sas de Fez," *AM* 18 (1918): 257–372. For an account of the accomplishments of the Fez mission, see Le Chatelier, "G. Salmon, Chef de Mission."

25. Jonathan G. Katz, "The Most Parisian of Muslims: Kaddour ben Ghabrit (1873–1954)," paper presented at the Northwest World History Association annual conference, Vancouver, WA, October 16–17, 2004.

26. Aubin was the author of *La Perse d'aujourd'hui* (Paris, 1908); *Les Anglais aux Indes et en Égypte* (Paris, 1899); and *En Haiti* (Paris, 1910).

27. Fustel de Coulanges, *La cité antique* (Paris: Hachette, 1864); English trans., *The Ancient City*.

28. Aubin, *Le Maroc d'aujourd'hui*, 268–270, 312–355; Gaillard, *Une ville d'Islam: Fez*, 147–151, and 175–176.

29. Michaux-Bellaire to Colonel [Huot], Tangier, November 20, 1922, MAE, Maroc, Protectorat, Direction des affaires indigènes, vol. 228.

30. At the height of the first Moroccan crisis, the French foreign minister Delcasse assured his Tangier representative of his willingness to "buy" the acquiescence of key members of the Fez elite. See Documents *diplomatique français* 2, IV, No. 483.

31. The articles were also published separately as a book by the Comité de l'Afrique Française. See also G. Marchand, "La situation commerciale à Fez en 1906," *RC*, 1906, 421–422.

32. For Aubin's discussions, see *Le Maroc d'aujourd'hui*, chaps. 10–12. There is reason to believe that the pseudonym René Maudit, used by the author of "Le makhzan marocain," RC, 1903, 293–304, hides the pen of Gaillard. Cf. Gaillard's later article, "L'administration au Maroc: Le makhzen, étendue et limites de son pouvoir," *Bulletin de la Société de géeographie d'Alger*, 1909, 433–470, which was used to brief French diplomats at the Algerian's conference.

33. The influence of Sir James Frazer's *The Golden Bough*, a particularly important work that operates on the assumption of the existence of historical survivals, has been explicitly acknowledged in the case of Edmond Doutté. The Fez ethnographers operated in an intellectual environment in which evolutionary views dominated, even if unacknowledged.

34. Le Tourneau, *Fès*; and Jean-Louis Miège, *Le Maroc et l'Europe*, 1830–1894, 4 vols. (Paris: P.U.F., 1961–63).

35. Évariste Lévi-Provençal, *Les historiens des Chorfa: Essai sur la littérature historique et biographique au Maroc du XVIe au XXe siécle* (Paris: E. Larose, 1922); and Abdullah Laroui, *Les origines du nationalisme marocain*, 1830–1912 (Paris: Maspéro,1977).

36. On the organic fallacy, see, among others, Édouard Michaux-Bellaire, "L'organisme marocaine," *Revue du monde musulman* 9 (1909): 1–33.

37. Discussed in Burke, *Prelude*, 180–187.

38. On the role of the *ulama*, see Edmund Burke III, "The Political Role of the Moroccan Ulama, 1860–1912," in Saints, Scholars, and Sufis, ed. N. R. Keddie (Berkeley: University of California Press, 1972), 93–126. Also Muhammad Baqir al-Kattani, *Tarjamah al-Shaykh Muhammad al-Kattani al-Shahid* (Unpublished manuscript, 1962); and Laroui, *Les origines du nationalisme marocain*.

39. The only effort at a study is Michaux-Bellaire's remarkably biased effort, "Une tentative de réstoration idrissite à Fez," *Revue du monde musulman* 5 (1908): 393–423.

40. Édouard Michaux-Bellaire, "Fez et les tribus berbères en 1910," *Bulletin de l'enseignement publique du Maroc*, 1921, 3–10.

41. Michaux-Bellaire to Colonel [Huot], Tangier, November 20, 1922, MAE, Maroc, Protectorat, Direction des affaires indigènes, vol. 228.

42. Clifford Geertz, Hildred Geertz, and Lawrence Rosen, *Meaning and Order in Moroccan Society: Three Essays in Cultural Analysis* (Cambridge: Cambridge University Press, 1979).

43. The argument in this section is presented in greater detail elsewhere.

44. See above.

45. At least as important was Mme Mellier, know to Fasis as "Madame Bureau." She spoke Arabic fluently and was a tireless advocate for mutual understanding in the weeks that followed the siege. See MacLeod to foreign minister Grey, Fez, March 7, 1913, FO 174, No. 272, No. 1.

46. MacLeod to foreign minister Grey, Fez, March 7, 1913, FO 174, No. 272, No. 1.

47. Sultan Abd al-Aziz appointed the *majlis al-a'yan* at a critical point in the crisis in 1904. See Burke, *Prelude*, 81–82.

48. During the siege of Fez in 1911 there was a complete breakdown in relations between the *makhzan* and the population of Fez (who were inclined to take the side of the besiegers). With the traditional structures of governance not functioning, the heads of the quarters of Fez met to select a temporary leader, Maylay Idris al-Zarawti, as the *shaykh al-rabia* until the crisis was resolved. See Burke, *Prelude*, 161–162.

49. On the role of 'ar sacrifice, see Edouard Westermarck, *Ritual and Belief in Morocco*, 2 vols. (London: Macmillan, 1926).

50. For the legislation, see the Bulletin *Officiel du Protectorat* (1912).

51. The *majlis al-baladi* is discussed by Jean Vattier, "La municipality dé Fez," RC 12 (1924): 383.

52. For a discussion of the election results, see the correspondence of Fez consul James MacLeod. MacLeod to Kennard, Fez, September 12, 1912, FO 174, No. 272, No. 101.

53. Vattier, "La municipalité de Fez."

54. Daniel Rivet, *Lyautey et l'institution du protectorat français au Maroc, 1912–1925* (Paris: L'Harmattan, 1988), 2:157–159.

55. MacLeod to Grey, Fez, March 17, 1914, FO 413, No. 60.

56. Michaux-Bellaire to Colonel [Huot], Tangier, November 20, 1922, MAE, Maroc, Protectorat, Direction des affaires indigènes, vol. 228.

57. Michaux-Bellaire to Colonel [Huot], Tangier, November 12, 1922, MAE, Maroc, Protectorat, Direction des affaires indigènes, vol. 228.

58. Michaux-Bellaire to Colonel [Huot], Tangier, November 20, 1922, MAE, Maroc, Protectorat, Direction des affaires indigènes, vol. 228.

59. See Bourdieu, "Le champs scientifique," *Actes de recherche en sciences sociales* 2:2 (1976): 88–104; and Bourdieu, *Le sens pratique* (Paris: Minuit, 1980).

FAMILY, GENDER, AND SEXUALITY

Tamkin

Stories from a Family Court in Iran

by ZIBA MIR-HOSSEINI

IN IRAN, AS ELSEWHERE IN THE MIDDLE EAST, THE LAW DEFINES the institution of marriage and the relationship of a married couple in ways that do not conform very closely to the experiences of ordinary people. The legal and the popular understandings of marriage are neither mutually exclusive nor necessarily in conflict, but they can be seen as distinct and opposed forces, particularly when a marriage is under strain or breaks down, when one or both of the partners have recourse to the law in order either to repair the marriage or to bring it to an end.

This chapter tells the stories of three women, each of whom is going through a difficult phase in her marriage. I came to know them while working on a documentary film about women and family law.[1] We meet them in court and learn how they confront the legal understanding of marriage. But first, we need some background on the main ways in which the legal and the popular understandings of marriage differ.

In Muslim societies, marriage is not so much a sacrament as a contract regulated by a code of law rooted in religious precepts—in the *shariʿa*. The Islamic Republic of Iran, which is ideologically committed to the shariʿa, has codified it and grafted it onto a modern legal system.[2] It is based on a strong patriarchal ethos imbued with religious ideals and ethics.[3] This ethos defines marriage as a contract of exchange, whose prime purpose is to render sexual relations between a man and woman licit. Any sexual contact outside this contract constitutes the crime of *zina*, and is subject to punishment. The marriage contract is patterned after the contract of sale, and its essential elements are (i) the offer (*ijab*) made by the woman or her guardian, (ii) its acceptance (*qabul*) by the man, and (iii) the payment of dower (*mahr*), which is a sum of money or any valuable that the husband pays or pledges to pay the wife on consummation of the marriage.[4] Polygamy is a man's right; only a man can enter more than one marriage at a time, and he is permitted up to four permanent unions and as many temporary ones as he desires or can afford.[5]

The contract establishes neither commonality in matrimonial resources nor equality in rights and obligations between spouses. The husband is the sole provider and the owner of the matrimonial resources, and the wife remains the possessor of her mahr and her own wealth. The procreation of children is the only area the spouses share, and even here a wife is not legally obliged to suckle her child unless it is impossible to feed it otherwise. With the contract, a wife comes under her husband's *'isma* (a mixture of authority, dominion, and protection), entailing a set of defined rights and obligations for each party; some have legal force, others depend on moral sanctions, though the boundary between the legal and the moral is hazy and shifting. The main legally sanctioned, rights and duties are *tamkin* (submission, obedience) and *nafaqa* (maintenance). Tamkin, defined as sexual submission, is a husband's right and thus a wife's duty; whereas nafaqa, defined as shelter, food, and clothing, is a wife's right and a husband's duty. A wife is entitled to nafaqa after consummation of the marriage, but she loses this right if she is in a state not of tamkin but of *nushuz* (disobedience).

The patriarchal emphasis and inequality of men's and women's legal rights in marriage are sustained through the rules regulating the termination of the contract. *Talaq* (repudiation), the unilateral termination of the contract, is the husband's exclusive right: he needs no grounds, nor is the wife's consent or presence required. Although a wife cannot obtain release from marriage without her husband's consent, she can offer him inducements to agree to *khul* (divorce by mutual consent). According to Muslim jurists, the wife may ask for khul on the grounds of her extreme aversion to her husband; in return for his consent, the husband should receive compensation. This can mean the wife's forgoing her right to mahr (dower), or returning it if it has already been paid. Unlike talaq, khul is a bilateral act, as it cannot take legal effect without the husband's consent. If the wife fails to secure her husband's consent, then her only recourse is to the intervention of the court. If she can establish valid grounds, the judge may pronounce talaq on behalf of the husband.[6]

This, in a nutshell, is the sharia understanding of marriage in Iran. But the law is liable to be modified as a result of both manipulations by the state and conflicts with social practice and custom.[7] Marriage, as ordinary people live and practice it, involves a host of customary obligations and social relationships that go far beyond its legal construction. Some of these are rooted in the ideals of the shari'a and enjoy its moral support, though nut legal sanctions. Marriage in practice not only has a more egalitarian structure than the law allows, but varies greatly with individuals, their social origins, and their economic resources. In particular, men's unconditional legal rights to divorce and polygamy are checked in practice by the mores and pressures of the extended family, the social stigma commonly attached to both divorce and polygamy, and above all by the practice of mahr. In Iran, a wife's right to mahr provides her with a strong negotiating card. She does not receive it upon marriage, but can demand it whenever she wants. Its value varies with social class and the wealth of the family, but it is always beyond the husband's immediate means to pay. In this way, the unclaimed mahr acts as insurance: a wife can, by forgoing her mahr altogether, persuade her husband to consent to a khul divorce; or, by threatening to claim her mahr, she can dissuade her husband from either divorcing her or taking a second wife; or she can claim substantial material compensation if an unwanted divorce goes ahead.[8]

In most marriages, couples find ways of accommodating or circumventing the legal requirements. Yet the tension is there, and it surfaces when the marriage breaks down or is under strain. It is then that many women first come to learn what their marriage contract entails, and how their rights and duties are defined in law. How do women relate to this legal reality? Do they accept it? Can they defy it? As the following extracts suggest, there are no simple answers. Their responses depend on their force of character, their socioeconomic condition, and the options available to them.

These extracts are drawn from my transcripts of three cases that appeared in a court in central Tehran in November 1997. Judge Deldar, a cleric, ran his court in an informal way, so that at times we (the film crew) were involved in the procedures. All three cases are typical of marital disputes that come to court in that they revolve around tamkin, nafaqa, and mahr, the main elements in the legal understanding of marriage that have been translated into positive law and can be enforced.[9] All three, moreover, betray the tensions between the different understandings of marriage and of gender relations. The only understanding that can be articulated in court is that of the law; the popular, everyday understanding of marriage cannot be articulated directly. As in all other court cases, the tensions between these understandings emerge in the form of two distinct agendas. As we shall see, while these agendas and understandings interact with and redefine each other, there is a wide gap between them, which has deepened in recent years. This is because women's position in society and their expectations of marriage have changed radically, while Iranian family law has remained some way behind these changes.[10]

EXTRACT 1. MS. AHMADI, DO YOU KNOW WHAT TAMKIN IS IN LAW?

Ms. Ahmadi[11] stands in front of the judge. She is small, and probably in her early fifties. He is busy reading a file. She waits for some time for him to raise his head. When she gets the chance, she starts to talk to the judge, handing him her file. Her voice is low, and her tone hesitant. She says that her husband recently took another wife, a sixteen-year-old girl. For the past five months he has not paid her any nafaqa; she made a petition for it, which was rejected. She has come to ask the judge why, and to ask what to do next. She adds that she has been married for twenty-eight years and has five children, two of them still at home. The judge looks at her file and tells her, "Here it says that you weren't in tamkin." She looks lost. I know that look; I have seen it many times. She is unfamiliar with the court and its language. I ask her, "Ms. Ahmadi, do you know what tamkin is in law?" "No," she answers.

Judge:	Then why did you say [probably in a previous session] you weren't in tamkin, if you didn't know what it is? It says here [in her file] that you said you weren't in tamkin; when you neglect your duties in marriage, you lose your right to nafaqa.
Ms. Ahmadi:	I never neglected my duties, I kept house for him, raised five children. Isn't that enough tamkin?
Judge:	No, tamkin is more than that. When he wants to sleep with you, you must agree. At night when he wants to come and

sleep with you, you must let him. That is tamkin. Are you prepared to do this or not?

She reddens, lowers her head, and answers, "No."

Judge:	Why not?
Ms. Al.:	can't ... I can't. ...

She must have reacted similarly in the previous session, which might explain why her petition was rejected. I am now convinced that she is new to the intricacies of the law. She is too honest, too naive. She doesn't know that legal facts are not necessarily about truth. She has now given the judge a reason to blame her for her husband's action.

Judge:	Why can't you? He's gone and taken another wife, you say he's married a sixteen-year-old. It's a wife's lack of tamkin that causes such a thing. Why aren't you prepared to be in tamkin?
Ms. A.:	Wasn't I in tamkin for twenty-eight years? Where have all these children come from?
Judge:	Yes. You must always be in tamkin. It was your lack of tamkin that caused him to take another wife. Encourage him a little, entice him back, if you are not in tamkin then you are not entitled to anything for yourself, and you can demand nafaqa only for the children.

She looks at the judge in horror. I can see the hurt in her face. I have to come to her aid once again, and tell her how the court defines tamkin. I address the judge: "I know the court's presumption is that a wife is in tamkin as long as she stays in the marital home. But what happens, for instance, if a wife says she is in tamkin but her husband says she is not? Whose word does the court accept?" The judge replies, "The wife's, of course," to make it crystal clear, I turn to her and say, "A wife can demand nafaqa when she says she is in tamkin, and she is still in the marital home. This is the meaning of tamkin. So you can file a new petition for nafaqa, and this time make it a penal one." She sighs and says, "Now I understand, but what can I say?"

We did not see Ms. Ahmadi again, which means that she did not take the course I suggested, to file a penal petition for nafaqa. If a wife submits such a petition at her local police station, it is dealt with that very day. If her husband is found, then he is brought to court, where he faces two options: either to pay the nafaqa calculated by the court, or to receive the penalty of a maximum of seventy-four lashes. Most men choose the first, and pay up then and there. But such radical action takes the dispute to a different level and almost always puts an end to the marriage, a step that many women of Ms. Ahmadi's generation and situation, lacking economic independence, cannot afford. A wife who takes this step is likely to be intent on teaching her husband a lesson, or exacting revenge after he has taken a second wife.[12]

Probably Ms. Ahmadi chose the softer option: to make a civil petition for nafaqa, to which she is entitled if she has not left the marital home and declares she is in tamkin. When her case duly appears in court (usually within three months), if the husband comes but refuses to pay, or if he fails to appear, then the court will issue a nafaqa order. With this order, she can take legal action to recover past nafaqa (if he is salaried, a sum is deducted monthly). But Ms. Ahmadi could obtain a divorce at any time, since her husband's taking a second wife without a court order constitutes valid grounds. Whatever she does, she needs knowledge of the law, or a lawyer, but above all she needs the financial means to survive outside marriage.

For many women like Ms. Ahmadi, tamkin is a way of life, going far beyond its narrow legal mandate. This is reflected in the dictionary definitions of tamkin: "giving power," "empowering someone to attain something," "accepting a situation." The word itself is seldom used in everyday language, and many women do not know its meanings, legal or popular; but it rules their lives, as they have little choice other than to be in tamkin—to submit to their husband.

But some women, as the next extract suggests, are able to refuse tamkin as a way of life and to challenge its legal link with nafaqa, the provision of food, shelter, and clothing. A wife with independent means and somewhere to go can circumvent the legal understandings of nafaqa and tamkin and assert her own. One of her options is to rewrite the terms of her marriage contract. She can obtain the right to choose her place of residence, either through a stipulation in the marriage contract or by a court order following a dispute. It is common, when a wife demands both nafaqa and a separate place of residence, for her husband to make a counterpetition for tamkin, though when she no longer resides in his house his power over her is substantially reduced and it is hard for him to insist on her submission, sexual or otherwise.

EXTRACT 2. MS. BEHROUZI: I WAS IN MY HOUSE, IT WAS UP TO HIM TO COME TO ME FOR MY TAMKIN

Ms. Behrouzi, middle-aged and wearing a *chador* (full-length veil covering the body and hair) and glasses, enters the courtroom with her lawyer, a younger woman wearing just a head scarf. Her husband follows them. They exchange greetings with us and take their seats. We have already met in the corridor, and they have agreed to be filmed. Ms. Behrouzi told me that two of her sons from her previous marriage live in London, and she wants them to see her in the film. She is more or less the same age as Ms. Ahmadi in the previous case, but unlike her is cheerful and full of confidence. We are delighted: very few cases that come to court involve lawyers, and we have been invited to film this one.

The lawyer starts to present the case to the judge.

"Your Honor,[13] I would like to inform the court that fifteen years ago my client contracted a permanent marriage with this gentleman. Both had children from their previous marriages. For six years, she lived in his house with his four children. But his children resented her, could not accept her taking their mother's place. There were frequent quarrels. Finally she went to the court and made a petition, demanding a separate residence and payment of nafaqa. The court found her demand reasonable, and issued an order to that effect. He too made a petition for tamkin [her return to his house] but it was rejected by the same court. You will find both orders in the file, which states that his house was not a suitable place for her to reside, and continuation of that situation could have caused her spiritual, psychological, and physical harm. In this way, she obtained the right to choose her place of residence and the husband was required by law to provide for her. At present she lives in a house in which she has a small inherited share. By law, this gentleman is required to pay her monthly nafaqa, and visit her there. But since New Year's Day [21 March 1997] he has failed to comply with his marital duties."

Ms. Behrouzi's husband, Mr. Amiri, is on the edge of his seat, looking more and more agitated. Several times he tries to get a word in, but the lawyer does not let him. Now, unable to contain himself any longer, he leaps up and approaches the judge's desk to tell his own side of the story.

"God be my advocate! This lady received nafaqa regularly until the New Year. In that court she used my children as an excuse. The court said, 'Provide her with a separate room.' I did that. But she said she wanted to go and live in her own house.

I said, 'Fine, as you like.' I even increased her nafaqa, and paid until the end of last year. Just before New Year, I telephoned her and said, 'New Year is approaching, husband and wife should be together, either you come to me or I come to you.' She said, 'I won't come, nor will you.' You yourself are a man, Your Honor. You know that we men work from morning to night, in hot or in cold weather. Is this how a wife should reward us? I was offended and had no intention of going to her for New Year. But she has a brother with whom I have lunch every other day. He said, 'My sister is not well, go and visit her, ask how she is doing.' I said, 'Just as you say.' So I went to see her on New Year's Eve. I swear by God, I am not lying to you. I bought two kilos of the best almond cookies that I could find in the bazaar, and I went to see this lady. It's 9:30 in the evening. I tell her I haven't eaten. She says, 'There's no food prepared in the house.' Then she goes and fries two eggs, and puts them in front of me. I say nothing. Eleven-thirty comes. I tell her, 'Aren't we going to bed?' She says, 'Are you going to sleep here?' I say, 'Yes, my children are away; and you are my wife in law and in religion. It is also written here [i.e., in the marriage contract].' She says, 'Not any more! If you want to spend the night here, I'll go downstairs to my son's flat, and sleep there.' So I said, 'Well, then, go and get your nafaqa from your son!' and I left. After all these insults, I asked her brother and others to mediate, and offered to send her money. But she told them she didn't want money, and she didn't want me to go to her. A wife who doesn't do tamkin is not entitled to any nafaqa."

The lawyer gets up and hands the judge two documents, saying, "Here is a copy of the nafaqa petition this lady made, and here is the summons sent to him claiming nafaqa, which he ignored." This infuriates Mr. Amiri.

Mr. Amiri: Your I honor, I swear to God I telephoned and said, "My girl, my lady, the light of my eyes, your nafaqa is ready, stop this nonsense." She said, "We'll talk in court." I said, "Fine, we'll see each other in court."

Ms. Behrouzi: Please, [let me say] only one word, please, Your Honor, let me. He telephones and says he wants to come at seven in the morning and then leave at seven-thirty [i.e., for quick sex], I said I wouldn't do such a thing.

The judge tries to calm them down, without success.

Judge:	No marriage can carry on with arguments and things like this. No one can be forced; there must be agreement. Madam, you must also be in tamkin, it's your duty.
Ms. Behrouzi:	When this gentleman says he wants to come for half an hour, what does this mean? This is an insult to me.
Mr. Amiri:	What insult? We agreed in court that I could go to her once a week, and have breakfast.
Ms. Behrouzi:	This gentleman wants to come to my house on Friday mornings.
Mr. Amiri:	That was our arrangement.
Ms. Behrouzi:	He has breakfast, and half an hour later … he knows what I am talking about, this is shameful, really! One wants a husband for companionship; I've been ill for two years, going to hospital, and he doesn't even know which hospital I've been to, where I go.
Mr. Amiri:	You didn't want me to come!
Judge:	How long since you last paid nafaqa?
Mr. Amiri:	Since New Year. If she's entitled to anything, by God, I'll give it to her right now.
Lawyer:	It's no good. The fact is that the condition for divorce has been fulfilled. In the previous court, they agreed that she could divorce herself if he failed to pay nafaqa. It's here in the court order. Whatever you do now does not change the past.
Mr. Amiri:	I won't give her a divorce, under no circumstances. From now on, I won't give any money; I'll go and buy whatever she needs; if she needs medical treatment, I'll take her to the doctors.
Judge:	Was she in tamkin to you?
Mr. Amiri:	No.
Ms. Behrouzi:	I was in my own house, Your Honor. It was up to him to come to me for my tamkin.
Mr. Amiri:	I come there, and at twelve at night, you tell me to go away. What sort of tamkin is this?

The session ends with the judge requiring Mr. Amiri to pay the nafaqa due to his wife. I do not know what happens later, but I learn that the underlying problem is Mr. Amiri's children, who, egged on by their mother, resent his remarriage to Ms. Behrouzi, refuse to let him visit her as often as she would like, and are determined to ruin their marriage. He is adamant that he will not give her a divorce, but if she is intent on it, he has little option but to agree to one or to try to accommodate her wishes. Legally he is bound to pay her nafaqa every month, but since she is living in her own house he has little chance of being able to enjoy what he is legally entitled to in return, i.e., his wife's tamkin, sexual and otherwise. The new court order has further improved her bargaining position, so that she can now negotiate her release from the marriage or insist on her own terms if it is to continue. For her, like most women, what is important in marriage is companionship and sharing; for her husband, like most men, it seems to be little more than sex, cooking, and personal services.

If older women like Ms. Behrouzi, with financial means and previous marital experience, can evade and subvert the legal mandate of tamkin, younger women are now challenging it in the name of religion and questioning its legal justification, as our third extract shows.

EXTRACT 3. MINA: DOES ISLAM SAY I MUST BE IN TAMKIN TO SUCH A MAN?

Mina and Javad, a young couple in their early twenties, sit next to each other. Throughout the court session, they never look at each other, and they speak only to the judge. Mina is wearing a black chador. Her face is pale, and her voice husky. Javad is wearing a sports jacket; his voice is rough and impatient.

Judge:	You say here that she left your house several times. Why? What is the problem in your marriage?
Javad:	From the very beginning of our marriage, I found certain things unacceptable. If I came home and objected to something, for instance, "Why is the food like this?" she would just say, "I have no duty to cook for you, to take your orders, or to raise your children." I found this too much to bear. Naturally,

I would get upset. You can keep quiet for a day or two, but finally you say something, you do something. Anyway, we went on like this for a while; and she left me four times.

Judge: What was the latest dispute about, this last time?

Javad: She's completely self-obsessed in her life. I think she has no respect for me—I mean, for her husband. She wants everything for herself: she goes wherever she wants, and she doesn't go anywhere she doesn't want. She does as she pleases, and then claims that I beat her. I came to the end of my tether, two or three times. Then she made a row, shouting and crying. Now I want her tamkin.

Judge: Your husband has petitioned for a tamkin order [for return to the marital home]. A wife must be in her husband's tamkin; if she leaves home it must be with his agreement, with his permission. A wife must have understanding, and not let things get to the point that her husband has to come here and petition for a tamkin order. Now tell me, why did you go back to your father's house?

Mina: From the very beginning—only three days after our wedding—he raised his hand at me. I was horrified. I am the last child of my family [usually the favorite] … I came to his house with hope. I did not expect that, only three days after the wedding, I'd get beaten because the food was not ready. He doesn't have the right to raise his hand at me because I didn't prepare this food. Islam doesn't give him that permission. A man can't compel his wife to do housework, according to the religion (*shar'*) that we have. God knows, since I went to his house, I've been beaten every three or four days. Once he hit me so hard that my eardrum was damaged, my thumb was broken. He insults me, he calls me names like—begging your pardon—"bastard." Does Islam say I must be in tamkin to such a man? What religion, what law allows this? This man does whatever he wants to me, he hits me. Your Honor, I fear for my life. He gives me assurances of safety, so I return to our marital home. He tells me, "In the court I say I love my wife and my marriage, and then at home I break your bones." This is his

	position, as I see it … What guarantee do I have if I remain in his house? Has the Prophet said I must do tamkin to such a man?
Judge:	You must live together in peace. You, too, you cannot order your wife to do things. She should do certain things in the house, from moral obligation; but a husband should not give orders … If [she] works on the husband's orders, she can demand wages … the domestic wages that women are entitled to [as part of a divorce settlement] are about this: the wife has done work and can demand wages for it. You, madam, if you do things on your husband's orders, you can demand wages. Does he give orders?
Mina:	He does, but I am not the type to demand wages for what I do at home. Every woman cares for her home. But he is unreasonable. For instance, one day we did not have hot water, so I couldn't do the washing up. Because of this I was badly beaten. Does Islam allow such a thing?

Clearly Mina has been following current debates over women's rights in parliament and the journals, particularly over what a wife's duties in marriage are, as well as the issue of wife-beating. Since the Revolution and the return to the shari'a there have been attempts to give legal sanction to shari'a moral injunctions. She knows the judge is referring to the 1992 amendments to the divorce laws, which enable the court to put a monetary value on women's housework, and to force the husband to pay *ujrat al-mithl* (like wages) for the work she has done during marriage. She also knows that this law is of no use to her, as it only applies when divorce is not initiated by the wife or is not caused by any fault of hers.[14] So she invokes the sacred, by appealing to Islamic ideals of justice and fairness. Is she alluding to the Quranic verse commonly interpreted as an endorsement of wife-beating (4[Nisal]: 34)[15] Has she been reading the women's magazines in which alternative Quranic interpretations and equality for women are aired and debated? Whatever the case, the judge does not react but avoids her question, dismisses her concern as trivial, and continues his attempt to make peace between them. Mina now reveals why her husband actually beats her: he wants her to give up her claim to mahr in return for a divorce.

Judge:	It is a shame to ruin your marriage for such trivial things. Now what's your problem with returning to your marriage?
Mina:	I don't want to live with him any more. He wants a divorce too. Two months ago, he agreed to give me a divorce by mutual consent; we discussed all this in my father's house. He signed it [the terms of the divorce settlement]; he agreed to pay the mahr in installments. The very morning we were to go to court for him to give me my divorce, he changed his mind and tore up the agreement. Then he filed a petition for tamkin, in order to put pressure on me to give up my claim mahr. If I go back, he will make life hell for me. He puts his foot on my throat to suffocate me, he pulls my hair; all this is causing me bodily harm.
Judge:	If such things happen, you can file a report and he will be prosecuted.
Mina:	I made a petition a month ago, and a hearing was set for six months ahead.
Judge:	The petition you made was for divorce. If he insults you, or if he causes you bodily harm, you should make a penal petition and your case will appear in court the same day. Civil cases, such as divorce, take a long time to appear. Young man, will you give her a guarantee here that, if she comes to live with you, there will be no insults, no maltreatment?
Javad:	Of course! I am not that type, Your Honor!
Judge:	He will give you a guarantee not to insult you under any circumstances, not to cause you bodily harm. Will you agree to go back?
Mina:	No! He has given such promises many times; the last time, when I came back from my father's house, he swore by Fatemeh Zahra,[16] but as soon as we got into the car, he started insulting me, and two days later he hit me.
Judge:	OK, you have no special problem, so go off and live together; God willing, nothing else will happen.
Javad:	If I insult her, she can come here and make a petition; but what can I do if she continues to paralyze my life and leaves for her father's house?

Mina: Why does she leave? Ask him, Your Honor. He hits me, and I have to leave. Tell him he's gone too far. He damaged my eardrum, he broke my thumb; he admits all that. Tell him there's a law, that no man can do just what he wants even within the four walls of his house.

The session ends with Javad signing a document guaranteeing to respect his wife and not to maltreat her. Both leave the courtroom in silence. I follow them, wanting to talk to her. I want to know whether she is going to return to the marital home and give him another chance, and to tell her that if he beats her again, she can bring a penal case against him by going to the police: they will send her for a medical examination, and if there is any physical injury, such as bruises or broken limbs, then a certificate will be issued and Javad will be summoned to court and forced to pay compensation. If she refuses to accept compensation, he will be imprisoned. Such a court order can strengthen her case later, if she chooses to apply for a divorce on the grounds of harm.

Outside the courtroom, I see Mina with her father, and tell them about the options. Her father says, "I'll never let her go back to that madman. I'm now going to make a petition for her mahr. He will pay for what he has done to my daughter, for ruining her life." They know that Mina's mahr—set at 140 gold coins—is their only negotiating card. Javad is legally obliged to pay it on demand, either in full or in installments, depending on his financial situation. Since the amount involved is substantial, he will probably agree to give her a divorce or to mend his ways, if they give up the claim. By law, there is nothing Javad can do to bring Mina back to the marital home, even if he succeeds in obtaining a tamkin order. A wife who refuses to comply with such an order merely loses her claim to nafaqa.

I never saw Mina or Javad again, and I don't know what the outcome was. But Mina's pale face and husky voice will remain with me forever.

What do these glimpses into the breakdown of three marriages tell us about law and social practices in post-revolutionary Iran? How do wives relate to the inequality inherent in their shari'a marriage contracts? What are their strategies to overcome it?

Like other marital disputes, these three stories must be interpreted in the context of different understandings of marriage and gender relations. By the time a marital dispute appears in court, it has already become a war of attrition. What causes and then fuels this war in Iran is the tension between the legal and the everyday understandings of marriage. While the marriage contract as defined by law concedes neither a shared area of ownership nor equality and reciprocity in conjugal rights and duties, marriage in social practice assumes all of these.

When this sharing and reciprocity is jeopardized by either spouse, the marriage comes under stress, and may end up in court. Each spouse will do whatever is possible to create a new balance. Husbands appeal to their shari'a prerogatives and demand their legal rights, especially the wife's submission; wives appeal to social practice and custom and try to offset their husband's legal power. Whatever the dispute, whatever her circumstances, a wife tends to resort to similar kinds of strategies, with the objective of making her husband pay for what she sees as a denial of her conjugal rights.

Men often retaliate with neglect and violence. A man can avoid confrontation with his wife and withstand social pressure by neglecting her. As our first two stories show, when confronted by his wife's demand for reciprocity in conjugal rights and duties, a husband tends to neglect his legal duty to provide for her. The more guilty he is in the eyes of his wife and of society—for example, if he takes a second wife—the more he stays away. Our third story shows how a man may try, through violence and physical domination, to assert an authority which the law bestows on him but which has little basis in social expectations of marriage. Physical violence then becomes a measure of the erosion of a man's authority in marriage: it is more frequent when a marriage is under stress, exactly because he feels a more acute need to assert his authority.

The wife then reacts by making financial demands. In this way, she makes her husband pay, both literally and figuratively. The very elements in the marriage contract that give men power can now be turned against them. The husband's authority over his wife, legally sanctioned and enforced through nafaqa, becomes a double-edged sword. A man who is unable to pay, or whose wife has her own income, can exercise little power over her, and he has no choice but to negotiate terms for either continuing or terminating the contract. The ways in which these negotiations take place, and women's choices and options, are shaped by their personalities, their conjugal circumstances, and the socioeconomic context in which marriage is embedded.

Thus a woman with no financial security outside marriage, like Ms. Ahmadi in our first story, comes to court either to get nafaqa from her straying husband or to preempt a divorce. Ms. Ahmadi's case was at an early stage of its court career. Soon she will learn that the most effective way to bring her husband to his senses is to take as much as she can. She can make one petition for nafaqa and another for mahr, but she can waive rights to these in return for a share of the marital home or custody of the children together with a set nafaqa payment for looking after them. A 1997 law requiring mahr to be revalued in line with inflation has put her in a better negotiating position. Now she can count on her mahr as an insurance in marriage.

Other women, like those in our second and third cases, come to court to negotiate the terms of a divorce. They have either economic means, like Ms. Behrouzi, or the support of their natal families, like Mina. By refusing to grant his wife a divorce, a man can hold on to his power, even though he knows that the marriage is over. This is often the only way he can realize his legal prerogatives if she leaves the marital home. She retaliates by bringing the case to court, and thus takes the marital dispute to another level. Her strategy is to resort to the contractual side of the marriage and to demand fulfillment of its terms. As we saw with Ms. Behrouzi, whose case had been in the courts for a good while, a wife can make the husband fulfil his legal duty (reduced to nafaqa) while evading her own (reduced to tamkin). But in most cases, like Mina's, a wife's main negotiating card is her mahr, since by leaving the marital home she has already lost her claim to nafaqa.

A large majority of divorce cases initiated by women never reach a decision; they are abandoned after two or three hearings. Either the couple succeed in reaching an out-of-court agreement or they give up, realizing the futility of their efforts. More than 70 percent of all divorces registered in any given year in Tehran are khul‘ (by mutual consent). Most if not all of these will have involved the wife waiving her claim to mahr in exchange for the husband's consent. As a Persian saying has it, *Mahram halal junam azad:* "Let my mahr go and my soul be free."

NOTES

1. *Divorce Iranian Style,* a film by Kim Longinotto and Ziba Mir-Hosseini (1998, distributed in the U.S. by Women Make Movies, in the U.K. by the Royal Anthropological Institute). We did not use any of the cases discussed here in the final version of *Divorce Iranian Style.* For the story behind the making of the film, see Ziba Mir-Hosseini, "Negotiating the Politics of Gender in Iran: An Ethnography of a Documentary," in *The New Iranian Cinema: Politics, Representation, and Identity,* ed. Richard Tapper (London: I. B. Tauris, 2001).

2. The Iranian state's appropriation and selective enforcement of the shariʿa pre-dates the establishment of the Islamic Republic in 1979, and it is not unique to Iran. Iran, however, is the only Muslim country in which the custodians of the shariʿa (the *ulama*) now control the machinery of a modern state and are able to pass and enforce laws in the name of the shariʿa. For the impact of this on gender rights, see Ziba Mir-Hosseini, *Islam and GenderI: The Religious Debate in Contemporary Iran* (Princeton: Princeton University Press, 1999).

3. Ten percent of all Muslims adhere to Shiʿa Islam; Iran is the only Muslim country in which it is the official religion. Family law in Shi'a Islam shares the same inner logic and patriarchal bias as Sunni schools of law. For differences among the schools of Islamic law, see John Esposito, *Women in Islamic Family Law* (Syracuse: Syracuse University Press, 1982).

4. Despite the uniformity that exists among all schools of Islamic law on the rules governing mahr, Muslim societies vary greatly with respect to its practice. In many societies mahr has a "prompt" portion, which is paid before marriage, and a "deferred" one, which is paid only upon divorce. In some countries, such as Morocco, the prompt portion constitutes the bulk of mahr, and is used by the bride's family to provide her with a trousseau; in others (including Iran), as we shall see later, mahr is prompt in form but deferred in function. See Ziba Mir-Hosseini, *Marriage on Trial: A Study of Islamic Family Law: Iran and Morocco Compared* (London: 1. B. Tauris, 2000).

5. Temporary marriage, or *mut'a*, exists only in Shiʿa law; see Shahla Haeri, *Low of Desire: Temporary Marriage in Iran* (London: I. B. Tauris, 1989).

6. For the different shariʿa modes of termination of marriage, see Mir-Hosseini, *Marriage on Trial,* 36–41.

7. For changes in Iranian laws relating to marriage and divorce, see Ziba Mir-Hosseini, "Family Law III. In Modern Persia," *Encyclopaedia Iranica* 9 (1999), 192–96.

8. For ways in which women use mahr in Iranian courts, see Ziba Mir-Hosseini, "Women, Marriage, and the Law in Post-revolutionary Iran," in *Women in the Middle Fast. Perceptions, Realities, and Struggles for Liberation,* ed. Haleh Afshar, 59–84 (London: Macmillan, 1993).

9. Most files contain a wife's petition for nafaqa or mahr, and a husband's counter-petition for tamkin. I have been doing research in Tehran family

courts since the early 1980s. For court procedures and the content of files, see Mir-Hosseini, *Marriage on Trial*, 28–31.

10. See Mir-Hosseini, "Women and Politics in Post-Khomeini Iran: Divorce, Veiling, and Emerging Feminist Voices," in *Women and Politics in the Third World*, ed. Haleh Afshar (London: Routledge, 1996), 142–70, and "Iran: Emerging Feminist Voices," in *Women's Rights*, ed. Lynn Walter (Westport, Conn.: Greenwood, 2000), 113–25.

11. All the names used are pseudonyms. In Iran, a woman does not take her husband's name on marriage, so although she may be addressed as *khanum Ahmodi*, Mrs. Ahmadi, this is her father's, not her husband's, surname.

12. See Mir-Hosseini, *Marriage on Trial*, 63–65.

13. The term most people use when addressing clerical judges, like this one, is "Hajji Agha."

14. For the 1992 amendments and gender debates, see Mir-Hosseini, "Women and Politics in Post-Khomeini Iran" and *Islam and Gender*.

15. For an alternative interpretation of this verse, see Ziba Mir-Hosseini, "Stretching the Limits: A Feminist Reading of the Shariʿa in Post-Khomeini Iran," in *Islam and Feminism: Legal and Literary Perspectives*, ed. Mai Yamani (London: Ithaca Press, 1996), 285–319.

16. Daughter of the Prophet and wife of Ali, the first Shiʿa imam, from whom the other Shiʿa imams are descended.

Reconstructing the Transgendered Self as a Muslim, Nationalist, Upper-Class Woman

The Case of Bulent Ersoy

by RÜSTEM ERTUĞ ALTINAY

WINTER OF 2007. ANOTHER SUNDAY NIGHT, A NEW EPISODE of *Popstar Alaturka*, a Turkish version of *Pop Idol*. Minority and human rights activist Hrant Dink has recently been assassinated by an ultranationalist youth and Turkey is experiencing one of the few notable instances of spontaneous collective action in the past two decades.[1] It has been only days since tens of thousands of people marched in the streets, chanting, "We are all Armenians!" to express their sympathy for Dink and the Armenian community. Hence, the TV show opens with the popular Armenian folk song "Sari Gelin"—which, later in the evening, will lead to a rather long and interesting monologue by one of the jury members. This member is a glamorous lady in her fifties, wearing a haute couture dress revealing her long legs and shapely breasts. She expresses her discontent with the slogan "We are all Armenians!" Underlining the fact that she is "the Muslim daughter of Muslim parents," she emphasizes that no one can ever make her say she is Armenian or Christian. Claiming that it would be more acceptable if the slogan had been "We are all Hrant," she deems it intolerable for a Muslim person to say that s/he is Armenian—and therefore Christian.

Rustem Ertug Altinay, "Reconstructing the Transgendered Self as a Muslim, Nationalist, Upper-Class Woman: The Case of Bulent Ersoy," *Women's Studies Quarterly*, vol. 36, no. 3, pp. 210–229. Copyright © 2008 by ProQuest LLC. Reprinted with permission.

But who is this glamorous woman who seems in desperate need to underline her Muslim, nationalist identity? For readers who take an even slight interest in Turkish popular culture, the answer would be quite obvious. The person is Bulent Ersoy: a self-proclaimed expert on classical Ottoman music—though a singer of the popular genre arabesk—one of the first Turkish men to undergo sex change and the very first one to ask for a female passport, and a hater of transgendered prostitutes. Ersoy has been an extremely popular public figure in Turkey since the early 1970s and is very likely to remain so.

Following Simone de Beauvoir's claim that "one is not born, but, rather, *becomes* a woman," in this essay I seek to trace how Bulent Ersoy has "become" a Muslim, nationalist, upper-class woman. In doing so, I aim to understand the strategies that define spaces of abjection reserved for transgendered individuals in Turkey in the post-1980s and examine the tactics for survival that are available to them.[2] I will try to explore Ersoy's personal history in the context of events in Turkey since the 1970s and discuss the cultural atmosphere and dynamics of gender in the country in the light of Ersoy's narrative.

A YOUNG, FLAMBOYANT MALE SINGER

The renowned singer of classical Turkish music Bulent Ersoy was born as Bulent Erkoc in 1952 in Istanbul. Named after a soccer player, Bulent was the only son of an urban middle-class family. He was introduced to classical Turkish music by his grandfather, who played the zither, and his grandmother, who played the lute. Shown to have talent, he took private lessons with acclaimed musicians at an early age and later attended the conservatory. While he was still a student, he began singing professionally under the stage name Bulent Ersoy—the name Erkoc, meaning "brave ram," was probably too masculine for this rather androgynous young man, so it was replaced by Ersoy, "brave lineage." Ersoy is also easier on the tongue.

Ersoy's first record came out in 1971. At that time, nightlife in the big cities, especially Istanbul, mainly consisted of Greek tavenas and nightclubs called *gazinos*. Those nightclubs provided the middle- and upper-classes with hours-long programs bringing together several singers as well as comedians and belly dancers. There would often be one lead singer, called an *assolist,* who would take the stage last and sing classical Turkish music. The extremely competitive atmosphere made it difficult to become a lead singer. At the time, many established lead singers sang arabesk, a genre influenced by Turkish folk and Middle Eastern music, that had come out in Turkey in the 1950s and 1960s. Martin Stokes, one of the leading experts on arabesk, claims that it is "a music inextricably linked with the culture of the *gecekondu,* literally the "night settlements" which mushroomed around Turkey's large industrial cities after the Menderes government program of rural regeneration in the 1950s produced a large rural labor surplus" (1989, 27). To the urban elite, arabesk was a new and lower-quality musical form. In this context, Ersoy decided to use this dissatisfaction with arabesk and constructed his public image as a "classicist." In other words, he appropriated Turkish classical music and made it his trademark so as to win a place in a highly competitive market. He catered to an audience that wanted to consume "authentic" or "elite" classical Turkish music as opposed to the "popular," "commercial" variety. With a singing style extremely similar to that of Muzeyyen Senar—a popular singer of classical Turkish music who at the time was at the height of her career and, in some sense, Ersoy's patron—he became the lead singer at Maksim, the most prestigious nightclub in the country. He was the second lead male singer at that time, after Zeki Muren (1931–96)—a flamboyant queer male singer, as was Ersoy. In fact, one could argue that Ersoy had appropriated an image with which the audience was already familiar, through Zeki Muren, who maintained it until the late 1960s, when he adopted a style that was an interesting combination of Elvis and Liberace. In other words, while Muren was adopting a new image, Ersoy was taking on Muren's previous one. After Ersoy established his name in the Turkish music scene, he started singing arabesk, for financial reasons (Tulgar 2004). This increased his both popularity and income immensely.

As was customary for such singers, Ersoy, like Muren, also made a number of movies with popular female stars of the Turkish cinema. In these mainstream love stories, Ersoy would act the young, naive, maybe somewhat androgynous, yet heterosexual, man. This accorded with his public image. Even though, later, Ersoy would claim that her friends had always seen her as a woman, at the time Ersoy would be visible in the press with his fake fiancées, constructing his image as heterosexual and male. Yet, as Pinar Selek argues, Ersoy and Muren challenged the codes of masculinity in Turkey with their public personas (2007, 111). They did not have the masculinity of other male singers such as Munir Nureddin Selcuk, Orhan Gencebay, or later, Ibrahim Tatlises. Ersoy's most significant attributes were probably his rather naive politeness and somewhat androgynous style. Thus, through a bodily and linguistic performance as a man who was openly gay in his private life, yet with a heterosexual public image, Bulent Ersoy opened a liminal sphere that challenged the codes of masculinity. According to Selek, this was why he was loved by women. In the Turkish movie *Evlidir Ne Yapsa Yeridir*, from 1978, women embark on a kind of feminist revolution; among their demands are male domestic help, new clothes, and listening to Bulent Ersoy.

EARLY POST-OPERATION YEARS

When Ersoy was physiologically male, he would usually wear a white tuxedo or a dark suit and bow tie. Unlike Muren, at the time, he never appeared in garments or accessories that challenged established masculine dress codes, such as mini-shorts, ostrich feathers, or sequins or wore hairstyles or jewelery that were normally seen on women. It was only after his hormone treatment began that he started to appear on stage in female attire. Arguably because Ersoy wanted to claim the female body, his costumes were particularly revealing. In 1980, after the military coup, when she was singing in a nightclub at the Izmir International Fair, Ersoy did not deny the audience its desire to see her newly developing breasts. Proving her femininity in this way resulted in her arrest and she served forty-five days in prison. In 1981, she underwent a sex change operation in London. This would change her life in ways that she probably never expected. Being a transsexual was not easy during the notoriously oppressive military regime. She had to go through several physical examinations as well as an exhausting legal case to be recognized as a woman. Her court defense was very significant for the construction of her public image as a transgender individual. She underlined that she was not an anarchist, but a loyal citizen who did not aim to do anything against the social order. By emphasizing her patriotism, she intended to avoid the fate of other victims of the military regime, during which 650,000 people were taken into custody, 230,000 were tried, fifty were executed, and 229 "died of unnatural causes" while in custody (Gunersel 2007).

Ersoy was not the only transgendered person who was at risk following the coup; and in fact, the trans community had been suffering from state violence since the 1960s. Back then, the community was quite small and most of its members lived in Istanbul (Cingoz 2007). As their chances for employment were extremely limited, they tried to survive by either doing odd jobs or taking up prostitution. As prostitutes working in the streets, they were always easy targets for the police. In 1973, the first brothels for transgendered prostitutes was opened in Istanbul's Beyoglu district. There, transgender people enjoyed relative security and regular health checks. In the late 1970s, the "social democratic" CHP government started a war against these brothels. It provided no alternative employment opportunity or any other support for the trans community, it just tore down the brothels—only for them to be reconstructed by the brothel workers. Transphobic policies intensified with the military coup of 1980. For one thing, the brothels were closed down for good. It was extremely difficult for a member of the trans community to find an apartment; they therefore had to share hotel rooms. When the brothels were closed down, many of the workers were subjected to verbal and physical abuse. Some were held in custody for weeks, and some were reportedly killed by police and their bodies were thrown into a river (Gunersel 2007). The approach of the military regime toward transgendered prostitutes was similar to that of the social democrats, but harsher: not only were the brothels closed down, but the doors of the only other sector that employed transgendered people, entertainment, was now closed to them. Performances by all transgendered entertainers were banned, and many had to take up prostitution as well.

In this political atmosphere, Ersoy was the only person who had the power to have her voice heard. What was striking in her attitude was that she was not making a claim in the name of queer people or the trans community—she was only trying to save herself. For one thing, she had found an interesting way to explain her gender status as a woman: "My mother thought I was a girl when she was pregnant with me. Maybe that is the reason why my male hormones did not develop." With such comments, she was clearly rejecting transgenderism as an opportunity to deny established gender codes. She desired only to be accepted as a woman. She did not have any intention to fight against heterosexism either. In an interview with the newspaper Gunaydin April 1981, Ersoy said: "The people whom I find most disgusting are homosexuals. I am so glad that I am not one" (Ersoy in Isiguzel 2000). With these statements and her own pseudoscientific theories, Ersoy claimed a female identity, and a strikingly homophobic one. But as far as the court was concerned, her efforts were in vain: her performances were banned, and she was unable to work in Turkey. Her right to work—a human right—had been violated. During this period, she had to work in Germany and France. She performed for Turkish migrant workers, singing what she now calls "market music," a position of lower status for a singer who had worked at the most exclusive nightclubs in Turkey. Among other things, she had to sell her jewelery, and at one point, she attempted suicide. While her public performances were banned, she still made albums and low-budget films for video. In Turkey, she would occasionally perform in nightclubs, where she would pretend to be part of the audience and sing from her table. She also worked as a model and continued giving interviews. Thus, she not only remained a popular public figure, keeping her fans remembering and missing her, but also persisted in affirming her female identity, in the clichéd heterosexual romances in which she acted, now taking the woman's part, and in the erotic photographs for which she posed.

In 1988, Ersoy was permitted by the neoliberal government of Turgut Özal to obtain a female ID and work in Turkey. It is worth noting that she had become a showpiece for the government. Before her sex change, he was a very popular singer and the public had been longing for her comeback. By giving her a female ID and allowing her to perform in Turkey, the government achieved two goals. First, to increase their own legitimacy, they presented the case of Ersoy as expressing the epitome of personal freedom.[3] Second, by granting Ersoy her work permit the Özal regime differentiated itself from the highly unpopular military regime that had preceded it. Thus, the neoliberal regime and its laissez-faire economic policies were legitimized in the eyes of Ersoy's fans, especially Turkey's new bourgeoisie, to whose tastes Ersoy catered, but also the general public. She had become the signifier of an era of freedom and tolerance.

The discourse of tolerance is crucial to understanding this process. Ersoy was given a female passport and the right to work not because this was her "right," but because she was "tolerated" by the regime. The discourse of tolerance is strongly related to the construction of spaces of abjection and their use for the definition and celebration of the "normal" or "legitimate" spheres as well as the nation or the state. Ersoy, as a transgendered individual, was the Other who was to remain in an abject space, yet enjoy the "tolerance" of the regime.[4]

Stokes notes that Ersoy made an album of classical Turkish music in 1987 "when the debate over the stage performance on [her] was at its height" and "this undoubtedly strengthened the case for the repeal of the ban" (1992, 227). After the ban was repealed, Ersoy again made a number of arabesk albums. It is feasible that Ersoy instrumentalized classical Turkish music to legitimize her singing in the eyes of people who did not enjoy arabesk.

When she managed to return to the stage, Ersoy climbed back to the top in no time. She resumed her work in prestigious nightclubs and gave concerts all over the country. Many of her songs became instant hits, and her films enjoyed success at the box office. The Turkish people had gladly accepted her back, and she enjoyed the support of the Özal family, particularly Semra Özal, the prime minister's wife, leading to Ersoy's appearing in a televised official celebration even though arabesk singers were rarely given the opportunity to appear on state-owned television at the time (Stokes 1989, 29). But this time, Bulent Ersoy was neither a young flamboyant boy nor the femme fatale of her early post-operation years. Although she was still loved dearly by her fans, her sex change operation was seen as a threat to the heterosexist patriarchal state hegemony during the military regime. She was cornered and had to face the tools of the homophobic and transphobic regime, from medicine to law. When she was back on the stage, she refused to use her transgendered status as a way to challenge gender codes, heterosexism, patriarchy, nationalism, capitalism, or conservatism. Rather, she refused to acknowledge her transgendered status and gradually started to advance an identity as a conservative, Muslim, nationalist, upper-class woman.

While she continued to sing at the most popular clubs and was dressed by some of the most prominent fashion designers, a significant change in her style became evident. Although glamorous, her costumes were not as revealing as they had been. She did not pose in lingerie or bathing suits anymore. She started to make films with important stars again.[5] But unlike her actions in the low-budget films in which she acted in her early post-operation years, when she would appear in lingerie, she did not even kiss the male lead. It would be plausible to say that she was following in the footsteps of Turkan Soray. Arguably the most popular actress in the history of Turkish cinema, Soray had adopted what came to be known as "Soray's rules": Don't undress, don't kiss, don't have sex in front of the camera (Buker 2002). Like Soray, Ersoy sought to present her sexuality as that of a woman, yet do it in a more discrete, almost "chaste" way to enjoy greater public acceptance in Turkey, where conservative Islam was on the rise, with the educational policies of the past three decades and the empowerment of the conservative Muslim small capital holders during the Özal regime. Her getting engaged with her boyfriend, Birol Gurkanli, in her early post-operation years also served to project the image that she adhered to the conservative heterosexual norms. Years later, in 1998, when she would marry the much younger Cem Adler, the public discussion would revolve around the age difference between the couple, rather than Ersoy's transsexualism.

In the late 1980s, Ersoy began to emphasize her Muslim identity, including references to Allah in her songs and during her performances, and she continues to wear a veil when she attends funerals. Her emphasis on this aspect of her identity peaked in 1995, when she recited the *adhan,* the Islamic call for prayer, in her album *Alaturka 95* and sparked a heated debate.

Normally, the *adhan* is called out by a muezzin from a minaret of a mosque five times a day to summon Muslims for prayers. In 1932, the Atatürk government imposed a Turkish-language *adhan* to replace the traditional Arabic, to promote Turkish as a liturgical language. This highly unpopular policy, implemented as part of the Kemalist project of modernization, was repealed in 1950. Today, although there are defenders of the policy among the Kemalist modernists, it is virtually impossible to hear the Turkish adhan.

By reciting the *adhan* in Arabic, Ersoy asserted her identity as a conservative Muslim. If she had recited the call to prayer in Turkish, she would have not only expressed her identity as a Kemalist/modernist but also led the media to focus on the language of the adhan. Instead, the media's focus was Ersoy's gender, and a huge debate started on whether a woman can recite the adhan or not. This gave Ersoy the opportunity to reaffirm her faith in Islam and also have others reaffirm her gender identity as a woman.

Ersoy's use of language, especially her choice of vocabulary, was also significant for the performance of her identity. What makes her vocabulary choices significant is her extensive use of Ottoman words. Having been virtually eliminated from the Turkish language with the modernizing Kemalist language reforms, this vocabulary is normally available to only a few elderly people who come from families that have social, cultural, and economic capital, or to people who learned it in university Turkish or history departments or in one of the few private language courses. In any case, it is an indicator of status and, to some extent, class. However, as this vocabulary was eliminated by the modernization project, its use has conservative connotations as well. As these words are borrowed from Arabic or Persian, they may also have a religious connotation. It is also possible to interpret this vocabulary choice as playing with the past. Ersoy aims to use a language that has been forgotten. When she uses this particular vocabulary, she seeks to perform her identity in a particular way. She reconstructs the time, and performs her identity not only as a person who brings a long forgotten knowledge from the past but also as someone who belongs to that past.[6] By constructing herself as an element of the past, she probably contests the social rejection that she faced because of her new status as a transsexual woman. This rejection of modernity is ironic because her sex change was made possible by medical technologies. By performing her identity as a conservative Muslim woman, Ersoy contests social rejection not only by rejecting a queer or transgender identity, but also by rejecting "modernity."

The developments in Turkish media were particularly instrumental in Ersoy's promoting her new public image. Previously, there was only state television; because her public performances were banned, Ersoy could not appear on television. Nor were there any private radio stations. Later, with the establishment of private stations for both television and radio, Ersoy started to appear frequently on television and radio. In fact, she even had her own talk show in one of the earliest private television channels, Kanal 6, owned by the Özal family. With the aid of these developments, Ersoy's new public image was established quite firmly by the mid-1990s.

THE OLDER SISTER

In 1992, Ersoy made one of her most successful albums. There was a song in the album that would turn out to be very important for Ersoy's personal history: "Ablan Kurban Olsun Sana" (Your Older Sister Would Sacrifice Herself for You). The song was about the sexual interest of an older woman in a younger person, but the most significant words it contained were those that formed the title. Using these lyrics as a term of affection in addressing her public, Ersoy was soon awarded the nickname *abla* (older sister). As noted by Sirman, while persons of the same generation and the same parents who are older than one are referred to as *agabey* (older brother) or *abla* (older sister) in Turkish, these words also serve as terms of address "not only with regard to persons one has filial and affinial ties to, but also with complete strangers. These terms provide a means of regulating relations between non-kin, thus extending the language of hierarchy and respect, age, and gender to cover a whole range of relationships within the society in general" (2004, 44). Ersoy's being given the nickname *abla* meant two things. First, her gender status as a woman had been strongly affirmed by her public. Second, she had managed to gain respect. Even though Ersoy did manage to gain the respect and love of her public as a popular singer, this would not be the ultimate status she would aim at.

THE DIVA

In the summer of 2004, Ersoy gave a concert in the Cemil Topuzlu open air theater in Istanbul. In this concert, she sang only classical Ottoman songs that were familiar to few people. In fact, she claimed that the scores for some of the songs could not be found in archives and she had had to make transcriptions from memory. She wore a dress inspired by the caftans of the Ottoman sultans and a headpiece that resembled an Ottoman turban. Ersoy did not earn any money from this concert. What she gained was social status.

Before the concert, she accepted an interview with the well-known journalist Ahmet Tulgar from the daily newspaper Milliyet. Ersoy was rarely giving interviews at the time, so even the existence of the interview was a sign of something important. In this interview, Ersoy claimed that she had caused a revolution in the 1970s by singing classical Ottoman music in nightclubs, yet betrayed her revolution as well as classical music by singing arabesk to be more popular and earn more money. Her desire was to "apologize to music." In other words, she was no longer satisfied with her status as an arabesk singer. She had earned enough money and could afford her albums to be less popular—which did not really matter at a time when most people could download music from the Internet anyway—but she wanted to regain her status as a classicist. This concert project was a result of this concern. With the costume as well as the songs she chose to sing in one of the most prestigious concert halls in Istanbul, underlining her status as a singer who could sing songs from the thirteenth-century that were known and understood by few, yet could fill that concert hall. With this performance, she claimed the past; just as she was legitimizing her identity with reference to the past in her use of Ottoman vocabulary while trying to avoid the rejection she might experience because of her transsexual identity, which is a modem, present-day possibility.

This was the beginning of a new era for Ersoy's public image. To the amusement of some, a term from classical music of the West was appropriated, and Ersoy became "the Diva" of Turkey. In many respects, not much had changed in the way she performed her identity. Yet things had intensified and her new title and her role as a member of the jury in *Popstar Alaturka* had provided her with a new forum to perform her identity.

Probably, the biggest change in Ersoy's public image was her approachability. She had already gained respect as the Older Sister, but being the Diva was something else. There was no real change in her music after the concert in which she sang classical Ottoman songs. In her television show as well as her concerts, Ersoy kept singing arabesk and pop music. But her expertise in a musical form that her public neither really knew nor could really stand, yet recognized as an indicator of status, as it was appreciated by a small elite group, did improve Ersoy's status.

In the construction of the Diva, class was also a key issue. Among signifiers of class were gift giving, conspicuous consumption, and discourses concerning consumption. Beginning with her relationship with Gurkanli, Ersoy had been famous for her lavish gifts. These became more and more visible after she became the Diva. Although expensive, some, such as the ring she gave her close friend Oya Aydogan on her birthday, fit within the established norms of gift giving in contemporary Turkish society; others, such as the bracelet she gave her patron Muzeyyen Senar when she was hospitalized, did not. All these sumptuous gifts helped to construct Ersoy's identity as an upper-class person. Her own expensive jewelery and clothing as well as shopping trips to Europe added to the indicators of class, yet the discourses concerning her consumption practices were even more influential. It was especially so in the case of jewelery. Even though jewelery has traditionally been a signifier of class, it is not always possible to tell whether it is real or fake. Ersoy started to insist that she never wears fake jewelery and to reveal the price of each and every piece she has.

As the importance of nationalism and Islam in Turkish public discourse has increased since the 1980s, the significance of these elements in Ersoy's construction of her identity has increased as well. Since the 1980s, Ersoy has been telling stories of rejecting European offers of citizenship. In 1997, she scolded a French interviewer who asked her about the ban on her public performances, saying that "it is a matter of domestic policy." But her aggressive response to the Dink incident, described at the beginning of this essay, was unprecedented. With it, she allied herself with the ultranationalists at a critical time in Turkish history as well as expressed her identity as a nationalist Muslim. With practices such as breaking her Ramadan fast on a live broadcast, she persisted in constructing a Muslim identity.

The last key aspect of the identity of the Diva was her womanhood. Even though her gender identity as a woman had largely been accepted, she still had a past to deal with. When her old friend, and new enemy, Sacit Aslan said that Ersoy had done her military service—which is compulsory for all men and only men—she furiously rejected the claim. She asserted that "her status" did not allow her to do military service, and waving her pink identity card, she said that she was "as female as Semra Özal." Here, she was using the female identity card (that was begrudged to her for so long) as a weapon with which to claim her womanhood. The reference to Semra Özal is also striking. By saying that she was "as female as Semra Özal," Ersoy not only claimed womanhood but also made a claim for power by equating herself with the former first lady, with whose help she had managed to get her pink identity card and work in Turkey.

The media helped Ersoy in the reconstruction of her past. In *Canli Hayat,* a television show presenting interviews with famous people and reenactments of important moments in their lives, Ersoy's pre-operation years were played by a young girl. Since her early post-operation years, Ersoy had been telling stories of how she would perform a female identity as a child. When he was alone at home, he would put on makeup, wear his mother's clothes, and take her cigarettes and cigarette holder and "pose like a woman" in front of the mirror (Tanis 2005). She would also claim that her friends had always seen her as a woman. In this show, the past had been reconstructed and the biggest "mistake" in Ersoy's life had been corrected: she had never been a man.

In an episode of *Popstar Alaturka,* Ersoy proved that she could not only claim a female identity but also claim the body of a particular woman. Like most stars, Ersoy occasionally undergoes plastic surgery, such as liposuction and face-lifting. In one episode of the show, she had recently undergone a series of plastic surgery. Having also borrowed the makeup artist of fellow singer Ebru Gundes, Bulent Ersoy had a striking resemblance to Gundes, a member of the jury on the show. Her class and status had enabled Ersoy to undergo plastic surgery in Germany, and also to borrow this makeup artist, which made it possible for her to claim not only womanhood but also the body of a much younger woman.

Popstar Alaturka also provided Ersoy with a new tactic to construct her identity. As a member of the jury, Ersoy was given the opportunity to criticize the contestants. Her comments were not limited to their singing. She would make sometimes friendly, sometimes harsh comments about their bodies and physical practices. She would often give examples from her own body. When the jury was discussing why one of the contestants preferred costumes that they found too conservative, Ersoy said that some women cannot wear dresses with a deep cleavage, as their bodies were not as fit for it as was hers. Later, she called a girl over and made her bend over, examining her body. Through these practices of criticism and evaluation, Ersoy constructed herself as an expert on the "ideal" female body and bodily practices and deemed her own body, at least in some respects, as the ideal body for a woman. It seems clear that Ersoy has internalized the restrictive discourses on gender and the body rather than resisting them. She constantly reproduces them while she constructs her body as desirable if not perfect and criticizes the bodies of the contestants of *Popstar Alaturka* as well as of other women, including the guests on her talk show, within the framework of stereotypes about gender and the body.

THE ANTI-MILITARIST MOTHER WITH NO CHILDREN

Although the preceding section was intended to be followed by the conclusion, a very significant incident in Ersoy's life occurred while this essay was in review and has led me to add one more section on Ersoy, as the anti-militarist mother with no children—an identity she briefly seemed to claim, then abandoned in haste.

An episode of *Popstar Alaturka* in February 2008 was devoted to soldiers who died in an operation to northern Iraq. While the host of the show and Ersoy's fellow singers sent their condolences to the soldiers' families, along with nationalistic and militaristic messages, Ersoy took an unexpected stance. Acknowledging that she could never be a mother, she stated that if she had a son, she would never send him to the army. This is a fairly popular discourse among Turkish mothers. Although they can't say it in public, as it is a crime punishable not only by the law but also by nationalists, many Turkish mothers tell their friends, relatives, or sons that they would never let them perform compulsory military service. In other words, while expressing her feelings about a war in which "Turkey has been instrumentalized by big powers," Ersoy sought to perform her identity as a mother by shifting the focus from reproductivity to feelings. This was a quite dangerous move, especially when combined with an antimilitarist comment. Fellow singer Ebru Gundes took the microphone to say that she could be a mother and she would only be happy to be the mother of a martyr if it was her destiny. Ersoy had opened a position that she could not fulfill and Gundes had used the opportunity to perform her identity as a nationalist mother, although she had no children either. But this would not be all. A public prosecutor filed charges against Ersoy for disparaging the military (Bax 2008). Interestingly, Ersoy enjoyed the support of many Turkish intellectuals, as well as—to her distress—the Democratic Society Party (DTP). As an antinationalist party that represents Kurdish people in the parliament, DTP was probably the last party whose support Ersoy would appreciate and enjoy. Still, the party's parliamentary group's deputy chairman, Ahmet Turk, praised her courage, the mayor of Batman offered to name a street after Ersoy, and her albums started to fly off the shelves in the southeast, where the majority of the population is Kurdish (DHA 2008). By contrast, a member of parliament from the ruling Justice and Welfare Party made fun of Turk and Ersoy, remarking that had Turk been as brave as Ersoy, he would "have his thing cut off" as well. This attitude was not unique to him. Thousands of people were making fun of Ersoy's transgenderism on the Internet. The one time she tried to perform her identity in a slightly different way, she was insulted by a member of parliament and thousands of people, and faced time in prison.

Ersoy was cornered once more, this time by the wrath of the government and nationalists, and the love of the Kurds. Therefore, she held a press conference. Stating that all she wanted was a "solution, instead of death" Ersoy reaffirmed her loyalty to the republic of Turkey. Arguing that "Turks are a soldier nation" and "one may give the God-given life for the motherland, for the nation" she stressed that she was not the public face or supporter of any group. Thus, she reembraced national- ism and militarism while rejecting any affiliation with or sympathy for the Kurdish community. Later, she stated once more that she was going to leave her wealth to the Turkish Educational Foundation (a secularist, nationalist foundation for educa- tion) and the Mehmetcik Foundation (a militarist, nationalist foundation that caters to the needs of disabled war veterans and the families of soldiers who lost their lives). Ersoy's choice of institutions was of particular significance, as the other queer star of Turkish music, Zeki Muren, had also left his considerable wealth to the same institutions. It appears that Ersoy was aiming at the acceptance that Muren always enjoyed in regard to the state and the military.

This example shows that while identity may not be a mere survival tactic, Ersoy's public performance of her identity is strongly related to survival in an hostile envi- ronment. Her transgenderism was such a sensitive issue that whenever she would do something that might challenge her established public image, she would be dispossessed of her womanhood and relive past stigmatization and humiliation.

CONCLUSION

This essay is being written in late 2007, twenty-six years after Ersoy's sex change operation. According to a recent study, 23 percent of urban gay/lesbian/bisexual identified people confirmed having been subjected to physical harassment and a distressing 87 percent confirmed having been subjected to verbal harassment (Ercivan et al. 2006, 112). On the cultural level, the popular drag performances of Seyfi Dursunoglu, which he has been presenting for more than forty years in nightclubs and more than thirty years on television, have been banned from television by the Radio and Television Supreme Council (Dundar 2007). The charge was that he promoted homosexuality to youth. This was not the only homophobic act by the council. Gay fashion designer Barbaros Sansal's talk show *Toplu Igne* was banned for the same reason. Virtually all depictions of homosexual physical intimacy on television, including kissing, are penal offenses. As a result, foreign shows such as *Dawson's Creek* or *Six Degrees* are often censored and Turkish productions have very few queer characters. As far as politics are concerned, there have been no openly gay politicians who have entered parliament in the history of the country. Even though the population is quite high in the big cities, only a handful of transgendered individuals work in the professions and, to my knowledge, none work in the public sector. All others work as indirectly forced sex workers.[7] And, leaving any affirmative action aside, the government even refused to ban "discrimination based on sexual orientation" in the new draft constitution.

In this sociopolitical and cultural context, there is only one transgendered person who enjoys success and popularity. Bulent Ersoy has two shows on prime-time television and earns millions of dollars every year, adding to her significant wealth. While she is indeed a talented singer and is highly knowledgeable about classical Turkish music, I contend that she owes her popularity, at least to some extent, to her earlier image as a heterosexual man and the tactics she employs against the strategies of the hegemony in contemporary Turkish society.

Like the first queer star of Turkey, Zeki Muren, Ersoy started her career with a heterosexual male image. Yes, he did not have the masculinity of other male singers, but he was in the press with his fake fiancées, and he acted as heterosexual men in movies. He attained fame as a heterosexual man. Muren had never dared to deny heterosexuality in public, although he was openly gay in his private life. His first stage performance was 1950, wearing a tuxedo. He had to wait for twenty years to become arguably the most popular and respected singer in the country to challenge the established dress codes for men with a costume he named "The Prince from Outer Space": platform heels, a miniskirt, and a sheer cape, with earrings and a kind of tiara. Muren had probably expected to use science fiction as an excuse for drag. If the prince was from outer space, it wasn't plausible to expect him to share the same codes of masculinity with earthlings. But things did not exactly work out that way. Muren had created a huge scandal and journalists were saying that he was "wearing women's clothes" (Alpman 2006). People had started to question his masculinity. At that time, Muren took an interesting turn and, leaving science fiction aside, chose to legitimize drag with the aid of history and nationalism. He said that his costume was inspired by Turkish heroes such as Baytekin and referred to Sultan Selim 1, who allegedly wore earrings. After that incident, Muren never performed in drag again, and even in his fifties he was holding meetings with the press at which he declared that he had "had affairs with 104 women" and that the allegations of homosexuality were nothing but ugly lies.

The sex change operation did not allow Ersoy to stick to a heterosexual male identity. Interestingly, when her hormone treatment began, Muren insulted her by asking, "I can walk with my head up, can Ersoy?" Being more successful in his bargain with the heterosexist hegemony, Muren did not refrain from allying with it to mock his rival. Soon, Ersoy was also going to adopt the language of the heterosexist hegemony, develop survival tactics that actually reproduce this hegemony and its strategies rather than resisting them. This can be interpreted as a bargain with the hegemony. I believe that this bargain is what gives Ersoy's story its particular significance. With the aid of the power she gained as a "heterosexual" man, Ersoy had the privilege to bargain with the heterosexual hegemony. This seems rather different from what Duggan calls "homo-normativity" or Puar's concept of "homonationalism," as the privileges Ersoy enjoys as well as the political views she defends are far from reflecting anything about the trans community in Turkey. While Ersoy enjoyed the support of the first lady, transgendered prostitutes were being tortured by the police, and they were being killed in the streets of Istanbul, Ankara, and Izmir. While Ersoy had two shows in prime time, LGBT organizations were being closed down by the state. Other than recognizing their new gender identity, the state has done nothing for members of the trans community. As noted earlier, there are only a handful of transgendered individuals in Turkey who are employed in any sector other than prostitution (Ogunc 2007).

Because of limited prior research, it is difficult to make any general statement about the political affiliations of the trans community. Berghan (2007) shows that they either tend to be apolitical or affiliate themselves with the Left. In fact, there are a couple of well-known leftist transgendered activists, among them Demet Demir, who was a candidate for parliament from a small leftist party, and Esmeray, who defines herself as a Kurdish feminist. LGBT organizations in Turkey, such as KAOS-GL and Lambdaistanbul, also tend to affiliate themselves with the Left. By performing her identity in the way that she does, Ersoy differentiates herself from contemporary leftist Turkish transgendered activists, as well as from transgendered performers such as Dana International, who embraces her transgender identity and openly supports the community, and performance artists, such as Kate Bornstein, who use their status to criticize heteronormative society and its tools, particularly medicine and law. Here, it is worth noting that while Ersoy has been embraced by the state and her public, she is openly rejected by one particular group: the trans community. These people, many of whom did identify themselves with Bulent Ersoy in their childhood and adolescence—particularly because she was the only transgendered person in the media—now feel cold toward her not only because of her homophobic and heterosexist comments and her apathy towards the problems of transgendered people but also because of her ultranationalism. In fact, Esmeray has said, "Bulent Ersoy is as transsexual as Michael Jackson is black" (Ogunc 2008). Thus, while Ersoy has rejected transgenderism and her transgender identity, she has in turn been rejected by the transgender community. While one may argue that this rejection was caused by the identity Ersoy chose to perform, it also serves the construction of this identity.

Bulent Ersoy, as a transgendered individual, has managed to survive and thrive in contemporary Turkish society thanks to the power she obtained as a "heterosexual" man, and only to the extent that she rejected her transgendered identity and opportunity to resist the dominant hegemony. The more she reproduced the dominant discourses, including the homophobic and transphobic ones, the more social acceptance she enjoyed. When she dared to deviate from the norm, she would be reminded of the bargain not only by the state but also by the people. This is how Ersoy's personal history has become the story of a Muslim, nationalist, upper-class woman and seems bound to remain so.

NOTES

1. Dink was a Turkish Armenian journalist and columnist who worked for Turkish-Armenian reconciliation and human and minority rights in Turkey. Being critical of both Turkey's denial of the Armenian genocide, and of the Armenian diaspora's campaign for its international recognition. Dink was prosecuted three times for "denigrating Turkishness" and received numerous death threats before his assassination by an ultranationalist.
2. Here, I borrow the terms "tactic" and "strategy" from Michel de Certeau (1984).
3. Previous political regimes had equally made use of popular singers as show-pieces. At the time of Ataturk, it was Safiye Ayla, a young girl who grew up

in a state orphanage. In the newly established republic of Turkey, Ayla was not only a beautiful voice but also a showpiece of the Kemalist revolution. Having grown up in a state orphanage, she was considered a daughter of the republic, someone who could represent the new woman with her education and professional success and also with her secular body. For Ayla as a leading female figure in the "Turkish Republican Enlightenment," see Ergun 1997. For other biographies of Ayla, see Seckin 1998 and Gungor 2006.

4. This is especially important in comparison with an incident that took place under the regime of Kenan Evren. In *Girgiriye*, a well-known Turkish comedy about the Roma community in Turkey made in the year in which Ersoy's public performances were banned, one of the characters appears on the stage of a nightclub in drag and is immediately taken to police headquarters. As a member of the Roma community, he exists in a space of abjection and enjoys the "tolerance" of the state, personified in the police chief. But this tolerance is not absolute; it is negotiated. Petty crimes can be forgiven as mischief perpetrated by these childish adults, especially because the crimes are of an apolitical nature. But when a male member of the Roma community appears on stage in drag, the situation is more serious, as transgendered people are less tolerable than the Roma. Therefore, the character has to promise the police chief that he would not do anything else that would be against "the moral order of the society," in order not to lose the tolerance he enjoys and be punished as Ersoy was.

5. *Biz Ayrilamayiz*, in 1988, and *Istiyorum*, in 1999, with their star-studded casts, helped Ersoy in her comeback; the former also launched the career of Gulben Ergen, who became one of Turkey's most popular stars.

6. A similar example of transgendered women legitimizing their existence with reference to the past—and using the examples of gay and bisexual men as well as transgendered individuals—can be found in the narratives of the transgendered people interviewed by Berghan (2007) and Kandiyoti (2002).

7. In Berghan 2007; Ogunc 2007; and Selek 2007, as well as numerous press releases by queer activists, transgendered individuals, virtually all of whom are sex workers, tell how it is not possible for them to find employment in any other sector, especially the public sector.

WORKS CITED

Alpman, Zazim. 2006.

Bax, Daniel. 2008 "Pop Diva Speaks Out Against Turkish Militarism: War Criticism in TV Casting Show." In *quantara. de.* Trans. Aingeal Flanagan. http://www.qantara. de/webcom/show_article.php/_c-478/_nr-738/i.html

Beauvoir, Simone de. 1974. *The Second Sex.* Trans. H. M. Parshley. New York: Vintage.

Berghan, Selin. 2007. *Lubunya: Transseksuel kimlik ve beden.* Istanbul: Metis.

Bomstein, Kate. 1994. "Gender Outlaw: On Men, Women, and the Rest of Us." New York; Routledge.

Buker, Secil. 2002. "The Film Does Not End with an Ecstatic Kiss." In *Fragments of Culture: The Everyday of Modem Turkey,* ed. Deniz Kandiyoti and Ayse Saktanber. New Brunswick: Rutgers University Press.

Cingoz, Yonca. 2007. "Bu isi yapmak ruhumda var." *Radikal,* 16 June.

de Certeau, Michel. 1984. *The Practice of Everyday Life.* Trans. Steven Rendall. Berkeley and Los Angeles: University of California Press.

DHA. 2008. "Batman Bulent Ersoy Caddesi." *Radikal,* March 3, http://www.radikal. com.tr/haber.php?habemo=249079

Dundar, Can. 2007. "Huysuz Viijin varolus mucadelesi veriyor." *Milliyet,* December 21, http://www.milliyet.com.tr/2007/12/21/pazar/yazdundar.html

Ercivan, Ali, et al. 2006. *Ne yanlis ne de yalniziz; Bir alan arastirmasi: Escinsel ve biseksuel-lerin sorunlari.* Istanbul: Lambdaistanbul.

Ergun, Perihan. 1997. *Cumhuriyet aydinlanmasinda oncu kadinlarimiz.* Istanbul: Tekin Yayinevi.

Gunersel, Tarik. 2007. "12 Eylul teroru hakkinda kamuoyuna duyuru," http:// www. pen.org.tr/tr/node/595.

Gungor, Necati. 2006. *Safiye Ayla'nin Anilari.* Istanbul: Heyamola Yayinlari.

Isiguzel, Sebnem. 2000. "Hanfendiler ve travestiler." Radikal, http://www.geocities. com/gayankara/hanfendiler.htm.

Kandiyoti, Deniz. 2002. "Pink Card Blues: Trouble and Strife at the Crossroads of Gender." In *Fragments of Culture: The Everyday of Modern Turkey,* ed. Deniz Kandiyoti and Ayse Saktanber. New Brunswick: Rutgers University Press.

Ogunc, Pinar. August 04, 2007. "Michael Jackson ne kadar siyahsa Bulent Er-soy O kadar transseksuel." Radikal, http://www.radikal.com.tr/ek_haber. php?ek=cts&habemo=6867.

Seckin, Nalan. 1998. *Musalladan sohrete Safiye Ayla.* Ankara: Bilgi Yayinevi.

Selek, Pinar. 2007. *Maskeler, suvariler, gacilar.* 2nd ed. Istanbul: Istiklal Kitabevi.

Sirman, Nukhet. 2004. "Kinship, Politics, and Love: Honour in Post-colonial Contexts—the Case of Turkey." In *Violence in the Name of Honour: Theoretical and Political Challenges,* ed. Shahrazad Mojab and Nahla Abdo. Istanbul: Istanbul Bilgi University Press.

Stokes, Martin. 1989. "Music, Fate and State: Turkey's Arabesk Debate." *Middle East Report* 160:27–30.

———. 1992. "Islam, the Turkish State, and Arabesk." *Popular Music* 11(2):213–227.

Tanis, Tolga. August 28, 2005. "Lirik Bir olaydir Bulent Ersoy." Hurriyet, http://webarsiv.hurriyet.com.tr/2005/08/28/693536.asp.

Tulgar, Ahmet. 2004. "Musikiden ozur diliyorum" Milliyet, June 1, http://www.milliyet.com.tr/2004/06/01/pazar/axpaz01.html.

On the Road

Travels with My Hijab

by MALIHA MASOOD

AT FIRST, IT FELT LIKE A BANDAGE WRAPPED AROUND MY skull. I had trouble hearing people speak unless I faced them head-on and watched their lips move (figure 1).

But what a difference it made. Two plus meters of snow-white georgette embossed with little stars. It was a present from my landlady in Cairo.

"You must wear the *hijab*," she admonished in a high-pitched shrill. "It is right thing for Muslim girl. You will feel more comfortable here."

Maybe she had a point. From the minute I arrived in my new neighborhood of al-Demerdash, I was conscious of the staring mafia. They just couldn't help themselves. Men, women, and children glued their eyeballs on me or, more precisely, my bare head. Maybe it was the novelty of a stranger's arrival. A Muslim stranger who could barely speak five words of Arabic. I willed the stares to go away. But they assaulted me every waking day, every minute of public appearance. I didn't have the thick skin to ignore them. And I certainly didn't want to remain confined with in the walls of my apartment. So I reached for the georgette and the headband. The five-minute walk from my tenth-floor high rise to the nearby subway station transformed into a stare-free zone. I rode

FIGURE 1: A woman wearing a *batula* or *burgu* appears to be hailing a cab, 2004. Photo by Sheryl B. Shapiro.

toward downtown Cairo celebrating my invisibility.

The gleaming tiled floors of the Sadat subway station astound me. They compete for my attention with a trio of giggly Egyptian debutantes in hiphugging jeans, black Spandex tops with matching lacy head scarves. My eyes gravitate toward the girls. One of them greets a friend who looks like she has just come from a photo session with French *Vogue*. Stiletto boots, side-slit skirt grazing the knees, fitted leather jacket, and a knockoff Hermès scarf as a head cover. Her face is an airbrushed Lancôme ad. Creamy beige skin, dark glossy lips, and gobs of mascara paired with pearly gray shadow. We lock eyes. She breaks into a smirk and elbows her cohorts. Here we go again. Stares and more stares. This time, it's not that I lack a hijab. The fashionistas are in shock about my baggy, celery green linen trousers, potato-sack jacket, and those fraying old Tevas. My scarf knots underneath the chin with two long ends dangling on my chest like seaweed. I cannot be bothered with hairpins and makeup or the plain white georgette. After all, I didn't come all the way to Cairo to win a beauty contest.

It's a beautiful station, as far as subway stations go. Clean, bright, and shiny. No one but me seems to notice, much less care. Commuters make a beeline for turnstiles and jam the escalators. The ticket window swarms with human traffic. I stride toward the exit. My ticket slides into a little slot. The turnstile refuses to budge.

I panic and throw my weight against the metal rod. It remains stuck. I try again and again. The only thing moving is my weak little body. No one is behind me, but as I look back, I see a small platoon of witnesses. The sexy hijabis are among them. Their smirks grow bigger along with the requisite stares. A security official watches my predicament and signals me to step into the stationmaster's office near the plat-form. The inspector volleys heated accusations at me in Arabic that no one bothers to translate. His sidekick squats on his haunches with a look that says, *I know what you're up to.*

"But you don't understand," I plead in English. "I am new in Cairo and made a mistake."

The stationmaster glowers and another stream of rapid-fire Arabic spews forth. The last guttural syllable of his tirade unleashes a wad of spit, the size of a dime, landing squarely on my right jaw. I wipe off the spittle with the back of my sleeve and catch a glimpse of my reflection in the streaky window behind his desk. A petite woman in a white head scarf blinks back. She has big scared eyes the color of espresso and charcoal-thick eyebrows. Her pale complexion contrasts with stray wisps of jet black hair poking from the sides of her veil. It seems to complement the gold pendant on her chain stenciled with the word Allah in stylized Arabic.

Oh no, oh no. A sinking feeling at the pit of my stomach. I know what this is all about. It's about my chameleon face, the kind that morphs into any society's gene pool, bestowing me the dubious honor of "You look so familiar, haven't I seen you someplace before?" It happens everywhere I travel. France, Spain, Italy. And now Cairo. So that's why the stationmaster has been raving like a lunatic. My appearance deceives him into believing the opposite of who I am. In that hijab, I look so, so *local,* for lack of a better word. I cannot possibly be a novice foreign tourist fresh off a transatlantic flight. It's a bit unnerving, the way a piece of fabric on my head erases the American in me. Strange consequences abound. I can't get away with cultural blunders or the failure to understand the intricacies of subway ticketing rules. If I happen to use a wrong token that jams the turnstile, then I must be an Egyptian smart aleck trying to cheat the system.

"Pay this amount." The stationmaster thrusts a form in squiggly Arabic handwrit-ing and draws a big circle in red ink around some cryptic numerals.

Congratulating myself for passing as a local troublemaker, I fork over 120 Egyptian pounds (about $30), assuming it is the bribe for my freedom. The station-master orders me to sit back down. I am already twenty minutes late for my first class at the Fajr Arabic Language Institute. Desperation mounts as I rifle through my bag and unearth my U.S. passport and the name of the Arabic school printed on a torn page of the weekly *Al-Ahram's* English edition. The stationmaster stares at them as if hallucinating.

"You *Amrikeyi?* You no look *Amrikeyi!*"

A speck of light dares to invade his eyes.

"Merhaba! Merhaba! Welcome, welcome to Egypt!"

The scowling face gives way to profuse handshakes.

"You come to office every day. I teach you Arabic and you teach me your English, yes?"

He beams like a proud papa.

"You want taxi, yes? Go with Yusuf. He get you nice clean taxi. Very cheap. You pay like Egyptian, not tourist, understand?"

I glance at Yusuf, the sidekick who treated me like a criminal fifteen minutes earlier. He is asleep on the floor, snoring loudly, his gaping mouth an open invitation to buzzing flies.

"You will share with me some *chai, yes?*"

My newfound friend pushes a button under his desk. A minute later, a little barefooted boy in a worn orange sweatshirt produces two chipped glasses of steaming black tea. I sip the heavily sugared brew and straighten out the folds of my crumpled georgette.

We all know that appearances are deceiving. Despite this knowledge, we still judge based on appearances. It is difficult not to when what we see on the outside is initially the only piece of available information about a person. It's not like we can get inside that person's head and figure out where she comes from, why she behaves the way she does, and what makes her tick in general. Appearances are our only clue.

Once when I was pounding away on my laptop at a Seattle public library, I overheard a conversation between two elderly women at a side table. It was about a six-year-old girl whom one of them had seen wearing the hijab.

"Why do they have to wear those things?" The voice sounded horrified.

Her friend responded. "It has to do with their Muslim religion. I hear it's very strict."

I thought of moving to a different part of the library so I wouldn't have to hear about Muslim rhymed with muslin once more. But I was in a lazy mood so I just stayed in my place, pretending to be deaf and ignoring something inside me that wanted to speak out and address those women. The longer I sat, the more conflicted I felt until I finally pushed back my chair and approached the adjoining table.

"Excuse me?"

"Why, hello, dear! Do sit down and join us. What a cute little dress you're wearing. Wherever did you get it?"

"It's from India."

"Ah, India! I just love Indian food. Don't you?" The silver-haired woman elbowed her companion.

"Umm. I wanted to say something."

"Yes?"

"Well, I don't really know how to say this. But I heard what you were talking about that little girl in her hijab. Well, I just ..."

"To cover up a small child. What an awful thing to do!"

"Yes, it's not an easy thing to understand. I have a hard time understanding it myself. You see, I'm also a Muslim."

"No, you're not!"

"You cannot be!"

"But I am!"

Both women scrutinized my kneelength batik sundress, my hijab-less head, my strappy kitten-heeled sandals.

"Well, you may be a Muslim. But at least you're not fundamental like that little girl."

I winced. And not just because of that mispronunciation again. I am all too familiar with their attitude, and the sadness and anger it evokes in me. As a Pakistani, born and raised Muslim, reared in Seattle for twenty three years, I have never gotten used to misplaced labels about Islam— not only the fable that wearing hijab automatically equals oppression, but the misapprehension that all Muslim men must be depraved polygamists and that the harsh austerity of our faith condones violence. Not that we Muslims have it all figured out. Some of us are downright allergic to questions and self-examination. But I don't recall a time when I did not feel immense pride in and open-ended curiosity about my cultural and religious heritage. As a teenager, I nearly drove my mother mad with whys.

One of my favorites was the why of veiling. Whenever I raised the issue with Ammi, she pointed me to the verse in the Qur'an advising women to cover their bosoms and hide their adornments.

"But it says nothing about covering the hair!" I challenged her.

"Isn't hair an adornment?" she countered.

"Well I suppose so. But it doesn't clearly say so."

My hijab-clad mother smiled and said, "It is clear enough to me."

That was nearly twenty years ago. Today, Ammi's eyes are just as radiant with faith. Her face continues to glow with *noor*, the sheen of inner light. She still makes it impossible for me to argue with the power of this much belief.

So I had a hard time explaining the significance of veiling to my newfound acquaintances at the library. As our discussion continued, I tried to hammer in the point that wearing the hijab is not an outright sign of the backwardness of Muslim females. It may have to do with cultural values or community peer pressure or at best a personal expression of faith.

The old ladies weren't so convinced. "Then why don't *you* wear it?" one of them asked.

I told her that I didn't think the head cover was religiously mandatory, but many Muslims, including my own mother, considered it otherwise. "How can any religion be so wishy-washy?" they wondered. Either something is required or it isn't. So which is it? I sighed and fumbled for a short answer, which of course does not exist.

The Muslim veil is full of meaning. At any given period of history, time or place, the idea and practice of veiling have led to clashing viewpoints—inclusion, exclusion; progressive, regressive; emancipating, humiliating; erotic, vulgar; trendy—the list goes on and on. One of the most contentious debates in some analytical circles underlies the assumption that feminists oppose the veil and antifeminists don't. That is to say, a covered Muslim woman cannot possibly have a mind of her own, that in order to improve her status and move forward, she has to reject Islamic traditions and adopt Western ways. According to the Egyptian scholar Leila Ahmed, this type of logic is not only ethnocentric and misguided, but it also overemphasizes the wearing or not wearing of the veil as the sole determinant of Muslim women's freedom and mobility or lack thereof. So pervasive is this fascination with the hijab that it inevitably dominates most discussions of women and Islam as if no other factors matter. Ahmed's argument does not negate the importance of the veil. But she compares it to Western women's struggles over gender justice where items of clothing such as bras were briefly in focus as symbols of contention yet did not take over the entire discourse on women's lib.[1]

Another outcome of the veil's hegemony in the public imagination is the idea, whether overtly or covertly expressed, of Islam as oppressor of women and the West as liberator. This idea was also internalized by Muslim rulers who introduced westernizing reforms that forcibly banned the veil, not because of what veiling said about women, but how it reflected on the *men*.

As an instrument wielding the gender politics of identity, the veil may have no equal. Whether enforced or forbidden, obsessive to the point of ridicule, the dialectics of a Muslim woman's head (covered or un-) are not without controversy. But it would be too simplistic to presume that veiling, in and of itself, renders passive submission. "Static" is the one word the veil refutes time and again.

A case in point is the colonial narrative of Algeria. In the initial phase, women wore the veil as a symbol of resistance against French occupation. The veil stood for the dignity and validity of all native customs under fiercest attack, particularly customs pertaining to women, ones the occupier was determined to control. The question of who ultimately controls how women look and dress was in many ways a pivotal battleground. As the Algerian struggle for liberation intensified, the veil was consciously abandoned during the course of revolutionary action in which women actively participated.

The Battle of Algiers (1965) is a film documenting their participation as attractive secret agents, carrying briefcases of false papers and huge sums of money, slinking through the Europeanized city streets where men, young and old, appraise the slim, brunette, bare-legged revolutionaries. When the French authorities discovered this form of militant female subterfuge, it marked a turning point in the Algerian war of independence.

Covert missions became increasingly suspect. As illustrated by the filmmaker Gillo Pontecorvo, in order to conceal packages, women were obliged to alter their body image. They became slouchy and shapeless and took back the protective cover of the veils under which they carried revolvers, bombs, and hand grenades. Enemy raids continued and it was not uncommon for these now-veiled revolutionaries to be shoved against walls to have their bodies passed over with magnetic detectors.

This is not to equate the struggles of Algerian women exclusively with the veil, then or now. The point is that veiling is a dynamic process, and during the Algerian revolution, women themselves dictated their appearances for strategic resistance. In a certain sense, the hard-won independence from France caused a turning back in society, wrestling with values already outmoded. Whereas the veil had been largely eschewed in the prerevolutionary era, it was resumed by many after the revolution and stripped of its traditional dimension. Interestingly, interaction with Western culture, in the form of colonization, also shaped the language of the veil as a distinct by-product of both East and West.

As my hijab and I ventured deeper into the Middle East, we encountered more contradictions. Traveling beyond Cairo in the winter of 2001, I still insisted on wearing the head scarf out of respect for the cultures I encountered, though the preponderance of high-society Arab girls flaunting their you-know-whats in people's faces was rather disconcerting. Don't get me wrong. I would have gladly cheered their right to wear skintight Spandex. But while Spandex paired with veils may appear to be a creative spin on Islamic modesty, my mind couldn't go beyond the hypocrisy.

In the Jordanian capital of Amman, I once saw a woman in full *niqab*, a thick black veil covering her entire face with a six-inch open strip around the eyes. She wore black from head to toe. But there was something odd about her, as she stood alone on a street corner, teetering on stilettos. After a while, a car drove by, screeched its tires, and stopped. A man got out, yelling profanities at the woman who was apparently his sister. She yelled back in defiance, protesting loudly as he clutched her wrist and dragged her toward the waiting car. She refused to get inside and her voice climbed decibels, occasionally breaking midsentence from hoarseness. There was a strange disconnect between the fury coming out of her mouth and her black-cloaked obscurity. Suddenly, she whipped out a cell phone from somewhere underneath her voluminous garments and furiously punched the numbers with a black-gloved finger. She spoke into it through her face veil, which fluttered with the movement of her hidden lips.

FIGURE 2: The author eschews hipster fashion in favor of traditional *hijab* in the old city of Damascus, Syria, 2001. Courtesy of Maliha Masood.

The brother went ballistic. He grabbed his sister's hand, yanked away the mobile, and smashed it with his feet. Then he tightened his grip, twisting her hand behind her back. The girl howled and kicked him in the shins with her spiky heels. He smacked her head and tried to push her to the ground. As their fighting continued, another car approached. A sleek white Mercedes with tinted windows. The passenger door opened and a tall, gray-haired man in a double-breasted suit stepped out and gestured to the woman with a curt angling of his head.

She was squatting on her haunches, a whimpering black huddle with teary eyes. The well-dressed stranger helped her up and led the still crying woman into the backseat of his car. Then he went up to the disgruntled brother, who was pummeling his fists on the car's roof. A lengthy speech followed. The older man took a wad of bills from his wallet, slipped them in the brother's front shirt pocket, and patted his cheek in a there, there kind of way.

The brother laughed sarcastically and hurled one final insult at his sister waiting inside the car. The one word I made out was *sharmuta,* Arabic for whore.

The next evening, I returned to the same street corner at the exact same time but there was no more drama. I waited at that spot for five consecutive nights but she never came back. Even if she was a prostitute, I wondered what drove her to it and why she was so heavily veiled. Maybe it was a way of ensuring her protection and anonymity. But that hadn't deterred her brother from recognizing her. Or did her niqab mean that she was in fact a pious woman, forced by circumstances to her current profession? Maybe, maybe not. After that incident, I was less and less sure of the real motives for veiling.

In the old city of Damascus, I was the star entertainment among the flared denims, boot-clad fashionistas snickering at my sensible Birkenstocks and navy *abaya* with cross-stitched embroidery that labeled me a local country hick instead of the American city slicker I wanted them to befriend. What I really wanted was to take pictures of these Damascene hipsters and show them to my American friends back home, who thought of themselves as the epitome of hipster style in Capri pants and tight midriff tops, without the slightest inkling of hipster competition in Syria. Yes, Syria, where I felt like a dork for the sake of Islamic modesty (figure 2).

Speaking of modesty, when I lived in Beirut, I had this roommate, Najma, a struggling architecture student, who sat in her room from dawn to dusk, fiddling with straight edges and blueprints. Whenever Najma was stuck on a problem, she would sing. I could have listened to her all day when she belted out classics by the Lebanese diva Fairuz, in a voice as clear as a bell.

Most days, Najma wore a purple paisley print head scarf folded into a triangle and knotted behind her nape. It kept a mass of thick corkscrew curls in check. She wasn't particularly religious. The only time we discussed Islam, Najma pointed out that she was an agnostic and we left it at that. I rarely got a chance to talk to her because she was so busy with her studies, often not returning home until two or three in the morning. For my birthday, she gave me homemade tapes of the music she listened to—funky fusion beats with hints of Sufi trance. I liked dancing to them in the tiny living room we shared.

Najma watched my attempts to shimmy my shoulders and wiggle my hips like a real belly dancer.

"You're trying too hard," she said.

"This is impossible!" I was trying to isolate my abs and shake them like Jell-O.

Najma stifled a giggle. *La habibi, la!*

"What then? What am I doing wrong?"

"You must learn to find your center. *Yallah,* I show you."

We wore gym clothes and dressed them up in gauzy veils, doubling as sarongs and bandanas to keep off the sweat. Najma blew me away with her graceful moves. What really surprised me was the smoldering sensuality that oozed from her limbs like sap from a ripe rubber tree. When I asked her how she learned to dance so well, she whispered in my ear, "La Souke."

La Souke turned out to be a nightclub where Najma performed Thursday and Saturday nights. Men went wild over her in thigh-high boots, wriggling in a cage, Madonna style. But she was best in her arousing Arabic numbers, all decked out in sequined halters and hip belts made out of little silver coins. In one routine, she added a sheer black veil, flinging it in the air and letting it fall flat on her face as she swayed and fluttered. Najma's dancing veil reminded me of an untrimmed sail, taunting the wind that fueled its flight. It defied definition. It could be anything one wanted it to be—just like Najma.

Demure student by day and sexy dancer by night—it was not my business, nor anyone else's, to judge her. The club gig paid well and Najma needed the money for college and rent. She could have had a "safer" job, but dancing was so much more lucrative. Wasn't she bothered by all those leering men, total strangers who probably went home and jerked off fantasizing about her pretty, dancing image? Najma laughed and said she could not care less. She was having a good time on that stage, proud of her sculpted body, and it emboldened her confidence to dance in public, to let people have fun, but the real entertainment was for herself! In a way I guess she was calling the shots.

When I left Beirut and vacated the apartment, Najma's goodbye present was a postcard-sized bundle and she told me not to open it until I got home. Five years later, I still have that chiffon veil of hers. Sometimes, I press my face into its black softness just to breathe the lingering scent of sweet tobacco smoke and Chanel No. 5.

By the time I reached Turkey, I had flung away my hijab. Yet there I met Turkish women who were clamoring to wear the head scarf in universities and government institutions where veiling was banned by law, making it a contentious battleground between individual self-expression and government policy. In the eyes of Turkish women demanding the right to cover their heads, the issue at heart was a matter of free will to dress as they pleased. And they were demanding this right even as they studied to be doctors, lawyers, and diplomats. Given Turkey's campaign to get into the European Union, the Turkish state has reinforced its anti-hijab laws, blatantly devoid of the concept of choice.[2]

If only choice could ever be simple. Back in the States, my traveling veils have converted to fashionable neck scarves and shawls. I have quite a collection in shades of burgundy, turquoise, and amethyst with patterns of polka dots and spiral chains. Most of them have been donated to my mother. We no longer argue about the whys of veiling. And she doesn't chide me for my uncovered head because she knows my faith is strong. Strong enough to muster the discipline to pray five times a day in a country where the azan or call to prayer does not blare from a neighborhood minaret but echoes inside the heart. What Ammi and I both resent are the judgment calls within our own Seattle community where an unveiled Muslim woman automatically earns the "secular" label, meaning she is nonobservant of practice. Is the presence of the hijab a surefire indicator of inner belief? Does the lack of hijab therefore signify none? Instead of an emphatic yes or no, my answer would be "it depends."

Recall the deceptiveness of appearances and our penchant to judge by them. In the United States, just as I discovered in the Middle East, appearance is everything. My ability to blend in has a reverse effect on my own home turf. Here, people have a hard time believing that I'm a Muslim just because I don't cover. They can tell by my funny sounding, hard-to-pronounce-name that I must be a "foreigner," but that's about it. The emphasis on image is so strong that if you don't look like a caricatured Muslim, you simply cannot be one.

A caricatured Muslim woman is undoubtedly veiled. But what are the implications behind that veiled image? Is she subservient, helpless, and weak? Feisty, determined, and ambitious? Not too long ago, I saw a PBS Frontline broadcast reissued from the 1980 film *Death of a Princess*. It is a dramatized documentary based on the true-life account of a Saudi princess, who was publicly executed for adultery. Justification for the punishment oscillated on the grounds of "Islamic law" and a violation of family tribal honor. The film suggested that the princess's murder was instigated by her own grandfather. Saudi uproar over the allegedly insensitive airing of their dirty laundry enflamed the controversy.

One unforgettable scene was especially criticized. The film describes how bored Saudi princesses cruise the desert highways in their chauffeured cars to pick up men. They could be married, young or old, beautiful or hideous. Black abayas and niqabs camouflage their identities, just as they did for that woman I had observed in Jordan, who may have been a prostitute. But unlike her, these rich royals are not at work. They are on a desert raid exploiting the anonymity of their covering for promiscuity. The car slows; the princess rolls down her window to eye a potential mate. Or she might sit inside a parked vehicle with a trio of others like her, silently observing men who are dancing for her pleasure with their swords, men wanting to please, men wanting to be chosen by the predatory veiled women who can see without being seen.

Much of the media attention and Saudi offensive centered on this scene's crudeness, which was said to be fiction and to have cheapened the film and insulted Saudi women, especially members of the royal family. Watching the scene unfold, I was struck by the image itself, for it made me think of how much power those Saudi royals wielded by virtue of being covered.

As a physical barrier, the veil denies men their usual privilege of discerning whomever they desire. By default, the women are in command. The female scrutinizes the male. Her gaze from behind the anonymity of her face veil or niqab is a kind of surveillance that casts her in the dominant position. It enables a woman to uncover with her eyes, to make visible that which is forbidden. So there seems to be an acute relationship between veiling and vision that undercuts the legacy of social, cultural, political, and religious meanings associated with the Muslim veil. It continues to fascinate me, the Rubik's cube of identities the hijab conceals and reveals.

A year of traveling alone in the Middle East and my upbringing as a Pakistani Muslim American have shown me that there is no formulaic way to describe the hijab. Even though I don't wear one as a rule, a part of me is stitched from its threads. Just because those threads are not always visible doesn't mean they don't count. The white georgette cloth that first felt like a bandage still floats in my eyes, sweeping layers of memory. We've had a long relationship, fraught with love, hate, confusion, and plenty of surprises. We've journeyed together and served each other well as travel companions—for the most part. My hijab gave me refuge from prying stares and possibly averted more serious dangers. It adopted me at sub-way stations and rejected me in trendy cafés. It has kept me warm on cold winter nights, it has wowed, titillated, and amazed, and it has also made me laugh, dance, sulk, and complain. As with most relationships, my hijab and I have had our spats and dramas. These days, we're in a mellow groove, content to leave each other alone, but always on the lookout for a rousing debate.

NOTES

1. Leila Ahmed, "The Discourse of the Veil," in *Veil: Veiling, Representation and Contemporary* Art, ed. David Bailey and Gilane Tawadros (Cambridge, MA: MIT Press, 2003).
2. In a noted case in 1999, politician and member of the Islamist Virtue Party Merve Kavakçi became the first veiled woman to be elected to the Turkish Parliament. She was prevented from making her parliamentary oath when she wore her head scarf to a swearing-in ceremony in defiance of the secular Turkish constitution. She was eventually stripped of her Turkish citizenship when it was discovered that she had earlier that year taken dual American citizenship.

EVERYDAY LIFE AND POPULAR CULTURE

Section four

Performing National Identity

by MIRIAM COOKE

When I look for my real self and can't find it, I say that it is lost in the terrors of a life where I am no longer myself. I have allowed the waves to toss my self to the right and to the left. Although I am in it, life has distanced me from my self ... When I wear my thawb [white gown], and gutra and walk on the earth of which I am a part ... the pebbles delight in my walking and they sing: Oh Arab! And the air of the earth embraces me and takes from my scent to spread it among the passersby. Every day I go to my friend the Stone and she knows me by my thawb, gutra and `uqal [headdress] and my perfume and I tell her all my secrets and we have become friends. One day, I changed clothes and left my thawb, gutra and `uqal at home and I sat on the Stone and she said: Who are you? And I said: I'm your friend who sits with you every day. She said: You're not my friend because your appearance and your thawb and your smell are not the same. And the Stone pushed me away violently and I fell into a lions' den and they tore my body to pieces, some from the West, some from the East and some from I don't know where. As I was drowning among my severed limbs, I heard a voice calling me. I looked up quickly and heard my thawb, gutra and `uqal saying, Come to us for we are your saviors, your features. If you abandon us you will be lost without identity and no one will know who you are.

THIS FAIRY TALE BY 'ABD AL-KARIM AL-'IZZAZI APPEARED IN THE
Qatari daily *Al-Raya* on September 7, 2010, three days before the end of Ramadan.
It narrates the important role national dress plays in marking Gulf Arabs' national
difference, authenticity, and identity. Gulf Arabs are increasingly donning a uniform
that turns every public appearance into a performance of national identity.[1] Men's
thawb, *gutra*, and `*uqal* and women's `*abaya* have become more than everyday
formal dress, they are the *sine qua non* of national performances (Longva 1997,
116–25).

Local dress signals not only the nationality but also the privileged status of Gulf
and Peninsula Arabs. It marks their difference from outsiders. In the second volume
of `Abd al-Rahman Munif's *Cities of Salt*, we read the consternation of tribal men
when they see an outsider wear their dress. On his way back from the Hajj, a Syrian
doctor establishes a clinic in Harran where he dispenses miracles. Despite his white
skin and elegant western clothes marking him as the outsider par excellence, Dr.
Mahmalji ingratiates himself with the Emir. The people not only accept him, they
come to believe in him (Munif 1989, 520–35). After caring for the dying ruler and
cozying up to his son, the new ruler, the doctor appears in the town wearing a
thawb: "He had discarded the foreign clothes that used to distinguish him from
those around him and had adopted wide, flowing Arab dress in which he drowned.
He did not know how to wear it properly and while he walked he kept tripping over
himself" (Munif 1986, 10). But, not for long. He soon learned how to walk in these
new clothes as though he were of them. At first the people did not recognize him,
but when they did, they became alarmed at how quickly this stranger had become
comfortable in their clothes. The disguise singled him out as someone to fear. He,
like all foreigners adopting Gulf Arab clothes, must be closely watched. He must
have an ulterior motive for going native.

An Emirati woman student I met in Abu Dhabi told me that restricting native
dress to Gulf Arabs is a survival mechanism in "countries where the local population is the minority."[2] Rejecting anonymity in the crowds of foreigners, Gulf Arabs
perform nationality and privilege through tribal dress. Men's national dress has become a sign of "cultural authenticity and connectedness to past traditions. Without
hesitation Emiratis will say that the *kandoura* is the dress of their ancestors and they
remain loyal to it, 'our dress is our identity.'" Displaying authenticity, wealth, power
and privilege, clothes "have become markers of a dominant ethnic class presiding
over the affairs of a multi-ethnic society in transition … current adherence to their
traditional national dress is a function of both tradition and modernity; modernity

in the sense that it is a reaction or protest to threatening global forces" (Khalaf 2005, 244–45). While the form of this national dress is said to be traditional, its meaning is modern inasmuch as it affirms a new national identity in the twenty-first century. For some, national dress also represents a protest against globalization, the flattening effects of jeans for everyone.

Denoting a collective construction of social boundaries, national dress is not a throwback but rather a conscious forward-looking reaction to the conditions of daily life. In fact, Bristol-Rhys contests the assumption that national dress is traditional. Citing some older women she interviewed, she observes,

> There was no possible way that a white *kandoura* would have been worn regularly before there was running water, washing machines, irons, starch and, to be honest, maids. A glimpse at any of the pictures taken of people before the late 1960s shows men dressed in various shades of brown and black, and not white. Only the rulers seemed to have managed white with any frequency. The `abaya was worn in the pre-oil days but, as one woman pointed out, you were never really in the 'public view' in the settlements and towns so it did not have to be worn all the time. 'It isn't national dress any more, it's the national uniform,' laughs Masifa. 'It is the only way to be recognized as citizens' (Bristol-Rhys 2011, 112).

This national uniform, Longva suggests, may be state-authorized. Unlike the assumption that the *thawb* and the `abaya were naturally and almost unthinkingly adopted by people under threat of disappearance, she claims that it is "a result of an ideological mobilization under the aegis of the state: the formation of a national identity" (Longva 1997, 125). The *thawb* and the `abaya have become vivid icons of a newly embraced, exclusivist, elitist national identity, and as such this national uniform is out of bounds for foreigners. *Gulf News* reported on September 15, 1996, Emiratis' concern about non-nationals wearing their clothes "so that they could pass off as nationals, hoping that they would get preferential treatment" (Khalaf 2005, 263).

The nationalist aspect may be as blatant as adorning `abayas "with portraits of Sheikh Muhammad al-Maktoum and Sheikh Maktoum al-Maktoum, the current and former rulers of Dubai, along with a map of the United Arab Emirates and the colors of its flag [ … ] these `abayas present a reification of national symbols" (Al Qasimi 2010, 69). The display of a modern, national subjectivity through dress "may be as old as human society ... the modern self may be less a matter of the content of an individual subjectivity than that of the insertion of that subjectivity into a particular regime of historicity and sociopolitical management" (Trouillot 2002, 853). In Jordan, for example, tribal dress differentiates Jordanians from the Palestinian refugees who migrated en masse after two wars with Israel in 1948 and 1967.[3]

TRIBAL DRESS IN GULF HISTORY

During the 1960s and 1970s when tribes were being disaggregated, western clothes performed modernity. Traditional dress became almost taboo because it emphasized connection to the past and thus impeded modernization. Today it is western dress that is virtually taboo for Gulf Arabs, at least when they are at home. According to Marxist theorist Fredric Jameson, the quintessential modern gesture is taboo: "what look like innovations are in the modern, the result of a desperate attempt to find substitutes for what has been tabooed. It is a model and a restructuration that shifts the burden of proof from the future to the past ... the taboo is very explicitly a taboo on previous kinds of representational form and content" (Jameson 2002, 127). In the midtwentieth-century Arab Gulf, the tribal was taboo; individual and collective modernization/westernization was the mandate.

Replacing the tie and suit in the twenty-first century, "tribal" dress is modern, national but, above all, it is also patriotic, as the founder and owner of "Al-Motahajiba" told his daughter, a student of mine in the VCUQ class. Today, one of the largest `abaya franchises in the region with its own international fashion shows (Al Qasimi 2010), "Al-Motahajiba" began modestly. Mr. Al Emadi had launched his business in a nine-square-meter location in the old commercial district that Muhammad `Ali `Abdullah's Suq Waqif replaced.

"The preservation of our culture and traditions started for me as a summer project in the year 1983 but it is now my mission against the winds of change blowing through our region. How to maintain your fashion edge against western trendy designers? ... Our notion is as Henry Ford once noted: If your attention is focused on what you give for a dollar worth of sales rather than what you get, your business is bound to succeed. 'Al-Motahajiba' is a brand that we intend to preserve for centuries to come hoping to be a small contributor in a sacred cause, our culture."[4] Al Emadi's brother added that Al-Motahajiba "is the most famous and glamorous brand name in the fashion design sphere among Arab women." Note the use of the words "brand" and "sacred." Like Jaidah and Bourennane's attribution of patriotism to their research into vernacular architecture, Al Emadi believes his `abaya franchise has made a patriotic contribution to indigenous culture, and the culture he is referencing is not religious but national. At the same time, in its scope and intent it exceeds national boundaries. As Al Emadi's daughter Sara commented, "Al-Motahajiba may seem to be a brand, which grew from a small shop in the souq, but in reality it is a tribal network spanning borders and cultures."[5]

The connection between tribal dress, modernity, and patriotism is widespread. A respondent to the survey that my VCUQ students designed about the wearing of the thawb or the `abaya wrote: "I am comfortable wearing the `abaya wherever I travel and that is my choice. Often I am asked about it and my identity and I feel as though I am an ambassador for my country." When I spoke with an Egyptian friend about this glorification of the `abaya she was amazed. She had always thought, she told me, that these super-rich women looked shabby in their black wraps. Clearly Gulf Arab women disagree. Far from shabby, tribal dress as national brand marks aristocracy. It distinguishes citizens from non-citizens, but it is also for international consumption.

Whereas Gulf men wear similar white gowns that are nonetheless nationally recognizable by collar or sleeve detail, women's black `abayas are not nation-specific. Fashions are often set in Saudi Arabia and then spread throughout the Peninsula where the `abaya plays not only a political but also a socio-economic role. Sulayman Khalaf writes, "The `abaya, when viewed within the Emirati elaborate system of ethnic stratification, becomes invested in multiple ways with social and cultural attitudes, meanings, images and symbols that help in the construction of the Emirati identity. The black `abaya has become the symbolic protected space for the Emirati woman, her spatial bubble, as it were, that not only protects but also differentiates and identifies" (Khalaf 2005, 242).[6] Men's dress code represents the national identity of individual states, while women's fashions are linked to the region as a whole.

A remarkable example of tribal dress as national icon was designed into one of Dubai's most iconic buildings: the 2007 Burj al-Arab that most believe is shaped like a dhow sail. The developers modeled this building on "a figure fitted with a kandura (long robe-like garment), gutra (headscarf), and egal (rope used to tie the gutra in place)" (Mitchell 2007, 136). Tribal dress, however stylized in architecture, makes a modern and immediately political statement.[7] Writing about Emirati dress "and the dynamics associated with its discourses," Khalaf confirms, "there are in our contemporary world different versions of modernity and different paths to it" (Khalaf 2005, 235).

While dress is one way of noting the mutually reinforcing overlap of the tribal modern, still another is Bedouin poetry.

THE MILLION'S POET

One of the most visible performances of the tribal modern is *Sha`ir al-Milyun*, or the Million's Poet competition. A reality TV competition, it assembles 18- to 45-year-old poets skilled in composing Nabati poetry, the colloquial poetics of the desert Bedouins, known for its improvisational spontaneity. The show has become very popular throughout the Arab world.[8]

Nabati poetry has always been an important part of tribal life; it was "the pinnacle of their aesthetic, creative ability, as an aesthetic relief from the starkness of the desert … They were also clearly proud to hear aspects of their culture elevated into verse … Bedouin poetry, like Bedouin culture, is heir to a Middle Eastern desert tradition that goes back four thousand years" (Bailey 2002, xii, 7, 15). Love of poetry is not new, but what is new is the interest in a poetic language that until recently Generation Twitter considered old-fashioned and taboo in the sense that it was connected to a past irrelevant to people intent on moving forward.

The brainchild of the crown prince of Abu Dhabi Shaikh Muhammad Bin Zayid Al Nahayan, the Million's Poet is a television talent show that the Abu Dhabi Authority of Culture and Heritage launched in November 2006. Performing the mutually constitutive tribal and modern in language, forty-eight contestants try to dazzle the jury honor the one who displays the greatest facility with the tribal language and millennial poetic conventions. Bedouin tribal poetry, with its obsolescing vocabulary, has stepped into the limelight. The winner, usually a man in his thirties, is awarded 1,000,000 Dinars and the title of the Million's Poet.[9] This is not an old-fashioned recital for elders. Young, hip Gulf Arabs attend this wildly popular competition in rhetorical tribal extravagance.

So popular has the show become among young people that some call it the Gulf Idol of poetry, á la American Idol. Poets stride on stage with music blaring, audience screaming, and lights flashing. They declaim their lines bombastically and then exit with equal pomp. Winners become national icons.

For a sense of the spectacle and also its incongruence a year into the Arab Spring, read this February 28, 2012, description of the fifth competition by Hugh Miles for the BBC News Middle East:

> The show is filmed live on Tuesday evenings in the Rafha Beach theatre, a heavily illuminated edifice in the desert on the road to Dubai. Inside, on the highly polished black stage bathed in gently shifting coloured lights, is what looks like a huge revolving flower with an oversized video screen at its centre. The auditorium is nearly full with a neatly self-segregated audience of men on one side, wearing traditional white dishdashas, and veiled women on the other in black abayas. Incense hangs pleasantly in the air, as from my seat behind the gold VIP tables I watch a qahwaji, a traditional coffee maker, serve the three judges Arabian coffee from a large ornamental brass pot ... All the poetry is proudly Arab, Islamic and tribal, and none of it expresses the slightest desire for either westernisation or democracy.[10]

Beyond pure entertainment, this competition integrates the language and lyrics of the Bedouin elders into the high-tech media world, and in so doing it bolsters the power of tribal leaders and their new nations.[11] The competition trumpets the coveted tribal modern brand. In April 2012, Shaikh Muhammad Bin Zayid Al Nahayan, Crown Prince of Abu Dhabi and Deputy Supreme Commander of the UAE Armed Forces, attended the finals, and Rashid Ahmed Al Rumaithi became the first Emirati poet to win first prize.

The selection process is quite elaborate. Every November, the jury of Gulf poets and literary critics selects forty-eight Nabati poets from several different Arab countries, including the desert regions of Jordan, Syria, Iraq, and Libya. In December, they gather at the al-Raha Beach Hotel Theater in Abu Dhabi to begin the six-week television knockout contest. Chosen poets are given a week to compose a poem on a given subject. The jury's verdict is worth 30 percent, while the remaining 70 percent depends on public votes.

It is important to note that, like other heritage projects, this competition has a commercial, and political, aspect. Every person who calls in her vote knows that she will have the equivalent of a dollar deducted from her phone bill. The more calls, the happier the telephone company. It has been rumored that big donors have bought thousands of calls. Like camel racing, a tribal poetry performance is thus underwritten by twenty-first-century capital and technology.

During the first year, one of the several subjects imposed on contestants was "Loyalty to the Homeland." The winner of that 2006 competition was Qatari Muhammad bin Futas of the Al Murrah tribe. Like all competitors, he first proclaimed his identity to be national, and then tribal: "Qatar is my homeland and I am like any other person who grew up in it, the cameleer, the shepherd, the rich, the pearl diver and the farmer … Men in danger respond as a man willing to sacrifice their pride [the word used was *gutra*] and lives to save their country's dignity and glory." Again, a tribal heritage project links to nationality, and national pride is symbolized by the men's traditional headdress, the *gutra*. [12]

The next year's winner was also a Qatari, but Qatari with a twist. Khalil Al Shibrimi Al Tamimi was in fact a Saudi with a recently acquired Qatari citizenship. A member of the legendary Al Tamim tribe, he asserted kinship with the ruling Al Thanis, who also claim descent from the Al Tamim. He asked to be brought back into the bosom of the tribe. His wish was granted, and he brought home the coveted prize.

On October 18, 2011, "Middle East Online" reported that Saudi, Kuwaiti, Qatari, Moroccan, Iraqi, Yemeni, and Egyptian poets, some of them women, had come to Amman to audition: "Some of them defied all circumstances experienced by their countries and traveled thousands of kilometers to attend the event. One Libyan poet took a huge risk, traveling through the dangerous roads from the violence-torn Libyan capital and then by air to make it to Jordan. Many Yemeni poets also braved the ongoing unrest in their country as well as poets from Iraq, Syria and Palestine to meet the jury." [13] With the eyes of the world on the revolutionaries overthrowing their ensconced dictators, intrepid poets from Libya and Yemen were undeterred.

NEO-BEDOUIN LANGUAGE

The competition is flourishing. A grassroots version of the Million's Poet was exported to the Yemeni archipelago of Socotro: "a geographically diverse body of contestants; a seated jury of experts; an audience seated on the ground of the Hadiboh public schoolyard; a grand prize of 100,000 Yemeni riyals ($450); and a glass trophy." [14] During the Yemeni uprising of 2011, contestants used the competition to air grievances against President `Ali `Abdallah Salih.

Filmmakers and writers have created stories about Nabati poetry and the competition. In the early 1990s, Dubai short story writer Muhammad al-Murr wrote about a young man who hoped to inherit his uncle's talent for Nabati poetry. A television program about Nabati poets inspired him, and he composed a poem he had penned by a skilled calligrapher and sent it to a local paper. Three weeks later, the editor printed a dismissal of the poem as "feeble in content and flawed in its metre. It is a long way from Nabati poetry but we would like to praise you for your beautiful handwriting" (al-Murr 1991, 70). Tribal poetry has strict rules; only skilled poets should dare compose it. In 2012, the Abu Dhabi company Imagenation released "Million's Poet," a film about Salamah, a Bedouin girl who defied her father's prohibition on her participation in the Million's Poet competition.[15]

It is remarkable how popular the language of this wildly popular poetic endurance contest has become.[16] The revival of the Bedouin Nabati language coincides with a linguistic crisis among young Gulf Arabs. A Qatari student once confided that her English was better than her Arabic and her English was not native. She was ashamed, she said, that she had not mastered any language.[17] Dana Abdulla Al Khalaf echoes this sentiment: "In the past, the dialect in Qatar was a pure local Arabic, Khaliji [Arab Gulf] dialect, but it kept changing ... some of the causes of change in our dialect are the languages we learn in school, multiculturalism, mass media, trade with different countries ... and globalization ... most young people now don't even understand words our grandparents used" (Al Khalaf 2010).

The words their grandparents used now pepper the language of the Million's Poet aspirants. Newspapers "carry weekly sections exclusively dedicated to *Nabati* poetry, and more than five hundred Internet sites and blogs publish, discuss and circulate Bedouin poems. These sites are growing by the day, along with satellite programs and poetry contests ... this genre is treated as an object for consumption and fetishism in a rapidly and alarmingly evolving consumer culture in the Gulf region" (al-Ghadeer 2009, 14). The celebration of Bedouin oral poetry challenges the domination of English, but it also serves as a counterweight to what many consider to be the diluted Arabic of the media, today's lingua franca across the Arab world.

Conferences deplore the disappearance of formal Arabic. During "The Arab Cultural Project" conference held in Doha, November 12, 2010, linguist Faruq Shusha commented that young people seem to think that their "modernity begins with a break from their language." The mission of the Sharjah-based Arabic Language Protection Association is the preservation of "the Arabic language from an awkward mix of foreign vocabularies and dialects, and to limit the negative influences of the multicultural environment on the UAE's official language … The new generations are becoming more and more distant from their native tongue. This has given rise to a new form of broken language that combines various accents emerging on the surface" (Davidson 2008, 201, 202). The popularity of the Million's Poet contest sparks the hope that Arabic in its unadulterated form may yet return.

This search for the pure language of desert Bedouin recalls the role of eighth-century Basra in the formative period of Arabic philology and linguistics. Basra scholars "were not content to collect samples of speech from Bedouins from the desert, or Badiya, the steppes of Suria and Iraq, who came to their cities; they also took themselves into the desert to gather them from the mouths of other Bedouins, the authenticity of whose speech they judged to be intact because they had lived far from the centers of urban life … The beginning of the tenth century marked the emergence of a neo-Bedouinism that re-established a connection with the past of the Basra school by putting a stay in the desert on the agenda for scientific reasons" (Touati 2010, 51, 67). This tradition continued until the twentieth century, with "many urban families sending their children to live among the Bedouin for a few seasons in order to learn the lore of the Bedouin and to absorb the positive values of living in a simple society in the purity of the desert" (Cole 1975, 53). Now, Bedouin Arabic is being brought to the capital, even though some still believe that it is only by living among the Bedouin that they will be able to learn this language in its pure form.

In 2008, the Abu Dhabi Cultural Foundation, inspired by the success of the Million's Poet, opened the first Nabati poetry academy. According to its founder Mr. Amimi, "Nabati is not a new kind of art, but Million's Poet has brought it into more popular culture, not just here but across the region."[18] In fact, it is new. Like camel racing, Nabati poetry has been reintroduced in a way that looks quite different from its predecessor. Academy scholars travel throughout the region recording Bedouin poetry In 2009, the Emir of Sharjah, Shaikh Sultan Bin Mohammad Al Qasimi, opened the Sharjah Nabati Poetry Centre "built to serve present and future generations."[19]

Tribal dress and poetry are performing the brand in spectacular ways, and in the final chapter I will look at how women are engaging with the tribal modern brand as they become increasingly visible in the public sphere.

NOTES

1. Lisa Wedeen discusses a similar phenomenon in Yemen, where the repetition of performative practices constitutes individuals and constructs the twenty-first-century nation (Wedeen 2008, 15, 17).
2. Conversation with Zayed University student in Abu Dhabi, December 5, 2008.
3. In her article about the return of the tribal in Jordan and the dialogic relationship between national and local performances of tribal culture, Linda Layne writes about "the changing meanings of the dilig, the traditional embroidered dress, for the tribes of the Jordan Valley ... In concert with the national valorization of tribal culture, the marked wearing of dilig by young women has become a symbol of tribal identity and, by extension, of Jordanian identity ... Because dilug symbolize "Bedouinness" and, by extension, "Jordanianness," their selection for wear by young women is a political statement and one that meets with public nods and comments of approval" (Layne 1989, 28–29). The dilig is both tribal and modern because it is national.
4. Sara Al Emadi, interview with her father and uncle, Doha, November 5, 2010.
5. Final paper in the tribal modern project at VCUQ, December 2010.
6. In 2010, Islamic banks in the Arab Gulf required its female employees to wear an `abaya regardless of their nationality.
7. In his article about the continued use of khadi, or the spun cloth that Gandhi advocated as a return to the true values of Indian society, Dipesh Chakrabarty writes that it is the "site of the desire for an alternative modernity" (Chakrabarty 2002, 64). Although alternative modernities are not the thesis of this book, what is interesting about this statement is the claim to modernity for heritage dress.
8. Nimah Nawwab claims that for some the show "has led to a rise in pride and tribalism," while others lament "the caliber of the work." Nawwab goes on to situate this poetry competition in its historical context: "Pre-Islamic poetry competitions at renowned sites such as Suq Ukaz drew poets from all parts of the area as they engaged in poetic battles that often included work composed on the spot" (Paine, Lodge, and Touati 2011, xxiii).
9. In Abu Dhabi there is a street lined with camel sculptures that was recently called Shari `al-Milyun—note the metathesis of the root letters ra and `ain

from sha`ir to shari`. The connection between these two heritage events, the poetry recitation and camel racing, is evident.

10. http://www.bbc.co.uk/news/world-middle-east-17178072, accessed February 28, 2013.

11. Unpatriotic poets pay a high price. German PEN reported that on November 16, 2011, the Qatari state security summoned Muhammad ibn al-Dheeb Al-Ajami to be interrogated about his "Tunisian Jasmine." In this January 2011 poem, he had criticized governments across the Gulf, stating "we are all Tunisia in the face of the repressive elite." On November 29, 2012, he was sentenced to life imprisonment on charges of "inciting the overthrow of the ruling regime" and "criticising the ruler." On February 25, 2013, the life sentence was reduced to 15 years. http://www.pen-deutschland.de/en/themen/writers-in-prison/aktuelle-ehrenmitglieder/mohammed-ibn-al-dheeb-al-ajami-katar/, accessed March 1, 2013.

12. With thanks to Hissa Zainal for help in finding the poem and then translating it.

13. With thanks to Pernille Arenfeldt for drawing my attention to this notice.

14. Nathalie Peutz, "Revolution in Socotra. A Perspective from Yemen's Periphery." (See http://www.merip.org/mer/mer263/revolution-socotra, accessed June 3, 2012).

15. http://www.movieweb.com/movie/millions-poet, accessed January 21, 2012.

16. "There is a remarkable similarity between the vocabulary of Bedouin Nabati poetry and the classical poetry that was being composed before Islam" said Prof. Clive Holes, the Khalid bin `Abdullah Al-Sa`ud Professor for the Study of the Contemporary Arab World at the University of Oxford. http://www.middle-east-online.com/english/?id=51475, July 10, 2013.

17. In 2012, the Qatari government made Arabic the compulsory language of instruction in K–12 schools and at Qatar University, in order to deal with the problem of illiteracy in Arabic. Despite strong resistance, the policy was implemented in September.

18. http://www.thenational.ae/news/uae-news/education/creation-of-nabati-poetry-academy-prompted-by-success-of-tv-shows, accessed November 27, 2010.

19. http://www.uaeinteract.com/docs/SultanopensSharjah_NabatiPoetryHouse/34357.htm, accessed November 27, 2010.

REFERENCES

Al Khalaf, Dana Abdulla. 2010. "Our Changing Language." In *Hazawi: Stories from Qatar*, Volume 4. Doha, Qatar: Carnegie Mellon University.

Al-Qasimi, Noor. 2010. "Immodest Modesty: Accommodating Dissent and the `Abaya-as-Fashion in the Arab Gulf States." *Journal of Middle East Women's Studies* 6(1): 46–74.

Bailey, Clinton. 2002 (1991). *Bedouin Poetry from Sinai and the Negev* (Foreword by Wilfred Thesiger). London: Saqi Books.

Bristol-Rhys, Jane. 2011. *Emirati Women: Generations of Change.* New York: Columbia University Press.

Cole, Donald Powell. 1975. *Nomads of the Nomads. The Al Murrah of the Empty Quarter.* Chicago: Aldine Publishing.

Davidson, Christopher. 2008. *Dubai: The Vulnerability of Success.* New York: Columbia University Press.

al-Ghadeer, Moneera. 2009. *Desert Voices: Bedouin Women's Poetry in Saudi Arabia.* London: I. B. Tauris.

Jameson, Fredric. 2002. *A Singular Modernity. Essay on the Ontology of the Present.* New York: Verso.

Khalaf, Sulayman. 1999. "Camel Racing in the Gulf. Notes on the Evolution of a Traditional Cultural Sport." *Anthropos* 94: 85–106.

Longva, Anh Nga. 1997. *Walls Built on Sand: Migration, Exclusion, and Society in Kuwait.* Boulder, CO: Westview Press.

Mitchell, Kevin. 2007. "In what style should Dubai build?" In *Dubai: Stadt aus dem Nichts*, edited by Elisabeth Blum and Peter Neitzke. Bauwelt Fundamente,143: 130–140. Basel: Birkhaeuser.

Munif, `Abd al-Rahman. 1986. *Mudun al-Milh. Al-khandaq*, Vol. 2. Beirut: Almu'assasa al-`arabiya lil-dirasat wa al-nashr.

al-Murr, Muhammad. 1991. *Dubai Tales.* Translated by Peter Clark. London: Forest Books.

Touati, Houari. 2010. *Islam and Travel in the Middle Ages.* Translated by Lydia G. Cochrane. Chicago: University of Chicago Press.

Trouillot, Michel-Rolph. 2002. "North Atlantic Universals: Analytic Fictions 1492–1945." *South Atlantic Quarterly* 101(4): 839–858.

Table Manners in Yemen

Eat! Do Not Talk!

by FUAD KHURI

FOLLOWING MY RESEARCH ON BAHRAIN, I BEGAN TO DO consultancy work in Yemen, Oman, Bahrain, and the United Arab Emirates. In Yemen (1980 and 1988) and in Oman (1982), I was a member of a World Bank team assessing the viability of various developmental projects. I welcomed the opportunity not only for its financial rewards, but more importantly, because it provided me with a closer look at the Zaidis of Yemen and the Ibadis of Oman, two Islamic sects about which I had been reading a great deal while researching *Imams and Emirs*, trying to extrapolate principles of religious organization from a corpus of historical data. What a privilege it was to be a member of the World Bank team. While pursuing the work for which I was being paid, I was learning about these people firsthand; researchers normally have to raise funds to support such research. I quickly found out that under the rubric of studying development, I could inquire about anything and claim it was relevant to the purposes of the mission. Development is indeed an open-ended ideology. We had access to official files and to officials who were apologetically helpful. The World Bank did not promise much, but people expected it to deliver milk and honey.

Fuad I. Khuri, "Table Manners in Yemen: Eat! Do Not Talk!" *An Invitation to Laughter: A Lebanese Anthropologist in the Arab World*, ed. Sonia Jalbout Khuri, pp. 127–138. Copyright © 2007 by University of Chicago Press. Reprinted with permission.

As soon as I arrived in Yemen, I felt, as I had in Bahrain, that the world around me was made a long time ago. Everything—people, houses, cars, roads, *sūqs*, fruit and vegetables—was tinted with dust, and dust is the beginning and the end: "from dust to dust." Inside the Sheba Hotel, where we stayed, the world was different. Except for some Yemeni craftworks that decorated the walls and a tribal shaikh sitting cross-legged on a Regency-style couch fiddling with his toes, you would think that you were at the Ritz. What a magnificent figure that Yemeni shaikh was! He was full of native pride, talking to his associates in a very loud pitch, unmindful of Western manners and acting as if the hotel were his own private domain. The Yemenis are simple, pure, and proud people—proud of their history, culture, food, and *qāt* chewing but not arrogant.

During my first visit to Yemen, in 1980, I was assigned the task of assessing local development associations (LDA) and examining their capacity to effect change at a local level. ("Association" was translated into Arabic as "cooperative.") Initially, I thought that LDAs were market structures intended to protect and promote the interests of specialized production or consumption groups. They turned out to be branches of a political party, designed by the ruling military regime to marshal support across the country. These structures were hierarchically arranged, with headquarters in Sana, the capital city, and were presided over by officials holding ministerial positions. Military regimes in the Middle East have always relied upon monolithic political parties to rally support among civilians, thus linking central government to local communities. For this purpose, the Yemeni regime chose to adopt the political language of "cooperation" and "development," taking as its motto the Qur'anic verse "Help one another to piety and godfearing; do not help each other in sin and enmity" (Qur'ān 5:2).

To assess the LDAs, I had to travel throughout what was called, prior to 1990, the Yemen Arab Republic, from Sa'da in the north to Ta'izz in the south via Ṣan'a, Mocha, and Ḥodeida. Unlike our stay in Ṣan'a at the luxurious Sheba Hotel, our accommodations elsewhere were very modest: in public schools, in guest houses of local dignitaries, or in the residential quarters of local governors, the *wālīs*. In general, we were well received by the *wālīs* and the heads of the LDA branches, who went out of their way to please the World Bank visitors. Being special guests, we were always offered the traditional Yemeni meal, consisting essentially of bread topped with honey and butter, followed by the main course, which always included meat, rice, and salads. We never had the legendary whole roast lamb cooked underground, which the Arabs are reputed to serve their guests. I have traveled extensively in

Arab countries from Casablanca to Bahrain, and lived among nomads, villagers, and city dwellers, but I was offered the whole roast lamb only once, in Morocco.

Food, the Arabs believe, is the barometer of health and moods. How a person feels—happy or sad, lively or lazy, healthy or sick, sexy or not—is related to the foods he eats. Food is the source of disease and the prescription for cure. I have heard people telling conflicting stories about the roast lamb ritual. Some say it follows a fixed pattern: the host "breaks" (eats of) the dish first to assure the guests that the food is not poisoned; then he offers each guest the organ of the lamb that suits his image of the guest. A highly regarded guest may be offered the lamb's eye, meaning that the host views the guest as one of the "eyes" (*'a'yān*) of society. If the host admires the guest's mind, he will offer him the lamb's brain. The tongue signifies the power of language; the liver, unity of purpose; the testicles, courage. The expression *'indu baydāt* ("he has balls") means that someone has courage. Contrarily, the host may take advantage of the ritual to mark the guest's undesirable qualities, in which case the meanings are reversed. The eye might then signify jealousy; the brain, irrationality; the liver, hatred; the testicles, cowardice; and the tongue, gossip. Eating is a poker game, where bluffing and counterbluffing follow lines of conflict. I experienced this ritual in 1966 at Fez, Morocco, where I and four other professors from AUB were invited to deliver lectures to college and secondary school teachers. The roasted lamb was served to us whole over a tray of rice flavored with dried plums. Elsewhere in the Arab world, I have been served rice topped with lamb cut into small pieces; in those cases the organs were often consumed by the host's household, especially by the women and children, and rarely found their way to the ritualistic meal. The head of the lamb, however, is sometimes placed whole on top of the pile of rice. It happened once that the host offered me the eye, which I, in turn, offered to a colleague, giving the excuse that he was in fact the eye of the delegation. I supported my behavior, which otherwise would have been disrespectful, with the Lebanese saying *al-'ain mā bti'lā'alā al-hājib"* ("the eye does not supersede the eyebrow").

I mentioned in a previous chapter that to the Arabs eating is a full-time job. Talking while eating, the "business luncheon," is not appreciated; the dictum is "When you have had the meal, disperse" (Qur'ān 33:53). The clearest illustration of this custom in my experience took place in Ṣa'da, a tribal city in northern Yemen, while we in the World Bank team were having dinner at a local restaurant that served one single dish, a lamb broth called *maraq*. In my hometown in Lebanon, we say, "The Arabs' soap is their beards, and *maraq* is their meat," meaning that they eat broth and clean their hands and mouth afterward with their beards. How true this saying was in Sa'da. *Maraq* is prepared by dumping small chunks of lamb, often richer in bone than in meat, into a big pot, then boiling them with a variety of spices for hours. My four colleagues and I sat on a bench extending across the restaurant. No à la carte menu was available; we had to order the *plat du jour, maraq,* which was served with four thick loaves of bread. We soaked the bread in the broth and nibbled at it. Suddenly we heard a stream of loud and confusing cries from outside the restaurant; around fifteen ferocious-looking men armed with machine guns entered and sat down haphazardly among us. Some of them had dyed their grey mustaches and beards with reddish brown henna and their eyebrows and eyelashes with blue kohl. This rather feminine makeup did not hide their totally masculine looks.

As soon as they took their seats, silence settled over the house. The owner of the restaurant, who was also the chef, hastily added more chunks of lamb to the pot, which was positioned at the end of the hall, visible to all the clients. One of the newcomers sat beside me and, without uttering a single word or looking at me, invited himself to my dish. He grabbed one of my loaves and started to eat my broth. Eager to start a conversation, I turned to him and said in Arabic, "What an honor it is to have you share my food, brother!"

He did not respond, but looked at me with a gentle eye. I continued, "Ṣa'da is a great town, quite impressive: its history, its people, its tenacity to survive against all kinds of hazards!"

Still no response; he did not utter a word but continued to partake of my dish. I tried to explain that the five of us were a World Bank team visiting Yemen to assess the country's potential for development. Ignoring me, he kept on eating. When my dish was empty, he took the plate, walked to the cooker, filled it with broth and meat, brought it back with a pile of bread, pushed the food in front of me, and said with some serenity, *"Kul"*—"Eat."

He and the others left the premises in the same manner in which they arrived. I ate and left with my colleagues, wondering about the eating habits across cultures. I was told that talking while eating might invite the jinn to partake of the food, leaving nothing for the others. This explained the reaction of my kohl-eyed guest.

I have witnessed two more examples of this behavior during my career. One was at a conference entitled "Man and Society in the Gulf," which was held in Baṣra, Iraq, and attended by an international audience of about 250 people. The opening session was devoted to formalities and included, among other things, a lengthy address by a leading Ba'th politician, Munīf al-Razzāz. After the speech, which lasted some two and a half hours, we were invited to lunch in a nearby building. On our way, my colleague and I came across al-Razzāz, who wanted to know our reaction to his speech. This delayed our arrival to the luncheon hall by about half an hour. By the time we got there, the dishes were scraped clean—this is what happens when people do not talk over meals. However, I should not complain, as we were offered instead a very special, private lunch.

The other experience was in 1988, during my second visit to Yemen with a World Bank team. Accompanied by about fifteen employees from the ministries of planning and agriculture, we visited a demonstration farm in the country's eastern province. After touring the farm, we were served lunch at the *wālī's* headquarters. By the time the World Bank team sat down to eat, the other guests had, with remarkable swiftness, devoured all the food. The next day, at the same time and place, I was ready to be among the first to plunge his hand into the dish of meat and rice. However, the presence of the *wālī* made a difference. No guest would start eating before the host had "broken" the food in the name of God, the Merciful and Compassionate.

In traditional Arab houses, food is served, not on a table surrounded with chairs, but on a large tray placed on a mat or a blanket spread on the floor. Guests sit cross-legged around the tray—in a circle, thus stressing the principle of equality— and eat without utensils, using their hands. As soon as the name of God has been mentioned, guests in Yemen help themselves to the food, with no deference given to one over the other. To be shy or to follow Western etiquette, that is, to wait until all are ready to eat, is to miss the most tender pieces of meat; everyone rushes to get the fillet.

Mr. Cook, the head of the World Bank team, complained jokingly that he always finished his meal with the leftovers. I advised him that Western etiquette does not work in Yemen and that he should reach for a piece of meat as soon as the name of 'Alla was pronounced. Born in Kenya to British parents who adhered to British habits more rigorously than do the British at home, he was hesitant to reach for the food on his own. I passed a message to the *wālī*, saying that Europeans like Mr. Cook felt embarrassed plunging into the dish of rice and meat without being invited to do so by the host. Eager to help, the *wālī* took a big chunk of meat and tossed it to Mr. Cook. Bewildered by the "natural" Yemeni way, Cook opened his eyes wide and the food fell into his lap. He should have opened his hands instead. Unmoved, the *wālī* took another piece of meat and threw it to me. Not without excitement, I rushed to catch the piece in the air—and in the process scattered it all over the place. The *wālī* and his Yemeni guests continued to eat as if nothing had happened. How sophisticated is the Yemeni way! In Lebanon, the incident would have caused hysterical laughter and much fuss.

The Lebanese overdo their hospitality by insisting that a guest keep on eating, even after he has had his fill. "Food is a measure of love," they say: the more food the guest eats, the deeper the affection he displays. To urge the guest to eat more, the host resorts to many tactics, the most common of which is to appeal to him to have an additional bite for the sake of his loved ones, whether friends or close relatives. An anecdote is repeatedly told of Cornelius Van Dyck, an American medical missionary who went to Lebanon in 1840 and who may have persuaded Daniel Bliss, the founder of the American University of Beirut, to include a school of medicine in his curriculum. Once, Van Dyck was invited to a dinner where *kibbeh* was served. *Kibbeh* is made of meat and burghul, which expands when cooked. The host was insistent: "For my sake have this bite"; "For my wife's sake have another"; "You do not like us if you do not have this one"; "Have this last piece." Inevitably, Van Dyck ate more than his fill, which caused him some discomfort. While returning home riding his mule, he stopped at a river crossing to allow the animal to drink. The mule drank his fill and stopped. Van Dyck, tired and aching, turned to the mule, saying sarcastically, "For my sake have a little more. You must have another sip!" The animal kept his head up, ready to proceed. Van Dyck then said to the mule, "Let us go. You are wiser than your master."

Natural as it was, the Yemeni way was comfortable: you are given food to eat, so eat it. In Yemen, the host's honor is fulfilled when the guests sit around the *mansaf*, ready to eat. Whether or not a guest actually eats makes little difference. In Lebanon, by contrast, the honor is done only when the guest actually partakes of the food. To accept an invitation to a meal and decline to eat is insulting.

During the two trips I made to Yemen, I had to play a double role. While working on a specific problem of development, I found myself also acting as an interpreter of language and culture. The teams I joined were made up of professional men specializing in agriculture, farm management, economics, or engineering. Many of them did not speak Arabic, and the Arabic speakers did not know much about local customs and the fabric of society. Again and again, I found my knowledge of Arabic poetry and Islamic law, dogma, and history to be of the utmost importance in building rapport between the researcher and the researched. In Ma'rib, my task was to examine water rights and assess the use and distribution of irrigation water following the construction of a dam in the late 1980s. The first Ma'rib Dam is said to have been built by the Queen of Sheba, who visited King Solomon to witness his reputed wisdom. Since then, it has been rebuilt and destroyed several times, the last rebuilding carried out by Shaikh Zāyid of Abu Dhabi, who donated the necessary funds as a memorial to his mother, who was of Ma'rib origin.

The dam is nourished by the monsoon rains that fall heavily in the valley at the southeastern corner of Yemen. In the days before it was built, the floodwater was distributed on the basis of proximity—that is, the higher plots, closer to the source of the floods, had priority over lower ones. Since the powerful 'Ashrāf tribes, who trace their origin back to the Prophet's family, owned the higher lands, they had the right to take irrigation water before others. Perhaps they became' Ashrāf (sharaf means honor; 'ashrāf, the honored) because they controlled the higher lands; it is a chicken-and-egg question. By contrast, the 'Akhdām, who are lowest on the social scale (khādim means servant), controlled the bottom end of the valley. Curiously, skin color darkens as one moves from the upper to the lower parts of Ma'rib Valley. Many of the 'Ashrāf and tribal chiefs are relatively tall with fair skin; the 'Akhdām are short and dark. Water rights were owned by tribal segments or lineages, locally called 'uzlats, and rights of use ('ihyā') were determined by an intricate system of shareholdings that passed from father to son through inheritance.

The newly constructed dam, impressive as it was, presented many technical problems: rapid sedimentation, intensive evaporation, and consequently high salinity. Using a computer model, one World Bank expert estimated the amount of water lost to evaporation to exceed by far the amount used for cultivation. Consequently, he advised that the valley would be better off allowing the water to sink naturally into underground reservoirs, from which it could be pumped, than storing it in the open air. His advice went unheeded: the pragmatic was overwhelmed by the symbolic. The reconstruction of the ancient Ma'rib Dam, one of the wonders of human civilization, was more a source of national pride than an irrigation project. Many of our Yemeni counterparts looked at the huge volume of water behind the dam with obvious nostalgia and deep admiration, always uttering the phrase 'Allāhu' akbar (God is greater), "blessed be the Creator." Arabs are charmed by what they lack in the desert: massive amounts of water and grass.

Perhaps more importantly, though, the implementation of the dam project created a number of social problems. How could the traditional system of water rights and usages be adapted to the new system, when sufficient water would be available to all? It had happened more than once that some 'Ashrāf did not allow the water to flow down to the 'Akhdām's cultivated fields until they had finished irrigating their fallow land in accordance with their traditional rights. It was not a question of farm management and efficient water usage as much as of honor and power ingrained in different forms of religious and social stratification. Traditionally, water rights were arranged according to written contracts, referred to locally as *baṣā'ir* or *faṣā'il*, which specified in detail the shares distributed annually between 'uzlats and among households within the same 'uzlat. In my previous researches on different communities in Arab countries, I had learned that questions of rights are normally addressed in the *sharī'a* courts. It did not take me long to locate the *sharī'a* court in Ma'rib, where I held lengthy meetings with the *qāḍī*, the head of the court. The first thing the *qāḍī* wanted to know was whether or not I was a close relation to Bishara El-Khoury, the first president of independent Lebanon. I tried to explain that the family name Khuri comes from a common religious title in Lebanon—so common that there is hardly a Christian village that does not contain a Khuri family—but before I could point out these families may not be related, the *qāḍī* interjected: "The Khuris then are a big tribe!"

"Yes, a big tribe." I realized that this was going to be the better answer.

The *qāḍī* was obviously flattered by having a member of both a big Lebanese tribe and a World Bank team consult with him on water rights and usages. I understood later that many teams had visited Ma'rib town, but none had thought to check the documents at the *sharī'a* courts or to interview the *qāḍī*. It turned out that the *qāḍī* came from a distinct line of religious specialists who had been handling contracts related to water rights and land usages for centuries. Having no land of their own, and consequently no stakes in the intertribal conflicts over land and water, they served as middlemen, reconciling conflicts between tribes or segments of tribes. They lived off *zakāt* (alms), honoraria, and the fees they exacted for the preparation of water and cultivation contracts. These contracts were so treasured that people carried them in the broad belts they wore on formal occasions.

When I inquired about water rights, the *qāḍī* referred repeatedly to *baṣā'ir* and *faṣā'il* contracts, the legal meanings of which I did not initially know. In the Arab countries of the Fertile Crescent, contracts are called *'uqūd*, from *'aqada*, meaning "to tie," or *ṣukūk*, from *ṣakka*, meaning "to coin." I only recognized the *baṣā'ir* and the *faṣā'il* to be contracts when I saw examples of them. Oh, yes! The verb roots, *baṣura* and *faṣala*, from which these words are derived, mean respectively "to recognize" and "to separate"—to recognize and then to separate the right from the wrong; in other words, to establish justice. Here is another case of the importance of justice. Once we knew the legal meanings of these contracts, we were able to help in resolving the conflict over water rights between the 'Ashrāf and the 'Akhdām.

The ability to play with words, trace their origins, cast derivations, and search for meanings, especially in poetic texts, was highly admired by the Yemenis. A good part of the *qāt* chewing ritual was spent on linguistic derivations, poetry, and politics. During the ritual, formalities were suspended, thus creating an atmosphere of free interaction between participants. Perhaps this is the reason that people of the same social order chew *qāt* together: men with men, women with women, literati with literati, traders with traders, 'Ashrāf with 'Ashrāf, and 'Akhdām with 'Akhdām. It has never been easy to cross social lines in Yemen.

The Yemenis believe that chewing *qāt* eliminates personal inhibitions, enhances virility, and raises the levels of people's wit and wisdom. My initial experience, however, did not confirm these generalizations: after a four-hour session of *qāt* chewing, I felt dizzy, tired, and lethargic. When I told my Yemeni companion about these symptoms, he snapped, "You did not know how to store the *qāt* [in your mouth]; you simply ate it."

The whole ritual is highly stylized. Each participant brings his own bundle of *qāt* to the session, which is often held in the host's reception room. Top officials have special rooms in the government houses designated for this purpose and hold their chewing rituals on Thursday afternoons. The ritual usually follows a pattern: the participants sit cross-legged on low cushions in a circle or semicircle, each placing his bundle of *qāt* on the floor in front of him for all to see. After subtly examining each other's bundles, they proceed to appraise the supply of *qāt*, its quality, freshness, tenderness, and texture—reminding one of the way the French appraise wine. To keep the *qāt* fresh, they continuously sprinkle it with water. Then, without any formal announcement, they begin; simultaneously each picks up a branch from his bundle, examines its leaves, throws the hard ones away onto the floor, takes a single tender leaf, cleans its surface by rubbing it very gently with the tips of his fingers, and then pushes it slowly into his mouth. Unlike eating, which is often done in a hurry, *qāt* chewing is carried out in slow motion. The art of chewing involves grading the leaf into smaller bits without grinding it, and then placing it along with other pieces between the lower gum and the cheek.

Literally speaking, the Yemenis do not chew *qāt*; they store it (*khazzana*). And storing *qāt* is an art in itself. Once all the tender leaves have been stored, the chewer slowly and gently presses on it using the tongue and the cheek muscle in order to extract the juice. A professional chewer will keep the stored stuff in his mouth for many hours (during which time he might appear, to a stranger, to be infected with mumps). Storing the *qāt* for long periods is a source of pride. Some Yemenis boast about storing it for eight hours, from the early afternoon to around midnight. Our Yemeni driver in the World Bank team used to drive, converse, recite poetry, and even sing while holding the *qāt* ball in his mouth. It is believed that nothing softens the effects of *qāt* chewing better than fresh camel milk.

The Yemenis believe that many foods—*qāt*, fresh camel milk, bread topped with butter and honey, lamb testicles and spinal cords—reinforce virility and enhance sexuality. These beliefs are not unique; they are simply an instance of a general Arab obsession with sex and food. In Lebanon, for example, it is believed that shellfish, almonds, honey, lamb's testicles, and a whole variety of herbs induce sexual excitement. I had never had fresh camel milk and told our Yemeni companion 'Abdalla al-Durjān that I would like to taste it. What a nice man al-Durjān was; following a *qāt* chewing session, he drove me for about two hours to a camel-herding camp so that I could try fresh camel milk. We arrived at the camp at 8 p.m., about the time the camels were milked. Driving in the desert in the moonlight was intoxicating. I felt as though the whole place was mine.

As we approached the camp, al-Durjān stopped about half a mile away and called in a full, loud voice for his friend 'Abdalla—half the Yemenis are called 'Abdalla (*'bd-Allāh*, "the slave of God"). Recognizing al-Durjān's voice, 'Abdalla's wife responded and invited us to enter the open camp. She spread a blanket on the sand, invited us to sit down, and dispatched her son to fetch her husband. Losing no time, she then turned to al-Durjān and inquired, "What news?" Immediately, al-Durjān introduced me as "Brother Fuad from Lebanon" and without going through any formality told her the purpose of our visit. She glanced at me and with a hidden smile informed us that her husband would be back soon.

When her husband came back, he invited al-Durjān and me to accompany him to the corral where the camels were kept at night. He called a milk camel by name, and she came closer. After evoking the name of God, the Merciful and the Compassionate, he milked half a bowl and offered it to me: "Drink." I drank my fill, but could not tell whether the special taste was due to the milk itself or to the bowl in which it was served. The taste was good, but the consequences were not; cold milk always gives me indigestion.

I felt that night that there was something very special about the desert: everything in it acquired higher value. A bunch of grapes at the Ma'rib hotel is just fruit; in the desert, just ten miles away, it is a gem. I was so taken by the empty expanse of the desert, quoting a wide range of ancient Arabic poetry, that al-Durjān sincerely thought I wanted to settle there and offered to help me find a Yemeni wife. I laughed, which he took as a positive response. Two days later he drove me to the edge of the desert to visit a family of two, a mother and her unmarried daughter. He insisted that day that I wear the Yemeni headgear, al-'amāma, which signified that I was a free man, and he told me, "You will see, doctor, the daughter is slim, relatively tall, and has wide green eyes." Green eyes are considered to be the height of beauty. One of the most revered saints among the Arabs (Christians, Muslims, and Druze) is al-Khudr, "the green." By contrast, blue eyes, especially if there is also a gap between the front teeth, indicate that the person possesses the evil eye, highly feared in Arab culture. Many parents adorn their children with blue beads in order to ward off the evil eye.

The daughter was naturally charming, exactly as al-Durjān had described her. While she was preparing coffee, al-Durjān talked a lot about camel breeds, pasture, and the art of herding and told the mother that I owned a big herd of camels. As we were leaving, the mother asked whether I had liked the coffee prepared by her daughter. I told her I had.

"Will you visit us again?" she asked.
"God willing!" I responded.

In truth, the idea of marrying in Ma'rib and settling there indefinitely, far from the bustle of civilization, did cross my mind. That was about the time that I was diagnosed with Parkinson's disease, and I felt like I just wanted to disappear. But, of course, feeling is one thing and reality another.

Against Hybridity
The Case of Enrico Macias/
Gaston Ghrenassia

by TED SWEDENBURG

ARAB JEWS PLAYED A MAJOR ROLE IN THE DEVELOPMENT OF modern Arab culture during the first half of the twentieth century, particularly in the realm of music. After the creation of the state of Israel and the subsequent emigrations, forced or otherwise, of Jews from Arab countries, the vital Jewish role in the Arab musical tradition gradually diminished. In Arab countries this story has largely been forgotten, expunged from official history, or rewritten according to the imperatives of a simplistic anti-Zionist ideology. Meanwhile, Arab Jewish, or Mizrahi, artists have continued to perform and record in Israel, where their brand of music has not only survived but has undergone a revival and today enjoys crossover popularity. A number of scholars have investigated this phenomenon and argued effectively that Mizrahi music represents a kind of challenge to hegemonic Ashkenazi-dominated and Eurocentric conceptions of Israel's national identity.[1] By contrast, little attention has been paid to the ongoing but mostly underground reception in the Arab world of music produced by Arab Jews.[2]

The failure of scholars to consider this quite remarkable phenomenon is understandable, given that the dynamics of Arab reception of Jewish Arab music are quite different from those that characterize the position of Mizrahi music in Israel. There, Mizrahi music has been produced in the context of ethnic identity construction and the emergence of local political movements. Mizrahi music can be meaningfully studied by attention to performers, spaces of consumption, mass media dissemination, and audience reception. It also makes sense, methodologically and theoretically, to examine the effects and meanings of Mizrahi music in the framework of the Israeli nation-state.[3] In sum, music produced in Israel by Arab Jews, even though theirs has been regarded by hegemonic forces as an "inferior" culture, is readily available for ethnographic, historical, and ethnomusicological study.

By contrast, the investigation of the reception of Arab Jewish music in the Arab world since Israel's creation defies conventional research methods. Not only has it been illegal in most Arab countries for over fifty years to import *any* goods from Israel, it also is widely considered an act of treason to enjoy or consume commodities produced by "the enemy." Nonetheless, despite the hostilities, Arab audiences for Arab Jewish music do exist. However, they are understandably invisible and unconnected to any social movements, and there exist virtually no social spaces where such audiences might regularly congregate to consume such music.[4] Arab Jewish performers do not, with few exceptions, produce their music with audiences in Arab countries in mind.[5] Quite often, as in the case of contraband Dana International cassettes sold in Egypt, Arab Jewish music circulates in the Arab world through informal or black market channels. All of these factors render it difficult to study such phenomena and to gauge the music's social and political effects. In most cases, the only available evidence consists of negative reactions penned by commentators and reporters in Arab newspapers and magazines. From this negative evidence, one can deduce that some Arabs in fact *are* listening to Arab Jewish music, otherwise, why would writers bother raising the alarm about the dangers of Zionist cultural influence? In most instances, however, it is difficult to deduce precisely what the existence of such Arab audiences *means*. Does the act of listening to Mizrahi music signify resistance to official or oppositional rhetorics of Arab anti-Zionism? Political apathy when it comes to the question of Palestine? Sympathy for the state of Israel? A critique of monolithic notions of Arab identity? A nostalgia for the time when Jews were an important presence in the Arab countries? Or simply the appreciation of good music?

My task here is not to provide definitive answers to these questions. But the case I have chosen to investigate, that of French variety star Enrico Macias, has the advantage of offering much more evidence to the researcher than do most other examples of Arab Jews with Arab audiences.[6] Macias's musical master, Cheikh Raymond Leyris, was a giant of the Algerian *malouf* tradition, and as we shall see, his own career was entangled in important ways with Zionism and the question of Israel. Macias is an artist with a global reputation, whose ties to Israel are well documented and whose career has been punctuated by controversies regarding his positions in support of Zionist projects. He has received massive press coverage over the past four decades, has been the subject of several biographies, and has authored two autobiographies.[7]

INTERZONE

To suggest something of the context that produces a figure like Enrico Macias, I want to evoke the concept of the "interzone," about which I have written elsewhere, and stress three of its key aspects.[8] The notion of the interzone refers, first of all, to the long history of Jewish presence in the Middle East and to the Jews' active participation in Arab Islamic civilization. Until the creation of the state of Israel in 1948, Arabic-speaking Jews were native inhabitants of the Arab regions of the Middle East and cocreators of (if not always fully equal participants in) Arab culture.[9] Second, the notion suggests that classical Arab Islamic civilization at its height was a kind of mercantile crossroads, an intermediary between civilizations in Africa, Europe, and South and East Asia. As such, Arab Islamic civilization was rooted in long-distance trade and travel, cultural exchange and interconnections, cosmopolitan and polyglot cities, and far-flung connections, a reality that Ghosh evokes vividly in his book *In an Antique Land*. Third, during the colonial period in the Arab world, the racial and social lines separating European and native were more fluid than in other zones of European colonialism that are usually cited as typical colonial cases (e.g., southern Africa and India). A distinct hierarchy of European colonials existed in which those hailing from the Mediterranean (Italians, Greeks, Corsicans, Maltese, Spaniards, etc.) were regarded as inferior to those from northern Europe. Although Mediterranean Europeans certainly made every effort to distinguish themselves, the boundaries separating them from the "natives" were nonetheless often rather fluid, even in settler colonies such as Algeria.[10]

I do not mean to suggest, however, that the interzone was a premodern golden age of tolerance, cosmopolitanism, and flexible boundaries. European colonialism in the Middle East was as cruel and deadly as anywhere else in the globe. It is estimated, for instance, that 1 million Algerians lost their lives in the course of the Algerian independence struggle.[11] In addition, Jews and Christians were not the full political or juridical equals of Muslims under Islamic law, and the character of their treatment frequently depended on the whim of the particular ruler and the socioeconomic context. The second-class position occupied by Arab Christians and Jews under Islamic rule and their vulnerability to various forms of persecution and discrimination help explain the receptivity of many of them to colonial intervention. Moreover, in many instances, European rule in fact improved the position of Arabic-speaking Jews and Christians.[12]

The relatively weak position of Jews who participated in Arab civilization also helps make sense of their complicated relationship to Zionism. For contemporary Arab Jews, memories of times of persecution and humiliation frequently coexist with nostalgia for the music of Umm Kulthum and traditional Arab foods like *foul* and *couscous*. The fact that Mizrahi musicians in Israel are problematizing the Eurocentricity of hegemonic Ashkenazi culture is in no way inherently contradictory to a trend of Mizrahi political support for right-wing Zionist parties. Indeed, since the 1970s, the main base for the Likud in Israel, the party of Begin, Shamir, Netanyahu, and Sharon, has been the Mizrahi community. In some senses, therefore, Enrico Macias represents an entirely typical Arab Jewish cultural figure: the fact that he is a supporter of Zionism who at the same time is one of the foremost practitioners of the canonical Arab musical tradition is not a paradox, but entirely normal in the post-1948 context.

It is for such reasons that I employ the notion of the interzone rather than concepts such as cultural hybridity, so often invoked today in the postcolonial and cultural studies literature. Hybridity is not an appropriate term for this case, especially as it is so frequently employed to suggest new forms of identity or cultural resistance. Arab Jewish culture is not novel, but has deep roots going back over a thousand years. Nor is it inherently a form of resistance against colonialism or Jewish nationalism. It is also not useful here to regard the Mizrahim as a natural bridge between Arab and Jew, as is sometimes done in the critical literature on Israel and Palestine. On the other hand, the argument offered by some Arab critics that Arab Jews like Enrico Macias are guilty of "appropriating" Arab culture is equally unhelpful, given that we are speaking of a shared, Arab Muslim-Jewish heritage.

I am drawn to the case of Enrico Macias precisely because of the difficult questions it poses. His is clearly not an instance of exemplary cultural or political practice. Macias's story resists romanticization, and it provides no clear model for action. Instead, his case raises a number of thorny, and recalcitrant, questions about identity and politics. How is it possible to be a Zionist and a master practitioner of traditional Arab music? To be proud of one's background as a *pied-noir* (one of the European Algerian settlers who left Algeria after it gained independence) and a leftist? To be a supporter of Israel's conquest of East Jerusalem and a backer of a Palestinian state? The story of Macias offers no easy solutions, but instead forces us to confront tough questions.

LAYLA MURAD, DANA INTERNATIONAL, AND OTHERS

Enrico Macias is certainly not the only prominent Arab Jewish singer to have won over audiences in the Arab world after 1948. It is impossible here to give any kind of complete accounting of this phenomenon. It is not a consistent story, for Arab Jewish musicians have at times aroused great opposition and controversy in the Arab countries and at other moments been warmly welcomed by Arab audiences. The great Egyptian vocalist and cinema star Layla Murad, a Jew who converted to Islam in 1946 when she married Egyptian actor Anwar Wagdi, represents an early example. In 1952, while on vacation in France, rumors circulated in Egypt that she had visited Israel and contributed money to the Israel Defense Forces. Murad returned to Egypt to give a few more concerts, but then, at the height of her brilliant career, she went into retirement rather than continue to face the ugly rumors. The Damascus-based Arab Boycott Committee banned Murad's music on the basis of the allegations of her support for Israel. Egyptian President Gamal Abdul Nasser, however, was able to convince Syria to lift its embargo of Murad in the course of negotiations over unification with Syria in the United Arab Republic in 1958.

Murad is, of course, a transitional case, from the 1948–1967 period during which Jews gradually disappeared from the Arab countries. Since 1967, the story of Arab Jewish music has mostly concerned Mizrahim located in Israel. In some instances, their music has been welcomed in the Arab world. For instance, in the 1980s, Yemeni Israeli singer Haim Moshe's hit "Linda, Linda" was broadcast over Israeli radio and enthusiastically greeted by listeners in neighboring Arab countries.[13] The late Israeli Yemeni singer Ofra Haza's recordings of traditional Yemeni music circulated on smuggled cassettes throughout Cairo in the late 1980s without setting off any contentious response from the media. During the second half of the 1990s, the Mediterranean fusion group Alabina, which features Israeli vocalist Ishtar (born Eti Zach) singing in Arabic, Spanish, and English, achieved great popularity in the Arab world and even performed in Tunisia and Morocco. Mizrahi music has been well liked among Palestinians in the West Bank and Gaza Strip since at least the 1970s, and Mizrahi cassettes and CDs circulate widely there. The Israeli Moroccan singer Zehava Ben played a number of well-publicized concerts in Palestinian cities in the Palestinian Authority between 1995 and 2000, entrancing audiences with her interpretations of the repertoire of Egyptian diva Umm Kulthum. I am told that the Mizrahi singer Sarit Haddad is now more favored in the Palestinian territories than Zehava Ben, and others, like Avi Cohen, said to be "the voice of Muhammad 'Abd al-Wahhab," enjoy popularity among Palestinians as well.[14]

Other Israeli Mizrahi singers whose music has circulated in the Arab countries have been far more controversial. Dance diva Dana International, of Yemeni origin, achieved massive popularity and notoriety in Egypt in 1995 and 1996, when it was estimated that Egyptians purchased roughly 1 million of her cassettes on the black market. For months, the Egyptian media was full of denunciations of Dana as a key weapon in Israel's plot to undermine and corrupt Egyptian youth. (The sexual innuendo of some of Dana's Arabic songs, as well as her transsexuality, also played a role in the Egyptian campaign against her.) Egypt's government banned her music again in 2001 as part of an antinormalization campaign.[15] The outbreak of the al-Aqsa Intifada has heightened Arab sentiment for a total embargo of Israeli culture. In July 2002, for example, Algerian rai star Khaled was threatened with boycotts when he toured Lebanon and Jordan because he had sung a duet in concert at a Meeting of Peace concert in Rome with Yemeni Israeli singer Noa (known in Israel as Achinoam Nini).[16]

Meanwhile, France has served as an important site for the revival of the careers of prominent Algerian Jewish musicians, including the late Reinette l'Oranaise (d. 1998), Lili Boniche, Maurice El Medioni, Line Monty, and Luc Cherki. After arriving in France from Algeria such artists mostly either went into retirement or performed solely on the ethnic Algerian Jewish wedding circuit. But over the past decade such artists have been drawing large audiences to public concerts and enjoying crossover success in France. The Beurs, the North African Arab residents and citizens of France, constitute an important part of the audience for these Arab Jewish artists, whom they regard as part of their own cultural formation.

It is in this larger context that it makes sense to turn now to the great French variety star Enrico Macias, and to the controversy, as well as acclaim, that attended his recent return to the classical Andalusian tradition of his Jewish Algerian youth. The controversy has been entangled with the issue of his ties to Israel as well as to the related question of the role of Algerian Jews in the history of French colonial adventure in Algeria.

THE CONSTANTINE POGROM OF 1934

In 1934, four years before the birth of Gaston Ghrenassia (later known as Enrico Macias) in Constantine, that city witnessed the massacre of twenty-five members of its Jewish community by Muslim residents. Among the dead were some close relatives of Macias's mother.[17] The proximate cause was a rumor that a drunken Jew had profaned a mosque, but the deeper reasons were an accumulation of resentments between Jews and Muslims of Constantine. These were rooted in the fact that, although both communities spoke the same language (the Algerian Arabic vernacular), the Jews enjoyed the privileges of French citizenship, while the Muslims did not. According to several observers, the French far-right anti-Semitic organization Croix-de-Feu probably manipulated the pogrom from behind the scenes.[18]

Despite their long history of residence and integration into Algerian life, albeit in a second-class position prior to the French occupation, Algerian Jews retained a sense of vulnerability and unease during the colonial period.[19] The Jews' memories of events like the Constantine massacre help make sense of their attitudes toward the Zionist movement and the state of Israel. According to Macias, during the Palestine war of 1948, he and his Constantine family listened attentively to Kol Israel (Israel Radio) and were very concerned about the condition of the Jewish community.[20] But despite their sympathy for the Zionists, in general Algerian Jews were not inclined to make *aliyah* to Palestine (pre-1948) and later Israel, chiefly because they held French citizenship and were heavily invested in French culture and it was easy to settle in France. Between 1931 and 1961, it is estimated that only 7,600 Algerian Jews migrated to Palestine-Israel.[21]

It was not just memories of the humiliations of the precolonial era or the ongoing fear of violence at the hands of Muslims that fostered the unease of Algerian Jews, but also the anti-Semitism of European Algerians. It would be a mistake, therefore, to regard the Algerian Jews simply as the indigenous beneficiaries of colonialism, as pieds noirs traitors to the Algerian nation. They may have been French citizens, but many French Algerians did not regard Jews as fully legitimate French nationals. Anti-Semitism was rampant among the colonialists in Algeria, and according to Raphaël Draï, fights and disputes between Jews and anti-Semitic Christian Europeans were everyday occurrences in the city of Constantine.[22] Algerian Jews suffered a heavy blow in 1940 with the German occupation of France and the establishment of the Vichy regime of Marshall Pétain. Jews lost their citizenship during the Vichy period, and Algerian Jews numbered among the victims of the Shoah.[23]

CHEIKH RAYMOND, COLONIALISM, AND ZIONISM

In 1961, during the last year of the Algerian independence struggle, Gaston Ghrenassia/Enrico Macias's musical master and future father-in-law Cheikh Raymond Leyris began receiving anonymous threats. Raymond responded to the warnings, and to the deteriorating position of the Jewish community in Constantine, by travel-ing to France that May to investigate a possible relocation there. While he was away, rumors circulated in Constantine that Raymond had been jailed for belonging to the OAS (Secret Army Organization, the ultra-right *colon* terrorist organization) or that he had taken refuge in Israel. Raymond returned to Algeria, having decided against moving to France, and on June 21, a few days after he came back, he was assassinated in the streets of Constantine. Within a few weeks of Raymond's death, the Jewish community of Constantine had by and large abandoned the city.

Why was this great master of Algerian malouf, the classical musical tradition of Andalusia, assassinated, and why did his murder lead to the rapid evacuation of Constantine's Jewish community? Raymond Leyris was born out of wedlock in Aurés in 1912 to a Jewish father named Jacob Lévy and a Catholic mother named Céline Leyris. Because at the time mixed marriages were inconceivable, Céline had been forced to abandon Raymond after naming him, and he was adopted and raised as a Jew by the Halimis, a poor and pious Jewish family from Constantine (93). Raymond was a francophone, but his language of everyday speech was Arabic, he knew Hebrew from his religious studies, and he sang in classical Arabic. He apprenticed with Constantine malouf master and 'ud player Cheikh Abdelkrim Bestandji, a Muslim and a member of a family with a long musical history. Raymond later started his own musical group, in which he sang and played the 'ud, the Arab lute, and rapidly gained acknowledgment as one of Constantine's leading malouf practitioners. This musical tradition (malouf means "faithful to the tradition") was the classical music of Andalusia, of Arab Spain, composed by Jewish and Muslim Arab masters during what has come to be known as the Golden Age, between the ninth and fifteenth centuries (24). It was transmitted orally, from father to son, across the generations, and had been preserved in Constantine, more or less intact, for at least five hundred years, although some instruments (such as the European-style violin) had been added. Eventually, the title Cheikh ("master") was conferred on Raymond after he demonstrated to a panel of Muslim sages that he had memorized over five hundred verses of poetry. (Macias claims Raymond knew thousands of classical Arabic qasa'id [poetry verses].)

The musicians, Muslim and Jewish, who played with Cheikh Raymond con-stituted a kind of supergroup, all masters of their instruments in their own right. Raymond's violinist was Sylvain Ghrenassia, Gaston's father. Sylvain came from a musical family whose repertoire, like Cheikh Raymond's, was malouf. Born in 1938, Gaston (the future Enrico) grew up listening to Raymond's orchestra. His Algerian Jewish family had resided in Constantine since its expulsion from Arab Spain during the reconquista in the fifteenth century. Constantine was home to one of the most important Jewish communities in Algeria, and about one-third of its population was Jewish. The Cremieux Decree of 1870 had made the Jews of Algeria French citizens, and the Ghrenassias, like Cheikh Raymond, were francophones who believed in Algérie Française. Gaston's parents and grandparents spoke Arabic at home among themselves and French with their children. Although there were Muslim quarters and Jewish quarters in Constantine, the Ghrenassias lived in a mixed quarter of Jews, Muslims, and Europeans.

Young Gaston was apprenticed to Cheikh Raymond at age fifteen and played guitar in Raymond's group between 1954 and 1961. It was Raymond's, and Gaston's, innovation to incorporate guitar for the first time into malouf. Although the years of Gaston's work with his master are the same as those of the Algerian War, Cheikh Raymond's group retained its favored position during this period, playing concerts and at life cycle celebrations (weddings, circumcisions) in both Muslim and Jewish communities throughout the conflict. In his 2001 autobiography, Macias asserts that the Jews of Algeria did not, for the most part, support the Algerian revolution-aries of the Front de Libération National (FLN), because they were ignorant of their own history and had been francisé (148). Neither, he says, did they generally belong to the extreme rightist, paramilitary OAS. However, he adds, the Jews ignored the OAS's true nature and did nothing to stop its abuses (156).

Macias's representation of the Jewish position during the war is somewhat selective. The Jews of Algeria were for the most part neutral during the war, but, led by local Zionists, they did organize to defend themselves. The Zionists in Algeria, in fact, were more significant as organizers of self-defense than as orchestrators of aliyah. In May 1956, Algerian Muslims attacked a Jewish café in Constantine with a grenade, injuring thirteen Jews. The next day, when a group of Muslims entered another Jewish café, its patrons, fearing another attack, pulled out revolvers and killed the Muslims.[24] Local Zionists not only organized Jewish self-defense but also served as army interrogators whose knowledge of Arabic facilitated the questioning of suspected Algerian FLN sympathizers (321). In 1961 a number of young Jews joined the OAS, despite the fact that one of its most important elements was the ardently anti-Semitic Jeune Nation group (331). When the OAS attacked Muslims, however, it was Algerian Jews who bore the brunt of the revenge attacks, because their districts frequently straddled Muslim and European districts and many Jewish enclaves were located in Muslim quarters. In Constantine, the war between the OAS and Muslims was especially fierce and the Jewish quarter subject to repeated Muslim attacks (332).

It is still unknown who gave the order to assassinate Cheikh Raymond, but it is fairly clear that the action was carried out by FLN elements. According to Macias, Raymond was apolitical, although he was in favor of Algeria remaining French. Macias and others argue that Raymond was killed because he represented a kind of cultural bridge between the two communities, Muslim and Jewish, a symbol of the *convivencia*.[25] But it might also make sense to see Raymond as representing the epitome of the contradictory position of Algerian Jews, who were, at one and the same time, French citizens, supporters of keeping Algeria French, speakers of Arabic, pieds noirs, Israel sympathizers, francophones, and upholders of traditional Arab culture. It is hard to imagine, in fact, how a national liberation movement, mobilized on the basis of quite homogeneous notions of Arab and Muslim identity, could, after a very bloody anticolonial struggle, have accommodated Algeria's 140,000 Jews, despite the best intentions of some FLN leaders.

MACIAS, THE JUNE 1967 WAR, AND THE ARAB BOYCOTT

Gaston Ghrenassia was part of the Jewish and colon exodus from Algeria, and he landed in Marseille in July 1961. By 1964, he had adopted the name Enrico Macias and become one of France's leading singers of variety. That same year, he played his first dates in Israel, and thenceforth, he continued to visit Israel nearly every year to give concerts or take vacations. Macias happened to be in Israel in late May 1967, during the crisis with Syria and Egypt, and he performed at kibbutzim near the "hot borders." His wife's pregnancy forced him to return to Paris, where he participated in pro-Israel demonstrations.[26] On the night of June 4–5, Macias reports, Cheikh Raymond appeared to him in a dream and told him to pack his bags and return to his country, which he took to mean Israel. Macias and several of his musicians quickly boarded a plane bound for Tel Aviv; they entertained Israel's victorious troops in the Sinai and at the Suez Canal. Accompanied by Generals Moshe Dayan (minister of defense) and Uzi Narkis (the conqueror of Jerusalem), Macias was one of the first Jews to pray at the Wailing Wall in June 1967; he asserts that this was one of the two most important moments of his life.[27] In addition, Macias met with Prime Minister Levi Eshkol, who personally thanked him for the role he had played in Israel's victory.[28]

Macias's activities in support of Israel's victorious troops were widely publicized, and so it is unsurprising that his music was soon banned in the Arab world on the grounds that it represented pro-Israeli propaganda. In 1969, Radio Cairo asserted that Macias was being boycotted because he was a paid agent of Israel and a supporter of Israeli expansionism.[29] This did not dissuade him from continuing in his high-profile support for the Jewish state. On a 1970 visit he performed in several frontier kibbutzim; during the October 1973 war he was again in Israel with his musicians, playing for troops at the Sinai front and for wounded soldiers at Hadassah Hospital in Jerusalem.[30]

Macias, however, was anything but a stereotypical Zionist. Shortly after arriving in Marseille, still known as Gaston Ghrenassia, he married Cheikh Raymond's daughter Suzi and began to relaunch a musical career. At first, he and his father, Sylvain, performed the Andalusian repertoire of Cheikh Raymond, but French audiences greeted this classical Arab music with hostility and racism. So he opted for a more mainstream, acceptable route. In Constantine, he had mastered not only malouf, but also French variety music, particularly the Mediterranean-inflected brand performed by artists like Luis Mariano (the son of refugees from the Spanish Civil War),Charles Aznavour (born Varenagh Aznavourian to Armenian refugees from the Turkish massacres of 1915), and Dalida (born and raised in Egypt). In addition to playing with Cheikh Raymond, the teenage Gaston had joined a gypsy musical ensemble in Constantine. The band's leader was named Enrico, and Gaston was known in the group as "little Enrico." On the boat from Algiers to Marseille, Gaston composed a song about his sorrow over leaving Algeria called "Adieu Mon Pays," which he recorded for Pathé-Marconi in 1962, adopting the recording name Enrico. He planned to use the last two syllables of his family name, Nassia, as his second name, but the Pathé-Marconi secretary with whom he spoke on the phone mistranscribed it, so "Adieu Mon Pays" was released under the name Enrico Macias.

In October 1962, the song was broadcast on a national radio program focusing on the pieds noirs. It became an immediate sensation, selling 50,000 copies in just a few days, and Enrico Macias became the singer in France of the pieds noirs. In 1963, he cut another record, and in July of the same year, he was booked into the most famous cabaret in Beirut, where he was received as a star. Macias remained a favorite throughout the Mediterranean for the next thirty years, despite boycotts and bannings in the Arab world. In 1963, he received a letter from Algeria's minister of culture informing him that he was banned in Algeria—for his support for French colonialism, not because of his Zionism.

His variety music, he asserts, was from the start tinged with Andalusian sounds. In concert over the years he has played 'ud for one number, or featured belly dancers, or spotlighted his father Sylvain on Andalusian violin for one song.[31] He was not able to experiment in this vein a great deal, and the Andalusian element remained at the level of frills and embellishments rather than forming the musical basis for his work. An emphatic Arabic sound invariably incited negative reactions from French audiences. However, the pieds noirs (who have a reputation for being fiercely anti-Arab) typically greeted Macias's use of Andalusian features (and even his singing in Arabic) with enthusiastic applause and shouts of approval.[32]

MACIAS AND SADAT

In September 1979, Egypt's president Anwar Sadat organized a festival of peace on the first anniversary of the Camp David Peace Accords. The Egyptian government invited Enrico Macias to participate, and contacted him—significantly—via the

Israeli government.[33] Clearly, President Sadat did not see Macias as simply a knee-jerk supporter of Israel. During the 1970s, Macias continued to insert small doses of Arabic music into his live performances and recordings. In 1977, he composed and recorded "La Folle Esperance," a song based on a folkloric Arab melody that Cheikh Raymond had played. The song's lyrics praised Sadat's November 1977 visit to Jerusalem, and asserted, "We [Muslims and Jews] are brothers." Macias reports that, when he first performed the song, on French television, it was a big success and that the studio audience included many Maghrebis, who clapped and sang along enthusiastically.[34] Another song Macias composed in the early 1970s, "Le Grand Pardon," expressed his hopes that the "sons of Abraham" would achieve peace. In a 1974 interview, he went so far as to assert his sympathy for the Palestinians because they had been uprooted. He did not agree, however, that the Jews were responsible for the Palestinians' dispossession.[35]

Macias writes that when Sadat met him in Egypt, he "said first he invited me because his people like me. But he also said to me, 'I made peace with Israel, but I want also to make peace with all Jews in all the world, and for the moment you are the representative of these Jews.'"[36] The fact that Sadat chose an Algerian Jew who spoke Arabic to represent world Jewry at the peace festival, rather than an Ashkenazi, is certainly significant; this was not a choice based on European notions of Jewish "representativeness." Macias was warmly greeted in Egypt where, despite the boycott, his music was well-known due to the underground market. In Egypt, he did not simply perform his variety hits, but felt comfortable enough to indulge in his Arabic repertoire. At a private concert, for instance, he performed a song by one of Egypt's most beloved stars, Farid al-Atrash, in Arabic.[37] He played his third show in Egypt at Gazira Stadium for the general public, with his father joining the band on violin. The crowd of 20,000 was enthusiastic, knew the lyrics to his songs, and went wild when Macias took up the 'ud. He and his father were invited to an audience with Sadat at his winter palace in Ismailiya, and Macias performed a few songs for the small gathering, including "La Folle Esperance," which he sang in Arabic. Macias has called his encounter with Sadat "the crowning achievement" of his life.[38]

THE BEURS AND LIBERAL HUMANISM

Macias has always represented himself as a kind of liberal humanist who, due to his own exile experience, is deeply concerned about the plight of migrants, refugees, and exiles everywhere. Many of his most beloved songs deal with the issues of diaspora and displacement, such as "Spanish Jew" and "L'Etranger." Moreover, he has been a prominent advocate of the civil rights of Arabs in France, the traditional targets of ultrarightist violence and antipathy. During the mid-1980s, the Beurs mounted major mobilizations against endemic French racism and police brutality. In 1983, young Beurs organized a two-month-long walk across the country, from Marseille to Paris. Their march culminated with a huge demonstration in Paris, and Macias was among the "celebrity" participants.[39]

Even though Macias has been regarded as the singer of the pieds noirs, over the years he has had frequent run-ins with extreme rightists, particularly due to their anti-Semitism and anti-Arabism (222). In 1983 he confronted the wrath of the far right when Algerian president Chadhli Benjedid visited France and some pied noir organizations demonstrated against his visit. In a newspaper interview, Macias asserted his hopes that Benjedid's visit would help settle the problems of the *harkis* (Algerians who fought on the side of the French during the war of national liberation and who were exiled to France) and the pieds noirs. But it was time, he added, to turn the page and move ahead. The extreme right reacted by accusing him of treason (223). On another occasion, in July 1988, Macias was scheduled to sing at Marignane in the Midi. The extreme-right party, the Front National (FN), led by some of its pied noir members, called for a boycott of the concert. The FN castigated Macias for fighting racism and defending the rights of immigrants, and it distributed leaflets that went so far as to label him a "henchman [*suppôt*] of the Arabs" and a "Youpin" (Yid), a classic anti-Semitic epithet (69). In 1992, in his one venture into French electoral politics, he ran unsuccessfully for Parliament as part of Bernard Tapie's Energie Sud list in the south, in the Var department. (At the time, Tapie was the highly controversial president of the Olympique Marseille soccer team and the chief executive of Adidas). Macias participated in the elections as part of a larger and ultimately failed effort on the part of the left to block the political rise of the extreme right in the south.

During this period, Macias continued to be active in the Israel-Palestine issue and in characteristically complicated ways. In 1994, Israeli president Ezer Weizmann asked him to represent Israel at a meeting in Gaza, where Yasser Arafat addressed a gathering of about 150 journalists, intellectuals, and artists from the Arab world. Macias was the only Jew and the only emissary from Israel (232–233). According to Macias, in his address to the gathering Arafat called on the Arabs to retake Jerusalem and make it the capital of Palestine; Macias subsequently met with

FIGURE 1: Enrico Macias (left) and Taoufik Bestandji in concert.

Arafat and told him that he rejected the idea that Jerusalem could be the capital of any country other than Israel. Macias was also active as a global humanitarian. In July 1997, UN Secretary General Kofi Annan named him as his first UN goodwill ambassador, a mostly celebrity appointment whose numbers have included such luminaries Magic Johnson, Luciano Pavarotti, Natacha Atlas, and Danny Glover.

THE CHEIKH RAYMOND REVIVAL AND ANTINORMALIZATION

In 1999, Macias made an unanticipated return to the Constantine malouf tradition of his master and father-in-law, Cheikh Raymond. The move resulted in the revival of his musical career but also plunged him into renewed controversy, revolving, once again, around the troubling and complex questions of his strong backing of Israel and the apparent contradiction of his being an Arab Jewish Zionist who is also a master practitioner of the Arab musical tradition.

By 1998, Enrico Macias had sold an estimated 60 million records worldwide. In Europe and the Mediterranean, he had achieved a stature comparable to that enjoyed by Frank Sinatra in the United States. In addition, he was a celebrity humanitarian, a prominent defender of the rights of immigrants and North Africans in France, a man of the left, and a champion of Israel who also believed that Palestinians had the right to their own state. But at the age of sixty, his musical output was regarded as somewhat old-fashioned and passé, especially by the younger generation in France. Moreover, the fact that Enrico Macias was viewed as a representative of pieds noirs culture also contributed to his has-been image.

As noted earlier, on his arrival in France Macias had tried to carry on the malouf tradition in the company of his father, but the French audience response was overwhelmingly hostile. Although the music he produced between 1962 and 1999 was frequently spiced with the Andalusian spirit and occasionally marked by the use of "Oriental" instruments, according to Macias, for the most part malouf, the essential part of his cultural formation, remained dormant and sleeping, and he had "forbidden" himself from returning to what he considered a "sacred repertoire." One factor that slowly drew him back to his heritage was the Beur mobilization, particularly its cultural dimensions. North African music, especially Algerian rai, gradually achieved mainstream status in France during the 1990s, in the face of tremendous anti-Arab sentiment. The Beur struggle had helped foster an increasing openness among French audiences, particularly among progressive youth, toward North African and Middle Eastern culture. Such tolerance and acceptance had simply not existed in the 1960s and 1970s.[40] Macias himself was an early supporter of rai music and rai artists in France, and the French public regarded him as an integral part of the North African cultural wave. Meanwhile, other Algerian Jewish singers were gaining prominence and wider publics in France, chief among them the great *hawzi* vocalist and 'udist Reinette L'Oranaise (d. 1998). Another significant factor that encouraged Macias's re-embrace of malouf was the new official receptivity in Algeria of him and his music. The Algerian government's overtures were motivated in part by its keen interest in currying favor with the French government and public at a time when it was engaged in a very bloody and repressive war with Algerian Islamists, which had broken out in 1992. Whatever the Algerian government's motives, its initiatives did offer important opportunities and incentives for Macias.

The first signal from Algeria came in 1993. In September, the Algerian ambassador to France organized an evening of solidarity with the people of Algeria. Enrico Macias was officially invited as a representative of Algerian culture and was warmly received. As was typical on such occasions, journalists asked for his opinion regarding the Palestine question. He asserted that as he himself was in exile, he understood "perfectly" the Palestinian refugee problem. As for Jerusalem, he asserted once again that it was the capital of Israel, but he added that the Palestinians had a right to their own state with their own capital (22–23).

The next official overture on the part of Algerian officialdom occurred in March 1999, when the Algerian cultural center in Paris organized a concert in honor of Cheikh Raymond. This was truly a remarkable event, given the fact that Raymond's memory had essentially been obliterated from Algeria's cultural history after his assassination. Among those present was Leila Shahid, the PLO's representative in France. Macias attended the concert together with his brother-in-law, Cheikh Raymond's son Jacques Leyris. The Constantinois violinist Taoufik Bestandji led the group. Macias recounts that, after Raymond's death, he had been certain that no one possessed the necessary talent to revive his master's music, but the playing of Bestandji's group proved him wrong (24). At the close of the concert, Bestandji invited Macias onstage, and he sang two of the Cheikh's songs to great acclaim.

Jacques Leyris subsequently encouraged Macias to continue his collaboration with Bestandji. Leyris had known Bestandji since 1990, when the latter had moved to France, and together they had brought out four CDs of Cheikh Raymond's music.[41] Taoufik is the grandson of Cheikh Abdelkrim Bestandji, who was Cheikh Raymond's master. Bestandji and Macias were determined to reestablish the centuries-old cultural link between Jews and Arab Muslims in Algeria that had been broken since the early 1960s, and they began to rehearse for a concert in Brouges in April.[42] Macias reports that he had no trouble returning to the music as a guitarist, but that because he had not sung with Raymond's group, he had to work extremely hard to master the difficult task of performing vocals in classical Arabic. He seems to have succeeded, because his concerts with Bestandji were great triumphs, performed in front of mixed audiences (Arabs, Jews, and French non-Semites). Macias and Bestandji's group released a live double CD, entitled *Hommage à Cheikh Raymond* (recorded at Brouges in April) as well as a concert DVD.[43] The CD's sales of 100,000 were double the normal sales of Macias's recordings over the past few years. The tribute to Cheikh Raymond also brought Macias renewed credibility with younger audiences, including North Africans. One song from the album, "Koum Tara," is a duet with rai singer Cheb Mami, who became a global star that same year on the strength of his "Desert Rose" duet with Sting.

Macias was quite explicit about what he considered to be the political implications of his collaboration with Bestandji. At the opening of the concert recorded on DVD, he tells the audience, "From this night the two communities, Jews and Muslims, are reconciled and *retrouvés*." Although his statement rang true insofar as

the concert audience, in other domains his "return" underscored, despite his opti-
mistic hopes, the existence of continued divisions and an absence of reconciliation.
At first, Macias's concert statement seemed prescient. Soon after Bouteflika's election in April 1999 (the same month as the Macias-Bestandji concert at Brouges), the
Algerian president made a point of paying public tribute to Cheikh Raymond, to the
Jews of Algeria, and to Enrico Macias. That summer, on the occasion of Constantine's
2,500th anniversary, Bouteflika again paid homage to Cheikh Raymond and called
on Macias to return to his country of birth (33–34). In October, Macias, his family,
and the family of Cheikh Raymond attended a very amiable dinner at the Algerian
ambassador's residence. Finally, in February 2000, President Bouteflika met Macias
at an official reception in Paris and formally extended him an invitation to visit
Algeria, which he had not seen since 1961. Bouteflika told Macias that the assassination of Raymond had been a grave mistake, representing the death of a part
of Algerian culture. He added that when Macias visited Cheikh Raymond's tomb in
Constantine, he would be by his side (39–40).

Macias began to make plans to tour Algeria in mid-March 2000, where he would
give several performances featuring both his variety and his malouf repertoires,
accompanied by the Bestandji group as well as his regular group. He was to be
joined on the trip by a group of one hundred Algerian Jews, including members
of his own family. The trip was to include a visit to Constantine, where he would
stay overnight in his birth house at the invitation of the family who lived there
(40). But news of Macias's impending visit quickly touched off loud opposition in
Algeria. Several groups there, mostly Islamists and conservative members of the
FLN opposed to normalization with Israel, objected that Macias's presence was the
first step toward the establishment of diplomatic relations between Algeria and the
Jewish state. Algerian MP Mohieddin Ameimour asserted that Macias's visit "had to
be stopped" because it "was nothing more than an [Israeli] attempt to gain access to
Algerian society and create an atmosphere conducive to normalizing relations with
Israel." Macias's concerts, claimed Ameimour, "were designed to act as a launching
pad for the [Israeli] penetration of the whole Maghreb."[44] Those opposed to the visit
spread rumors that Macias's family had committed crimes during the Algerian war
of liberation. Some accused Macias himself of having belonged to the ultra-right
OAS or to the Territoriale, the pied noir organization that fought on the side of the
French army. Abdallah Djaballah, former head of the moderate Islamist party An-
Nahda, declared at a meeting in Constantine that the singer's visit was forbidden
by Islam, and one of Djaballah's aides accused the Jewish nation of being at the

root of all the ills of the Muslim nation.[45] The former leader of Ahmed Ben Bella's dissolved Movement for Democracy in Algeria (MDA), Khaled Bensmaïn, recalled that Macias had sung for Israeli soldiers during the 1967 war.[46] Bensmaïn also claimed that Macias's aim of visiting the tomb of Raymond Leyris would "touch the values of the [Algerian] revolution," as Leyris had been executed for belonging to the OAS.[47]

Other opponents raised suspicions about President Bouteflika's intentions regarding Israel. They asserted that he had been undertaking "secret contacts" with Israel since the previous year, when he met Israeli officials at the funeral of Moroccan monarch Hassan II in July 1999 and shook the hand of Israeli prime minister Ehud Barak.[48] More nonpartisan observers saw Bouteflika's initiatives regarding Macias and Israel as part of a strategy to open up Algeria to the West and to attract foreign investment, particularly from the United States.[49] In any case, the outcry over Macias eventually forced Bouteflika to cancel the visit. In the aftermath, journalist Addi Lahouari wondered "why, each time the question of Enrico Macias and Algeria comes up, [Algerian] journalists, consciously or unconsciously, speak of Israel? What does Israel have to do with this case?"[50] Lahouari is of course correct to suggest that the case was about more than simply Israel, although this should not blind us to Algerian sentiments regarding the plight of the Palestinians. Israel served as an important ideological weapon the opposition forces were able to use in political struggles with Bouteflika. In addition, the uproar over Macias is symptomatic of the anxiety that exists in Algeria over the possibility that Algerian Jews might make legal claims regarding properties lost in the wake of independence.

INTIFADA AND ROUBAIX

During the same period, the issue of Enrico Macias and his relation to Israel erupted into controversy in France as well. Shortly after the outbreak of the al-Aqsa Intifada in Palestine, on October 10, 2000, pro-Israel groups in Paris organized a demonstration of 8,000–10,000 in support of the Jewish state and to protest an upsurge of anti-Semitic incidents in France. Henri Hadjenberg, president of the Representative Council of Jewish Organizations in France, was prevented from speaking at the demonstration because he had shaken the hand of Yasser Arafat. Macias did address the crowd and sang "Yerushalaim."[51] In statements to the Jewish media, he asserted that because the French media were failing to do their job and were doctoring news information with regard to Israel and the Palestinians, he tunes into CNN.[52]

The following month, Macias and the Bestandji group were scheduled to give a concert of Cheikh Raymond's music in Roubaix, a town located near the Belgian border with a population composed of roughly 40 percent immigrants. A number of Arab groups called for a demonstration and a boycott of the concert to protest Macias's pro-Israel stance. They accused Macias of participating in a demonstration alongside rightist Zionist parties, especially the Likud, and of refusing to denounce the massacre of Palestinians. Local socialists condemned the "blackmail directed at the singer's visit" and the Greens asserted that Macias had "nothing to do with the Israeli right wing and bears no responsibility for the present situation in the Middle East."[53] Two hundred pro-Palestinian protestors picketed the concert, chanting, "Stop the massacres, free Palestine, Barak assassin." The demonstration was as much a sign of the tremendous alienation of unemployed young Beurs, the victims of severe racism in France, as a sign of solidarity with Palestine.[54] Inside the Roubaix concert hall, meanwhile, an audience of about one thousand, including Arabs and Jews, enjoyed the music of Cheikh Raymond.

Since the furor over these controversies has died down, Macias has continued with his usual activities. After his Cheikh Raymond tribute, he has gone back to variety-style recording, but now with a more obvious integration of Andalusian elements. He continues to be active on both the Beur/Algerian and pro-Israel arenas, playing benefits in both camps. Recently, for instance, he performed at a benefit organized in November 2002 for the victims of the November 10 floods in Algiers that took over one thousand lives. Among those performing on the same stage were such well-known Arab artists in France as Khaled, Cheb Mami, and Djamel Allam.[55]

CONCLUSION

We have not learned much in this essay about the Arab audiences for the music of Enrico Macias and other Arab Jewish artists. The fact that such audiences exist, despite the ongoing violence in Palestine-Israel, offers at least one slim thread of hope for reconciliation. But music alone cannot bridge the gap, although it may be a beginning. Given the widespread dissemination of crude anti-Semitic discourse (mostly drawn from European sources) in the Arab world, the fading of memories of people's everyday experiences with Arab Jews prior to their emigration, the lack of decent books or research on Arab Jews or translations of studies written in other languages, ignorance about Arab Jews is on the increase in the Arab world. The escalating levels of Israeli violence against the Palestinians, the occupation of the West Bank and Gaza—now nearing its fourth decade—and the Zionist ideology which asserts the total identification of the category "Jew" with Israel, only heighten prevailing tendencies in the Arab world toward binary thinking and black-and-white categorization when it comes to Israel and Palestine, Arab and Jew.

To realize the promise that the Arab audiences for Macias might portend, established modes of thinking will have to be radically shifted. It is in this spirit that I advance the notion of the interzone. It suggests that we conceptualize Arab Islamic civilization and tradition as cosmopolitan and open rather than closed and homogenizing. The interzone proposes regarding Arab Islamic civilization as one in which Jews and Christians actively participated in developing. But the interzone also reminds us of the abuses and persecutions to which Jews and Christians living under Islam frequently fell victim. Only by taking this history seriously, acknowledging the realities of Jewish life in the Arab world rather than romanticizing the Golden Age of Andalusia, can one begin to comprehend the apparent complexities of someone like Enrico Macias. Jews in Algeria may have benefited from colonialism, but they also suffered greatly from the pogrom of Constantine, their loss of French citizenship during the Vichy era, and the death camps of the Shoah (which, despite hegemonic definitions, did not just eliminate European Jews).

The interzone also proposes a shift in our binary thinking about colonialism.[56] Otherwise, how are we to make sense of the colons, the pieds noirs, in France, who since the 1960s have greeted Enrico Macias's forays into Andalusian music, including his use of Arabic language, with wild enthusiasm?[57] To stereotype France's estimated 1 million pieds noirs as simply anti-Arab racist Le Pen supporters is to crudely oversimplify.[58] The case of Enrico Macias, as well as that of his remarkable master and father-in-law, Cheikh Raymond Leyris, calls for a radical rethinking of the nature of French colonial experience in Algeria, a reexamination that would stress the heterogeneity, contradictions, and internal divisions within colon society, as well as the nature of everyday pieds noirs, and especially Jewish, interactions with Muslim Algerians.[59]

All this is not, however, to suggest in any way that the politics of Enrico Macias are exemplary. I find his blind spots when it comes to Palestine-Israel to be quite disturbing, particularly the fact that he can claim to identify with Palestinian exiles while denying the fact that Zionist violence produced those refugees. The circumstances that engendered the historical plight of the Palestinian refugees deserve to come to light and be acknowledged just as much as do the circumstances of Cheikh Raymond's murder. I fully appreciate, however, Macias's courage in defending the rights of France's estimated 4 million Arabs and the role he has played in making Arab culture more acceptable in France. Moreover, in his recent autobiography, *Mon Algérie*, he acknowledges that French colonialism manipulated the Algerian Jews and expresses empathy for the Algerian national movement. Although there is not space to discuss this subject here, France at present represents the most hopeful site for the development of a dialogue between Arab Muslims and Arab Jews on such issues.

Despite Macias's recent moves, and despite his leftist and humanitarian instincts, he remains someone deeply concerned about anti-Semitism in France and willing to stand next to members of the Likud Party in support of Israel. Given the history and context discussed here, I would argue that it makes sense that Enrico Macias is both a strong (if Labor-leaning) Zionist and a preeminent master of Arab Andalusian music. This is not a paradox but a normal condition for tens of thousands of Arab Jews. If the normality of this situation is to be changed, it will take a tremendous amount of hard political and intellectual work.

NOTES

An earlier version of this paper was presented at the International Summer Academy on "Cultures of Conflict: Reflections on Middle East Dilemmas," sponsored by the Institute for the History of the Jews in Austria and the Austrian Institute for International Affairs, July 2, 2003, Vienna. Thanks to Rebecca Stein and Sari Hanafi for their very tough and useful comments. Thanks as well to David McMurray for general inspiration and assistance with the finer points of French; to Ammiel Alcalay, for prompting my initial interest in the music of Arab Jews; and to Bruce Masters, for warning me against romanticizing the picture of Arab-Jewish relations in the Middle East.

Unless otherwise noted, all translations are mine.

1. See, for instance, Ammiel Alacalay, *After Jews and Arabs: Remaking Levantine Culture* (Minneapolis: University of Minnesota Press, 1993) and "Israel and the Levant: 'Wounded Kinship's Last Resort,'" *Middle East Report* 159 (July–August 1989): 18–25; Amy Horowitz, "Performance in Disputed Territory: Israeli

Mediterranean Music," *Musical Performance* 1, no. 3 (1997): 43–53, and in this volume; Motti Regev and Edwin Seroussi, *Popular Music and National Culture in Israel* (Berkeley: University of California Press, 2004); Motti Regev, "*Musica mizrakhit*, Israeli Rock and National Culture in Israel," *Popular Music* 15, no. 3 (1996): 275–284, "Present Absentee: Arab Music in Israeli Culture," *Public Culture* 7, no. 2 (1995): 433–445, and "The Musical Soundscape as a Contest Area: 'Oriental Music' and Israeli Popular Music," *Media, Culture and Society* 8, no. 3 (1986): 343–355.

2. The only exception I am aware of is my own study of Dana International's (earlier known as Danna International) reception in Egypt; see Ted Swedenburg, "Saida Sultan/Danna International: Transgender Pop and the Polysemiotics of Sex, Nation, and Ethnicity on the Israeli-Egyptian Border," in *Mass Mediations: New Approaches to Popular Culture in the Middle East and Beyond*, edited by Walter Armbrust (Berkeley: University of California Press, 2000), 88–119.

3. There are, however, important Mizrahi communities outside of Israel. Kay Kaufman Shelemay's ethnomusicological study of the liturgical music of Syrian Jews in Brooklyn is one of the few examinations of such diasporic musical communities of which I am aware; see *Let Jasmine Rain Down: Song and Remembrance among Syrian Jews* (Chicago: University of Chicago Press, 1998).

4. Exceptions are Mizrahis who perform in the Palestinian territories, Arab Jews who play for Arab audiences in Europe, and the odd Mizrahi or Israeli who give concerts in the Arab world, like Enrico Macias in Tunisia at the Carthage Festival (Tunis) and the Hammamet Festival and Noa at the Sacred Music Festival in Fez, Morocco, both in summer 1999 (before, significantly, the outbreak of the second Palestinian Intifada).

5. Exceptions include the Arab songs recorded by Dana International, aimed at least in part at Arab audiences outside Israel, and analyzed by Swedenburg, "Saida Sultan/Danna International." Ishtar of the group Alabina also seems to have had Arab world audiences in mind when she recorded songs in Arabic; during its existence, the group was quite popular in the Arab world.

6. The exceptions I am aware of are Mizrahi singers who perform for and are appreciated by Palestinians in the West Bank and Gaza, some of whom are discussed briefly below.

7. Because biographies of popular music stars are not considered serious and therefore are not regularly collected by academic libraries, I have been able to consult only one Macias biography: Martin Monestier, *Enrico Macias: L'enfant de tous pays* (Paris: Encre Editions, 1980). Autobiographies are Enrico Macias with Jacques Demarny, *Non, je n'ai pas oublié* (Paris: Éditions Robert Laffout, 1982); Enrico Macias with Florence Assouline, *Mon Algérie* (Paris: Plon, 2001). Subsequent references to the latter are cited in parentheses in the text.

8. Ted Swedenburg, "Musical Interzones: The Middle East and Beyond," paper presented at the Center for the Humanities, Wesleyan University, September 23, 2000. I borrow the term interzone from William Burroughs's fictional writings on Tangier, most notably *Naked Lunch* and *Interzone*. My use of the concept is inspired by his vision of Tangier but has a much wider historical, geographic, and sociological reach.

9. Of the voluminous sources on this subject, among the most accessible are Alcalay, *After Jews and Arabs*; Amitav Ghosh, *In an Antique Land* (New York: Vintage Books 1994); and S. D. Goitein, *Jews and Arabs, Their Contacts through the Ages* (New York: Schocken Books, 1964). For a very fine comprehensive review of the literature, see Sarah Abrevaya Stein, "Sephardi and Middle Eastern Jewries since 1492," in *The Oxford Handbook of Jewish Studies*, edited by Martin Goodman (Oxford: Oxford University Press, 2002), 327–362.

10. Although there is no space here for a definitive comparison between the racialist character of European colonialism in the Arab world as opposed to more canonical cases of colonialism, it is clear that the kind of obsessive racial boundary maintenance that was developed in the Dutch colonies and is described by Ann Laura Stoler did not, for the most part, characterize European colonies in the Middle East. *Race and the Education of Desire: Foucault's History of Sexuality and the Colonial Order of Things* (Durham, N.C.: Duke University Press, 1995).

11. According to Ali Ahmida, .5 million Libyans died in battle or lost their lives due to starvation, disease, or thirst during the Libyan independence struggle. *The Making of Modern Libya: State Formation, Colonization, and Resistance, 1830–1932* (Albany: State University of New York Press, 1994), 1.

12. For an account dealing with Christians and Jews in the Arab provinces of the Ottoman Empire, see Bruce Masters, *Christians and Jews in the Ottoman Arab World: The Roots of Sectarianism* (Cambridge, England: Cambridge University Press, 2001).

13. Horowitz, this volume.

14. Personal communication, Pnina Motzafi-Haller, May 2003. Muhammad 'Abd al-Wahhab (d. 1991) was one of Egypt's most renowned singers and composers of the twentieth century.

15. Reported by United Press International, August 6, 2001.

16. The song they performed was John Lennon's "Imagine." A recorded version of the duet was released on Khaled's 1999 album *Kenza*. (The song is conspicuously absent, however, from the U.S. version of the album.) In the Israeli context, Noa is well-known as a partisan of peace, of the Peace Now variety.

17. Two Muslims died as well. Dozens of Jews were wounded, and hundreds of stores in Jewish neighborhoods sacked. See Jean-Luc Allouche, "Constantine, La Necessaire," in *Les Juifs d'Algérie: Images et Textes*, edited by Jean Laloum and Jean-Luc Allouche (Paris: Éditions du Scribe, 1987), 122.

18. Raphaël Draï, *Lettre au président Bouteflika* (Paris: Éditions Michalon, 2000), 52.

19. The Constantinois Jew Raphaël Draï writes that his grandmother recounted to him (in Arabic) that the Jewish community of Constantine welcomed the coming of French troops because Turkish rule was oppressive to the Jews. Draï writes as well that the image that Constantine Jews retain in their memory of the French assault on Constantine is of the dey (the local Turkish ruler) tying local Jews to the stock of his cannons in the hopes of keeping French troops from firing on them (Draï, *Lettre au président Bouteflika*, 49).

20. Macias, *Non, je n'ai pas oublié*, 83.

21. Joelle Bahloul, "Les Pionniers de Regavim," in *Les Juifs d'Algérie*, 304.

22. Draï, *Lettre au président Bouteflika*, 50.

23. Among them, the great doyen of classical Andalusian singing from Oran, Saoud El Medioni, popularly known as Saoud El Oranais. El Medioni, who was the master of the next generation of Algerian Jewish artists from Oran, including Reinette l'Oranaise and Lili Boniche, and was the uncle of Maurice El Medioni, met his end at Sobibor concentration camp (Poland) in March 1943. See Annie Teboul, "Les Musiciens," in *Les Juifs d' Algérie*, 278.

24. Michael Laskier, *North African Jewry in the Twentieth Century: The Jews of Morocco, Tunisia, and Algeria* (New York: New York University Press, 1994), 320–321.

25. Other observers have noted that Raymond also represented a bridge with Christianity, given that his mother was French Catholic.

26. Monestier, *Enrico Macias*, 87.

27. The other moment was meeting Anwar Sadat in 1979, discussed below.

28. Macias, *Non, je n'ai pas oublié*, 288–291.

29. Monestier, *Enrico Macias*, 11.

30. Macias, *Non, je n'ai pas oublié*, 311, 316.

31. To my ears, the Arab influence on his variety recordings is quite subtle and requires some effort to hear.

32. Monestier, *Enrico Macias*, 55.

33. Ibid, 178.

34. Macias, *Non, je n'ai pas oublié*, 327.

35. Monestier, *Enrico Macias*, 145.

36. Richard Cromelin, "Macias: Singer for the Dispossessed," *Los Angeles Times*, November 22, 1985, part 6, p. 1.

37. Farid al-Atrash (d. 1974) was a Syrian Druze whose entire career as singer, 'udist, and movie actor was based in Egypt. He is one of the most renowned Egyptian singers of the twentieth century.

38. Monestier, *Enrico Macias*, 183.

39. Frank J. Prial, "Parisians March Against Racism," *New York Times*, December 5, 1983, section 1, p. 20.

40. Josette Alia, "La france et la culture arabe," *Nouvel Observateur* 1726, December 4, 1997; David McMurray, "La France Arabe," in *Post-Colonial Cultures in France*, edited by Alec G. Hargreaves and Mark McKinney (London: Routledge, 1997), 26–39.

41. Cheikh Raymond, *Concert Public De Malouf*, Vols. 1–3, CD (Paris: Al Sur, 1995); *La Desirée* (Paris: Al Sur, 1999). On these recordings you can also hear the teenage prodigy Gaston Ghrenassia (Macias) playing guitar.

42. Interestingly, Macias claims that plo representative Leila Shahid informed him ahead of time that she would attend his Bourges concert in tribute to Cheikh Raymond. Veronique Mortaigne, "Enrico Macias, ambassadeur de la reconciliation des juifs et des musulmans," *Le Monde*, April 19, 1999.

43. Enrico Macias accompanied by Taoufik Bestandji and the Foundok Ensemble, *Hommage à Cheikh Raymond*, CD (Paris: Trema/Sony Music, 1999); Enrico Macias accompanied by Taoufik Bestandji and his ensemble, *Enrico Macias en concert en hommage à Cheikh Raymond*, DVD (Paris: TFI Video, 2000).

44. Mohieddin Ameimour, "Bouteflika Hit 'Several Birds with One Stone' by Rapping Algerian Journalists over Israeli Trip," *Mideast Mirror* 14, no. 125 (July 3, 2000), translated from *Al-sharq al-awsat*.

45. Hassane Zerrouky, "Enrico Macias déchaîne les passions," *L'Humanité*, March 7, 2000.

46. Agence France Presse, "Un parti islamiste dénonce la visite d'Enrico Macias en Algérie," February 15, 2000.

47. Hassane Zerrouky, "Constantine attend l'enfant du pays," *L'Humanité*, March 4, 2000.

48. Françoise Germain-Robbin, "Enrico Macias reporte sa tournée en Algérie," *L'Humanité*, March 6, 2000.

49. Nitzan Horowitz, "Algerian President Warms to Israel," *Ha'aretz*, October 31, 1999.

50. Addi Lahouari, "Abdelaziz Bouteflika a du renoncer à inviter Enrico Macias," *Liberation*, March 9, 2000, 9.

51. "Yerushalaim Shel Zahav" (Jerusalem the golden), one of Israel's most beloved folk anthems. Curiously, Macias was not prevented from speaking, although he too had met Arafat, in 1994.

52. Henri Tincq, "Les fils de la diaspora defilent à Paris devant l'ambassade d'Israel," *Le Monde*, October 12, 2000.

53. Bertrand Bollenbach, "Concert by Singer for Peace Sparks Mideast Boycott Rumpus," Agence France Presse, November 25, 2000.

54. Sara Daniel, "Enrico Macias et la 'haggra,'" *Nouvel Observateur* 1882, November 30, 2000.

55. Amel Bouakba, "Beur FM vient au chevet des sinistrés de Bab El Oued," *La Tribune* (Algiers), February 11, 2002, available at: http://allafrica.com/stories/200202110457.html.

56. Of course, many postcolonial theorists have advocated such a move. My interest here is in using the interzone concept to think through some of their proposals. For a useful account of antibinary thinking with regard to colonialism, see Michael Hardt and Antonio Negri's chapter on "The Dialectics of Colonial Sovereignty," in their *Empire* (Cambridge, Mass.: Harvard University Press, 2000), 114–136.

57. Monestier, *Enrico Macias*, 55.

58. This is to suggest that not only are the pieds noirs not all racists, but that even the "racists" among them might have quite an ambivalent relation to

both French and Arab culture. A useful analogy here might be the contradictory position of the Mizrahim in Israel.

59. I am a great admirer of the work of Ann Laura Stoler, but I do not think that
her *Race and the Education of Desire* serves as a useful model of colonialism
in this instance.

RELIGION

section five

The Idea of an Anthropology of Islam

by TALAL ASAD

I

In recent years there has been increasing interest in something called the anthropology of Islam. Publications by Western anthropologists containing the word "Islam" or "Muslim" in the title multiply at a remarkable rate. The political reasons for this great industry are perhaps too evident to deserve much comment.[1]

However that may be, here I want to focus on the conceptual basis of this literature. Let us begin with a very general question. What, exactly, is the anthropology of Islam? What is its object of investigation? The answer may seem obvious: what the anthropology of Islam investigates is, surely, Islam. But to conceptualize Islam as the object of an anthropological study is not as simple a matter as some writers would have one suppose.

There appear to be at least three common answers to the question posed above: (1) that in the final analysis there is no such theoretical object as Islam; (2) that Islam is the anthropologist's label for a heterogeneous collection of items, each of which has been designated Islamic by informants; (3) that Islam is a distinctive historical totality which organizes various aspects of social life. We will look briefly at the first two answers, and then examine at length the third, which is in principle the most interesting, even though it is not acceptable.

Eight years ago, the anthropologist Abdul Hamid El-Zein struggled with this question in a survey entitled "Beyond Ideology and Theology: The Search for the Anthropology of Islam."[2] This was a brave effort, but finally unhelpful. The contention that there are diverse forms of Islam, each equally real, each worth describing, was linked in a rather puzzling way to the assertion that they are all ultimately expressions of an underlying unconscious logic. This curious slippage from an anthropological contextualism into a Levi-Straussian universalism led him to the final sentence of his article: "'Islam' as an analytical category dissolves as well." In other words, if Islam is not an analytical category, there cannot, strictly speaking, be such a thing as an anthropology of Islam.

So much for an answer of the first kind. One adherent of the second point of view is Michael Gilsenan, who, like El-Zein, emphasizes in his recent book Recognizing Islam that no other form of Islam may be excluded from the anthropologist's interest on the grounds that it is not the true Islam.[3] His suggestion that the different things that Muslims themselves regard as Islamic should be situated within the life and development of their societies is indeed a sensible sociological rule, but it does not help identify Islam as an analytical object of study. The idea he adopts from anthropologists—that Islam is simply what Muslims everywhere say it is—will not do, if only because there are everywhere Muslims who say that what *other* people take to be Islam is not really Islam at all. This paradox cannot be resolved simply by saying that the claim as to what is Islam will be admitted by the anthropologist only where it applies to the informant's *own* beliefs and practices, because it is generally impossible to define beliefs and practices in terms of an isolated subject. A Muslim's beliefs about the beliefs and practices of others *are* his own beliefs. And like all such beliefs, they animate and are sustained by his social relations with others.

Let us turn then to an answer of the third type. One of the most ambitious attempts to address this question is Ernest Gellner's *Muslim Society*, in which an anthropological model is presented of the characteristic ways in which social structure, religious belief, and political behavior interact with each other in an Islamic totality.[4] In what follows, I shall deal in some detail with this text. My purpose, however, is not to assess this particular work, but to use it to extract theoretical problems that must be examined by anyone who wishes to write an anthropology of Islam. As it happens, many elements in the overall picture presented by Gellner are to be found also in other writings—by anthropologists, Orientalists, political scientists, and journalists. In looking at this text one is there fore also looking at more than a unique account. But the picture it presents is of less interest than the way it has been put together—the assumptions it draws on and the concepts it deploys.

II

There is in fact more than one attempt to conceptualize Islam in Gellner's text. The first of these involves an explicit comparison between Christianity and Islam, each broadly conceived as differing historical configurations of power and belief, one essentially located in Europe, the other in the Middle East. Such a conceptualization is central to Orientalism, but it is also to be found implicitly in the writings of many contemporary anthropologists.

One sign of this is the fact that anthropological textbooks on the Middle East—such as Gulick's or Eickelman's—devote their chapter on "Religion" entirely to Islam.[5] Although Christianity and Judaism are also indigenous to the region, it is only Muslim belief and practice that Western anthropologists appear to be interested in.[6] In effect, for most Western anthropologists, Sephardic Judaism and Eastern Christianity are conceptually marginalized and represented as minor branches in the Middle East of a history that develops elsewhere—in Europe, and at the roots of Western civilization.

My disquiet about this notion of Europe as the true locus of Christianity and the Middle East as the true locus of Islam does not come primarily from the old objection to religion being represented as the essence of a history and a civilization (an objection which even some Orientalists like Becker advanced long ago).[7] My concern as an anthropologist is over the way this particular contrast effects the conceptualization of Islam. Consider, for instance, the opening paragraphs of Gellner's book. Here the contrast be tween Islam and Christianity is drawn in bold, familiar lines:

> Islam is the blueprint of a social order. It holds that a set of rules exist, eternal, divinely ordained, and independent of the will of men, which de- fines the proper ordering of society. … Judaism and Christianity are also blueprints of a social order, but rather less so than Islam. Christianity, from

its inception, contained an open recommendation to give unto Caesar that which is Caesar's. A faith which begins, and for some time remains, without political power, cannot accommodate itself to a political order which is not, or is not yet, under its control. … Christianity, which initially flourished among the politically disinherited, did not then presume to *be* Caesar. A kind of potential for political modesty has stayed with it ever since those humble beginnings. … But the initial success of Islam was so rapid that it had no need to give anything unto Caesar. (MS, 1–2)

If one reads carefully what is being said here, one must be as sailed by a variety of doubts. Consider the long history since Constantine, in which Christian emperors and kings, lay princes and ecclesiastical administrators, Church reformers and colonial missionaries, have all sought by using power in varying ways to create or maintain the social conditions in which men and women might live Christian lives—has this entire history nothing to do with Christianity? As a non-Christian, I would not presume to assert that neither liberation theology nor the Moral Majority belong to the essence of Christianity. As an anthropologist, however, I find it impossible to accept that Christian practice and discourse throughout history have been less intimately concerned with the uses of political power for religious purposes than the practice and discourse of Muslims.

I want to make it clear that I have nothing in principle against comparisons between Christian and Muslim histories. Indeed, one of the most valuable features of the recent book by Fischer on Iran is the inclusion of descriptive material from Jewish and Christian histories in his account of the *madrasa* system.[8] This is one of the very few anthropological studies of contemporary Islam that employs implicit comparisons with European history, and consequently enrich our understanding.

But one should go beyond drawing *parallels*, as Fischer does, and attempt a systematic exploration of *differences*. For this reason, my own research over the past few years has been concerned with detailed anthropological analyses of monastic ritual, the sacrament of confession and the medieval Inquisition in twelfth-century Western Europe, institutions that stand in contrast to the very different connections between power and religion in the medieval Middle East.[9] Of particular note is the fact that Christians and Jews have usually formed an integral part of Middle Eastern society in a way that is not true of non-Christian populations in Europe. My claim here is not the familiar and valid one that Muslim rulers have in general been more tolerant of non-Muslim subjects than Christian rulers have of non-Christian subjects, but simply that medieval Christian and Muslim authorities ("religious" and "political") must have had to devise very different strategies for developing moral subjects and regulating subject populations. This is too large a subject to be expounded here, even in outline, but it is worth touching on by way of illustration.

Modern historians have often observed that Muslim scholars in the classical and post-classical periods displayed no curiosity about Christianity, and that in this their attitude was strikingly different from the lively interest shown by their Christian contemporaries in the beliefs and practices not only of Islam but of other cultures too.[10] What is the reason for this intellectual indifference toward Others? The explanation given by Orientalists such as Bernard Lewis is that the early military successes of Islam bred an attitude of contempt and complacency toward Christian Europe. "Marked by the imposing military might of the Ottoman Empire, the peoples of Islam continued until the dawn of the modern age to cherish—as many in East and West still do today—the conviction of the immeasurable and immutable superiority of their civilization to all others. For the medieval Muslim from Andalusia to Persia, Christian Europe was still an outer darkness of barbarism and unbelief, from which the sunlit world of Islam had little to fear and less to learn."[11] Perhaps that was so, but our question is best approached by turning it around and asking not why Islam was un-curious about Europe but why Roman Christians were interested in the beliefs and practices of Others. The answer has less to do with cultural motives allegedly produced by the intrinsic qualities of a world-view or by the collective experience of military encounters, and more with structures of disciplinary practices that called for different kinds of systemic knowledge. After all, Christian communities living among Muslims in the Middle East were not noted for their scholarly curiosity about Europe either, and Muslim travelers often visited and wrote about African and Asian societies. It does not make good sense to think in terms of the contrasting attitudes of Islam and Christianity, in which a disembodied "indifference" faces a disembodied "desire to learn about the Other." One ought instead to be looking for the institutional conditions for the production of various social knowledges. What was regarded as worth recording about "other" beliefs and customs? By whom was it recorded? In which social project were the records used? Thus, it is no mere coincidence that the most impressive catalogues of pagan belief and practice in early medieval Christendom are those contained in the Penitentials (handbooks for administering sacra mental confession to recently converted Christians) or that the successive manuals for inquisitors in the later European Middle Ages describe with increasing precision and comprehensiveness the doctrines and rites of heretics. There is nothing in Muslim societies to parallel these compilations of systematic knowledge about "internal" unbelievers simply because the disciplines that required and sustained such information are not to be found in Islam. In other words, forms of interest in the production of knowledge are intrinsic to various structures of power, and they differ not according to the essential character of Islam or Christianity, but according to historically changing systems of discipline.

Thus, beyond my misgivings about the plausibility of historical contrasts in terms of cultural motives—such as "potential for political modesty" on the one hand, and "theocratic potential" on the other—lies another concern, namely that there may well be important differences which the anthropologist studying other societies ought to explore, and which may too easily be obscured by the search for super-ficial or spurious differences. The problem with the kind of contrasts of Islam with Christianity drawn by Gellner is not that the relations between religion and political power are the same in the two. Rather, the very terms employed are misleading, and we need to find concepts that are more appropriate for describing differences.

III

So far we have looked very briefly at one aspect of the attempt to produce an an-thropology of Islam: the virtual equation of Islam with the Middle East, and the defi-nition of Muslim history as the "mirror image" (Gellner) of Christian history, in which the connection between religion and power is simply reversed. This view is open to criticism both because it disregards the detailed workings of disciplinary power in Christian history and because it is theoretically most inadequate. The argument here is not against the attempt to generalize about Islam, but against the manner in which that generalization is undertaken. Anyone working on the anthropology of Islam must be aware that there is considerable diversity in the beliefs and practices of Muslims. The first problem is therefore one of organizing this diversity in terms of an adequate concept. The familiar representation of essential Islam as the fusion of religion with power is not one of these. But neither is the nominalist view that different instances of what are called Islam are essentially unique and sui generis.

One way in which anthropologists have attempted to resolve the problem of diversity is to adapt the Orientalist distinction between orthodox and non-orthodox

Islam to the categories of Great and Little Traditions, and thus to set up the seemingly more acceptable distinction between the scripturalist, puritanical faith of the towns and the saint-worshiping, ritualistic religion of the countryside. For anthropologists, neither form of Islam has a claim to being regarded as "more real" than the other. They are what they are, formed in different ways in different conditions. In fact, the religion of the countryside is taken as a single form only in an abstract, contrastive sense. Precisely because it is by definition particularistic, rooted in variable local conditions and personalities, and authorized by the uncheckable memories of oral cultures, the Islam of the unlettered country folk is highly variable. "Orthodoxy" is therefore, for such anthropologists, merely one (albeit invariable) form of Islam among many, distinguished by its preoccupation with the niceties of doctrine and law, claiming its authority from sacred texts rather than sacred persons.

This dichotomy has been popularized by two well-known Western anthropologists of Moroccan Islam, Clifford Geertz and Ernest Gellner, and by some of their pupils. But what made it interesting was the further argument that there was an apparent correlation of this dual Islam with two types of distinctive social structure, something first proposed by French colonial scholarship on the Maghrib. Classical Maghribi society, it was claimed, consisted on the one hand of the centralized, hierarchical organization of the cities and on the other of the egalitarian, segmental organization of the surrounding tribes. The cities were governed by rulers who continually attempted to subdue the dissident, self-governing tribes; the tribesmen in turn resisted with varying degrees of success, and sometimes, when united by an outstanding religious leader, even managed to supplant an incumbent ruler. The two categories of Islam fit nicely into the two kinds of social and political structure: *shari'a* law in the cities, variable custom among the tribes; 'ulama in the former, saints in the latter. Both structures are seen as parts of a single system because they define the opponents between whom an unceasing struggle for political dominance takes place. More precisely, because both urban and tribal populations are Muslim, all owing at the very least a nominal allegiance to the sacred texts (and so perhaps also implicitly to their literate guardians), a particular style of political struggle emerges. It is possible for urban rulers to claim authority over the tribes, and for tribes to support a country-based leader who aims to supplant the ruler in the name of Islam.

To this broad schema, which was initially the product of a French "sociology of Islam," Gellner has added, in successive publications, a number of details drawn from a reading of the classical sociologies of religion, Ibn Khaldun's *Muqaddimah*, and British anthropological writings on segmentary lineage theory. And he has extended it to cover virtually the whole of North Africa and the Middle East, and almost the entire span of Muslim history. The resulting picture has been used by him, and drawn on by others, to elaborate the old contrast between Islam and Christianity in a series of inversions—as in the following crisp account by Bryan Turner:

> There is a sense in which we can say that in religion "the southern, Muslim shore of the Mediterranean is a kind of mirror-image of the northern shore, of Europe." On the northern shore, the central religious tradition is hierarchical, ritualistic, with strong rural appeal. One corner-stone of the official religion is saintship. The deviant reformist tradition is egalitarian, puritan, urban and excludes priestly mediation. On the southern shore, Islam reverses this pattern: it is the tribal, rural tradition which is deviant, hierarchical and ritualistic. Similarly, saint and shaikh are mirror-image roles. Whereas in Christianity the saints are orthodox, individualistic, dead, canonized by central authorities, in Islam the shaikhs are hetero-dox, tribal or associational, living in recognized local consent.[12]

Even as it applies to the Maghrib, this picture has been subjected to damaging criticism by scholars with access to indigenous historical sources in Arabic (e.g. Hammoudi, Cornell).[13] This kind of criticism is important, but it will not be pursued here. While it is worth asking whether this anthropological account of Islam is valid for the entire Muslim world (or even for the Maghrib) given the historical informa-tion available, let us instead focus on a different issue: What are the discursive styles employed here to represent (a) the historical variations in Islamic political structure, and (b) the different forms of Islamic religion linked to the latter? What kinds of questions do these styles *deflect* us from considering? What concepts do we need to develop as anthropologists in order to pursue those very different kinds of ques-tions in a viable manner?

In approaching this issue, let us consider the following interconnected points:

1. Narratives about culturally distinctive actors must try to translate and represent the historically situated discourses of such actors as responses to the discourse of others, instead of schematizing and de-historicizing their actions.

2. Anthropological analyses of the social structure should focus not on typical actors but on the changing patterns of institutional relations and conditions (especially those we call political economies).
3. The analysis of Middle Eastern political economies and the representation of Islamic "dramas" are essentially different kinds of discursive exercise that cannot be substituted for each other, although they can be significantly embedded in the same narrative, precisely because they are discourses.
4. It is wrong to represent types of Islam as being correlated with types of social structure, on the implicit analogy with (ideological) superstructure and (social) base.
5. Islam as the object of anthropological understanding should be approached as a discursive tradition that connects variously with the formation of moral selves, the manipulation of populations (or resistance to it), and the production of appropriate knowledges.

IV

If one reads an anthropological text such as Gellner's carefully, one may notice that the social and political structures of classical Muslim society are represented in a very distinctive way. What one finds in effect are protagonists engaged in a dramatic struggle. Segmentary tribes confront centralized states. Armed nomads "lust after the city," and unarmed merchants fear the nomads. Saints mediate between conflicting tribal groups, but also between the illiterate nomad and a remote, capricious God. Literate clerics serve their powerful ruler and try to maintain the sacred law. The puritanical bourgeoisie employs religion to legitimize its privileged status. The city's poor seek a religion of excitement. Religious reformers unite pastoral warriors against a declining dynasty. Demoralized rulers are destroyed by the disenchantment of their urban subjects converging with the religious and military power of their tribal enemies.

A representation of social structure that is cast entirely in terms of dramatic roles tends to exclude other conceptions, to which we shall turn in a moment. But even a narrative about typical actors requires an account of the discourses that orient their behavior and in which that behavior can be represented (or misrepresented) by actors to each other. In a dramatic play in the strict sense, these discourses are contained in the very lines the actors speak. An account of indigenous discourses is, however, totally missing in Gellner's narrative. Gellner's Islamic actors do not speak, they do not think, they *behave*. And yet without adequate evidence, motives for "normal" and "revolutionary" behavior are continually being attributed to the actions of the major protagonists in classical Muslim society. There are, to be sure, references in the text to "partners who speak the same moral language," but it is clear that such expressions are merely dead metaphors, because Gellner's conception of language here is that of an emollient that can be isolated from the power process. In the context of his description of the circulation of elites "within-an-immobile-structure," for example, he writes that "Islam provided a common language and thus a certain kind of smoothness for a process which, in a more mute and brutalistic form, had been taking place anyway." In other words, if one re moves the common language of Islam, nothing of any significance changes. The language is no more than a facilitating instrument of a domination that is already in place.

This purely instrumental view of language is very inadequate? inadequate precisely for the kind of narrative that tries to describe Muslim society in terms of what motivates culturally recognizable actors. It is only when the anthropologist takes historically defined discourses seriously, and especially the way they *constitute* events, that questions can be asked about the conditions in which Muslim rulers and subjects might have responded variously to authority, to physical force, to persuasion, or simply to habit.

It is interesting to reflect on the fact that Geertz, who is usually regarded as having a primary interest in cultural meanings as against Gellner's preoccupation with social causation, presents a narrative of Islam in his *Islam Observed* that is not, in this respect, very different. For Geertz's Islam is also a dramaturgical one. Indeed, being more conscious of his own highly wrought literary style, he has made explicit use of metaphors of political theater. The politics of Islam in "classical" Morocco and in "classical" Indonesia are very differently portrayed, but each, in its own way, is portrayed as essentially theatrical. Yet for Geertz, as for Gellner, the schematization of Islam as a drama of religiosity expressing power is obtained by omitting indigenous discourses, and by turn ing all Islamic behavior into *readable gesture*.

V

Devising narratives about the expressions and the expressive intentions of dramatic players is not the only option available to anthropologists. Social life can also be written or talked about by using analytic concepts. Not using such concepts simply means failing to ask particular questions and misconstruing historical structures.

As an example, consider the notion of tribe. This idea is central to the kind of anthropology of Islam of which Gellner's text is such a prominent example. It is often used by many writers on the Middle East to refer to social entities with very different structures and modes of livelihood. Ordinarily, where theoretical issues are not involved, this does not matter very much. But where one is concerned, as at present, with conceptual problems, it is important to consider the implications for analysis of an indiscriminate usage of the term "tribe."

It is the case not only that so-called tribes vary enormously in their formal constitution, but more particularly that pastoral no mads do not have an ideal-typical economy. Their variable socioeconomic arrangements have very different implications for their possible involvement in politics, trade, and war. Several Marxists, such as Perry Anderson, have argued for the concept of a "pastoral mode of production," and following him Bryan Turner has suggested that this concept should form part of a theoretically in formed account of Muslim social structures because and to the extent that Middle Eastern countries have pastoral nomads living in them.[14]

The assumption that pastoral nomads in the Muslim Middle East have a typical political and economic structure is misleading.[15] The reasons for this are too involved and tangential to consider here, but a brief look at the issue will remind us of concepts of social structure different from those still being deployed by many anthropologists and historians of Islam.

Any study of the military capabilities of pastoral nomads in relation to townsmen must begin not from the simple fact that they are pastoral nomads, but from a variety of political-economic conditions, some systematic, some contingent. Types of animals reared, patterns of seasonal migration, forms of herding arrangements, rights of access to pastures and watering points, distribution of animal wealth, degree of dependence on returns through sales, on direct subsistence cultivation, on gifts and tribute from political superiors or inferiors—these and other considerations are relevant for an understanding of even the basic question of how many spare men can be mustered for war, how readily, and for how long. Among the pastoral nomadic population I studied in the deserts of northern Sudan many years ago, for example, the possibilities for mobilizing large numbers of fighting men had altered drastically from the middle of the nineteenth century to the middle of the twentieth primarily because of a large increase in small livestock, a shift to more intensive and complex herding arrangements, greater involvement in animal sales, and a different pattern of property rights. The point is not that this tribal grouping is somehow typical for the Middle East. Indeed, there are *no* typical tribes. My argument is simply that what nomads are able or inclined to do in relation to settled populations is the product of various historical conditions that define their political economy, and not the expression of some essential motive that belongs to tribal protagonists in a classic Islamic drama. In other words, "tribes" are no more to be regarded as agents than "discursive structures" or "societies" are. They are historical structures in terms of which the limits and possibilities of people's lives are realized. This does not mean that "tribes" are less real than the individuals who comprise them, but only that the vocabulary of motives, behavior, and utterances does not belong, strictly speaking, in analytic accounts whose principal object is "tribe," although such accounts can be embedded in narratives of agency. It is precisely because "tribes" are differently structured in time and place that the motives, the forms of behavior, and the import of utterances will differ too.

Representations of Muslim society that are constructed along the lines of an action play have, not surprisingly, no place for peasants. Peasants, like women, are not depicted as *doing* anything. In accounts like Gellner's they have no dramatic role and no distinctive religious expression—in contrast, that is, to nomadic tribes and city dwellers. But, of course, as soon as one turns to the concepts of production and exchange, one can tell a rather different story. Cultivators, male and female, produce crops (just as pastoralists of both sexes raise animals) that they sell or yield up in rent and taxes. Peasants, even in the historical Middle East, *do* something that is crucial in relation to the social formations of that region, but that *doing* has to be conceptualized in political-economic and not in dramatic terms. The medieval agricultural sector underwent important changes that had far-reaching consequences for the development of urban populations, of a money economy, of regional transcontinental trade.[16] This is true also for the later pre modern period, even though economic histories talk of the changes in terms of decline rather than growth. One does not have to be an economic determinist to acknowledge that such changes have profound implications for questions of domination and autonomy.

This approach to writing about Middle Eastern society, which pays special attention to the long-term working of impersonal constraints, will be sensitive to the indissoluble but varying connections between the social economy and social power. It will also continually remind us that historical Middle Eastern societies were never self-contained, never isolated from external relations, and so never entirely unchanging, even before their incorporation in the modern world system. Unlike those narrators who present us with a fixed cast of Islamic dramatis personae, enacting a predetermined story, we can look for connections, changes, and differences, beyond the fixed stage of an Islamic theater. We shall then write not about an essential Islamic social structure, but about historical formations in the Middle East whose elements are never fully integrated, *and never bounded by the geographical limits of "the Middle East"*[17] It is too often forgotten that "the world of Islam" is a concept for organizing historical narratives, not the name for a self-contained collective agent. This is not to say that historical narratives have no social effect—on the contrary. But the integrity of the world of Islam is essentially ideological, a discursive representation. Thus, Geertz has written that "It is perhaps as true for civilizations as it is for men that, however much they may later change, the fundamental dimensions of their character, the structure of possibilities within which they will in some sense always move, are set in the plastic period when they were first forming."[18] But the fatality of character that anthropologists like Geertz invoke is the object of a professional *writing*, not the unconscious of a subject that writes itself *as Islam* for the Western scholar to read.

VI

The anthropology of Islam being criticized here depicts a classic social structure consisting essentially of tribesmen and city dwellers, the natural carriers of two major forms of religion—the normal tribal religion centered on saints and shrines, and the dominant urban religion based on the "Holy Book." My argument is that if the anthropologist seeks to understand religion by placing it conceptually in its social context, then the way in which that social context is described must affect the understanding of religion. If one rejects the schema of an unchanging dualistic structure of Islam promoted by some anthropologists, if one decides to write about the social structures of Muslim societies in terms of overlapping spaces and times, so that the Middle East becomes a focus of convergences (and therefore of many possible histories), then the dual typology of Islam will surely seem less plausible.

It is true that in addition to the two major types of religion pro posed by the kind of anthropology of Islam we are talking about, minor forms are sometimes specified. This is so in Gellner's account, and in many others. Thus there is the "revolutionary" as opposed to the "normal" Islam of the tribes, which periodically merges with and revivifies the puritan ideology of the cities. And there is the ecstatic, mystical religion of the urban poor that, as "the opium of the masses," excludes them from effective political action—until, that is, the impact of modernity when it is the religion of the urban masses which becomes "revolutionary". In a curious way, these two minor forms of Islam serve, in Gellner's text, as markers, one positive, one negative, of the two great epochs of Islam—the classical rotation-within-an-immobile structure, and the turbulent developments and mass movements of the contemporary world. So this apparent concession to the idea that there may be more than two types of Islam is at the same time a literary device to define the notions of "traditional" and "modern" Muslim society.

Now, the anthropologist's presentation of Islam will depend not only on the way in which social structures are conceptualized, but on the way in which religion itself is defined. Anyone familiar with what is called the sociology of religion will know of the difficulties involved in producing a conception of religion that is adequate for cross-cultural purposes. This is an important point because one's conception of religion determines the kinds of questions one thinks are askable and worth asking. But far too few would-be anthropologists of Islam pay this matter serious attention. Instead, they often draw indiscriminately on ideas from the writings of the great sociologists (e.g., Marx, Weber, Durkheim) in order to describe forms of Islam, and the result is not always consistent.

Gellner's text is illustrative in this regard. The types of Islam that are presented as being characteristic of "traditional Muslim society" in Gellner's picture are constructed according to three different conceptions of religion. Thus, the *normal tribal religion*, "that of the dervish or marabout," is explicitly Durkheimian. "It is ... concerned," we are told, "with the social punctuation of time and space, with season-making and group-boundary-marking festivals. The sacred makes these joyful, visible, conspicuous and authoritative" (MS, 52). So the concept of religion here involves a reference to collective rituals to be read as an enactment of the sacred, which is also, for Durkheim, the symbolic representation of social and cosmological structures.[19]

The concept that is deployed in the description of the *religion of the urban poor* is quite different, and it is obviously derived from the early writings of Marx on religion as false consciousness. "The city has its poor," Gellner writes, "they are uprooted, insecure, alienated. ... What they require from religion is consolation or escape; their taste is for ecstasy, excitement, an absorption in a religious condition which is also a forgetting" (MS, 48).[20] If one looks at this kind of construction carefully, one finds that what is called religion here is the psychological response to an emotional experience. What was indicated in the account of tribal Islam was an emotional *effect*, but here it is an emotional *cause*. In the one case the reader was told about collective rituals and their meaning, about ritual specialists and their roles; in the other attention is directed instead to private distress and unfulfilled desire.

When one turns to the *religion of the bourgeoisie*, one is con fronted by yet other organizing ideas. "The well-heeled urban bourgeoisie," remarks Gellner, "far from having a taste for public festivals, prefers the sober satisfactions of learned piety, a taste more consonant with its dignity and commercial calling. Its fastidiousness underscores its standing, distinguishing it both from rustics and the urban plebs. In brief, urban life provides a sound base for scripturalist Unitarian puritanism. Islam expresses such a state of mind better perhaps than other religions" (MS, 42).[21] The echoes from Weber's *Protestant Ethic* in this passage are not accidental, for its authority is invoked more than once. In this account, the "bourgeois Muslim" is accorded a moral—or, better, an esthetic—style. His distinguishing feature is the literacy that gives him direct access to the founding scriptures and the Law. In this latter respect one is urged to see him as immersed in a moralistic, literate enterprise. Neither collective rituals nor unquenched desire, neither social solidar-ity nor alienation, religion is here the solemn maintenance of public authority that is rational partly because it is in writing and partly because it is linked to socially useful activities: service to the state and commitment to commerce.

These different ways of talking about religion—the tribal and the urban—are not merely different aspects of the same thing. They are different textual construc-tions that seek to represent different things, and that make different assumptions about the nature of social reality, about the origins of needs, and about the rationale of cultural meanings. For this reason, they are not merely different representations, they are incompatible constructions. In referring to them one is not comparing like with like.

But the main difficulty with such constructions is not that they are inconsistent. It is that this kind of anthropology of Islam (and I want to stress here that Gellner's eclecticism is typical of very many sociological writers on Islam) rests on false conceptual oppositions and equivalences, which often lead writers into making ill founded assertions about motives, meanings, and effects relating to "religion." More importantly, it makes difficult the formulation of questions that are at once less tendentious and more interesting than those which many observers of con-temporary Islam (both "conservative" and "radical" Islam) seek to answer.

An instructive example is the hoary old argument about the totalitarian character of orthodox Islam. Like Bernard Lewis and many others, Gellner proposes that
scriptural Islam has an elective affinity for Marxism, partly because of "the inbuilt
vocation towards the implementation of a sharply defined divine order on earth"
(*MS*, 47) and partly because of "The totalism of both ideologies [which] precludes
institutionalized politics" (*MS*, 48).[22] Quite apart from the empirical question of
how widespread Marxist movements have been among twentieth-century Muslim
populations, it must be said that the notion of a totalitarian Islam rests on a mistaken
view of the social effectivity of ideologies.[23] A moment's reflection will show that
it is not the literal scope of the *shari'a* that matters here but the degree to which
it informs and regulates social practices, and it is clear that there has never been
any Muslim society in which the religious law of Islam has governed more than a
fragment of social life. If one contrasts this fact with the highly regulated character of social life in modern states, one may immediately see the reason why. The
administrative and legal regulations of such secular states are far more pervasive
and effective in controlling the details of people's lives than anything to be found
in Islamic history. The difference, of course, lies not in the textual specifications of
what is vaguely called a social blue print, but in the reach of institutional powers
that constitute, divide up, and govern large stretches of social life according to
systematic rules in modern industrial societies, whether capitalist or communist.[24]

In 1972 Nikki Keddie wrote: "Fortunately, Western scholarship seems to have
emerged from the period when many were writing ... that Islam and Marxism were
so similar in many ways that one might lead to the other."[25] Perhaps that period of
Western scholarly innocence is not entirely behind us. But the point of this example
will be lost if it is seen as merely another attempt to defend Islam against the claim
that it has affinities with a totalitarian system. Such a claim has been challenged in
the past, and even if rational criticism cannot prevent the claim from being reproduced, the matter is in itself of little *theoretical* interest. Instead, it is important to
emphasize that one must carefully examine established social practices, "religious"
as well as "nonreligious," in order to understand the conditions that define "conservative" or "radical" political activity in the contemporary Muslim world. And it is to
this idea that we will now turn.

VII

My general argument so far has been that no coherent anthropology of Islam can be founded on the notion of a determinate social blueprint, or on the idea of an integrated social totality in which social structure and religious ideology interact. This does not mean that no coherent object for an anthropology of Islam is possible, or that it is adequate to say that anything Muslims believe or do can be regarded by the anthropologist as part of Islam. Most anthropologists of Islam have defined their scope too widely, both those appealing to an essentialist principle and those employing a nominalist one. If one wants to write an anthropology of Islam one should begin, as Muslims do, from the concept of a discursive tradition that includes and relates itself to the founding texts of the Qur'an and the Hadith. Islam is neither a distinctive social structure nor a heterogeneous collection of beliefs, artifacts, customs, and morals. It is a tradition.

In a useful article, "The Study of Islam in Local Contexts," Eickelman has recently suggested that there is a major theoretical need for taking up the "middle ground" between the study of village or tribal Islam and that of universal Islam.[26] This may well be so, but the most urgent theoretical need for an anthropology of Islam is a matter not so much of finding the right scale but of formulating the right concepts. "A discursive tradition" is just such a concept.

What is a tradition?[27] A tradition consists essentially of discourses that seek to instruct practitioners regarding the correct form and purpose of a given practice that, precisely because it is established, has a history. These discourses relate conceptually to a past (when the practice was instituted, and from which the knowledge of its point and proper performance has been transmitted) and a future (how the point of that practice can best be secured in the short or long term, or why it should be modified or abandoned), through a present (how it is linked to other practices, institutions, and social conditions). An Islamic discursive tradition is simply a tradition of Muslim discourse that addresses itself to conceptions of the Islamic past and future, with reference to a particular Islamic practice in the present. Clearly, not everything Muslims say and do belongs to an Islamic discursive tradition. Nor is an Islamic tradition in this sense necessarily imitative of what was done in the past. For even where traditional practices appear to the anthropologist to be imitative of what has gone before, it will be the practitioners' conceptions of what is apt performance, and of how the past is related to present practices, that will be crucial for tradition, not the apparent repetition of an old form.

My point is not, as some Western anthropologists and Westernized Muslim intellectuals have argued, that "tradition" is today often a fiction of the present, a reaction to the forces of modernity—that in contemporary conditions of crisis, tradition in the Muslim world is a weapon, a ruse, a defense, designed to confront a threatening world,[28] that it is an old cloak for new aspirations and borrowed styles of behavior.[29] The claim that contemporary ideas and social arrangements are really ancient when they are not is in itself no more significant than the pretense that new ones have been introduced when actually they have not. Lying to oneself, as well as to others, about the relationship of the present to the past is as banal in modern societies as it is in societies that anthropologists typically study. The important point about tradition is simply that all instituted practice's are oriented to a conception of the past.

For the anthropologist of Islam the proper theoretical beginning is therefore an instituted practice (set in a particular context and having a particular history) into which Muslims are inducted *as* Muslims. For analytical purposes there is no essential difference on this point between "classical" and "modern" Islam. The discourses in which the teaching is done, in which the correct performance of the practice is defined and learned, are intrinsic to all Islamic practices. It is therefore somewhat misleading to suggest, as some sociologists have done, that it is *orthopraxy* and not *orthodoxy*, ritual and not doctrine, that matters in Islam.[30] It is misleading be cause such a contention ignores the centrality of the notion of "the correct model" to which an instituted practice—including ritual—ought to conform, a model conveyed in authoritative formulas, in Islamic traditions as in others. And I refer here primarily not to the *programmatic discourses* of "modernist" and "fundamentalist" Islamic movements, but to the established *practices* of unlettered Muslims. A practice is Islamic because it is authorized by the dis cursive traditions of Islam, and is so taught to Muslims—whether by an *'alim*, a *khatib*, a Sufi *shaykh*, or an untutored parent.[31] (It may well be worth recalling here that etymologically "doctrine" means teaching, and that orthodox doctrine therefore denotes the correct process of teaching, as well as the correct statement of what is to be learned.)[32]

Orthodoxy is crucial to all Islamic traditions. But the sense in which I use this term must be distinguished from the sense given it by most Orientalists and anthropologists. Anthropologists like El-Zein, who wish to deny any special significance to orthodoxy, and those like Gellner, who see it as a specific set of doctrines "at the heart of Islam," both are missing something vital: that orthodoxy is not a mere body of opinion but a distinctive relationship—a relationship of power to truth.

Wherever Muslims have the power to regulate, uphold, require, or adjust *correct* practices, and to condemn, exclude, undermine, or replace *incorrect* ones, there is the domain of orthodoxy. The way these powers are exercised, the conditions that make them possible (social, political, economic, etcetera), and the resistances they encounter (from Muslims and non-Muslims) are equally the concern of an anthropology of Islam, regardless of whether its direct object of research is in the city or in the countryside, in the present or in the past. Argument and conflict over the form and significance of practices are there fore a natural part of any Islamic tradition.

In their representation of "Islamic tradition," Orientalists and anthropologists have often marginalized the place of argument and reasoning surrounding traditional practices. Argument is generally represented as a symptom of "the tradition in crisis," on the assumption that "normal" tradition (what Abdallah Laroui calls "tradition as structure" and distinguishes from "tradition as ideology"[*CI, 33*]) excludes reasoning just as it requires unthinking conformity. But these contrasts and equations are themselves the work of a historical motivation, manifest in Edmund Burke's ideological opposition between "tradition" and "reason," an opposition which was elaborated by the conservative theorists who followed him, and introduced into sociology by Weber.[33]

Reason and argument are necessarily involved in traditional practice whenever people have to be taught about the point and proper performance of that practice, and whenever the teaching meets with doubt, indifference, or lack of understanding. It is largely because we think of argument in terms of formal debate, confrontation, and polemic that we assume it has no place in traditional practice.[34] Yet the process of trying to *win someone over* for the willing performance of a traditional practice, as distinct from trying to demolish an opponent's intellectual position, is a necessary part of Islamic discursive traditions as of others. If reasons and arguments are intrinsic to traditional practice, and not merely to "a tradition in crisis," it should be the anthropologist's first task to describe and analyze the kinds of reasoning, and the reasons for arguing, that underlie Islamic traditional practices. It is here that the analyst may discover a central modality of power, and of the resistances it encounters—for the process of arguing, of using the force of reason, at once presupposes and responds to the fact of resistance. Power, and resistance, are thus intrinsic to the development and exercise of any traditional practice.

A theoretical consequence of this is that traditions should not be regarded as essentially homogenous, that heterogeneity in Muslim practices is not necessarily an indication of the absence of an Islamic tradition. The variety of traditional Muslim practices in different times, places, and populations indicate the different Islamic reasonings that different social and historical conditions can or cannot sustain. The idea that traditions are essentially homogeneous has a powerful intellectual appeal, but it is mistaken.[35] In deed, widespread homogeneity is a function, not of tradition, but of the development and control of communication techniques that are part of modern industrial societies.[36]

Although Islamic traditions are not homogeneous, they aspire to coherence, in the way that all discursive traditions do. That they do not always attain it is due as much to the constraints of political and economic conditions to which the traditions are related as to their inherent limitations. Thus, in our own time the attempt by Islamic traditions to organize memory and desire in a coherent manner is increasingly remade by the social forces of industrial capitalism, which create conditions favorable to very different patterns of desire and forgetfulness.[37] An anthropology of Islam will therefore seek to understand the historical conditions that enable the production and maintenance of specific discursive traditions, or their transformation—and the efforts of practitioners to achieve coherence.[38]

VIII

I have been arguing that anthropologists interested in Islam need to rethink their object of study, and that the concept of tradition will help in this task. I now want to conclude with a final brief point. To write about a tradition is to be in a certain narrative relation to it, a relation that will vary according to whether one supports or opposes the tradition, or regards it as morally neutral. The coherence that each party finds, or fails to find, in that tradition will depend on their particular historical position. In other words, there clearly is not, nor can there be, such a thing as a universally acceptable account of a living tradition. Any representation of tradition is contestable. What shape that contestation takes, if it occurs, will be determined not only by the powers and knowledges each side deploys, but by the collective life to which they aspire—or to whose survival they are quite indifferent. Declarations of moral neutrality, here as always, are no guarantee of political innocence.

NOTES

1. See, for example, Edward W. Said, *Covering Islam* (New York: Pantheon Books, 1981).
2. Abdul Hamid El-Zein, "Beyond Ideology and Theology: The Search for the Anthropology of Islam," *Annual Review of Anthropology 6* (1977): 227–54.
3. Michael Gilsenan, *Recognizing Islam* (London: Croom Helm, 1982). Hereafter cited as *RI*.
4. Ernest Gellner, *Muslim Society* (Cambridge: Cambridge University Press, 1981). Hereafter cited as *MS*.
5. John Gulick, *The Middle East: An Anthropological Perspective* (Pacific Palisades, CA: Goodyear, 1976); Dale E Eickelman, *The Middle East: An Anthropological Approach* (Englewood Cliffs, NJ: Prentice-Hall, 1976).
6. There are a few exceptions, such as Suad Joseph and Barbara Pillsbury, eds., *Muslim-Christian Conflicts* (Boulder, CO: Westview Press, 1978).
7. See Josef van Ess, "From Wellhausen to Becker: The Emergence of Kulturgeschichte in Islamic Studies," in *Islamic Studies*: A Tradition and Its Problems, ed. Malcolm H. Kerr (Malibu, CA: Undena, 1980).
8. Michael M. J. Fischer, *Iran: Front Religious Dispute to Revolution* (Cambridge, MA: Harvard University Press, 1980).
9. Talal Asad, "Anthropological Conceptions of Religion: Reflections on Geertz," *Man* 18, no. 2 (1983): 237–59; Talal Asad, "Notes on Body Pain and Truth in Medieval Christian Ritual," *Economy and Society* 12, no. 3 (1983): 287–327; Talal Asad, "Medieval Heresy: An Anthropological View," Social History 11, no. 2 (1986): 354–62; Talal Asad, "On Ritual and Discipline in Medieval Christian Monasticism," *Economy and Society*, 16, no. 2 (1987): 159–203.
10. For example: Gustave von Grunebaum, *Modern Islam* (Berkeley: University of California Press, 1962), 40.
11. Bernard Lewis, "The Muslim Discovery of Europe," in *Islam in History*, ed. Bernard Lewis (New York: Library Press, 1962), 40.
12. Bryan Turner, *Weber and Islam* (London: Routledge and Kegan Paul, 1974), 70.
13. Abdallah Hammoudi, "Segmentarity, Social Stratification, Political Power and Sainthood: Reflections on Gellner's Theses," *Economy and Society* 9, no. 3 (1980): 279–303; Vincent J. Cornell, "The Logic of Analogy and the Role of the Sufi Shaykh in Post-Marinid Morocco," *International Journal of Middle East Studies* 15, no. 1 (1983): 67–93.

14. Bryan Turner, *Marx and the End of Orientalism* (London: George Allen & Unwin, 1978), 52.

15. Talal Asad, *The Kababish Arabs: Power, Authority and Consent in a Nomadic Tribe* (London: Hurst, 1970); Talal Asad, "The Beduin as a Military Force," in *The Desert and the Sown*, ed. Cynthia Nelson (Berkeley: University of California Press, 1973); Talal Asad, "Equality in Nomadic Systems?" in *Pastoral and Production and Society*, ed. Equipe Écologie et Anthropologie des Sociétés Pastorales (Cambridge: Cambridge University Press, 1983).

16. Andrew M. Watson, *Agricultural Innovation in the Early Islamic World* (Cambridge: Cambridge University Press, 1983).

17. The changing networks of intercontinental trade that linked *DarulIslam* to Europe, Africa, and Asia differentially affected and were af fected by patterns of production and consumption within it (see Maurice Lombard, *L'Islam dans sa première grandeur: VIII–XIe siècles* [Paris: Flammarion, 1971]). Even the spread of contagious disease with its drastic social and economic consequences con-nected Middle Eastern political units with other parts of the world (see Michael W. Dois, *The Black Death in the Middle East* [Princeton, NJ: Princeton University Press, 1977], especially 36–37). It would not be necessary to refer so baldly to well-known historical evidence if it were not still common for eminent schol-ars to write of "Islam" as a mechanically balanced social structure, reflecting its own dynamic of cause and effect and having its own isolated destiny.

18. Clifford Geertz, *Islam Observed* (New Haven, CT: Yale University Press, 1968), II.

19. Gellner's resort to the Durkheimian viewpoint on religion is not quite as consistent as it ought to be. Thus, in one place we read that "the faith of the tribesman *needs* to be mediated by special and distinct holy personnel, rather than be egalitarian; it *needs* to be joyous and festival-worthy, not puritanical and scholarly; it *requires* hierarchy and incarnation in persons, not in scripts" (MS, 41; emphasis added). But a dozen pages later, when Gellner wants to introduce the idea of "revolutionary" tribal religion, these *needs* have to be made to disappear: "It is a curious but crucial fact about the social psychology of Muslim tribesmen," he writes, "that their normal religion is for them *at one level* a mere *pis aller*, and is tinged with irony, and with an ambivalent recognition that the *real* norms lie elsewhere" (MS, 52; emphasis in original).

20. Such phrases might be more plausible (but not therefore entirely valid—see, e.g., Janet Abu-Lughod, "Varieties of Urban Experience," in *Middle Eastern*

Cities: A Symposium on Ancient, Islamic, and Contemporary Middle Eastern Urbanism, ed. Ira M. Lapidus [Berkeley: University of California Press, 1969]) if applied to the condition of poor rural migrants in a modern metropolis. To describe the lower strata of medieval Muslim cities, with their organization into quar ters, guilds, Sufi brotherhoods, etc., as being "uprooted, insecure, alienated" is surely a little fanciful, unless, of course, one takes the mere occurrence of bread riots in periods of economic hardship as a sign of mental disturbance among the poor. Yet, oddly enough, when Gellner does refer to the urban masses in twentieth-century cities, a totally new motivation is imputed to the uprooted migrants: "The tribal style of religion loses then much of its function, whilst the urban one gains in authority and prestige from *eagerness of the migrant-rustics to acquire respectability*" (MS, 58; emphasis added). Now the religion of the urban poor is attributed no longer to a desire for forgetting, but to a desire for respectability.

21. Most Muslims for most of their history, as Gellner himself acknowledges, cannot be described as scripturalist puritans, yet "Islam," he claims, expresses a scripturalist, puritan state of mind better than other religions. There is surely some fuzziness here. It is clear that Gellner is identifying the *essential* tendency of Islam with what he regards as the life-style of the "well-heeled urban bourgeoisie." This equation may be appealing to some Muslims, but the attentive reader will wish to ask in what sense this social group is naturally "puritan," and indeed in what sense they are "better" puritans than, say, seventeenth-century Puritans in England and America. A natural "distaste for public festivals"? Anyone who has lived in a Muslim community, or read relevant historical accounts (e.g., Edward Lane's *Manners and Customs of the Modern Egyptians* [London: Dent (Everyman edition), 1908], or Snouck Hurgronje's *Mekka in the Latter Part of the 19th Century* [Leiden: Brill, 1931]), will know that the rites of passage are more elaborate among the "well-heeled urban bourgeoisie" than among the lower urban social strata. "Scripturalism" based on literacy? But the literacy of merchants is very different from the literacy of professional "men of religion" (see Brian V. Street's excellent book, *Literacy in Theory and Practice* [Cambridge: Cambridge University Press, 1984]). Besides, the traditions of Qur'anic exegesis developed by Muslim "men of religion" are far richer and more diverse than the blanket term "scripturalist" suggests.

22. In reproducing the view that there is an "elective affinity" between Islam and Marxism, Gellner appears to have missed the fact that Ibn Khaldun, the

only classical Muslim theorist who deals in detail with connections between political power and the economy, warns explicitly against the government's trying to control trade or produc tion—see *The Muqaddimah*, abridged edition (London: Routledge and Kegan Paul, 1967), 232–34. Since the idea of government control of the economy has never been part of classical Muslim theory, but is central to classical Marxism, there is here a crucial opposition between the two.

23. Apart from the important communist parties in Iraq and Sudan (neither of which commanded a massive following), Marxism has had no real roots among contemporary Muslim populations. States like the People's Democratic Republic of Yemen are exceptions that prove the rule. (See also Alexandre A. Bennigsen and S. E. Wimbush, *Muslim National Communism in the Soviet Union* [Chicago: University of Chicago Press, 1979] for an account of protracted resistances against Russian imperial power.) Marxist ideology has been associated with some Westernized intellectuals and *some* authoritarian states, but never with 'ulama or the well-heeled urban bourgeoisie, who are supposed by Gellner to be the historical carriers of scripturalist, puritan Islam. It is his mistaken attempt to connect this latter kind of Islam with "Marxism," "Socialism," or "Social radicalism" (terms used indiscriminately) that leads him to make the implausible argument that "scripturalist rigorism or fundamentalism" is admirably suited to bringing about modernization in the Muslim world.

24. As a succinct evocation of the powers of the modern state, the following memorable passage from Robert Musil's great novel has scarcely been bettered: "The fact is, living permanently in a well-ordered State has an out-and-out spectral aspect: one cannot step into the street or drink a glass of water or get into a tram without touching the perfectly balanced levers of a gigantic apparatus of laws and relations, setting them in motion or letting them maintain one in the peace and quiet of one's existence. One hardly knows any of these levers, which extend deep into the inner workings and on the other side are lost in a network the entire constitution of which has never been disentangled by any living being. Hence one denies their existence, just as the common man denies the existence of the air, insisting that it is mere emptiness." *The Man without Qualities*, vol. 1 (London: Seeker and Warburg, 1954), 182.

25. Nikki Keddie, *Scholars, Saints and Sufis* (Berkeley: University of California Press, 1972), 13.

26. Dale F. Eickelman, "The Study of Islam in Local Contexts," *Contributions to Asian Studies* 17 (1984): 1–16.

27. In outlining the concept of tradition, I am indebted to the insightful writings of Alasdair MacIntyre, in particular his brilliant book *After Virtue* (London: Duckworth, 1981).

28. Thus Gilsenan: "Tradition, therefore, is put together in all manner of different ways in contemporary conditions of crisis; it is a term that is in fact highly variable and shifting in content. It changes, though all who use it do so to mark out truths and principles as essentially unchanging. In the name of tradition many traditions are born and come into opposition with others. It becomes a language, a weapon against internal and external enemies, a refuge, an evasion, or part of the entitlement to domination and authority over others" (*RI*, 15).

29. Or as Abdallah Laroui puts it in *The Crisis of the Arab Intellectual* (Berkeley: University of California Press, 1976), 35, hereafter cited as *CI*: "one might say that tradition exists only when innovation is accepted under the cloak of fidelity to the past."

30. For example, see Eickelman, *Middle East*, chapter 9. In a short paper written many years ago, "Politics and Religion in Islamic Reform" (*Review of Middle East Studies*, no. 2, London: Ithaca Press, 1976) I emphasized that orthodoxy is always the product of a network of power.

31. Incidentally, it is time that anthropologists of Islam realized that there is more to Ibn Khaldun than his "political sociology," that his deployment of the Aristotelian concept of virtue (in the form of the Arabic *malaka*) is especially relevant to an understanding of what I have called Islamic traditions. In a recent essay, "Knowledge, Virtue and Action: The Classical Muslim Conception of *Adab* and the Nature of Religious Fulfillment in Islam," Ira Lapidus has included a brief but useful account of Ibn Khaldun's concept of *malaka* (in Barbara D. Metcalf, ed., *Moral Conduct and Authority: The Place of Adab in South Asian Islam* [Berkeley: University of California, 1984], 52–56).

32. Cf. "Doctrine" in *New Catholic Encyclopedia*, vol. 4 (New York: McGraw-Hill, 1967).

33. See Alasdair MacIntyre, "Epistemological Crises, Dramatic Narrative, and the Philosophy of Science," in *Paradigms and Revolutions*, ed. Gary Gutting (Notre Dame, IN: Notre Dame University Press, 1980), 64–65.

34. See John Dixon and Leslie Stratta, "Argument and the Teaching of English: A Critical Analysis," in *Writers Writing*, ed. A. Wilkinson (Milton Keynes, UK: Open University Press, 1986).

35. Thus, in an essay entitled "Late Antiquity and Islam: Parallels and Contrasts" (in B. D. Metcalf, *Moral Conduct and Authority*), the eminent historian Peter Brown quotes with approval from Henri Marrou: "For in the last resort classical humanism was based on tradition, something imparted by one's teachers and handed down un-questioningly … it meant that all the minds of one generation, and indeed of a whole historical period, had a fundamental homogeneity which made communication and genuine communion easier" (24). It is precisely this familiar concept, which Brown employs to discuss "the Islamic tradition," that anthropologists should abandon in favor of another.

36. For an introductory discussion of some problems relating to the control and effects of a typically modern form of communication, see Raymond Williams, *Television: Technology and Cultural Form* (London: Fontana, 1974).

37. The result among Muslim intellectuals has been described by Jacques Berque thus: "Dans le monde actuel et parmi trop d'intellectuels oude militants, on se partage entre adeptes d'une authenticité sans avenir et adeptes d'une modernisme sans racines. Le français traduit mal, en l'espèce, ce qui en arabe vient beaucoup mieux: ançâr al-maçîr bilâ açîl wa ançar al-açîl bilâ maçîr." *L'Islam: La philosophie et les sciences* (Paris: Les Presses de l'Unesco, 1981), 68.

38. It should be stressed that the problem indicated here is not the same as the one treated in the many monographs that purport to describe the recent "erosion of the old unity of values based on Divine Revelation" that has accompanied the disruption of the "stable, indeed static, social world" of traditional Muslim society (cf. Michael Gilsenan, *Saint and Sufi in Modern Egypt* [Oxford: Clarendon Press, 1973], 196, 192). I have argued that that world was never stable and static, and hold that the concept of a complex and evolving Islamic tradition does not presuppose a simple unity of values.

The Private Performance of Salat Prayers

Repetition, Time, and Meaning

by NILOOFAR HAERI

BETWEEN 2007 AND 2009, DURING ANNUAL VISITS TO TEHRAN, I talked to a group of Muslim women about their performance of the five daily prayers (*salaat* in Arabic, hereafter "*salat*;" and *namaaz* in Persian).[1] The results of these conversations led me to revisit some of the debates about rituals—in particular, those that involve language. In 2010–2011, I went back to Tehran and carried out an additional four months of fieldwork on the salat. Ethnographic studies of the salat remain few in number (Bowen 1989, Parkin 2000, Henkel 2005, Mahmood 2001), but those that concern themselves with its private rather than public performance are even more rare. The prevalence of images of the public performance of salat have made it appear as the unmarked form of prayer for Muslims. Yet, notwithstanding the weekly visibility of Friday and communal prayers in holy sites whose images are broadcast to most corners of the world, over a day and a lifetime, most prayers are performed at home with various degrees of privacy.

The public performance of the salat in small agricultural communities or large urban metropolises, in ethnically homogeneous or heterogeneous places, and in revolutionary or more quiet times can have a range of symbolic and political meanings as has been demonstrated by several scholars (Gilsenan 2000, Mottahedeh 1985, Fischer 2003, Bowen 1993, Lambek 2000, Starrett 1998, Mahmood 2005, Varzi 2006, Deeb 2006, Torab 2007, among others). But, performed in private, in the presence of God alone, the salat calls our attention to dimensions that are crucial to a better understanding of the ritual itself, to a deeper appreciation of sources of variation within Islam, and to the multiple roles that language plays in shaping this experience.

The focus on public performance has skewed the study of the salat towards men (Parkin 2000), since women pray in mosques far less often. Mosque attendance in all social classes is more of a male than a female practice, but especially so in the higher social classes. None of the women in my group pray on a regular basis at the mosque. Even their male relatives pray at home most of the time. The influence of class on mosque attendance is similar in Egypt, but in the context of social movements with religious aims (whether or not connected to oppositional politics), women attend mosques more often (Mahmood 2005). In Iran, after the revolution of 1979, urban lower class women's mosque attendance increased (Torab 2007). For Turkey, Henkel reports that "women generally do not use mosques" to perform the salat (2005: 494; see also Gilsenan 2000: 167).

The aim of this article is to consider the implications of a ritual that is performed alone (see also Silverstein 2009, Du Bois 2009). I will offer an ethnography of private prayer—what I have been able to observe and what I am told about it by the women I interviewed. It is difficult to conceive of what a ritual would mean or be like beyond the public eye. But this central ritual of Islam is both private and public. The salat falls under what are called "ibadaat" (sing. ibaada, in Persian ibaadat)[2]—practices that are undertaken for the purpose of concentrating on being in the company and in the thought of God. These refer to the salat as well as other obligations (Graham 2010: 94). Among Muslims, it is not controversial to undertake ibaadat at home (or outside) (Parkin 2000).[3] Hence, the term "ritual" is not a fully adequate translation. This non-equivalence should hover over ethnographies and analyses of Muslim rituals. At the same time, ibaadat does have a significant partial overlap with ritual as is evident in the literature on the salat within and outside of anthropology. I will therefore carry out an analysis of the salat as a ritual, bearing in mind the problematic translation.

Returning to the question of private prayer, I ask what are individuals doing when they follow a ritual requirement of their religion without the presence of fellow reciters and a leader to emulate?[4] In considering the "linguistic individual," Barbara

Johnstone (1996: 3) argues that most work on language has relied on theorizations of the abstract social system, following Saussure, without adequate attention to the individual speaker. In this way, we have yet to answer the question of "when, how and why individual speakers are connected with discourse and language in particular historical, cultural, and generic context" (Johnstone 2000: 406, 1996). One can pose the same question with respect to the performance of rituals: How does each reciter get connected to the ritual (language) at a given historical moment, in a given cultural context? It is this question that I try to address in the following.

In attempting to understand the experience of individual prayer, I will examine some of the central debates in anthropology with regard to the roles of language in ritual performance: first, the consequences of repetition of formulaic language and the relation between repetition, formality, and meaning (Bloch 1974, 1975, 2005; Tambiah 1985; Irvine 2001; Johnstone 1987; Keane 1997a; Stasch 2011); second, possibilities for creativity in the face of seeming linguistic and structural rigidity (Csordas 1987, Bloch 2005, Du Bois 2009, Silverstein 2009); and third, the related question of agency, co-presence, and authorship in the performance of rituals (Bloch 2005; Keane 1997a, 1997b, 2007a; Mahmood 2001, 2005; de Certeau 1988; Bialecki 2011).

Each salat is made up of *suuras* ("chapters") from the Qur'an. The suuras are recited in a prescribed order—certain orders have become standard. However, the only suura that is required to be recited at the beginning of each prayer is *al-Fatiha* (Iranians refer to it as *al-Hamd*), the opening chapter of the Qur'an. In theory, any suura that the reciter chooses can follow al-Fatiha (see also Graham 1993: 103). The opening chapter is described as a *keliid*, a "key" that lets the reciter into a hoped for sacred spacetime. There are five daily recitations: at dawn, noon, afternoon, evening, and night. Each one of these has a standard number of prayer cycles or "*rak'ats*"—the dawn prayer has two, evening three, and the others four. In addition to the recitation of the suuras, the performance of each prayer involves four body postures: standing, bending forward with hands on knees ("*rukuu*"), prostrating ("*sujuud*"), and sitting. People who are incapable of these physical movements may perform the whole prayer in any one posture they find comfortable. Those who would like to add to the number of prayer cycles can do so, and those who are traveling are allowed to decrease that number.

Depending on the personal context of the reciter, there are a number of non-standard suuras that are chosen by these women for the prayers: for seeking refuge in God in times of distress, *al-Falaq* ("The Dawn," Suura 113) and *al-Naas* ("The

People," 114) are recited; when feeling light and in good relations with God, having been given what one asked for, *al-Nasr* ("The Victory," 110); when one needs to be patient, *wal-Asr* ("The Time," 103) and "for when you need to be reminded that after every period of hardship comes a period of ease and comfort," some choose *al-Sharh* ("The Relief," 94). These suuras—all of which are between 3–6 ayas—are examples of non-standard suuras that were mentioned more frequently. The choice can be any chapter of the Qur'an.

Within the structure of each prayer, in particular that of dawn, there is a non-obligatory act that is *mustahabb* ("favored") and that is to recite a *qonuut*. The content of what one recites in the qonuut can vary greatly. The women in this group all like to include the qonuut. One might recite a few verses of a suura, talk to God in Persian, recite a du'a, or as a few told me, recite a few verses of poetry. Qonuut is often said to be an exclusively Shi'ite practice. However, Arab Iranian Sunnis from Qeshm (an island in the south of Iran) told me that they do include it in their salat. Bowen (1993: 69) mentions that the question of its inclusion was debated in Indonesia among Sunnis.[5] According to Ayatollah Taghi Modaressi, qonuut, meaning obedience, is a special du'a and must be performed in the following manner: hands must be raised and held in front of the face such that "the palms are facing the sky and the backs of the hand the earth."[6] Hence, the qonuut is another occasion for creativity. Individual performance seems to be a major site of variation and innovation in part because one is not following a prayer leader, as is the case in congregational prayer.

I begin by contextualizing the women and their lives in present day Tehran and go on to offer an ethnography of prayers performed by them. Before going further, it should be noted that there are two main kinds of prayer for Muslims: the obligatory salat and the non-obligatory du'a—often glossed as "personal prayer, supplications." There are different kinds of du'a: prayers written by various Shi'ite imams, spontaneous requests or talks with God, or recitation of a few verses of a Qur'anic chapter. In English, one uses the word "prayer" for several kinds of prayers that have distinct names among Muslims. In any case, while on some days a believer might not recite a du'a, she is required to do the salat daily.

The language of rituals is usually characterized as "formal"—meaning that it is different from the everyday language of the performer and that the latter has not "chosen" its words (see Irvine 2001). For many, formality seems to imply rigidity—at times they are used synonymously (see below). Repetition in ritual and its consequences for meaning continue to be debated (Asad 1993, Bowen 2000, Keane

2007a, Bloch 2005, Robbins 2001, Du Bois 2009). Building on this literature, I pose a number of questions that require further debate. For example, does the concept of repetition imply sameness of context at each performance? And, if not, can there be such a thing as pure repetition—an exact copy of what one has done previously? Are all repetitions comparable so that repeating a phrase "to a bewildering extent" (Bloch 2005: 124) can be compared to repeating "Amen" in Christian rituals or to reciting the same chapter of the Qur'an at the beginning of each salat? In a review of studies of repetition in the social sciences and humanities, Johnstone (1987) found that "mainstream Americans and other Westerners" view repetition negatively, even though it is used all the time in everyday language, in talking to children, and in poetry and songs.

In pursuing a line of inquiry into the questions I posed above, it is crucial to take the temporality of the salat—in several senses—into account. The repetition of formal language over time lessens the formality—in fact, repetition undermines the stiffness and rigidity associated with formality. It potentially removes one of the hindrances to creativity. In addition, the age at which the salat is performed matters greatly. The salat of an 18-year-old is not the same as that of a 65-year-old. The worlds stretching in front of them are clearly distinct. What the salat has to offer as ibaadat, as meaning, resonances, and knowledge are not once and for all matters. And the length of time one has been praying is crucial to understanding how, over time, the salat changes. For the women among whom I did my fieldwork, the fact that they had been praying for more than three decades is central to their religious experiences. Over a lifetime, what the salat means in terms of providing a particular form of being in the thought of God, what its verses signify, and how the reciter finds spaces of creativity and presence in its performance, go through transformations. As the individual's intellectual and emotional conditions change, as she makes and remakes a variety of relationships with friends and family, as she experiences births and deaths, her interactions with the salat also undergo changes, including the contribution of the salat to the cultivation of a certain interiority. With increases in religious knowledge, different chapters of the Qur'an other than the standard ones are chosen, depending on particular concerns and anxieties of any given moment. To do this also requires confidence and practice, all of which are implicated in the length of time the prayers have been performed.

The meanings of what is recited are in part dependent on whether the reciter is literate and aware of continuing theological debates and the layers of meanings of the repeated verses. Without knowing whether an individual is literate, and to what degree, whether she is part of a community in which literacy is a dominant mode of knowledge acquisition, whether relevant debates (about the ritual) are part of television and radio programming and so on, we cannot answer the question of the relation between repetition and meaning (or loss of meaning). The skepticism that a number of anthropologists have voiced over having a general category called "ritual" (Asad 1993, Bowen 1993, Robbins 2001) is highlighted when literacy is taken into account. In communities where the semantic and theological meanings of a frequently performed ritual like the salat are regularly debated, the verses of the prayers remain, year after year, perhaps too meaningful for those who are literate enough to participate in such discourse. What happens to meaning in any given ritual has to be analyzed *over time* and with respect to its specific users, uses, and histories. In his discussion of "private ritual encounters" and the "general category" of ritual communication, Silverstein asks whether the "'communication' authorized and licensed by the ritual [must] be denotation-centered" (2009: 272). As I will suggest below, the answer to this question is negative in the experience of the women that I studied. What emerges in the course of the private performance of the salat is that it's stipulated poetics do not preclude possibilities for reflexivity.[7]

There is another sense in which the temporality of the salat needs further contemplation. When one stands to pray, I was told, one does not know where the session will end up. Will the reciter manage to communicate to God and feel close to him?[8] Will she be able to muster the necessary concentration? Will she be able to be as honest as possible? I will return to this discussion later in this article. For now, it should be noted that my interlocutors described an efficacious prayer as one that ends with them feeling particularly close to God, having managed to be "honest" with him and having communicated what is on their minds. However, one does not know how any given prayer session will proceed. Some women told me that whenever they start to pray and realize shortly afterwards that their mind has wandered, they "break" their prayer and start over. If they still do not succeed, they will not pray for a few hours, or even a whole day, until they can marshal the necessary concentration.

THE WOMEN AND THEIR RELIGIOUS ACTIVITIES

The women I spoke to in Tehran are middle class[9] and well-educated. Almost half were born and raised in other parts of Iran but have ended up living in the capital. I interviewed about 25 women. Each interview lasted for approximately two hours and I was able to talk to some of the women more than once. I held a number of group discussions as well. I interviewed the women's Qur'an teacher and attended lessons frequented by a different group of women. Over the years, however, I have been talking to and observing a larger group of Muslim men and women. Therefore, while I mostly rely on the views and statements of these 25 women, I also draw on a larger set of interlocutors and a longer time span. My interlocutors do not comprise a "representative sample" of Iranian Muslim women; however, their approach to following the requirements of their religion is fairly representative of professional, middle class women who have gone to university and pursued economic independence. Their insights are worth analyzing because they challenge our ideas about the possibilities of ritual when performed beyond the public eye and outside a congregational context. With few exceptions, most of these women are in their 60s. Among the older group are women who have known each other for a long time, The Private Performance of Salat Prayers: Repetition, Time, and Meaning bound by kinship ties and long-standing friendships. They are retired now and receive pensions. After finishing high school, some went on to teacher training colleges (for two years) and/or to universities where they specialized in fields such as psychology, literature, and language. They held long-term jobs as high school teachers (mostly in public schools, but also a few in private ones), head mistresses, editors of dictionaries, and other similar posts requiring linguistic and cultural expertise. A few wear a headscarf both inside and outside the house, but most take their scarf off as soon as they enter a private home, whether or not they expect to see unrelated men. Outside the home, covering the hair is obligatory for women under the laws of the Islamic Republic. None wears a head-to-toe veil (*chador*) except when inside mosques, shrines, and for special gatherings. Most of the women engage in extensive and systematic charity work, which offers them a wide network of friends and acquaintances in several parts of Iran with whose lives they become intimately familiar.

They take a number of classes during the year, the most regular being Qur'an classes. The Qur'an classes are generally year round and one can join at any time.

Many are offered inside people's homes and require a personal introduction. The Qur'an classes that I went to were not publicly advertised and, because political discussions of daily events inevitably came up (though not routinely), the teacher and the students wanted to make sure that those who join will not report on such discussions. The classes are free and teachers rarely accept money. However, students bring sweets, free copies of the Qur'an and other publications, and at times make voluntary payments so that the classes can go on. They start from the first Chapter of the Qur'an and discuss each word and verse, then move on to the next chapter. In any given class, there are at least five or six different editions of the Qur'an with different Persian translations. The teacher reads a verse in Arabic, then its translation, and asks: "What do others have?" Those with different translations then read their versions and a discussion ensues over particular words or verses—are the translations adequate, clear, apt, weak, or misleading? In the long debates that ensue, problems of translation and interpretation merge so that the inadequacy of a word in Persian for a particular one in the original Arabic leads to further considerations that have to do with theological precedence, likelihood, and coherence. There are also weekly poetry classes that most of these women attend. These are classes on Mowlavi (Rumi), Hafiz, and other poets.[10]

Some of the women in this group come from religious families among whom scholarly knowledge of Islam is highly valued. They learned how to pray and read the Qur'an and other religious texts from family members. It is important to note that, as in other Muslim countries, there are many low cost salat manuals, as well as manuals on other rituals. However, their mere availability does not mean that those who pray actually use them. If the believer is not literate, she cannot read the manuals. If the believer is literate, more often than not, she learns the prayers either at home or from a teacher. Until a few decades ago, instructions about how to pray were parts of books on various religious topics and not separate manuals. These books were sometimes given by (grand) parents or other relatives to children to read and later be tested on. This allowed the parents to "correct" or change what some of the books said. Ultimate authority lay with the parent or relative, not with the book. This is still the case and those who use manuals generally seek another person's guidance as well. One woman commented that prayer manuals are for "foreigners who convert." There are probably others, besides converts, who use the manuals, but their general use should not be assumed from their existence on the market (Henkel 2005: 492).

How and from whom one learns to pray—whether from family members, at school, from religious figures, or from books and manuals—is important because it has implications for structures of authority and the practice of variability in the performance of salat and other rituals. Those who have learned about their religion from kinship networks see themselves as authorized to engage in variation. There is a great deal of awareness of the hierarchies of religious knowledge. The kind of pedagogical process (Mahmood 2001, 2005) that one experiences—family, friends' families, teachers, classes, manuals, books, and combinations thereof—can make a fundamental difference both in the ways in which rituals come to be embodied and in the legitimacy of variation and sources of authority. To learn to pray from a kinship network is to learn variability because inevitably there are individual differences that are explicitly commented on and discussed.[11] Short manuals and pamphlets on doctrinal matters are produced for those with lower levels of literacy and religious knowledge, and they are designed as teaching tools, hence simplified. They rarely present the possibilities for variation in performing a ritual. The pedagogical process can result in distinct forms of embodiment depending on who (and what) mediates that process.

In addition to praying, the women in this group organize and participate in a variety of religious gatherings. These include *mowludis* (celebrations of the birthdays of the Prophet and other imams) where the exclusively female participants arrive dressed up. At these events, they read from the Qur'an, sing, clap, dance, and recite praise poetry (Torab 1996, 2007; for Pakistan, see Hegland 2003). A mix of classes and generations attend these gatherings. Younger women who become interested in expanding their religious knowledge make friends with the older women present at these ceremonies—facilitating future meetings that enable them to pose questions or read certain texts together. Another kind of gathering which takes place once a month in some homes (its time being decided based on the lunar calendar) is called a *rowzeh*. In a rowzeh, a professional reciter, *rowzeh khan*,[12] comes to recite religious songs, verses of the Qur'an, and du'as appropriate to specific occasions. In the homes of some families, rowzehs can turn into literary evenings where, after the rowzeh khan is finished, individuals who are present read their own poetry or choose verses from the poetry and prose of others to move listeners to a debate. The poems or passages do not have to be religious and most often they are not. Literary and political discussions round out the evening. In some homes, rowzehs have separate male and female sections, while in others men and women sit in the same room (see Fischer 2003: 100 for a description of a more strictly religious rowzeh).

At times, small groups of close friends (sometimes just two women) get together to recite special prayers specifically designated for Friday evenings—du'as on behalf of themselves or others, for the sick, deceased, and anyone in need. If there are women present who cannot read the verses, they still take part by sitting close and listening (Haeri 2003, Hirschkind 2006)—listening being itself a religious act. Often, the larger gatherings involve cooking and the distribution of special kinds of food and sweets.

Some women organize what is called a *khatmeh an'aam*. The An'aam suura has 165 aya ("verse") and is said to be special because it is the only one that was revealed to the Prophet all in one moment, unlike other suuras whose "descent" (*nozuul*) occurred at different times. Khatmeh an'aam means finishing the reading of this suura in one *majlis*, or sitting. Ideally, 40 women should gather together and take turns in reading the ayas out loud. In practice, the number of reciters is often lower and each individual recites several verses and then the next person picks up where she left off. It is believed that reading and finishing this suura is appropriate when one has made a special request of God. So women who have a *"nazr"* ("vow") may organize khatmeh an'aam. Other women believe that one should do the reading *before* one has any wishes.

For Persian speakers, one fundamental difference between the salat and the various du'a is linguistic. The salat is the word of God and hence *always* in Arabic, but a du'a can be in either Arabic or Persian.[13] The Arabic du'as are published in prayer books such as *Mafaatih al-Janan* ("keys to paradise"). This prayer book seems to be the most popular and is available in many editions. It includes prayers written by Shi'ite imams. Note that a few verses of a suura can be used as a du'a. In addition, at the end of the salat, reciters often sit cross-legged and "talk to God in Persian"— this is also du'a. For example, if praying for someone to regain his health or wishing to thank someone for a generous deed they have done, a reciter might say "I did lots of du'a for his health" or simply "I did lots of du'a for her" (*barash kheili du'a kardam*), meaning "I thanked her in front of God for the great thing that she had done," i.e., "I prayed for her."

Having achieved decades of consistency in the discipline of performing the salat, fasting during Ramadan, going to the *hajj* ("pilgrimage") when they could, doing charity work, and so on, the women characterize their struggle as learning to get closer to God. This involves learning to communicate with him in more candid and intimate ways—telling him what is in their *del* ("heart") and increasing their understanding of various aspects of their religion. In terms of the salat, they talk about their struggle as in part consisting of reaching utmost *tamarkoz* ("concentration"). It is reasonable to suggest that the particular aims of one's struggles in (religious) self-formation and the variety of experiences one has while praying, change as one grows older and enters different stages of life. The women I talked to witnessed changes in the political uses of the salat (especially after the revolution of 1979) and the ways in which it found a series of new symbolic meanings depending on the particular configurations of post-revolutionary regimes. In their long religious lives, they have attempted to be pious and, in a sense, one can say that attempts to become increasingly pious are lifelong, meaning that piety can encompass many different struggles. But at this point in time, their specific reasons for the performance of the salat and other rituals are not articulated in terms of piety. Explaining the contents of their struggles, several told me that "one has to *learn* to become intimate with God," to which another added, "it is not always easy to be totally honest with God."

PRIVATE PERFORMANCE OF THE SALAT

Unless there are guests in the house and rooms must be shared at prayer time, the women in this group perform their prayers alone in their rooms. The salat is recited while standing on a *sajjadeh* ("prayer rug") which contains the *janamaaz* (small square or round cloth that includes the prayer stone, *mohr*) and the *tasbiih* ("prayer beads"). At times, rose petals or a few jasmine (*yaas*) flowers are thrown inside the janamaaz. The sajjadeh, janamaaz, and tasbiih are objects to which the women have an emotional attachment. While they may lend their sajjadeh to guests who have come without theirs, the sajjadeh is personal, like an item of clothing. The whole set is wrapped into a bundle and placed carefully on beds or chairs. People avoid sitting on them or throwing clothes on them. Parkin (2000: 1) asks whether the spaces in which prayers are performed outside the mosque are considered sacred. I happened to ask some women this question. It seems that there is a *ravaayat*[14] that on *roozeh qiyamat* ("day of judgment"), the particular spot where one has always prayed bears witness that the reciter has in fact been praying. As such, that place can be considered special and meaningful, if not sacred. With some interesting exceptions,[15] I noticed that the exact place where the women pray never seems to change. Indeed, they often leave the sajjadeh open for the next prayer.

As I mentioned earlier, none of the women in my group pray on a regular basis at the mosque. Even their male relatives pray at home most of the time. In their bedroom at home, they lower the lights, partially draw the curtains, close their doors, and are left alone by others who know they are praying. They whisper their prayers, but the whispering is audible.[16] People hold off on calling each other at prayer times. In one of several group discussions, I asked whether there are differences between praying at home and at a mosque. One woman said:

> There is a big difference. I don't like praying with a prayer leader (*pish-namaaz*) at all. It does not put me in the right state of mind. First of all, women can't even *see* the prayer leader and so there is the *mokabbir* who is usually a young boy who says things out loud to help the women know what is going on like "*qad qaamat il-salat*" so you know that you have to stand up at that point. And then for the noon and afternoon prayer, they don't even recite them out loud [as opposed to the prayer at dawn] so you don't hear anything in addition to not seeing anything. They really don't think about women …

The other women present expressed similar views. However, those who had grown up in cities such as Isfahan and Yazd said that when they were in elementary school, their mother or grandmother used to take them to their local mosques. They loved that experience. The mosques were beautiful and they saw their neighbors there—it was almost like going to a party. At times, as children, they were allowed to stand in front of the older women and lead the salat, but that kind of atmosphere does not exist in mosques any longer. In any case, to better understand the women's reasons for not praying at mosques, we should remember that praying behind a prayer leader implies a hierarchy of knowledge and spiritual achievement that may dissuade them because the pish-namaaz is not necessarily more accomplished in those realms. One must consider him as at least an equal and "accept" his qualifications.[17] At times, one may disagree with his politics and not pray behind him for that reason.[18] They find praying in public generally less conducive to concentration[19] (with some exceptions)—hence a series of factors make praying in public as a regular activity undesirable.

We should pause here on the possibility of *degrees* of publicness and private-ness in the performance of the salat. At one end of the scale, there is the mass Friday prayer on the grounds of Tehran University that is led by a senior cleric and in which thousands of people participate. It is also broadcast on television inside and outside of Iran. The choice of the *"imam jom'eh"* ("Friday imam") is often a political matter and the topics he discusses are rarely just matters of religion. The seating arrangement (before and after the prayer people sit on the ground) is decided on the basis of political rank, though religious rank is also important. Hence, the Friday prayer is at the extreme end of both publicness and politiciza-tion. Then there are group prayers in smaller mosques that are not televised. On Fridays, mosques usually have a prayer leader, but on other days they may not necessarily have one for every prayer time. In each city and in each neighbor-hood, there are more or less important mosques. There are individuals who pray at their local mosque by themselves—in a "favorite corner" in an attempt to cre-ate some measure of privacy while enjoying the purity or holiness of the mosque atmosphere. There are also group prayers at home on special occasions, for ex-ample, the prayer performed on Id al-Fitr, the end of the month of Ramadan.[20] To celebrate this day, some families gather with friends and pray in the same room. Finally, there is the most private prayer performed in one's room with no one else present except oneself and God.

The woman quoted above stated that she is not put in the right state of mind when praying behind a pish-namaaz. But she and others had experiences in the mosque where the pish-namaaz was a respected scholar (at times, an elder ac-quaintance) who had a beautiful voice, recited the verses with a melody, and guided them towards a connection with God. A crowd is not necessarily antithetical to the possibility of experiencing transcendence, as Sufi gatherings clearly demonstrate. The importance of the style of the delivery of verses along with the beauty of the voice are particularly commented on with respect to the *azaan*, the call to prayer. There are a few famous azaan reciters, such as the late Mu'azzin Zadeh Ardebili, whose voice continues to be heard everyday on radio and television as well as in some mosques. In fact, these calls to prayer may begin the process of mediating the relationship that the worshipper hopes to build to the divine during prayer. Hence, depending on one's relationship to a pish-namaaz, the scale of the public space, and whether one is being watched by multiple publics while praying, the public/private dichotomy loses its starkness and becomes mediated by a variety of factors. If this argument is tenable, then one cannot characterize every prayer outside the home as "public" tout court. The reciter standing in a favorite corner in a mosque and praying by herself probably has a different experience from one who prays in the front row of televised Friday prayers. In order to understand this, we need more ethnographies of the experience of the salat under distinct conditions. Perhaps, what we can learn from Sufi gatherings is that privateness and concentration are related to each other or are similar states.

After the revolution of 1979, there emerged a reflexive turn in Iranian society—a still continuing interest in understanding "ourselves" better. The revolution brought about a great desire to understand Iranian identity, culture, history, and religion. This reflexive turn has contributed to debates on a variety of matters, chief among them religion (see also Adelkhah 2000). The large number and kinds of mostly informal classes on different aspects of religion and literature that are offered is a direct reflection of this change in Iranian society. Many, though not all, of the women I spoke to in the course of my fieldwork could manage to live abroad, but they do not want to leave Iran. What seems to be providing great meaning to their lives is precisely this kind of searching stance vis-à-vis their religion. Their regular gatherings, charitable activities, and the many classes that they attend cannot be characterized as belonging to a strictly private sphere. These women consider themselves to be Muslims whose religion is at the center of their lives, private and public. It is a kind of religious devotion that seeks debates, and of course one of those debates revolves around the experience of living under a government that identifies itself as Islamic. They do not characterize their religious practices as political opposition. At the same time, they are critical about certain sanctioned approaches that they come across in the public square and the public sphere. There are religious scholars that have television and radio programs representing views and practices that are congruent with those of the women in this group. Hence, the public sphere is not uniformly discounted. The religiosity of the more political public figures is often displayed in the media, and this provides occasion for spontaneous commenting. The television broadcast of the Friday prayer elicits a variety of comments, always said with a shaking of the head along with surprise, that you can pray all your life without becoming a "true Muslim." Some routinely assert that while praying is a necessary condition for becoming a true Muslim, it is not sufficient, as the examples on television demonstrate daily. Among other things, this highly visible religiosity gives greater currency to reams of poetry that express dismay against outward displays of piety. Those who suddenly "jump up" and pray in a gathering as soon as they hear the call to prayer are not automatically regarded as more pious than those who do not (Deeb 2006, Parkin

2000). In fact, they often elicit comments to the contrary, being judged as "insincere." Another difference that the women see between themselves and the public figures shown praying on television is that they believe that "one prays for oneself, not for God." That is to say that God wants people to pray so that they become better human beings, stay away from lies, learn to be more compassionate and less hypocritical, and so on. But he "does not need our prayers." The implication is that if people prayed for themselves then prayer would not be merely a matter of doing *"dolla raast"* (mindless bending and standing up)—a reference to the bodily positions one assumes in the course of the salat. Dolla raast is the expression used to refer to the very opposite of mindful, sincere salat. Thus while it is true that the state has appropriated, and to a large degree co-opted, the public sphere to conform to only certain kinds of practices and interpretations of Islam, the large number of women—and men—who pray outside the mosque, take part in debates, and exchange readings, CDs, and cassettes in various "private" gatherings are also engaged in a certain kind of appropriation, albeit one less visible.

AL-FATIHA DOES NOT ALWAYS MEAN THE SAME THING

I return now to a more detailed discussion of formality, repetition, rigidity, and meaning. All these terms should be put in quotation marks to call attention to the fact that different scholars mean different things by them and see distinct implications. Does formality necessarily imply rigidity and absence of the possibility for creativity? Does repetition mean a gradual loss of (propositional) meaning? Among the group of women with whom I carried out my fieldwork, what appears to take place over time is that while the forms of the verses—the words that make them up—remain unchanged (they are God's chosen words after all), their meanings proliferate. At different times, some meanings come to dominate, others recede and become less important, and still others may come to be rejected. There are the semantic meanings and theological interpretations of the verses. There are also meanings that emerge as a result of the personal matters conveyed to God while uttering any given suura. And in addition, some suuras and verses acquire resonances and associations over time with people, places, experiences, and events.

Years of reciting the same suuras—the practice of reciting them five times a day, everyday, for decades—enables these women to tell God what is on their mind while enunciating the words of the suuras. That is to say, that they use God's chosen words to tell him what *they* want to share: requests, gratitude, questions, anxieties, or remembrance of a person who is ill or has passed away. To make sure that I was grasping what one interviewee was explaining to me, I asked her: "so you are saying that in reciting the same suura, you say different things to God?" She replied rather emphatically and in a louder voice: "you say *a thousand things* to God. Over the course of a day and throughout your life there is so much that comes up that you want to tell him." This was explained to me repeatedly by my interlocutors—that "things happen," "things come up," and you need to talk to God about them.

Many of my conversations began with variations on the following questions: Do you feel that you are communicating with God when you pray? In what ways are you communicating if you are not choosing the words? The women in this group know the meanings of the words in the suuras and know what the suuras are about so that while they are reciting them, they understand what they are saying. This is not necessarily the case with less educated Persian and other non-Arabic speaking Muslims. Even among Arab Muslims, a certain level of effort, repetition, and education is required for them, as the prayers are in *Classical* Arabic (Haeri 2003).[21] I was told that the prayers are indeed acts of communication with God:

> What else am I doing? Of course I am communicating with God but I tell him different things depending on what is happening in my life. I do not immediately begin to pray as soon as I stand on my sajjadeh. I pause and gather my thoughts. I do my *niyyat*[22] and *takbir*. Then I try to concentrate on each word that I am saying and while doing that I am also telling God what I need, what I am afraid of, I ask for guidance. Al-Hamd [al-Fatiha] does not always have the same meaning.

I think her last assertion bears repetition: that the most repeated chapter of the Qu'ran "does not always have the same meaning." It is in part the implications of this view that I try to elucidate. Another woman, echoing the point that this suura does not always mean the same thing, offered the following example: "today, the phrase 'those who have gone astray' for me means Mubarak [former President of Egypt], tomorrow it may be someone else."

Analyses of the consequences of repetition and formulaic language are based on the assumption that linguistically, nothing else is happening: the reciter simply repeats the formal language each time the ritual is performed. This model of ritual is quite unlike the experiences of these women. If we conceive of the salat as a speech event that is multi-functional, then what opens up before us is the simultaneity of several functions that potentially make any given prayer efficacious to various degrees. There is, for example, a metapragmatic focus on the pronunciation of each word (Silverstein 1993, Caton 1993)—taking care to pronounce them carefully. The resonances of the ways others pronounce them are also present at times. One woman told me, "I cannot perform the morning [dawn] prayer without hearing my father's voice." Another said that she prays out loud because hearing her own voice helps her concentrate better and because that is how her father prayed. He was familiar with the modes of Classical Persian music and he almost *sang* the verses. In regards to what she shares with God, the reciter speaks of her anxieties, poses questions, or makes requests.[23] Hence, there is not *simply* a repetition—a re-production of a copy of what has been recited before. These resonances, memories, and associations are part and parcel of what we call, almost always rather vaguely, "the meaning" of a ritual.

There is an equally compelling reason for conceptualizing the performance of the salat as a speech event: each recitation is, in the words of Du Bois, a meeting between the "ritual text" and the "voice of the individual who enacts it"—"the encounter of a seemingly timeless text with the unique personal voice of its present performer calls into question some of our most basic assumptions about the separation between the worlds of ritual and ordinary discourse" (2009: 317). Du Bois' analysis is of particular relevance to the concerns of this article because he examines an instance of a "ritual in solitude." To these assumptions about ritual and ordinary discourse, we might add one that presumes a necessary forfeiture of agency and intentionality in any ritual performance. In her review of the ways in which the concept of formality has been employed by anthropologists, Irvine identifies four uses and highlights the implicit but prevalent assumption that formality is equated with rigidity and is timelessly resistant to change:

> But formalization can be thought inimical to change only if one has a certain view of the social system to which formal occasions call attention—a view that the social system is monolithic, that the structure of a society prevents its members from conceiving of alternatives, and that all members of society have exactly identical conceptions of the social order. (Irvine 2001: 202)

We assume that those who pray are a monolithic group who are "prevented from conceiving alternatives." And we further assume that the individuals' particular attributes and dispositions do not make any difference to the form and content of the ritual. Yet, even when a ritual entails the repetition of formulaic verses, it still makes a difference whether she is young or old, literate or illiterate, has knowledge of Arabic or not, is aware or unaware of theological debates, has achieved various degrees of devotion and intimacy with God or not, and what she is going through at any particular moment. The question is what happens to a set of conventions, and to their forms and contents, as enacted by different groups of people throughout their lifetimes and under different social and political conditions. Among this group of women, variation and creativity are precisely what have rendered the salat of continuous relevance to their daily lives. Although speaking of Christianity and the oral reading of the Bible, what Du Bois (2009) finds in terms of the "semiotic openness" of scripture resonates with my observations of the salat as performed by these women as well as with their readings of the Qur'an.

There was a general surprise almost every time I asked the question about communicating with God: "Well I am not choosing the words of the suura but I concentrate on pronouncing them well, not hurrying through them, and I try to learn to tell God what I want to." Specifically, one of the women gave the following example to explain what is happening in her prayers (at least at times) when she is reciting al-Hamd (al-Fatiha). She said:

> In the first four ayas, you are praising God and God is in the third person—
> you feel that he is rather far from you.
>
>   1. In the Name of God, the Beneficent, the Merciful
>
>   2. All Praise be to God, Lord of the Worlds
>
>   3. The Most Beneficent, the Most Merciful
>
>   4. Sovereign of the Day of Resurrection
>
> But suddenly in the next verse you address God directly and you feel
> closer to him, you say:

5. It is You we Worship and You we Ask for Help

These you say very slowly and calmly because now you have reached a station (*jaygaah*)[24] where you are talking to God *directly*, you are addressing him. Here you are saying that I seek your aid. Only yours. Now you say what it is you want, what is in your del (heart). You seek his aid on behalf of yourself, say if your child is sick, or on behalf of a friend who needs help …

Although I had heard previously that "you tell God what is on your mind" while enunciating the words of the suura, this was the first time someone offered such a meticulous and detailed description of how that can happen. Perhaps the simultaneity is possible precisely because these words are utterly familiar to the reciter. Having told God what the reciter has in mind, she went on:

Then, at this point, while you are still addressing God directly, you go on to say:

6. Guide us to the Straight Path

7. The Path of Those you have Blessed, not Those who Have Provoked Your Anger and Those who Have Gone Astray.

Now this is the path of God but you don't know exactly what that means, does that just mean you pray and you fast? One constantly asks God and oneself this question: What path is that? What is it you have to do to be on that path?

In her experience, although for years she repeated the words of this suura over and over, they have neither "drifted out of meaning" nor become semantically impoverished or "fetid" (Bloch 1975; see also Bowen 1989 and Keane 1997a for a critique). On the contrary, they have served as vehicles for intimate conversation with God—telling him of concerns and worries and posing questions. My interlocutor continued:

There is a certain answer to that: it says the path of those that you have blessed. But who are the ones God has blessed? I think it is those that God never leaves alone, never forgets. We ask God not to leave us to ourselves even for a second because without that overseeing, we would be lost, be without protection. So even if we can't or don't know what it means to be "blessed," we ask of God simply to not forget us.

It would not be reasonable to claim that everyone who prays achieves this kind of "intimacy" with God or arrives at this station, especially for those who have just started praying. But such descriptions of what sometimes happens during the prayer for some people challenge received notions of the linkage between authorship, agency, and formal language. I asked whether there could be a certain contradiction between concentrating on the words of the prayer on the one hand, and then also telling God other matters. No one saw this as a contradiction. The two are not separate communicative acts—they are intertwined. In fact, they pointed out that they find the higher their level of tamarkoz ("concentration"), the better they are able to tell God what they want.

I argue that, precisely because praying involves more than simple repetition, in time repetition actually *overcomes* the formality. Formality does not act to block a multiplicity of meanings from emerging. Through repetition, the form becomes, to various degrees and at different times, a vehicle for conveying many different meanings. This seems to be a move away from concentrating on the purely de-notational meaning of the verses. In this way, the reciter creates a presence in the words of the prayer and the prayer transforms into a space of co-presence. In using God's words to tell him what the reciter wants, she comes to co-exist with the divine in the very words that belong to him. It is easier to see that the act of repetition allows the repeater a presence if we imagine the consequences of the repetition of, for example, playing a musical instrument. A cello concerto played over and over, everyday, for years does not become "rote." The musical piece is not repeated, but *practiced*. I suggest that the salat is *practiced* everyday, not always simply repeated.[25] Perhaps, the co-presence that can be achieved through practice is similar to Alter's analysis that repetition in the Hebrew Bible expresses the "inescapable tension between human freedom and divine historical plan" (2011: 141). One could argue that the intentionality of the reciter does not reside merely in the ability to choose the words of the prayer, but in the fact that she comes to breathe new meanings into the same words. As Culler points out, meaning is "context bound but context is boundless" (Culler 1983: 123).

In my interpretation that these women at times reach a co-presence with God in the space of the prayer, I am inspired by Michel de Certeau's discussion of voice as being a "presence in the signifier" (1988: 137).[26] I am not suggesting that the reciter, in fact, arrives at a *voice* co-existing with God's but that she creates a co-presence. She is present in the very words that belong to God because through their utterance she tells God what *she* wants to. And it is this co-presence that makes her feel that a particular prayer session was so much deeper, better, and more efficacious than others. Speaking of Christian Europe, de Certeau states:

> The sacred text is a voice, it teaches … it is the advent of a "meaning" (un *"vouloir-dire"*) on the part of a God who expects the reader (in reality, the listener) to have a "desire to hear and understand" (un *"vouloir-entendre"*) on which access to truth depends. (1988: 137)

He goes on to argue that this voice "no longer reaches us" and explains his position by analyzing the dominance of writing[27] in the last few centuries and the "gigantic effort of 'modern' societies to redefine themselves without that voice"[28] (1988: 137). In the case of Persian speaking Muslims who pray, that voice—still in its original Classical Arabic and not having undergone "corruptions" through repeated translations[29]—seems to reach the reciters. Those who pray do have a vouloir-entendre—they have a desire to hear and understand, but at the same time there is a vouloir-dire in which God is not the only one who speaks and creates meaning. This is a vouloir-dire that is shared between God and those who pray. I suggest that in repetition the actor achieves a certain presence in the very form of what she is repeating. Hence repetition as *practice* offers the possibility of creativity—the possibility of undermining the rigidity and formality that form imposes. Speaking of medieval monks, Asad states that the "proper performance of the liturgy is regarded not only as integral to the ascetic life but also as one of the 'instruments' of the monk's 'spiritual craft,' which he must acquire by practice" (1993: 62–63). It would not be an exaggeration to say that for these women the practice of the salat is in fact a "spiritual craft" at which they hope to become better in the course of their lives. It seems to me that we would conceptualize the salat differently if we thought of it as practice rather than as repetition. It is, of course, possible that for some the experience of repetition in prayer does render the ritual "mindless." But those I spoke to saw the repetitive nature of the ritual as a challenge and an opportunity, through practice, to achieve a more perfect communication with God.[30] In his critique of views of formalization, Asad states that "Increasing formalization [of speech and behavior in the monastic program] did not signify increasing subordination: on the contrary, those less adept in the performance of prescribed forms were placed under the authority of the more adept" (1993: 135).

The semiotic ideologies underlying the ways in which different religious communities distinguish between spontaneous prayers and formulaic ones—that is, prayers "coming from the heart" as opposed to ones that are already formulated by others—have been discussed by a number of scholars (Keane 2007b, Bialecki 2011, Mahmood 2005, Engelke 2007, Targoff 2001). In the literature on the anthropology of Christianity (Cannell 2007), this discussion has proved highly productive and led to a number of interesting formulations. A full treatment of how the ethnographic material presented so far might contribute to this debate is outside the scope of the present article, particularly because the semiotic ideologies that are local to the Iranian context need a lengthy discussion.[31] I would, however, like to relate my formulation of co-presence as discussed above to the ways in which sincerity is seen as predicated on assuming an interior state (Keane 2007b: 316, Bialecki 2011: 682).

Keane argues that the "concept of sincerity thus seems to assume a clear distinction between words and thought, as parallel discourses (interior and exterior) such that they either could or could not match up" (2007b: 316). Recall that in the case of the salat, the words are those of God's. While one's own words may or may not match one's thoughts, in the case of God's words, the challenge to utter them with sincerity and pure intentions is one that is explicitly articulated by these women as part of their struggle. What does it mean to utter God's words with sincerity? If sincerity is an inner state but the words do not spring from it, what then is entailed for Muslims in performing the salat? It seems to me that a part of the ethical cultivation of these women is the interiorization of the word of God and its utterance, each time, with full concentration and pure intention. This struggle entails both arriving at a disciplined disposition in relation to the salat (Mahmood 2005) and simultaneously arriving at an interiority that succeeds in creating a co-presence in the words that belong to God.

PRACTICE, ITERATION, AND AGENCY

As I have argued, practice may be a more suitable concept for the performance of the salat (at least for the women in this group) and perhaps for other rituals because it underlines the continuous honing of skills, sentiments, and goals such as intimacy. It highlights the possibility that at each turn, the performer may arrive at a new understanding, a different way of making connection with God, of concentrating, finding new things to say, using a chapter of the Qur'an that she had never recited before, and so on. I find a similarity here between the idea of practice and that of iteration as explored by Derrida (1985). They both look back but have implications for what is to come, so they also look forward. There is, in a repeated act, a trace, a memory, but at the same time, each iteration of the act is open. Arguing against Searle that a citation or use must be "serious" rather than in jest, Derrida claimed that on the one hand, the serious could be a special case of that which is acted rather than the opposite. And on the other, that each iteration is open to new meanings because each time, the citation is (re)contextualized. While Derrida does not deny that a convention must be recognized for it to be a convention (or a performative), he calls attention to the fact that the recognizability does not render the meanings of the convention as closed to further possibilities. The insight captured by the openness of iteration seems to me to be similar to the conceptualization of the salat as practice rather than repetition.

As applied to rituals, each iteration might accomplish the goal of the ritual differently. For example, the salat is supposed to be an act of "submission" to God but each submission might be a different experience. We do not know the contents of any given submission—what do people experience in the acts of submission? Butler states that "an account of iterability of the subject ... shows how agency may well consist in opposing and transforming the social terms by which it is spawned" (1997: 29 as quoted in Mahmood 2005: 21). Mahmood points out that Butler's conceptualization of agency "tends to focus on those operations of power that resignify and subvert norms" (2005: 21). In other words, we read "agency primarily in terms of resistance" (2005: 23). Mahmood goes on to argue that there is agency also in "ethical self-formation" (2005: 32)—in acts that would be regarded as submission rather than resistance. This is a significant observation and Mahmood argues that the submission/resistance dichotomy needs to be re-thought. What I would add is that "submission" as a practice of ethical self-formation is iterable, and may be accomplished differently each time and over time. Submission in public or private, at age 18 or age 70, in sickness and in health, in revolutionary contexts or outside of them can span many different experiences. What I have described in terms of the experiences of the women in my group cannot be characterized as either submission or resistance. We need non-binary conceptualizations and a wider vocabulary for what individuals are doing when they follow the requirements of their religion. Perhaps taking into account sets of simultaneous norms—norms that are often contested by different groups—would lead us to that wider conceptualization.

CONCLUSION

The salat is both a public and a private ritual. In Islamic terms, it is an ibaadat that is meant to put the believer in the thought of God regardless of place and the number of people it is performed with. What individuals experience in performing it under a variety of circumstances, alone, together, in times of peace and quiet or otherwise, is in need of further ethnography. One salat session might be entirely different from another. The experiences of these women can hardly be captured in any binaries of doctrine or practice. The text of the salat, being comprised of suuras from the Qur'an, can be characterized as "formal" in several senses. However, the repetition of these forms brings about a familiarity that in time undermines their formality. There is an emergence and a proliferation of meanings rather than a fading of it: denotational, theological, personal experiential (as memories of persons and events), and personal interpretive. Any given verse can have indexical significance that might correspond to the particularities of the life of the reciter in the moment of the performance. And as those particularities change, the indexical significance can change as well. The stipulated poetics of the salat do not prevent thematic choices of non-standard suuras or the communication of questions and anxieties to God. In fact, it is often these very possibilities that give moral and emotional force to the salat. The struggle to achieve efficacy is an on-going one. Reciters strive to arrive at a station where they are able to create a presence in the words of the prayer and achieve a certain companionship with the divine.

ACKNOWLEDGMENTS

I thank the group of women whose insights I share with readers in this article, as well as their Qur'an teacher. Maurice Bloch, John Bowen, Steve Caton, Michael Jackson, Shirin Haeri, Michael Lambek, Anand Pandian, Tom Porteous, Joel Robbins, and Rupert Stasch kindly read earlier versions of this paper and gave me comments. I thank Steve Caton and Michael Silverstein for their comments on the poetics and the metapragmatics of prayer. The comments of the reviewers enhanced my thinking. I thank them for their suggestions.

NOTES

1. For Persian speakers, the word is namaaz but the term salat is more familiar to anthropologists, hence my choice to use salat (its second vowel is long: salaat).
2. In English, this term is often translated into "worship." I avoid this term because I do not find it a good translation for ibaadat. My interlocutors rarely use this term. This might be because the translation of "worship" into Persian is a verb that brings to mind most readily idolatry—the verb is *parastidan* (infinitival form). The *ta marbuuta* of Arabic borrowings is pronounced in Persian, hence *rak'at* and *ibaadat*; the latter term has a pharyngeal 'ain at the beginning but this turns into a glottal stop in Persian. I only indicate it when it occurs in the middle of a word.
3. Parkin states that prayers outside the mosque are "fragmented" and "suspicious," adding: "Mosque-based prayers denote a large measure of Islamic piety while those outside the mosque provoke questions: was there no choice but to pray away from a mosque …" (2000:1). While this might be the case in the community Parkin studies, it should not be generalized to views of "Islamic piety." What is meant by "fragmented" and "suspicious" remains unexplained. One could get a general agreement among Muslim Iranians that performing Friday prayers at the mosque (for men) accrues more *sawab* ("reward") in the eyes of God, but no one that I spoke to would say that praying outside the mosque is in any way "less pious."

    Chapter 62, verse 9 of the Qur'an says to believers to leave their shops and go to the mosque to pray on Fridays when they hear the call to prayer to remember Allah. This is followed by the verse "That is better for you, if you only knew." Two verses further (62:11) we read about what it is that is "better": "But when they saw a diversion or transaction [O Muhammad], they rushed to it and left you standing. Say, 'What is with Allah is better than diversion and than a transaction, and Allah is the best of Providers.'" So what is better is to pray when it is time to do so and "be with Allah." The "better" is not referring to praying in the mosque, at least not exclusively (www.quran. com).

4. I hasten to add that we also do not know the answers to these questions for public prayer. In other words, we do not know about the experience of individuals while praying in public, beyond the symbolic and political meanings that public prayers might convey in some contexts.

5. The subject of qonuut brought up mention of Sunni practices—a very rare topic in the many discussions that I have had. I was told by several that Sunnis do not include qonuut in their prayer. This was not a criticism but, as they saw it, a fact. As it turns out, some Sunnis do, but perhaps most do not. The fact that these women rarely discussed sectarian differences might be because Sunnis in Iran are a minority and practically any statement about them can feed into unforeseen but feared sectarian rifts. Some go out of their way to make positive statements. The Qur'an teacher told me that he prefers the body posture of Sunnis in prayer and so he stands to pray like them. Having said that, I do not want to imply that the experiences and views I describe here have nothing to do with the fact that these women are Shi'ites. When we have comparable studies of private prayer among Sunnis, we would be in a position to tease out differences that stem from Shi'ite/ Sunni doctrinal differences.

6. Accessed from http://www.almodarresi.com/Persian/fbook/42/pl0tx6xz. htm on September 25, 2010. There are many websites that discuss the qonuut.

7. I am stealing "stipulated poetics" from Michael Silverstein.

8. Persian does not have gender in third person singular—there is no "he" or "she." Hence God is never referred to as "he."

9. However, they do not all live at the same level of comfort. Some are better off than others. Indeed, a few have deep financial worries. What they have more in common is the social class milieu in which they grew up and their levels of education.

10. At times, weekly classes are offered in neighborhood *farhang-sara* ("Cultural Centers") and if the teacher proves popular, they become events with full houses, Q and A, and tea and sweets served later. Somewhat more frequent are the classes that are organized inside people's homes. The pattern is that someone finds out (or shares with others) that a friend/acquaintance is particularly knowledgeable about a poet. This person is then asked to offer classes. These are often at least two hours long and go on for months, rotating in being hosted in different members' homes. Poetry and prayer have been longtime neighbors in Iran. An early exploration of the crossings between the two among Bedouins in Egypt is Abu-Lughod's (1986) *Veiled Sentiments: Honor and Poetry in a Bedouin Society.*

11. One hears many stories such as "my grandmother told me 'I like to say *sobhan allah* three times when I go to sujuud but your grandfather preferred *ya latif* ...'" and so on.

12. To organize a rowzeh once a month, a family must have some means at its disposal. At a minimum, the rowzeh khan must be paid various sums depending on how professional he is. The "khan" in this term comes from the Persian verb *khandan*, "to read, recite, sing."

13. Among Muslims whose mother tongues are not genealogically related to Arabic, the semiotic ideologies about Arabic and the local languages show some interesting and perhaps expected similarities (see Bowen 1993:82–87).

14. When there are certain ideas—stories (ravaayaat, pl.)—that people are unwilling or unable to give the status of *hadis* (Classical Arabic *hadith*, the acts and words of the Prophet Mohammad) to (whether belonging to the Prophet or Shi'ite Imams), they use the rather non-committal term "*ravaayat*," thereby also implying that perhaps this is just a superstition. From Arabic r-w-y, "to narrate," and *rawaaya*, "a story." Note that hadis can also mean a story.

15. A few women told me that they do change the place of their prayers, depending on where there is natural light, a better breeze, bigger space, and so on.

16. In Cairo, when I was present during the prayers of my women friends, I could not hear anything at all. I could see their lips moving, but did not hear any sound.

17. The women in this group believe that women are equal to men in religious knowledge and capacities for leadership, similar to the groups of Muslim

and Jewish women that Lahav (2009) spoke with on limitations to religious leadership.

18. See Torab 2007:148 for a description of ambivalence towards the pish-namaaz as discussed among a group of women with lower levels of literacy than the group discussed in this article.

19. There are a series of hadis in which the Prophet underlines full concentration as the most important aspect of the performance of salat. For example, in one hadis, the Prophet says: "two rak'ats that are accompanied by active thought and concentration are better than a whole night of praying when one's heart is playful and uninvolved" (as cited in Khomeini 1943).

20. See also Deeb 2006:105 on group prayers among Shi'ites in al-Dahiyya, Lebanon.

21. But even those who do not know what the words of the suuras mean, learn, for example, that in al-Fatiha, one is praising God. Still the question of what it means to "understand" something like a suura has not received adequate attention.

22. Niyyat (Arabic *niyya*) means "intention." It is necessary to *do* niyyat in the performance of the salat. One concentrates, discarding all other thoughts, on the prayer and says that she will perform, for example, two prayer cycles for the dawn prayer *waajib qurbatan ilallah*, "to be close to God, or as God has asked," followed by *"allaho akbar."*

23. An educated middle class man in his 50s told me that when he was in the last year of high school and had difficult exams, he would recite one of the salat prayers while walking to school. He said this alleviated his anxiety.

24. There is a great deal of writing on the idea of stations that one may reach in practicing the salat in the course of a lifetime. Many theologians have written about stations in their *"asraar il-salat"* ("secrets of the salat"), including Ayatollah Ruhollah Khomeini. In his *Adabu Salat*, Ayatollah Khomeini discusses various subjects, including stations of the salat, covering topics that have to do with ritual purity, the clothes one must wear, and moving on to the spiritual stations, and the particular understandings that the one who prays should hope to arrive at. In the second chapter of *Adabu Salat* entitled "The Stages of the Stations of the People of Suluk," he begins with this passage:

> Know that there are for the people of *suluk* [journey], in this station
> (i.e., paying attention to the humility of servitude and the Glory of His
> Lordship) and other stations, countless stages and degrees, only to a
> few of which we can generally refer, since comprehensively knowing
> all their aspects and counting all the stages are beyond the capacity of
> this humble creature: "*The ways to Allah are as numerous as the breaths
> of the creatures.*" (Khomeini 1943:82)

The last statement, in bold in the original, is a reference to a hadis. I thank
Sylvain Perdigon for calling my attention to the French translation of
Ayatollah Khomeini's original book.

25. In French, to practice an instrument is "*répéter*" and each practice is a
    "*répétition.*"
26. This is similar to Du Bois' definition of voice as being present when the
    speaker invests a text with his "stance" (2009:324), but the two are not the
    same. To be present in the signifier, the reciter can give each signifier a "new"
    meaning, whereas to have a stance in uttering a signifier, it must be audible
    to be analyzed as a stance.
27. Tambiah makes a similar point about the influence of writing in his *Culture,
    Thought and Social Action* (1985:25–26).
28. Without further explanation he also speaks of "textual corruption and the
    avatars of history" (1988:137).
29. There are in fact tens of translations of the Qur'an into Persian. But these
    have not become the Qur'an itself. They are read and consulted, but in order
    to perform a religious duty one must read the Qur'an in its original language.
30. Some women discuss the fact that they go through periods where they are
    not satisfied with their praying.
31. I have argued elsewhere that in communities where the language of the di-
    vine book is considered God's word and sacred, reciters are the "custodians"
    of that language and not its "owners." This distinction has implications for
    viewing languages like Classical Arabic or Biblical Hebrew as exhibiting non-
    arbitrariness (Haeri 2003:13–21). I think addressing how "sincerity" figures
    into language use in such communities might offer interesting insights, in
    particular with respect to implicit separations of aesthetics and conven-
    tions from what comes to be considered as sincere linguistic practices.
    I addressed this question in a presentation at the American Anthropological

Association's meetings (November 14, 2012) in a paper entitled "The Words of Others: Sincerity, Prayer and Poetry.

REFERENCES

Abu-Lughod, Lila. 1986. Veiled Sentiments: Honor and Poetry in a Bedouin Society. Berkeley: University of California Press.

Adelkhah, Fariba. 2000. *Being Modern in Iran*. New York: Columbia University Press.

Alter, Robert. 1994. *Hebrew and Modernity*. Bloomington: Indiana University Press.

——. 2011. *The Art of Biblical Narrative*. New York: Basic Books.

Asad, Talal. 1993. *Genealogies of Religion: Discipline and Reason of Power in Christianity and Islam*. Baltimore: Johns Hopkins University Press.

Bialecki, Jon. 2011. "No Caller ID for the Soul: Demonization, Charisms, and the Unstable Subject of Protestant Language Ideology." *Anthropological Quarterly* 84(3):679–703.

Bloch, Maurice. 1974. "Symbols, Song, Dance and Features of Articulation or Is Religion an Extreme Form of Traditional Authority?" *Archives Europeennes de Sociologie* 15(1):55–81.

——. 1975. *Political Language and Oratory in Traditional Societies*. New York: Academic Press.

——. 2005. *Essays on Cultural Transmission*. Oxford: Berg Publishers.

Bowen, John. 1989. "*Salat* in Indonesia: The Social Meanings of an Islamic Ritual." *Man N.S.* 24(4):600–619.

——. 1993. *Muslims Through Discourse: Religion and Ritual in Gayo Society*. Princeton: Princeton University Press.

——. 2000. "Imputations of Faith and Allegiance: Islamic Prayer and Indonesian Politics Outside the Mosque." In David Parkin and Stephen Headley, eds. *Islamic Prayer Across the Indian Ocean: Inside and Outside the Mosque*, 23–38. Surrey: Curzon Press.

Cannell, Fenella. 2007. *The Anthropology of Christianity*. Durham: Duke University Press.

Caton, Steve. 1993. *"Peaks of Yemen I Summon": Poetry as Cultural Practice in a North Yemeni Tribe*. Berkeley: University of California Press.

Csordas, Thomas. 1987. "Genre, Motive, and Metaphor: Conditions for Creativity in Ritual Language." *Cultural Anthropology* 2(4):445–469.

Culler, Jonathan. 1983. *On Deconstruction: Theory and Criticism after Structuralism.* Ithaca: Cornell University Press.

de Certeau, Michel. 1988. *The Practice of Everyday Life.* Berkeley: University of California Press.

Deeb, Lara. 2006. *An Enchanted Modern: Gender and Public Piety in Shi'i Lebanon.* Princeton: Princeton University Press.

Derrida, Jacques. 1985. *Margins of Philosophy.* Chicago: University of Chicago Press.

Du Bois, W. John. 2009. "Interior Dialogues: The Co-Voicing of Ritual in Solitude." In Gunter Senft and Ellen Basso, eds. *Ritual Communication,* 317–340. London: Berg Publishers.

Engelke, Matthew. 2007. *A Problem of Presence: Beyond Scripture in an African Church.* Berkeley: California University Press.

Fischer, Michael. 2003 [1980]. *Iran: From Religious Dispute to Revolution.* Madison: University of Wisconsin Press.

Gilsenan, Michael. 2000 [1982]. *Recognizing Islam: Religion and Society in the Modern Middle East.* London: I.B. Taurus.

Graham, William A. 1993. *Beyond the Written Word: Oral Aspects of Scripture in the History of Religion.* Cambridge: Cambridge University Press.

——. 2010. *Islamic and Comparative Religious Studies: Selected Writings.* Burlington: Ashgate Publishing Company.

Haeri, Niloofar. 2003. *Sacred Language, Ordinary People: Dilemmas of Culture and Politics in Egypt.* New York: Palgrave Macmillan.

Headley, Stephen. 2000. "Afterword: The Mirror in the Mosque." In David Parkin and Stephen Headley, eds. *Islamic Prayer Across the Indian Ocean: Inside and Outside the Mosque,* 213–238. Surrey: Curzon Press.

Hegland, Mary. 2003. "Shi'a Women's Rituals in Northwest Pakistan: The Shortcomings and Significance of Resistance." *Anthropological Quarterly* 76(3):411–442.

Henkel, Heiko. 2005. "Between Belief and Unbelief Lies the Performance of *Salat*: Meaning and Efficacy of a Muslim Ritual." *Journal of the Royal Anthropological Institute* 11(3):487–507.

Hirschkind, Charles. 2006. *The Ethical Soundscape: Cassette Sermons and Islamic Counterpublics.* New York: Columbia University Press.

Irvine, Judith. 2001. "Formality and Informality in Communicative Events." In Alessandro Duranti, ed. *Linguistic Anthropology: A Reader*, 189–207. Malden: Blackwell Publishers.

Johnstone, Barbara. 1987. "Introduction. Perspectives on Repetition." *Text* 7(3):205–214.

———. 1996. *The Linguistic Individual: Self-Expression in Language and Linguistics*. New York: Oxford University Press.

———. 2000. "The Individual Voice in Language." *Annual Review of Anthropology* 29:405–424.

Keane, Webb. 1997a. "Religious Language." *Annual Review of Anthropology* 26:47–71.

———. 1997b. *Signs of Recognition: Powers and Hazards of Representation in an Indonesia Society*. Berkeley: University of California Press.

———. 2007a. *Christian Moderns: Freedom and Fetish in the Mission Encounter*. Berkeley: University of California Press.

———. 2007b. "Anxious Transcendence." In Fenella Cannell, ed. *The Anthropology of Christianity*, 308–323. Durham: Duke University Press.

Khomeini, Ruhollah. 1943. *Adabu Salat*. Accessed from http://www.al-islam.org/adab/ on May 1, 2011.

Lahav, Pnina. 2009. "Seeking Recognition: Women's Struggle for Full Citizenship in the Community of Religious Worship." In Hanna Herzog and Ann Braude, eds. *Gendering Religion and Politics: Untangling Modernities*, 125–152. New York: Palgrave Macmillan.

Lambeck, Michael. 2000. "Localising Islamic Performance in Mayotte." In David Parkin and Stephen Headley, eds. *Islamic Prayer Across the Indian Ocean: Inside and Outside the Mosque*, 63–98. Surrey: Curzon Press.

Mahmood, Saba. 2001. "Rehearsed Spontaneity and the Conventionality of Ritual: Disciplines of 'Salat.'" *American Ethnologist* 28(4):827–853.

———. 2005. *Politics of Piety: Islamic Revival and the Feminist Subject*. Princeton: Princeton University Press.

Mottahedeh, Roy. 1985. *The Mantle of the Prophet: Religion and Politics in Iran*. New York: Simon and Schuster.

Parkin, David. 2000. "Inside and Outside the Mosque: A Master Trope." In David Parkin and Stephen Headley, eds. *Islamic Prayer Across the Indian Ocean: Inside and Outside the Mosque*, 1–22. Surrey: Curzon Press.

Robbins, Joel. 2001. "Ritual Communication and Linguistic Ideology: A Reading and Partial Reformulation of Rappaport's Theory of Ritual." *Current Anthropology* 42(5):591–614.

Silverstein, Michael. 1993. "Metapragmatic Discourse and Metapragmatic Function." In John Lucy, ed. *Reflexive Language: Reported Speech and Metapragmatics*, 33–58. Cambridge: Cambridge University Press.

———. 2009. "Private Ritual Encounters, Public Ritual Indexes." In Gunter Senft and Ellen Basso, eds. *Ritual Communication*, 271–292. London: Berg Publishers.

Starrett, Gregory. 1998. *Putting Islam to Work: Education, Politics and Religious Transformation in Egypt.* Berkeley: University of California Press.

Stasch, Rupert. 2011. "Ritual and Oratory Revisited: The Semiotics of Effective Action." *Annual Review of Anthropology* 40:159–174.

Tambiah, Stanley. 1985. *Culture, Thought and Social Action.* Cambridge: Harvard University Press.

Targoff, Ramie. 2001. *Common Prayer: The Language of Public Devotion in Early Modern England.* Chicago: University of Chicago Press.

Torab, Azam. 1996. "Piety as Gendered Agency: A Study of Jalaseh Ritual Discourse in an Urban Neighborhood in Iran." *Journal of the Royal Anthropological Institute* 2:235–252.

———. 2007. *Performing Islam: Gender and Ritual in Iran.* Leiden: Brill Publishers.

Varzi, Roxane. 2006. *Warring Souls: Youth, Media and Martyrdom in Post-Revolution Iran.* Durham: Duke University Press.

Reforming Religious Identity in Post-Khatami Iran

by ROXANNE VARZI

JOURNAL ENTRY, FEMALE TEHRAN COLLEGE STUDENT, SPRING 2000 *Recently I haven't been too concerned about making sure my hejab is ok at school (rayat nemeekunam). I want them to throw me out. I heard that if you're thrown out of the university in Iran, the United States will give you a visa. Once I have graduated I'll be like a donkey lost in the valley, so why not get kicked out?*

We told everyone about our relations with boys. I thought shit, whatever happens, fuck it. Everyone talks about us behind our backs, as if we were sluts, but when a girl wearing a chador speaks with a boy it's no big deal. Why is what we (who do not wear chadors) do is so much more important? Lately no one bothers with the hejab. People are more concerned with sandals and socks and light colors. Everyone shakes hands—boys and girls, which is great. One day we went to a restaurant and a man played all the songs from before the revolution on a violin and someone sang. It was great. My dad says everyone has gone crazy and no one can be normal and you see things that are shocking. In Africa they dance and stuff, in the twenty-first century, why can't we? No wonder everyone is crazy. I have decided to go abroad to continue my studies.[1]

With President Khatami's election in 1997, and the subsequent relaxing of social rules that resulted in a more open social atmosphere, came a battle of surfaces. Khatami's policies shifted the emphasis from religious national identity to an Iranian national identity, thereby spurring an ongoing conflict with the spiritual leader of the Islamic revolution, Ayatollah Khameini.[2] In a speech in summer 2000, President Khatami reassured the country that a shift in physical appearance did not signify a move away from Islam.[3] "Just because someone shaves his beard does not mean that he is not a practicing Muslim," he stated.[4] And yet the ongoing anxiety at the time that centered on changing the surface points to the level of investment held by the conservative clergy in keeping that surface, and thus in turn points to the power that resides in the image of an Islamic nation.

As the Islamic surface fades, efforts are being made to shift the emphasis back to the true nature of belief and identity. The baten has taken on a more powerful role than the zaher. But, as I noted earlier, that space may or may not include Islam. For a majority of Iranian youth, revolutionary ideology dampened a faith in the religion it used as a vehicle. Indeed, one former revolutionary told me that had revolutionary policy aimed at creating faithful Muslims and had it been less concerned with converting revolutionaries it would have been more successful. As he noted, "If a woman really has faith in Islam, covering would not be illogical or oppressive."[5]

This shift came about as youth raised under revolutionary dictate began to mature and question their surroundings. It also came about as a group of key revolutionaries known as eslah talaban, students of reform (who were supporters of President Khatami), began to question their own ideology and identities. Many eslah talaban remain practicing Muslims who no longer accept the dominant revolutionary ideology. They believe that religion should not mix with politics and that ideology is not the same thing as faith. In short, when mixed with politics, religion loses its core and becomes an ideology. This is especially true when riya comes into play, as politics is public and a public religion has the potential of becoming a deceptive act.

Many reformists were among the main cultural producers under the Islamic regime.[6] The key to understanding reform can be found in the fact that the major players (like Said Hajjarian) were once Basij and heavily active in the construction, propagation, or administration of the Islamic republic. This fact is important for two reasons: reform in the Islamic republic can only come from within, and there can be no reforms without addressing the legacy of the failure and the tragedy of the war and the culture of martyrdom that was born of it. Those who fought the war, who gave family members to martyrdom, and who expected to be taken care of by the government and the Islamic society they created have the most to lose should the Islamic republic dissolve. Among the veterans that I interviewed, some said in retrospect that they were thankful that they were not martyred and that God saved them from dying during a moment of insanity. Some, as we are increasingly seeing portrayed in contemporary cinema, would rather be dead or just numb.[7] The important shift in identity came not just in youth per se but also in the reform generation, who demonstrated for revolution, fought the war, and now have children who are part of a new and different generation. One reformist I interviewed during Ashura, also a former Basij, could no longer bear to observe the rituals surrounding Muharram. He remembered the days when he was immersed in these activities, and he not only regrets those days but also can no longer participate in the activities as a faithful Muslim because for him they hold only an ideology that he has left behind: "In the end, none of this mourning ritual kills the pain."

This particular reformist began to have marital problems when he lost faith in both Islam and the ideology of revolutionary Islam. He regretted wasting his youth fighting for Islam, especially at the front line of the war. His wife, although disillusioned with the ideology, remained a faithful believer. He hated what her outward practices, such as wearing Islamic covering, represented to him and he began to lose respect for her. In turn, she lost respect for him the further he moved away from Islam. However, as the political battle between the reformists and conservatives intensified, she found it harder to negotiate her faith in Islam and her dislike of the revolutionary ideology. And even though she still believed in the faith, she stopped covering because the hejab became inseparable from the ideology that she believes to be marring the name of Islam. For many, it is no longer necessary to show their belief or to propagate it by joining in the masses, and thus religion has left the public sphere and become privatized. Ideology, including ideological religion, however, thrives in the public sphere and cannot exist without a public show of support. According to one reformist, "Religion has not disappeared, it's merely slipped into the private sphere."[8] Further, as young people demand more autonomy, the survival of clerical rule will depend on the importance that youths place on the Islamic component of their identity. The idea of an Islamic democracy works when one is both Islamic and secular (and when a secular identity incorporates Islam, but the Islam component does not dominate that identity).[9]

One of the critical issues among politicians in Iran is whether the revolutionary government was successful in creating Islamic subjects. What institutions, practices, ideologies, and values from the revolution retain their legitimacy and remain useful for policy purposes? Both reformists and conservative politicians in Iran are vying for power by subtly debating the way in which an "Islamic citizen" is defined. The main concern of social planners and cultural producers in Iran, both in the government and outside of it, is how to continue implementing policy and producing culture for a nonresponsive mystery generation. While over 60 percent of Iran's population matured strictly under revolutionary Islamic law, there is no assurance that revolutionary Islamic values succeeded in affecting the identity of Iran's youth. There is overwhelming evidence that the twenty-seven-year effort to create Islamic citizens worked against itself and instead made the country more secular.

One cultural producer that I interviewed believed that objects of the familiar world—cars, trees, parks, and Iranian citizens—are Islamic by virtue of the fact that they exist inside an Islamic nation. Thus are these modern, self-certain subjects, by participating in an Islamic nation, also Islamic subjects?

Abdul Karim Soroush, a leading reformist philosopher and former revolutionary, claims that the experience of the past twenty years as an Islamic republic created a shift from a "modern" Cartesian subject to a "modern" Islamic one.[10] This might suggest that the government's attempt to form a monolithic Islamic identity was somewhat successful. But was it? What is interesting is the extent to which Western theories of the subject have permeated the Islamic intellectual scene. New notions of subjectivity and agency that support transmutable definitions of identity have supported the shift in contemporary Islamic thought from the realm of conservative Islamic politics based on a clerical government back to the early, more liberal, philosophy of the revolution that called for a democratic Islamic government. These philosophical debates question the notion of a singular Islamic subject (created by the Islamic republic's public policy) and in turn have allowed space for new versions of a secular Islamic citizen to emerge. The idea of a transmutable identity threatens the legitimacy of the conservative clergy for whom there can only exist a monolithic Islamic identity.[11] The reformists support the claim that Islam will remain a strong component of identity even after a shift toward secularism. The conservative clergy claims that a religious identity cannot be maintained in a secular state—that is, that one cannot simultaneously hold true to Islamic values and be secular. This is true if the notion of Islamic values functions as an ideology and not as a belief. (The ideology of political Islam runs counter to that of secularism, but the belief in Islam does not.)

Can killing the Islamic character of the nation change the true nature of Islamic identity? True Sufis do not identify themselves as Sufi. To be Sufi is to be pure of heart, something that is practiced privately and not announced as an identity or political or religious affiliation (and thus is akin to riya). Sufism is about the baten and not the zaher. This principle brings us back to the notion of riya and the belief in mystical Islam. As noted in Avini's project, the attempt to film or visually capture the essence of Islam is problematic and points to Islam as an invisible entity that resides not in the appearance of things, zaher, but in the essence of one's being, baten. One should not use personal practice to announce religiosity or morality, because when one does so Islam ceases to exist solely for the purpose of faith. Given the notion of riya, one should ultimately be more concerned with the space of inner faith rather than the surface of things, zaher.

Because of the strong illusion that revolutionary policy created, it is impossible for policymakers to claim any empirical evidence as to the true identity of Iranian youth. In order to continue their program and formulate policy, they need to look below the surface without shattering it or voicing the "public secret" (once the secret is voiced, it loses its power). As Khatami said, "This country needs calm now and real research (not slander). Instead of asking whether reforms are killing Islam, we need to ask ourselves what is Islam? How can we make it livable?"[12]

Revolutionary artists, philosophers, and other cultural producers realized that the culture they were working so hard to produce was not being consumed. For example, Iranian cinema was not popular in Iran until after Kiarostami won the Palm d'Or—international recognition gave Iranian cinema legitimacy as an art form where formerly it was dismissed as propaganda. These cultural producers thus became disillusioned, knowing that in forcing Islamization the youngest generations would turn away from it entirely.

Policymakers have begun to channel their efforts into sociological research (mainly polls) in order to discern what the masses need to remain happy Islamic subjects.[13] While I was doing my own research on secular youth in northern Tehran, the government was doing very similar research across the entire socioeconomic spectrum of the country, but using very different research methods (primarily polls, especially door-to-door types).

THE FOUNDATION FOR YOUTH AFFAIRS, TEHRAN, SUMMER 2000

The unbearable heat and humidity cause my rupushe to stick to my shirt and pants and thus outline my body, which defeats the whole purpose of wearing it. As usual I've been called at the very last minute, and I only have a short time to make it to a "casual" interview with the head of the Government Research Center on Youth.

At the center, the director of a provincial youth center is in town to discuss his budget and education programming. My host, a former Basij and an engineer, suggests that a toy missile-building kit might serve as an effective education tool: "It's a lot of fun and it teaches them engineering skills."

"Is there something else that is less violent and teaches them engineering?" I ask.

"They do not actually have explosives, they're just wood."

After spending the morning discussing popsicle-stick projects (my idea, because they are cheap, accessible, etc.) it's time for prayers and lunch. On the way to the lunchroom my host states: "Well, we have not discussed much about your research and there is not much to say about ours except that our general concern is that Iranian youth are under a great deal of stress primarily due to the economic situation, and if this stress is not kept inside it seeps out and spoils family life and public culture, and the government then has to step in.[14] We're looking for the most effective ways to help youth with their stress, we have found that television shows on psychology help a great deal."

I'm about to mention that many youth I know never watch Iranian television, when we abruptly turn the corner into a large lunchroom with two floors.

"I'm sorry, Ms. Varzi, the office abides by Islamic law, you'll have to eat upstairs with the women."

The men excuse themselves and leave me to pick at my sandwich and curse my social science skills and inability to have learned even a single thing about the government's research on youth after three uncomfortable hours in the president's office drinking tea and making sure my hejab was not falling off.

"Are you a sociologist?" asks one of the young women.

"I'm an anthropologist."

She smiles, "We're all studying sociology at Tehran University, this is our part-time job."

"Oh?" I perk up, "Are you learning a lot of sociological skills at this job?"

"Not really, we were hoping to do more practical training, like polling, or research, but we're only doing data entry."

"Really? Are you at least learning how sociologists do their work?"

"We enter all the data for the polls that the office is in charge of taking."

"Well, learning to ask the right question is one of the most important skills as a social scientist. What do you think of the types of questions being asked on the polls, are you able to at least offer feedback and suggestions? It's good to learn the reasons

why certain questions are asked and what the answers might indicate in terms of larger social import."

"The questions center around satisfaction, the quality of life, feelings of security, financial and physical security in the city, general feelings about the future, employment prospects, and whether youth think the state can provide these basic human necessities," the women tell me.

The polls appear to center around the question as to whether youth feel that the state can or do meet their needs, whether they feel safe and feel that the state provides that safety. This is what the Hegelian state promises and this Islamic state is struggling to deliver.

"Most people do not fill in the polls, or turn the pollster away when they come to their doors. People never know if the government is trying to corner them. Iranians do not like to give personal information."

"What if the polls were anonymous and not given at a person's house where they can later be found?"

"I do not know if they have tried that. They are anonymous, we type in location just for class markers."

On the way back upstairs I ask to use a washroom.

"You'll have to use the men's room. Until recently they did not employ women." I thank them and head home.

On another occasion I am introduced to a more open study.

TEHRAN UNIVERSITY, CENTER FOR SOCIOLOGICAL STUDIES OF YOUTH, 2000 *"I'm worried about this generation. We have nothing in common with them. This generation does not choose, they placate, they allow things to be done then they react or reject, but they never initiate anything. They have a notion that whatever evolves comes from the government and not the people, so why bother?"*

Mr. Daneshgu, a young Ph.D. student who is conducting a study on contemporary youth culture for Vezarat Irshad (the Islamic Guidance Ministry) is genuinely concerned about the young generation. He continues, "When I was in my late teens I was at the front, leading a battalion. I had responsibilities—heavy life-or-death responsibilities. There was camaraderie in our group. War gave responsibility to youth and confidence.[15] Being in charge of a battalion at the age of twenty gave youth something to protect and nurture, these youth are given nothing to protect, nurture, or be in charge of.[16] There was equality; we had uniforms, uniformity—a common cause. But this generation has no higher goals or purpose.[17] They are not interested in religion. Religion moves against pluralism, whereas choice gives one rules."

"Why do you think that is?"

"You know, religion had a function for my generation, we were thirsty for it. We needed it to bring the country together. We were thirsty for change, for higher aware-ness of spirituality and purpose. This generation does not see any function for religion in their lives.[18] This generation wants choice. They are a capitalist generation, they want the things they see on satellite TV. They have different desires and interests. The problem is we are their cultural producers and yet they do not consume anything that we produce. At the same time, neither do they attempt to produce anything of their own, they are extremely passive. We are the ones who are tired and they are the ones taking a break."

"Are you saying religion is done for? I think they retain a respect for religion and are still somewhat religious."

"There is a big age gap in this society. This generation does not care about morals. We want to know why. How do we turn this around? Our movement is trying to figure out where morality has gone and why good is replaced by evil and how to bring good back. This is the theme of our ten-volume study.[19] We are very concerned about this generation and morals. If our enemies [the West] give us the time and space to work with this generation we could save it."

Among conservatives the attitude remains that it is outside infiltration in the form of satellite dishes and black-market videos, and now ongoing communication via Web blogs, that is the cause for the failure of Islamic values. The blame is always directed to the outside. At the same time Daneshgu's research is somewhat self re-flexive in its attempts to discern where government policy may have taken a wrong turn with youth. In fact, the Tehran University study went to the heart of the matter. The poll on which the study is based was conducted with over fourteen hundred youths between the ages of eighteen and thirty. The general data on religion found that youths do not believe that a religious leader needs to rule a religious state, and that a religious state could just as easily be run by a religious intellectual who is not a trained cleric. The study further found that youths today have very little knowl-edge of Khomeini's life or any notion of Velayat-e Faqih (which is surprising given the education system which stresses this history), and that youths attend religious hey'ats (ceremonies) but do not pray. The polls also found that the religious section of the newspaper is the least read, though people have a positive view of religion.

Only 3 percent of youth are against Namaz Jumeh.[20] They do not agree that the reformists' papers were opened to steal youth away from religion. Most youth do not buy the paper, but do read it when their parents buy it (most youths get the news from the Internet or from satellite). They also believe that society is becoming less religious and more criminal, which they blame on economics and the clergy: "All the bad things clerics do is done in the name of religion." Their favorite pastimes are, in order of popularity, cinema, music, painting, and theater (cruising must not have been an option on the form, because from what I have seen that would be the first pick).[21]

When a reformist newspaper published the results of a poll indicating that 75 percent of the general public and 90 percent of schoolchildren do not pray, the clergy reacted by passing a law allowing women to become prayer leaders in segregated situations in order to encourage praying. Two additional laws passed as a result of the polls include one allowing bright colors to be worn in school, and another allowing young girls in segregated schools to go without the hejab in all-female classes. These came as a direct result of medical and psychological findings that point to overall depression on the part of young adults.

In my own research I found a very similar disregard for organized religion, but I also found that most youth at the college level knew a lot about Islam, Islamic law (including Velayat-e Faqih) and were well-versed enough in it to use it to their advantage. I also found that youth attend hey'ats for their own purposes, but they do not pray unless made to do so. I do believe that there is a major shift both in knowledge and worldview between those secular youths whom I worked with in the university and the generation below them in high school and in middle school. Indeed, the generation in high school is culturally completely different, in large part because they missed most of the war.

The most interesting part of the poll was aimed at determining the effectiveness of public discipline (amr be maruf).[22] Among the questions asked were, "Who should have the authority to tell you what to do?" and "Who would you listen to?" Students do not think that those who demand that youth act a certain way are practicing what they preach; both Basij and secular youth agreed that many clerics and their family members do not uphold the same moral standards for themselves.[23] When asked what they think about the type of person who does not respond positively to moral instruction on the street, most youths reasoned that such a person gets his or her morality from within and has his or her own inner structure and values (again, the emphasis is being shifted to the baten).[24]

JOURNAL ENTRY, FEMALE TEHRAN COLLEGE STUDENT, SPRING
2000 *I think I lack something others have. I am stupid and do not know a thing, and
I'm writing all this stupid stuff in this journal. The big words of my life are behind most
people, I will be twenty-two in a month and I know these words are stupid ... I feel
like life is just a dream, a dream without value ... it cannot have meaning with all this
depression. In elementary school they made us believe we should be intellectuals. I
do not have the patience. I feel empty one minute and the next I feel just normal like
everyone else. My thoughts are all mixed up and I forget everything (my father tells me
that he feels the same way, it's normal).*

*I have so much to do and I'm depressed and do nothing. One says write a list, so I
write it. I have things I want to do but do not know where to start. I think things were
better before the revolution, wish I lived then, when there was good music, dance, and
a nice atmosphere. I said this to someone once and they said "You're imagining Paris at
that time, not Tehran."*

*Time flies. I feel like it's too late to start anything and that I've lived a hundred years.
I feel like I'm on a dark road or dark valley looking for a light to show me the way, but
the light is also lost, sometimes from afar I see flashes. Furugh [Farokhzad] says such
light can as easily be the light of a wolf's eyes.*

*They just shut down all the newspapers, but that's fine. Now my father has more
time to talk to me without all his damn papers to read. Besides, even if they kill Khatami,
all the young people are leaving the country behind, who's left to construct this place? I
could care less. Descartes says that if a person imagines something exists then it comes
into existence. Makmalbaf says that truth is right in front of us, but it's not. That's too
easy.*

*My thoughts are heavy, busy. I'm going crazy, two more terms and my studies will be
over and I'm not sure what to do with myself. My college friends say go for the master's
concourse. I don't know. I wish someone would tell me what to do. I need to find someone to give me advice. I feel like a roach whose foot and hands are caught in a tree and
cannot move. I do not feel like doing anything. Even breathing is hard. God, I've filled
this notebook with so much garbage.*

*I am friends with three boys from the university; we're very good friends, but at
school I have to pretend that I do not know them. Imagine everyday you see someone
you are friends with but you pretend not to know each other. This play acting was hard
at first but now I'm used to it. I am a doruhi person (two-faced), hesabi (for sure). If we
had important things to say to each other at school we would write letters ... there is*

a place at school where we put our personal things, during lunch and prayer when no one is around we would put notes in each other's bags. [Prayer is a moment of suspension when the authorities are unavailable.] Still other psychological things remain. We sometimes put letters in those plastic eggs that hold chocolate and hide them in the university garden. I wonder what would happen if we were able to be normal around each other. The younger poru kids speak with each other. It's just my generation that is scared all of the time, we remember the days before Khatami.

Time is running out of my hands like water and I cannot contain it. I love the end of winter, life seems more valuable, and I love going to Tajrish, to the bazaar there, to shop. I love the new year, Nowruz, and all of its rituals ... I feel like I've been born again and everything is lovely. Greenery, newness, branches budding, rain that's new and fresh, tea, saffron candy, all these good things make me happy. This tree in front of our house has seen a few different Nowruz's, maybe even lovers under its branches from the old days. One day when I'm dead and gone this tree will be here and the river in Tajrish will also be here. [Will lovers gather then?] With all this breath I've taken and all the food I've eaten, all the happiness and unhappiness, how small I am. Our existence is a mystery, a puzzle.

While Khatami appears to have made a difference as gauged in the inches taken off of the hems of rupushes and the decrease in the number of martyr billboards, these surface differences do not make the ultimate difference necessary for real social change to occur. My research shows that as long as change remains concerned with the surface of things, zaher, there can be little change in inner identity, worldview, baten—the place where real change occurs. In many ways it will be up to the next generation to make a difference, but they have learned from their parents' mistakes that it does not pay to be political. Even the landslide vote for Khatami was not an overwhelming decision on their part to make a political difference. Perhaps the first election in 1997 gave them hope and a space to voice their concerns, but that changed by 2000. In the 2005 presidential election most reform-minded individuals did not bother to vote because they felt the outcome was inevitable.

JOURNAL ENTRY, TEHRAN COLLEGE STUDENT, WINTER 2000

A few days ago we went to vote. People were talking loudly about whom they planned to vote for. A Hezbollah guy was dictating his vote loudly to his daughter. He mentioned all the conservatives, foremost Hashemi-Rafsanjani. For some reason I took great pleasure in walking past him with my hair falling out of my russari. We all voted together for Khatami.

I did not want to vote for Khatami; he is no assurance for the future security of this country. I do not really care what happens to the future of this country. I voted for Faizeh Hashemi last time, and look at what happened. The only reason I voted at all was because we had to have a stamp on our student id cards indicating that we voted in order to take the college entrance exam, and now we need one in order to stay in school. No one in my family has voted since the revolution.

The registration line was full of people like my family who had not voted since the revolution. Our neighbors who were shah people even voted for the first time. The line was full of women wearing makeup and men in ties! Those against the regime were surrounded by clouds of perfume that mixed with the Hezbollah's clouds of rose water. Again the same group went and voted for city council members and I remember a lot of people in our group voting for a candidate just because he wore a tie.

For youth, public politics are not the proper platform for change. For them, change is something that has to come gradually from within the individual. This change might occur in much the same way Shariati espoused—as a return to self—only this self will not be obliterated but rather reconstructed through a phase of khodsazi. We see evidence of this in the self-help groups, the turn toward psychology and the twelve-step programs, but also in the choices of many youths to become teachers, psychologists, social workers, and lawyers.

The selflessness and martyrdom of bi-khodi has proven to be deadly. The political aspects have played out and proven to be empty; it is time to seek out a new kind of leader, not through elections or revolutions but from within. While it appears as though Iranian youth is on the verge of moving in this direction, of looking inward and concentrating on baten as opposed to zaher, there is much evidence that many young people continue to be concerned with appearances and the surface of things.[25] These youth make their statements by presenting themselves as differently as possible from what is deemed Islamic—rebelling without concern about inward self-awareness or change.

There is, however, a contingent of youth (as well as former Basij reformers) whose members are trying to see beyond the many layered surface in order to find a truth that they can live by. But even these youths are lost when it comes to the notion of a strong individual that is self-certain and autonomous. As illustrated in these pages, the movement of a strong Islamic public policy grinding against a strong private sphere has left most youths confused and alone.[26] While there has occurred a shift in the political landscape that lends validity to public opinion and locates the seat of political change within the individual and inner reality of baten as opposed to the revolutionary policy that concentrated on the surface of things, zaher, this shift is occurring gradually and with difficulty. Iranian youth are moving toward a stronger notion of self, even in the midst of bi-khodi and hopelessness, but they have yet to reach the peak. They are still on the long journey toward the peak, moving their way up the mountain toward the Simurgh. Not all of them will make it, and many will fly away to foreign lands like the generation before them, but the majority remain caught in a web of shifting and foggy visionary terrains in which they battle to see and be seen.

NOTES

1. This student left Iran for post-graduate study in France.
2. See Varzi, "Iran Gardi."
3. When visuals become benign, the state becomes the object of scrutiny.
4. Address to the nation, April 24, 2000, Seda Sima (the Islamic republic of Iran broadcasting).
5. Interview in Tehran, 2000.
6. Abdul Karim Soroush was a key ideologue in the Ministry of Education and President Khatami was the Minister of Culture; Mohsen Makhmalbaf's evolution can be traced from that of a revolutionary to a reformist by watching the thematic development of his films, and Ibrahim Hatamikia, once worked with Avini's project at the front. Makhmalbaf began his career with films like Boycott, which portrayed his own experiences as a young revolutionary in the shah's prisons. His next acclaimed work was on the war, titled Marriage of the Blessed, which also engaged in a critical view of the war and the struggle of veterans to reenter society. His films continued to emphasize social issues, and they are as critical of society during the revolution years as they had been before. Finally, in films like Gabbeh, Makhmalbaf moved over toward the reformist project of redefining Iran in terms of its nomadic and non-Islamic cultural heritage, where the very texture and emphasis on color in the film is a move against the all-black backdrop of a revolutionary Tehran.

7. Jafar Panahi's Crimson Gold is a wonderful portrayal of a war veteran (who plays himself) trying to make ends meet in postwar Iran.

8. Interview in Tehran, 2000. This resonates with the theorists of secularization who define a religious state in terms of making the public space a religious space. See Asad, "Religion, Nation-State, Secularism."

9. This is why empirical research is important to the project, as I demonstrate below.

10. In a presentation at the University of Washington in 1997, Abdul Karim Soroush, the controversial Islamic thinker, claimed that in Iran there has been a shift from a Cartesian subject position to an Islamic one, which will enable Iran to move away from an Islamic republic to an Islamic democracy based on a nation of independent Islamic subjects.

11. My training in anthropology has led me to be skeptical of a monolithic and essential "Iranian" or "Islamic" identity. I contend that no strong monolithic Islamic identity exists in contrast to the image that we have of Iran—even on the surface. What exists is a state of imposed "normalcy" in the context of the black mourning banners commemorating martyred imams and the imposing billboards of bloodied war martyrs and maimed POWs from the Iran-Iraq war.

12. Speech on Seda Sima, spring 2000 (my translation). Years later, this continues to be relevant.

13. Instead of taking polls, which people rarely answer correctly anyway, a day without mandatory Islamic covering would expose the percentage of the population who might choose not to wear Islamic cover. This, of course, is a dangerous idea, because masses of uncovered Iranian women would shatter the illusion of a strong Islamic Republic. In 2005 women are getting away with wearing the minimum requirements.

14. In 2000, the Department of Social Welfare stated that unemployment had risen in the last four years from 9.1 percent to 16 percent, while unofficial figures put it at almost double that figure. The department also stated that nearly one-fifth of all Iranians were living below the poverty line—in other words, making less than an average of one dollar per day. Meanwhile, personal savings have disappeared with the decreased value of the rial. The rial was close to 300 to the dollar when I was in Iran in 1993, but had more than tripled to almost 1,000 to the dollar in 2000.

15. Indeed, the war gave purpose to many boys who lacked direction. As noted earlier, Avini's project alone gave boys from villages and the south of the city, who were never given a chance to speak or be heard, an opportunity to be in the limelight and voice their feelings.

16. As noted elsewhere, the government never trusted this generation, and their parents never trusted the government to deal with them properly, so ultimately they were left without anyone's trust.

17. This view can be thought of in light of Hegel's discussion about a higher purpose for work.

18. Here, I would disagree; spirituality (self hypnosis and meditation classes, Jung classes, Sufi music, self-help culture, Hafiz's poetry) has the function of escape and protest.

19. The study took ten months and the efforts of sixty researchers. The form of the research was a questionnaire with yes or no answers, and the resulting report included many charts and tables with statistics.

20. Namaz Jumeh, or Friday prayers are as political as they are religious—recall that during the war they served as forums to encourage boys to martyr themselves.

21. Note that theater is fast becoming one of the most popular (and avant-garde) forms of entertainment. I saw a production of Genet's The Blacks that used body language to the absolute limit of Islamic possibility.

22. The theme of this questionnaire came at an interesting and important time, as the Basij who are those most likely to engage in public disciplining have become the brunt of a rare show by the general public of not just anger but violence. In spring and summer 2000 more than a few incidents of violence toward Basij, some resulting in death, were reported on the radio and in papers.

23. I heard endless tirades on the hypocrisy of classmates coming from religious families who owned bootlegged videos and western clothes; further, they could enjoy these things without the fear of the authorities because they were the authorities.

24. And, again, the components of outward identity and belief in an ideology are easier to measure than belief or faith in religion, because ideology is public and visible whereas faith is invisible.

25. To see how concerned people are with surfaces, all one needs to do is walk through Tehran and take note of the noses bandaged as a result of recent

cosmetic surgery, as well as the more straightforward evidence of botox and makeup.

26. The hours of material appearing on blogs alone gives an idea of the struggle of Iranian youth.

POLITICS AND PROTEST

section six

Weapons, Passports, and News

Palestinian Perceptions of U.S. Power as a Mediator of War

by AMAHL BISHARA

AN AMERICAN VISITOR TO THE WEST BANK IS LIKELY TO BE audience to the maxim that Palestinians are critical of the United States government but fond of the American people. One may hear a statement of this kind in taxi cab conversations or read it in post-9/11 political analysis (cf. Mansour 2005, 158). While this adage fits in a tidy sentence, Americans visiting the West Bank will find its implications to be far reaching. Palestinians' welcoming stance toward Americans is often elaborated in the form of carefully prepared meals or round after round of generously sweetened tea and coffee. At the same time, Americans may meet with voluminous expositions on how the U.S. position as the preeminent Middle East peace negotiator is belied by disproportionate U.S. political, military, and economic support for Israel.

Yet Palestinians' views of the United States and its power are more rooted in concrete experiences than these popular policy analyses suggest. I will show this by analyzing Palestinian practical assessments of American passports, weapons, and media during an Israeli incursion into the West Bank city of Nablus and in its aftermath. Especially during the hot moments of the second Intifada, the Palestinian uprising against Israeli occupation that began in

September 2000, manifestations of U.S. power have been available for Palestinians to see and hear: the gold flash of an eagle emblem on the navy passport of an American passing smoothly through an Israeli checkpoint, the boom of a U.S.-made warplane streaking across the sky. During the Intifada, Palestinians have also sought to make use of their own connections to the United States as they manage conflict with Israeli authorities.

The role of passports and weapons as objectifications of U.S. power that can mediate between Palestinians and Israeli authorities warrant attention in part because of the particular circumstances of the second Intifada. During this time, Israel expanded a system of checkpoints and other forms of closure that have isolated Palestinians from each other, Israelis, and much of the rest of the world.[1] While some forms of Israeli counterinsurgency involve close contact with individuals or a presence inside Palestinian cities, in general Israel has used weapons and strategies that maintain a distance between Palestinians and the Israeli army. In these circumstances, some of the most pivotal kinds of contact have occurred indirectly, by way of objects. That many of these objects were associated with the United States is a reflection of the robust role the United States has played in the Israeli-Palestinian conflict, the international arms trade, and Palestinians' emigration patterns, as well as in widespread Palestinian mappings of the concentrations of global power.

Palestinians sometimes do come into contact with American journalists or humanitarian workers. For a variety of reasons, the second Intifada has seen a growing presence of Western nongovernmental organizations, activists, and journalists in the West Bank and Gaza Strip (Bishara 2008; Hanafi and Tabar 2005; Seitz 2003). Their presence generates the kind of contact Anna Tsing describes as "friction." Tsing's concept of friction encourages analysis of how people with different interests, resources, beliefs, and skills can collaborate. Even when it may not seem that these global connections have come to fruition, Tsing encourages scholars to analyze "the unexpected and unstable aspects of global interaction" (Tsing 2005, 3) that may lead to transformations in power relations. Although the structures of power I describe in the northern West Bank city of Nablus are quite durable, Palestinians can sometimes mobilize objects of U.S. provenance or well-worn transnational circuits of media for their benefit.

THE VIEW FROM NABLUS

Nablus is a nearly 2,000-year-old city in the northern West Bank with a rich and well-documented history of regional and international trade in such items as soap and olive oil (Doumani 1992). It is home to one of the largest Palestinian universities, Al-Najah University, and to the Palestinian stock market. However, for long periods during the Intifada, it was the most inaccessible city in the West Bank. Its 134,000 residents live between two mountains, with the downtown deep in the valley and neighborhoods built on steep inclines (PASSIA 2008, 335). An Israeli checkpoint at each end of the valley and restricted roads virtually all around controlled access to the city.[2] Nablus was the only city in the West Bank to which I was repeatedly (although inconsistently) refused entry by Israeli soldiers during my fieldwork from 2003 to 2005. For internationals wishing to visit Nablus without special press or other institutional credentials, as for local Palestinians whose identity cards did not specify Nablus as a place of residency, access was often a question of negotiating with soldiers or finding an illicit route of entry. The mountains were a formidable barrier to passage by foot; donkeys and off-road vehicles were among the improvised means of traversing the difficult terrain.

Although Nablus residents inhabited a narrow space, they cultivated embodied means of situating themselves in more expansive geographies. On cool summer evenings, I would sit with Nablus residents on their porches overlooking the valley, and they would comment on the bustle of a wedding procession down the street and then moments later on the lights of Israeli factories farther off to the west. Many Palestinians had worked in these factories before the Israeli closure of the West Bank tightened. One night, as we pondered the view, my host told me that from her aunt's house up higher on the mountain they could even see the distant shimmer of sunset on the Mediterranean Sea. Its beaches have been emphatically off limits to the vast majority of Palestinians since 2000. When, overlooking the valley, I exclaimed that it seemed we were really high up already, my companion, a recent college graduate with a usually buoyant air, told me with a weary shrug of her shoulders that if I turned around and looked up, I would see how immense the mountains really were.

DEPLOYING U.S. WEAPONS AGAINST U.S. PASSPORTS IN NABLUS

Looking not only oriented Nablus residents with regards to their geographic location; sometimes it allowed them to locate themselves in global political networks. Attending to the particulars of the landscape as a "lively actor" (Tsing 2005, 29) reveals that people often gain the perspectives and traction that lay bare the structures of power through the specificities of terrain. During some nights of the second Intifada, Nablus residents watched Israeli forces bomb their city from the sky. On these nights, it was not just Israeli power that was on display. Palestinians knew that many of the most menacing of the weapons used against them during the second Intifada were U.S. made: F-16 aircrafts, Apache helicopters, Hellfire missiles, and armored Caterpillar D-9 bulldozers (Abrahams 2004). These are much more destructive weapons than were used in the first Intifada, which started in 1987. I often heard Palestinians tell heroic stories of artfully dodging bullets and throwing stones during either of the two Intifadas. From everyday asides, I knew that they tolerated much of the Israeli army's arsenal with an exhausted irritation, as when an old Israeli-made Merkava tank settled loudly outside one's house in the middle of the night during an arrest raid. Yet Palestinians described the palpable horror of hearing a low-flying helicopter roar overhead and even glimpsing its gun's red laser viewfinder on a nearby surface; they described the stunning crash of a missile falling a few cars ahead of their own as they drove through town. These new American weapons were distinctly frightening.[3]

It was not only the big weapons of the second Intifada that Palestinians knew to be from the United States; it was also many of the smaller ones. Palestinians were aware that the M-16 rifles that Israeli soldiers brandished were U.S. made. They were more powerful than the Soviet-designed Kalashnikovs, or AK-47s, that Palestinian Authority security forces were permitted to carry. Tear gas canisters were stamped "Federal Laboratories, Saltsburg, Pennsylvania" (Fisk 2001). In the wake of protests, children gathered spent canisters, and if they could not sound out the long words, if they did not know where exactly Pennsylvania was, they knew enough to associate the long strings of roman letters with the United States.

The use of warplanes and missiles drastically changed the kinds of contact that occurred between Palestinians and Israelis during the second Intifada. An iconic tactic of Israeli counterinsurgency during the first Intifada was the breaking of protesting youths' bones, which temporarily prohibited them from throwing stones

(Kifner 1988). This tactic required intimate contact between Israeli soldiers and Palestinian youth. Its effects were serious, but they were also limited. During the second Intifada, extrajudicial killings of Palestinian militants carried out by missiles or helicopter gunfire put noncombatants at tremendous risk, severely escalating the possibility of violence in Palestinian cities and contributing to the bloody and spectacular aesthetics of the second Intifada (Allen 2008). The technology of air-power obviously facilitates the goal of halting insurgency quite differently than do army batons.[4]

July 6, 2004, was one of those nights when much of Nablus was kept awake by the air war, as Israeli planes targeted two militants and an apartment building that they were said to have entered. If, as Allen Feldman writes, "the perception of history is irrevocably tied to the history of sensory perception" (Feldman 1994, 407), this was an acutely corporeal history in the making. I was not there that night, but in a visit to Nablus three months later while doing research about Israel's policy of extrajudicial killings, I interviewed several people: the widow of one of the victims, a doctor who lived on the top floor of the targeted building, a health worker who arrived on the scene as the attack was ending, a Nablus public relations official, the city's unofficial medical examiner, and three other people who heard and saw the night's events unfold from their homes.

As an anthropologist primarily studying journalism, I was undertaking this research in part in order to understand how people related to Western journalists. Because I was based in Jerusalem, I did not have many close contacts in the city, and my position there simulated that of foreign journalists. During these days of research, I found that the story of that night had become notorious in Nablus. While many had first-hand memories of watching the attack, they also knew details about the evening that they could not have witnessed but must have read about or heard. As they told me their stories, I realized that they were striving to expand this community of knowledge to and through me.

The geography of the city itself sharpened Nablus residents' perceptions of the events. Those on the southern mountain had a clear view of who was being hit on the northern mountain. Those on the northern mountain saw the planes as they spit out missiles above their city; they saw the missiles glide into range. And then they listened for the proximity of the impacts. That night, which apparently began as an Israeli attempt to either arrest or assassinate a leader from the leftist Popular Front for the Liberation of Palestine (PFLP), five people were killed in Nablus: an Israeli officer, two PFLP members, and two Palestinian noncombatants.

One man, a university professor who was on the southern mountain, chronicled the beginning of the incident in terms of the sounds of the weapons. He said that the character of a sound signaled the type of weapon that had made it, and from this, he could identify who was likely bearing the weapon. He said the clash started with the sound of a small explosion; he surmised this was a Palestinian pipe bomb. Immediately, he heard the dry, clear bursts of Israeli gunfire and the less distinct booms that he attributed to Palestinians' Kalashnikov rifles. This, he told me, is probably when the Israeli officer, Captain Moran Vardi, who was twenty-five, was hit.[5] Soon after, the Israeli air fire began. The professor's voice shook with fury as he articulated the names of the planes he heard and saw: Apache helicopters, F-16s.

After the conflict had erupted, wanted men from the camp had evidently taken refuge around the apartment building, so it had become a target. Inside, Khaled Salah, a professor of electrical engineering at Al-Najah University, huddled on the floor with his wife, Salam, their daughter, Diana, age twenty-three, and two of their sons, Muhammad, sixteen, and Ali, eleven. For hours, they read the Qur'an and watched the red glow of the bullet tracers that stuck in their walls slowly fade. Missiles hit the bedroom and the kitchen. Later, his wife told me that the air had smelled of perfume from broken bottles, that in the moments of silence between the gunfire, they could hear water dripping from pierced tanks on the roof. The family made desperate calls to the U.S. consulate pleading for intervention, because Diana was a U.S. citizen.

After several hours of fire, the city fell quiet, and people on both sides of the mountain heard the soldiers call out over loudspeakers in Arabic for the residents of the house to come downstairs. Khaled Salah tried to open the door to their apartment, but he found it jammed. According to his daughter, Diana, he went to the window and called down to the soldiers in English, "We can't open the door. The door is damaged. I am a peaceful man. We all are peaceful people. I have children. My daughter has an American citizenship. I have an American green card, I have no weapons. Only my children are here. Come and open the door. I can't open it."[6] She said he continued in Arabic: "Help ... help ... somebody come and open the door."

Passports are not only brought out or brought up when requested by an authority; they can also be actively deployed (Caplan and Torpey 2001). Certainly, in locations of violence, passports and other documents of identification have powers that exceed the licensing or restricting of movement (Gordillo 2006; Longman 2001). But in this case as in a handful of others (Chu 2008), it is the carrying of a foreign—and specifically a U.S.—passport that seemed to be imbued with protective qualities.

Under what local epistemologies of state, documentation, and warfare might a U.S. passport—or more tenuously, a permanent resident card—act as a shield against one of the world's strongest armies? Did Khaled Salah imagine that the soldier would believe it to be some kind of "friendly fire" for an Israeli soldier to shoot at a Palestinian-American family with weapons made in the United States? I doubt it. Nor was Khaled Salah invoking a legal privilege accorded by these documents. Pleas made with foreign passports, especially the use of foreign passports to pass through checkpoints, were common and occasionally effective during the second Intifada (Kelly 2006). But, legally, holding a foreign passport did not change the status of a resident, as it was the local status of a person—whether she was on a tourist visa, held an Israeli or Palestinian passport, or held an Israeli residency card—that determined one's status.[7]

Rather, I imagine that Khaled Salah attempted to use the U.S. passport, first, to intimate his status within Palestinian society and thereby assert his innocence and, second, to suggest that killing him would cause public relations problems for Israel. The first line of this argument, that Palestinians who were U.S. citizens or residents were much less likely to be militants than the general population, worked on the patchwork logic of a few widely held assumptions. U.S. passport holders and U.S. permanent residents were generally people who had some financial resources to travel and educational or familial connections through which documents could be obtained over time. Such a person of privilege, this logic suggested, would not be involved in militant operations. As Khaled Salah himself said, "I am a peaceful man," a characterization repeated by his wife when I interviewed her later. Moreover, if one had obtained U.S. documents recently, they quite literally served as a kind of certification of being "clean," because it is known that the United States does not give residency cards or passports to anyone with significant infractions in an Israeli security file. This was an argument about the divisions among different kinds of Palestinians that insinuated that the U.S. passport holder was a "good" Palestinian (Mamdani 2004).

The second line of argument, that killing a Palestinian American would create a negative public image of Israel, was also plausible but hardly ironclad. Rachel Corrie, the blond U.S. citizen who was crushed by a Caterpillar D-9 bulldozer in Gaza on March 16, 2003, as she tried to prevent the Israeli military from destroying a Palestinian family's house, was well-known and held in high esteem in the

Palestinian territories. But most Palestinians would have had no way of ascertaining the extent to which her death had gained notoriety in the United States. The Israeli soldiers on duty that night in Nablus might or might not have known that the driver of the bulldozer in Gaza had never been prosecuted.

Indeed, one difficulty in tracing out the logics of either of these arguments— that is, about local status or international public relations—is that Palestinians' perceptions of their validity might differ from Israeli soldiers' perceptions of them. But it is precisely the lack of a direct conversation on these and other issues that characterized such incidents and rendered objects like the passport so critical. The tenuousness of the logics in play is one (and not the only) reason that, as Khaled Salah called out into the night, it would have been utterly unclear how and on what basis the soldiers would respond. In this standoff between a person wielding a U.S. passport as a shield and an arsenal that included U.S. weapons, the power remained in the hands of Israeli soldiers, who controlled the weapons and whose discretion it was to recognize or ignore the U.S. passport.

On this night, chance was not in Salah's favor. The soldiers did not respond to his calls for help. Instead, a few minutes later, Israeli soldiers fired up at the apartment, killing him immediately and critically injuring his sixteen-year-old son, Muhammad. Salam and Diana Salah implored that an ambulance be summoned, but the Israeli soldiers dispatched only a neighbor to help open the jammed door. Salah's wife and daughter were forced to come downstairs with the rest of their neighbors.

By the time the building was evacuated, one of the two PFLP militants had already been killed during the ambush, while a second, Yamin Faraj, the commander of the military wing of the PFLP in Nablus, had survived injured. A doctor who lived on the top floor of the building recounted to me that the soldiers searched and bound all of the men of the building as they waited on the street. A short while later, he recalled, one of the handcuffed men was unbound and forced to drag Faraj from his hiding place. Then, he said, the Israeli soldiers shot Faraj in the head.[8] An ambulance was permitted access to the building only hours after the shooting, and by then Muhammad Salah was dead.[9]

MAKING NEWS OF CALAMITY

If the passport and residency card failed to provide the Salah family with protection from being fired at, would they provide the family any kind of recognition in the wake of tragedy? If the passport failed as a shield, might it later serve as a permit for representation, or at least for being represented? The incursion was covered by outlets including the Associated Press, the Agence France-Presse (AFP), the BBC, *Ha'aretz,* the *Washington Post,* and the *New York Times.* I surmise that one reason this night of violence received the coverage that it did was because of Khaled Salah's identity, mentioned in most of these reports. The aspects of his identity that warranted remark were his status as a professor, his family's U.S. residency cards and passports, and the fact that he had earned his Ph.D. at the University of California. That an Israeli officer had been killed also made headlines. In these international media, the extrajudicial killing of a militant was recorded only by the AFP.

Some of the articles that noted the Salahs' status were nevertheless framed in a language of just-the-facts detachment that would not likely generate readers' empathy.[10] For example, the *Washington Post* noted both Salah's education and his immigration status in ways that almost defied a (nonimmigrant) reader to recognize any qualities or experiences he might share with Salah:

> A statement by the university said that Salah earned his doctorate in electrical engineering from the University of California at Davis in 1985. A spokesman for the U.S. Consulate in Jerusalem said that Salah's wife said in a conversation Tuesday with consulate staff that he had a green card to work in the United States. (J. Anderson 2004)

Both the *New York Times* and the *Washington Post* articles cited Palestinian sources—the Salah family and medical workers—in sequence with the Israeli military spokesperson (J. Anderson 2004; Myre 2004), a common technique that can create the impression of balance and objectivity while refraining to offer an evaluation of the facts at hand (Mindich 1998). None of the articles mentioned that some of the weapons used in the attack were made in the United States. Perhaps this is because passports are meant to confer an identity upon their holders, while the provenance of an object seems less important once it has been sold. Perhaps it is because people are recognized as actors and victims—and thus news subjects—in a way that objects are not. And perhaps it is because the use of U.S. weapons in such conflicts is matter-of-fact and no longer newsworthy.

Two articles that were written based on reporting in Nablus were authored by Ali Daraghmeh, a Palestinian reporter for the Associated Press who lives in Nablus (Daraghmeh 2004), and Gideon Levy, an Israeli journalist working for the Israeli newspaper *Ha'aretz* who is known for his incisive coverage of Israeli occupation (Levy 2004). They too focused on the professor with ties to the United States rather than on the militants. The *Ha'aretz* article, published weeks after the attack, was the longest. It provided a chronicle of the night of the attack and extended quotes from Salam Salah. Levy's article circulated on the Web far beyond the *Ha'aretz* English Web site, both in repostings and as a source for further articles in outlets as diverse as the New England–based *Jewish Journal* (Arnold 2004) and Ramallah-On-Line (Fraser 2004a). My own initial article, based on the research I describe here, analyzed the impact of assassinations and targeted killings on Nablus (Bishara 2005).

Each of these longer features articulated a distinct political position, but their authors all built upon a face-to-face interview with Diana or Salam Salah or reinterpreted such an encounter after reading another source. Certain sensations recounted by Salam Salah, like the scent of broken perfume bottles, caught the attention of more than one author (Bishara 2005; Levy 2004). Certain sentiments passed through layers of mediation. When I interviewed Salam Salah, she recounted the hours of siege in detail; from her words, I imagined that as much as they were terrified in those moments, she treasured them as the last time her family sat close together. Levy's article captured this same sentiment: "They lay on the floor, folded into one another, five members of a family like one body" (Levy 2004). This passage was reframed in a poem by activist and playwright Genevieve Cora Fraser. It begins,

> Entwined as a ball
> Of thread the family
> Clung and enveloped
> One another in love In terror in their last
> Moments together (Fraser 2004b)

Fraser wrote the poem without meeting the Salah family, apparently drawing on other available media. Yet it contained remnants of Salam Salah's narrative. This poem then itself created a cycle of more contact and mediation. The Salah family read Fraser's poem online and invited her to visit. Fraser wrote again about the family's tragedy after she had met Salam, Diana, and Ali and asked for public support for the family's request of a U.S. inquiry into Khaled and Muhammad's deaths (Fraser 2005).

When I met Salam Salah, she remained despondent, and it was hard to tell whether media coverage was any real consolation. But her willingness to meet poets, journalists, and anthropologists suggests that coverage meant something to her. During our meeting, she showed me some of the few family photos that had not been destroyed during the attack. They portrayed a family trip to Colorado, her late son's birthday party, her husband shoveling snow. She was angry at the U.S. role in the operation—not because of the weapons' place of manufacture, but because the consulate had done nothing while they were under fire. But still, she told me that her eldest son, Amr, was in Massachusetts, studying to be an electrical engineer, like his father, and organizing the effort to demand a U.S. investigation into the attack.

CONCLUSIONS

While U.S. officials assert that the United States is the prime negotiator of peace, during the second Intifada, Palestinians have known objectifications of U.S. power to be mediators of war. These objects have been the means by which Palestinians and Israeli soldiers interact during a period when the possibilities for direct connection have been highly attenuated. In the West Bank, U.S. power is not abstract: Palestinians sense U.S. power and make sense of it in political analysis. This U.S. presence is evident for Palestinians, who viscerally know weapons by their sounds and appearances and who are intellectually aware that Israel acquires these weapons with U.S. military aid. Yet, in U.S. news media accounts of specific incidents of violence, the history of weapons is generally not recognized as playing an active role in conflict.

Palestinians do not only discern U.S. power, they act upon and with it. A U.S. passport can be a makeshift shield in a moment of peril. Given the limited resources at their disposal, Palestinians may feel that wielding their little piece of U.S. power is a worthwhile maneuver, even as they know there are no guarantees for success. After a crisis, a U.S. passport may be a kind of permit to representation of an event in Western news. In processes that are collaborative but not egalitarian, foreign journalists and researchers and Palestinian doctors, bureaucrats, militants, journalists, and others remediate and reframe incidents of violence. With vivid language, Palestinians may introduce their interviewers to the corporeal dimensions of living under siege, and they often remark to Americans that the weapons they faced were made in the United States of America. These moments of contact do not forestall violence. They do not even grant Palestinians permission to narrate their own stories (Said 1984), but at least they make space for Palestinians' statements to be read alongside those of the Israeli military spokesperson. Clearly, these developments happen within social and political hierarchies, but they also can be shaped by the distinct details of particular local stories: looming, rocky mountains and broken perfume bottles. They are fueled by the "grip of worldly encounter" (Tsing 2005, 1) that can give substance and meaning to universalist aspirations to justice. This is the generative unpredictability of friction about which Tsing writes. Although these media may not effect change, they can be "a hair in the flour [that] ruins the legitimacy of power" (Tsing 2005, 206). Whether horrifying or empowering, U.S. power is a palpable part of the Palestinian-Israeli conflict, as it is in many conflicts around the world. Under these circumstances, U.S. neutrality or invisibility is inconceivable. We can instead look to people in places like Nablus to learn about the far-reaching contours of American power and the multiple ways in which it is deployed.

NOTES

Acknowledgements: I am grateful to Beatrice Jauregui, John Kelly, Sean Mitchell, and Jeremy Walton for organizing the conference on Anthropology and Counterinsurgency and editing this volume. This paper benefited from discussion at the conference and from readings of various drafts by Lori Allen, Nidal Al-Azraq, Summerson Carr, and Julie Chu.

1. As of April 2008, the United Nations identified 608 obstacles within the West Bank alone, an area slightly smaller than the state of Delaware. This does not count the barriers to entering Israel itself. Gaza has been even more drastically isolated (United Nations 2008).

2. A map by the Israeli human rights organization B'Tselem, "The Forbidden Roads Regime," elucidates prohibitions on Palestinian use of roads in the West Bank (B'Tselem 2004).

3. Each year since 1985, the United States has given Israel an average of $3 billion, much of which has been military aid. At $2.4 billion in fiscal year 2008, military aid from the United States represents 20 percent of Israel's total defense budget. Of this amount, 75 percent must be used to buy U.S. defense

equipment (Sharp 2008, 3–4). Israel's use of Apache helicopters, F-16 planes, and M-16 rifles against Palestinians during the second Intifada has been documented elsewhere (cf. Human Rights Watch 2002, 2005).

4. *The Journal of Palestine Studies* found that in the first five years of the Intifada, 322 people were killed as targets of Israeli assassination attempts, while 240 bystanders were killed in assassinations or assassination attempts (Esposito 2006, 196).

5. A statement by the Israeli military spokesperson seems to confirm this account (J. Anderson 2004).

6. This quote is taken from the transcript of a press conference at Al-Najah University. A related quote can be found in "Death in a Cemetery" (Levy 2004), and Salam Salah gave me a similar account when I interviewed her.

7. Moreover, carrying a U.S. passport with a tourist visa did not itself guarantee free movement, as evinced by the difficulties I faced entering Nablus with my U.S. passport.

8. An eyewitness cited in an AFP report also confirmed that an execution took place (Saada 2004). Also, doctor Sameer Abu Za'rur, who had been serving as the city's volunteer medical examiner during the Intifada, went on the record when I interviewed him about Faraj's death: "I know there are rumors that he was shot point blank. I can't say anything about those rumors. But I can tell you that above his eyebrows, there was nothing."

9. In contrast, the Israeli army's statement about the incident suggested that their deaths were an unfortunate collateral effect of the operation: "Dr. Salah and his son Mohammed were apparently killed by IDF gunfire, but there was no intention to do them harm" (quoted in Levy 2004). This statement points to one aspect of another famous conceptualization of "friction" in warfare, Carl von Clausewitz's observation that circumstances of war must be expected to be unpredictable (Clausewitz 1989 [1832], 66). One political scientist suggests that within a theory of just war, friction should prohibit certain tactics like missile attack and air strikes simply because too much can go wrong when they are used (Smith 1994).

10. For more on the history and effects of detachment as a journalistic value, see McChesney (2004) and Mindich (1998).

REFERENCES

Abrahams, Fred. 2004. *Razing Rafah: Mass Home Demolitions in the Gaza Strip*. New York: Human Rights Watch.

Allen, George W. 2001. *None So Blind: A Personal Account of Intelligence Failure in Vietnam*. Chicago: Ivan R Dee.

Allen, Lori. 2009. Martyr Bodies in the Media: Human Rights, Aesthetics, and the Politics of Immediation in the Palestinian Intifada. *American Ethnologist* 36 (1): 161–80.

Anderson, John Ward. 2004. Top Militant among Five Killed in Raid in West Bank. Washington Post, July 7, A13.

Arnold, Mark. 2004. *Anatomy of a Tragedy: From Nablus to the North Shore*. http://www.jewishjournal.org/archives/archiveSept10_04.htm.

Bishara, Amahl. 2005. The Targeted and the Untargeted of Nablus. *Middle East Report* (235): 8–11.

Caplan, Jane, and John Torpey. 2001. Introduction. In *Documenting Individual Identity: The Development of State Practices in the Modern World*, edited by J. Caplan and J. Torpey, 1–12. Princeton: Princeton University Press.

Chu, Julie. 2008. Card Me When I'm Dead: Identification Papers and the Pursuit of the Good Afterlife in China. Paper Presented at the Department of Anthropology, University of Chicago.

Daraghmeh, Ali. 2004. Palestinian Professor, Son Killed in Israeli Raid. July 6 Associated Press.

Doumani, Beshara. 1992. Rediscovering Ottoman Palestine: Writing Palestinians into History. *Journal of Palestine Studies* 21 (2): 5–28.

Feldman, Allen. 1994. On Cultural Anaesthesia: From Desert Storm to Rodney King. *American Ethnologist* 21 (2): 404–18.

Fisk, Robert. 2001. Palestine: Death in Bethlehem, Made in America. *Independent*, April 15.

Fraser, Genevieve Cora. 2004a. Palestinian American Calls for US Investigation into Israeli Assault. http://archive.ramallahonline.com/modules.php?name=News&file=article&sid=2114.

Gordillo, Gastón. 2006. The Crucible of Citizenship: ID-Paper Fetishism in the Argentinean Chaco. *American Ethnologist* 33 (2): 162–76.

Hanafi, Sari, and Linda Tabar. 2005. T*he Emergence of Palestinian Globalized Elite: Donors, International Organizations, and Local NGOs.* Jerusalem: Institute of Jerusalem Studies.

Kelly, Tobias. 2006. Documented Lives: Fear and the Uncertainties of Law During the Second Palestinian Intifada. *Journal of the Royal Anthropological Institute* 12:89–107.

Kifner, John. 1988. Israel's New Violent Tactic Takes Toll on Both Sides. *New York Times,* January 22, A10.

Levy, Gideon. 2004. Death in a Cemetery. *Ha'aretz,* July 23.

Longman, Timothy. 2001. Identity Cards, Ethnic Self-Perception, and Genocide in Rwanda. In *Documenting Individual Identity: The Development of State Practices in the Modern World,* edited by J. Caplan and J. Torpey, 345–57. Princeton: Princeton University Press.

Mamdani, Mahmood. 2004. *Good Muslim, Bad Muslim: America, the Cold War and the Roots of Terror.* New York: Three Leaves Press, Doubleday.

Mansour, Camille. 2005. The Palestinian Perception of America after 9/11. In *WiThus or against Us: Studies in Global Anti-Americanism,* edited by T. Judt and D. Lacorne, 157–71. New York: Palgrave McMillan.

Mindich, David T.Z. 1998. Just the Facts: *How "Objectivity" Came to Define American Journalism.* New York: New York University Press.

Myre, Greg. 2004. Mideast Clashes Kill 6 Palestinians and Israeli Officer. *New York Times,* July 7, A3.

PASSIA. 2008. *Palestine Facts and Figures.* Jerusalem: PASSIA.

Seitz, Charmaine. 2003. ISM at the Crossroads: The Evolution of the International Solidarity Movement. *Journal of Palestine Studies* 32(4): 50–67.

Tsing, Anna. 2005. *Friction: An Ethnography of Global Connection.* Princeton: Princeton University Press.

Evading State Control
Political Protest and Technology in Saudi Arabia

by MADAWI AL-RASHEED

RECENTLY ANTHROPOLOGISTS HAVE BEEN CONCERNED WITH the concept of civil society and the prospect of its development in non-Western societies. The rediscovery of the concept is motivated by political changes that have swept 'traditional' societies now integrated into nation-states, most modelled on a Western pattern. The resulting debate has ramifications beyond the specific concept of civil society which touch wider issues at the heart of anthropological analysis and interpretation (Hann and Dunn 1996). Is civil society, the child of the European Enlightenment, an appropriate tool for the analysis of political processes in societies culturally and historically removed from the West? Classically, civil society implies that individuals and groups are free to form associations and organisations independent of the state, which can mediate between citizens and the state (Hann and Dunn 1996:1). This development is regarded as associated with interaction through market capitalism. With the exception of a few convincing applications in the Middle East (Norton 1995, 1996; Eickelman 1996), anthropologists remain sceptical. Gellner has led denials of its applicability and even the prospect of its appearance in the Muslim world. In his view, the underlying bonds of the Muslim *umma* (community) militate against it because Islam 'exemplifies a social order which seems to lack much capacity to provide political countervailing institutions and associations, which is atomized without much individualism, and operates effectively without intellectual pluralism' (Gellner 1994: 29).[1]

In this chapter I aim to expand our understanding of civil society in Saudi Arabia, here exemplifying the Islamic world although by no means representative of Muslim countries. If we retain a narrow definition of civil society (limiting it to the emergence of independent and formal non-kin-based organisations as buffer zones between the individual and the polity, guarding the individual interests of citizens, regardless of their kin or regional identities, against those of the state), then Saudi Arabia does not pass the test as the formation of such formal organisations is banned under the present regime. However, political protest has been voiced in the last decade through various mechanisms, ranging from the formation of non-kin-based dissident groups, through petitions to the ruling elite signed by a cross-section of society, to the electronic-transmission of critical literature, which are the seeds of an emerging civil society. Saudi Arabia, now immersed in modernity, is benefiting from new technologies used for purposes not anticipated by those who introduced them. Here I investigate the changing forms of political protest in Saudi Arabia, applying a historical perspective to highlight the transformation of the means of protest and their evolution over time. I contrast two periods: pre-state political structures and state structures. Pre-state politics was characterised by the fragmentation of authority and the genuine ability of people to contest and challenge their legitimate rulers. In pre-state Arabia and in the context of centralised tribal dynasties, political protest manifested itself in the arena of the tribal *majlis* (council). When this resource was exhausted, groups resorted to the old mechanism of fission and shifting alliances. In contrast, the state era was initially characterised by the state's ability to silence protest and curb its eruption, and by the failure of society to organise effective opposition. However, in the 1990s silencing opposition has become more difficult as a result of increased education, literacy, modernisation and the availability of new technologies of communication, and groups can organise themselves effectively along new, non-kin lines. As long as political parties remain banned, one has to look beyond the rigidity of the Western model to see an emerging civil society on the pages of the opposition press, faxes and electronic mail.

In the Middle East, the wide spread of mass higher education, printing and communication technology (videos, televisions, cassettes, personal computers, facsimile machines and electronic mail) has undermined traditional sources of knowledge and authority and created multiple political discourses and protests against absolutist states. This has led to the intensification of dispute and con-test, the polarisation of groups, the consolidation of multiple centres of power (Eickelman 1992), and has marginalised the traditional elite in the emergence of a new category of citizen—educated, urban and computer literate. While such new groups may retain the rhetoric of tradition, they are otherwise immersed in modernity, particularly the new Islamists of the Muslim world, including members of the Saudi Islamic opposition. Their Islamist discourse evokes a vision of society faithful to authenticity and genuine ancient tradition while simultaneously benefit-ing from modern technology and modern discourses on democracy, human rights, autonomy and equality. Islamist discourse and organisational strategies are both facilitating the emergence of civil society in the Muslim world, contrary to Gellner's assertion that they represent its antithesis.

PRE-STATE POLITICS

The central region of Saudi Arabia, Najd, is most interesting in terms of investigating local processes of political centralisation because it had a number of dynastic emir-ates *(imarah)* with characteristics resembling those of states. The Rashidi dynasty (1836–1921), based in the oasis of Hail in northern Najd,[2] was established among the sedentary population of the oasis, but included pastoral nomads.

The nineteenth-century founders of the Rashidi dynasty were a prominent lineage drawn from the Shammar, one of the major tribal confederations of north-central Arabia. While the majority of the tribe was nomadic, the Rashidi lineage was settled in the oasis. They assumed the title of *amirs* (princes) whose authority was recognised not only among members of their own lineage, but also among other Shammar lineages. The *amirs* coexisted with Shammar chiefs—known as *sheikhs*—whose influence was restricted to their own lineages. The *amirs,* as heads of the whole tribe, represented it to external powers such as the Ottoman Empire in adjacent areas, the Hijaz and Mesopotamia.

The *amirs* ensured the protection not only of their subjects, but also of vital trade routes into the oases they controlled using an armed force of Shammar volunteers, conscripts from the oases, mercenaries and slaves. This permanent force, paid in cash and kind, enforced the *amirs'* orders, punished transgressors, expanded their domain, and distinguished the *amirs'* leadership from that of the tribal *sheikhs* as leaders with no power to influence people's decisions. While all male members of the tribal section carried weapons, they neither served the *sheikhs'* personal interests, nor enforced their commands. Their voluntary participation in raids and in the defence of their section was a moral duty. In contrast, the *amirs'* armed men constituted a permanent professional force, giving them powers of coercion which tribal *sheikhs* lacked. Centralised oasis-based leadership was thus enforced and maintained.

However, the *amirs* had little control over the economic base of pastoral production. Shammar tribesmen grazed their animals in their traditional tribal territory and their *sheikhs* negotiated with their counterparts for access to other (including non-Sharnmar) sections' grazing land and wells. The *amirs'* economic power rested on their ability to control and protect caravan and pilgrimage routes within Shammar territory. Their armed force ensured the safe passage of both merchants and pilgrims to the holy cities of Arabia, Mecca and Madina, in return for caravan tolls.

The Rashidi dynasty was complex. It combined the fluid leadership of the Shammar *sheikhs* with the centralised leadership of the Rashidi *amirs*. Economically, the *amirs* depended on an economy combining pastoral nomadism, oasis agriculture and trade. These attributes distinguished the system from the tribal organisation of the nomadic groups. The Hail dynasty was a micro-polity characterised by an urban base, the appointment of local representatives, an independent military force, the generation of surplus and the imposition of taxes.

Fragmented authority and fluctuations in both territory and constituency distinguished this political system from modern states, as a dynasty with centralised power but no single authority. The *amirs* had to accommodate the authority of the tribal *sheikhs* with whom they coexisted. This resulted in tensions stemming from the coexistence of a centralising agency, the *amirs*, and a decentralised political tribal structure and fluid economic base, both militating against a durable polity. The contradiction between political centralisation and the inherently decentralised tribal organisation and pastoral economy generated political protest, managed through *majlis* politics—the negotiation and resolution of conflict within the confines of the *amirs'* council in Hail.

The Hail *majlis* attracted the attention of European travellers who visited the *amirs* in the nineteenth and early twentieth centuries. My description of this institution draws on their accounts and on the oral narratives of the Shammar and the descendants of the Rashidi *amirs*. Early maps of the *amirs'* residence in Hail, Barzan Palace, show its proximity to the oasis market and mosque (Euting 1983). Palgrave claims that the palace site occupied one-tenth of the oasis (Palgrave 1865:103). In Wallin's (1854:200) account, the palace was easily distinguished from other houses by its imposing size. It consisted of two court-yards, the first comprising a guest reception room, the *amir's* private rooms, stables, kitchen, prison and a private quarter, while the second held the main entrance overlooking the central square, al-Mishab. The regular public meetings of the *majlis* were held in al-Mishab, opposite the *amir's* warehouses and guest chambers. Maps show a slave market behind the fortified, walled palace.

The arrangement of space reflected the concerns of the *amirs*. The kitchen, the reception rooms and the *majlis* occupied a substantial part of the building. The kitchen was important to prepare meals for *majlis* attendants. These feasts crucially consolidated the *amirs'* leadership and enhanced their reputation as generous rulers, attracting new supporters and enhancing the loyalty of existing ones. The *majlis* received numerous visitors: Hail notables, Shammar and non-Shammar *sheikhs*, and ordinary tribesmen. The amir with his brothers, uncles, and cousins sat on a slightly raised bench, he himself occupying the central place. Often foreign visitors, such as Ottoman and British messengers, were received in the *majlis*, the arena linking the Rashidi dynasty to the outside world and the various external powers which influenced the course of political events in Arabia. Access to the *majlis* was not generally regulated by strict rules; anyone with a case, request or enquiry attended these open meetings.

The *majlis* was an arena for dispute settlement between individuals and groups, ranging from theft and trespassing to murder and vengeance. These disputes were resolved by applying both customary tribal law and the *sharia*, the Islamic legal code. In the latter, the *amirs* were assisted by a *qadi*, Islamic judge, who was often literate and knowledgeable in Islamic matters as a result of studying in Hail, or other centres of Muslim learning. The *qadis* dealt specifically with disputes relating to commerce, marriage, divorce and inheritance. Other cases, especially those involving the nomadic population, were resolved according to tribal customary law. The two legal codes coexisted:

> Where, however, quarrels are not settled by the intervention of friends, the disputants bring their cases to the Emir, who settles them in open court, the *majlis,* and whose word is final. The law of the Koran,though

often referred to, is not, I fancy, the main rule of the Emir's decision, but rather Arabian custom, an authority far older than the Musluman code. I doubt if it is often necessary for the soldiers to support such decisions by force.

(Blunt 1968:266)

The procedure for dispute settlement was simple:

Someone steps forward and announces that a couple of sheep have been stolen from him by such and such a person. The *amir* promises him that he will see to it that they are given back or replaced, and has the *sheikh* of the tribe to which the thief belongs informed of this with the observation that he must clear the matter up. This simple announcement implies the tacit threat that in case of delay, the *sheikh* in question, together with his tribe, may, at the next year's distribution of grazing grounds, be allotted a region inferior to their previous one.

(Euting in Ward 1983:467)

The *amirs* apparently sought the cooperation of the tribal *sheikhs* in close contact with their followers and with grassroots knowledge of their behaviour. The tribal *sheikhs* attending the *amir's majlis* were held responsible for returning stolen property and arranging for blood money to be paid in cases of murder. The failure of a *sheikh* to do so resulted in withdrawal of benefits from the whole group.

Settling disputes within the *majlis* thus involved a multiplicity of authorities and legal codes in their successful resolution. Although various accounts indicate that the amir was the final judge, the voices of both *qadis* and tribal *sheikhs* were heard and respected. Above all, participation of the *sheikhs* ensured enforcement of the decisions taken. However, power remained with the *amirs* who, thanks to their armed force, were able to exert pressure on those who did not abide by *majlis* resolutions.

In addition to its role in mediating disputes, the *majlis* was the site of political participation of multiple but equal centres of authority. Here again, *amirs* heading their own lineages and the Shammar tribe were elevated by their noble origin, economic and military power, but were regarded by Shammar *sheikhs* as equal partners. Shammar *sheikhs* regarded *amirs* as their equals by birth and common ancestry. Kinship ties between the *amirs* and the Shammar lineages equalised a relationship which had the potential to develop hierarchically. The *amirs* could not coerce the Shammar *sheikhs* nor could they impose their will on them, but sought their participation in negotiating alliances and cementing loyalty. Decisions to raid other groups to gain booty or territory followed prolonged consultation with the *sheikhs* during their regular visits to the *majlis*. As their participation in raids was essential for the *amir's* campaigns, the latter could not afford to antagonise them.

Direct coercion being inappropriate, the *amirs* resorted to indirect bribery and subsidies to tribal *sheikhs* attending the *majlis* through gifts of rice, sugar, flour, weapons, cash and other useful items. Tribal *sheikhs* also offered the *amirs* gifts of camels and other items drawn from their pastoral economy. The exchange, however, remained unequal. The *amirs* were more lavish, with their greater surplus from raids and conquest within Arabia, and their external relations with the Ottoman governors who occasionally offered them income in return for swearing allegiance to the Ottoman Sultan. However, authority remained diffused in the tribal structure, with no single *sheikh* or *amir* claiming supreme political authority.

The *majlis* was also the arena where political protest was voiced. Realising both their equality with the Hail *amirs* and the inability of the latter to coerce them, the Shammar *sheikhs* and other non-Shammar tribal leaders used the *majlis* to voice their protest against policies imposed on them by the Rashidi leadership, concerning the allocation of pasture and wells, and access to markets in oases under Rashidi jurisdiction, and also complained about raids against their sections, especially if they had paid the protection tax imposed on them by Hail. The *sheikhs* generally used the *majlis* to contest decisions against the interests of their lineages and were occasionally able to revoke them. While the *sheikhs* appreciated strong leadership in Hail, they were intolerant of weak, unjust and hesitant *amirs* who were not able to deliver security, prosperity and lavish subsidies.

Disenchanted tribal *sheikhs* resorted to fission to express their political protest. When *majlis* politics failed, tribal groups opted for the old strategy of shifting alliances. Fission allowed groups to maintain their autonomy and subvert their coercion by central authority. The ability of tribal sections to switch allegiance accompanied the development and consolidation of the Rashidi dynasty. However, its most devastating implications occurred in 1921 when the Rashidi *amirs* came under the attack of a rival dynasty, that of the Saudis, and some Shammar sections demonstrated their protest against their traditional Rashidi *amirs* (weakened by internal strife and competition over leadership within their own lineage), by switching allegiance to the Saudis. The Rashidi dynasty collapsed and Shammar territory was incorporated into the modern Saudi state. In the nineteenth century, the *amirs* were able to deal with such fission by resorting to diplomacy, negotiation and bribery. However, the weakened leadership of the first two decades of the twentieth century had neither the resources nor the skills to control the fragmentation of either their territory or their tribe.

The Rashidi dynasty demonstrates that pre-state Arabia witnessed varying degrees of centralised leadership. Tribal dynasties such as the Rashidis rested on a mixed economy of pastoralism, agriculture and trade, based on tribal organisation coexisting with multiple centres of authority. Although power was concentrated in the hands of an oasis-based lineage with economic and military resources, the exercise of power had to be negotiated with equally important tribal *sheikhs*. The latter had no economic, military or symbolic powers to match those of the *amirs*, yet they were important reservoirs of authority diffused in the tribal structure. Political protest was not silenced for two reasons. First, the mixed economic base militated against the exercise of absolute control over tribal sections. Second, the inability of the *amirs* to communicate effectively with the hinterland disallowed any durable supervision of distant territories and populations within their sphere of influence. *Majlis* politics was the mechanism by which the *amirs* maintained their position and accommodated the interests of their tribe.

STATE POLITICS

The emergence of the modern Saudi state in 1932 resulted in the triumph of one dynasty over others in Arabia through conquest assisted by a religious reformist movement, Wahhabism, and external support from Britain (which assumed a more important role in the region after the collapse of the Ottoman Empire after the First World War). The Saudis did not immediately establish the modern state of today (Kostiner 1993). In its early days, the Saudi state is better described as a dynasty, exhibiting characteristics little different from the political systems which had existed in Arabia such as the Rashidi dynasty described above. The major difference, however, stems from the fact that while the Rashidi dynasty was purely a tribal configuration, that of the Saudis was an amalgamation of tribal leadership and Islamic ideology. Saudi political hegemony was achieved through religious reform, which resulted in the Saudis emerging as the central political power and the Wahhabi *ulama* as the only interpreters of faith. The founder of the modern Saudi state, Ibn Saud, adopted the title of first Sultan and later King.

The adoption of this title was accompanied by major political transformations, thus altering traditional tribal dynastic government. The new state moved away from the historical pattern whereby a central power coexisted with other centres. The Saudi state was based from the very beginning on the elimination of other power centres. Prominent tribal *sheikhs* and *amirs* in Arabia were either eliminated or co-opted by this central power. This double process of elimination and co-option began to crystallise in the 1950s when oil revenues started flowing into the state treasury. Armed with enormous oil wealth, the state laid the foundation for an elaborate bureaucratic apparatus, a modern army, an educational infrastructure and an efficient transport network, linking the various regions in the country and facilitating the entry of Saudi Arabia into the modem world. This transformation was strikingly rapid. By the 1970s, the country had already benefited from the latest Western technological innovations at inflated prices. Even more striking was the fact that this material transformation was imposed on a society which did not adjust socially or culturally to the new era.

The race to enter the modern world economically and technologically was not matched by a similar race towards political modernisation. In the 1990s, Saudi Arabia is still an absolutist monarchical state, ruled by a royal lineage assisted by a number of appointed ministers, and a 60-member appointed consultative council, *majlis al shura,* created only in 1992. The country's constitution is the Quran and the law of the land is the *sharia,* the Islamic legal code, as interpreted by the Wahhabi *ulama.* Political parties are banned, freedom of assembly and expression virtually non-existent. The fiscal accountability of rulers cannot be checked in the absence of legitimate channels. The state controls the economy, supervises education, and generally restricts personal rights and freedoms. Political decisions remain top secret and are the monopoly of an elite, often composed of the king and other members of the royal family. Consulting the consultative council remains a formality given its unelected nature and composition.

This political system has made direct protest and opposition to central power difficult. The various tribal and non-tribal groups are unable to resort to the old mechanism of fission, the dominant form of previous protest. Ruling out fission as a mechanism of protest has narrowed the space for local autonomy and directed the attention of discontented groups towards other options within the limitations of the new state.

Despite the sophistication and rapid proliferation of the state bureaucracy, the princely *majlis* remains, quite separate from the formal consultative council, *majlis al shura* created in 1992. The princely *majlis*—a daily meeting held by the king and local governors, often princes of the royal family—is a survival of the traditional tribal *majlis*, at the heart of previous dynastic systems. The idea of the *majlis* has survived but its function, structure and meaning have been transformed with the consolidation of the state.

The *majlis* has lost its past main function as an arena for the free expression of opinions and political participation,[3] although disputes are still settled, and favours and subsidies demanded by the constituency are supplied by the king and the princes. The *majlis* is today a space for gaining loyalty in return for cash handouts, the allocation of resources and the smoothing of the rigidity of the state bureaucracy. Citizens frustrated by the impersonal state apparatus bypass it altogether by demanding the direct settlement of their cases by the *majlis*.

The underlying power structure of the *majlis* has also been transformed, into an hierarchical institution with a single head who makes the final decisions. Its hierarchy manifests itself through symbolic acts of greeting and elaborate seating arrangements, and the presence of armed bodyguards who not only represent the elevated status of the prince, but also ensure his security. Upon entering the *majlis*, attendants greet the prince by kissing his hand, forehead or shoulder, depending on their own standing in the new hierarchy. Kissing his hand is reserved for those of low status, whereas the forehead and the shoulder are reserved for attendants of noble origin. Attendants are then directed to seatsreflecting their social status— those of higher standing being seated on the right or left sides of the prince and those of low status further away from the central core of the *majlis*. This hierarchy is also preserved in the rules of the *majlis* dictating who is given the opportunity to speak directly to the prince. Low-status attendants may only hand a letter to the guards who take it to the prince. Anyone given the opportunity to speak, in addressing the prince must follow a formula. While in the tribal *majlis* participants could address the *amir* using first names, today this is replaced by the formula of *'jalalat al malik'* ('Your Majesty' for the king and 'Your Royal Highness' for princes). These symbolic expressions reflect the transformation of the *majlis'* underlying political structure from diffused tribal authority to hierarchical state power.

Given this transformation, political protest has been squeezed out of the *majlis*. Discontented groups within the kingdom resort to modern means of protest, previously unknown in the country because of the availability of traditional mechanisms. The demonstrations and strikes witnessed at various periods in the 1950s, 1970s and 1980s represented a shift towards new strategies. Demonstrations were always dealt with swiftly by the government. Political protest has also been expressed through petitions to the King and other members of the royal family. The most famous petitions were submitted during and after the Gulf War of 1991, and originated from both the religious establishment and 'secular' groups, reflecting discontent among those who previously supported the government.

In the 1990s, we witness the use of the fax machine and electronic mail—technological innovations appropriated by a whole spectrum of discontented groups to voice their political protest. My ethnographic data is based on an analysis of one Saudi Islamist opposition group, the Committee for the Defence of Legitimate Rights in Saudi Arabia (CDLR), which has employed such technological innovations in its struggle against the royal family.[4]

The CDLR was initially established in the capital, Riyadh, in May 1993 by six Saudis, and was immediately banned by the authorities; some of its supporters were arrested, including Dr al-Massari, the son of one of the founders. After his release, al-Massari and al-Faqih established new London headquarters for the Committee in exile. The CDLR started an active campaign to undermine the legitimacy of the royal family armed with the latest telecommunications technology linking them to Saudi Arabia. In addition to smuggling tapes and videos into the country, more recently the CDLR started satellite television broadcasts.

The CDLR relies heavily on fax machines and electronic mail to distribute weekly monitors to their supporters in and beyond Saudi Arabia. Through these channels the London office also receives information from Saudi Arabia, which is redistributed by fax and computer. The CDLR have thus challenged the Saudi state, whose agencies have so far failed to curb these flows of information.[5]

The rise of the CDLR,[6] and other organisations not considered here, needs to be contextualised within the Gulf War and its political, social and economic impact on Saudi Arabia. I have dealt with this context elsewhere (Al-Rasheed 1996, 1997). Suffice it to say that the expansion of the education system was critically important, especially the rise in student numbers in the Islamic and technological universities. During the economic boom of the 1970s and early 1980s, such students were recruited to jobs in the civil service, the oil industry and the religious institutions (graduates of Islamic colleges). However, the decline of oil prices in the 1990s, the heavy cost of the Gulf War and the general stagnation of the Saudi economy have meant that not all recent graduates have been absorbed into work. Today some respond to unemployment by giving their support to the Islamic opposition in return for a promise to ameliorate their economic situation under a regime more sensitive to their needs and concerns.

The number of unemployed university graduates with high expectations is likely to increase, given the demographic characteristics of the country (almost 60 per cent of the population is under the age of 21 and the annual population growth rate 3.8 per cent). This new category of citizen, computer literate and with technological and other valuable skills acquired in the country or abroad, is frustrated by the contradiction of being a national of a very wealthy state with a bleak employment future and no access to legitimate political channels to change his situation. His rising expectations of a secure future have been fuelled by his empowerment through education. Mass education tends to elevate such individuals above traditionally recognised authorities through their command of foreign languages, computer literacy, and scientific skills. Such young individuals have no experience of the historically recent tribal structure even though they may retain a tribal affiliation and identity. Excluded from the circles of princes, their prospects for economic prosperity are limited to patronage networks woven in the princely *majlis*.

This situation triggered a reaction resulting in the formation of the CDLR and other Islamist opposition groups. The educationally empowered individual searches for means to voice his protest. In the absence of alternative and legitimate channels such as political parties or pressure groups, he lends his ears to Friday sermons critical of the government, attends theological debates on the nature of the Islamic state in the centres of religious learning and participates in clandestine group discussions debating political issues, while he continues to communicate and receive messages from exiled and local opposition groups on his personal computer. He eagerly consumes news, broadcast on radio and television.

The long-term impact on society of mass education and the adoption of new technologies to express political protest still needs to be assessed. In Saudi Arabia, this strategy gathered momentum only after the Gulf War; as such, it is perhaps premature to predict the future on the basis of short experience. However, at the moment a number of trends can be observed and documented. The intensification of Islamist opposition to the regime and the identification of the newly emerging category of the young, literate, educated citizens with this opposition, have definitely contributed to the marginalisation of traditional political and religious authorities in the country. The old tribal groups who retained their elevated status were first marginalised by the centralised state, but today they cease to inspire deference or enjoy their vague authority under the patronage of the Saudi princes. Their old discourse emphasising blood ties, noble ancestry and respect for elderly authority, has waned in the face of new political concepts and ideologies. Today they present no real challenge to the state.

Equally, the traditional Wahhabi religious establishment whose authority crystallised over the last seventy years of Saudi rule find themselves challenged from within and below. The defection of young *ulama* and their support for the new Islamist groups through the Friday sermons, the circulation of critical tapes, leaflets and treatises, demonstrates that a unified religious discourse in support of the government is no longer possible. The old apologist *ulama* are constantly challenged by the young, who have adopted a more vigorous interpretive approach to crucial political questions such as those pertaining to the nature of the state, the status of the monarchy, the accountability of rulers and the importance of advice to government. These young *ulama* have gone beyond theological debates relating to how people should practise 'true Islam'; today they find themselves debating current political affairs, aided by increased literacy and the availability of new technologies of communication among the populace. Their debates are no longer confined to mosques and religious colleges, but propagated to a wider audience thanks to printing, electronic mail, fax machines, videos and cassettes.

What these new technologies allow is a serious evasion of state control. Today political protest cannot be curbed successfully unless it takes the form of an open confrontation with the state through demonstrations and strikes. The state coercive machinery remains intact to deal with such confrontations swiftly and efficiently. Arrests of suspected opponents and the execution of political activists have increased in the 1990s. However, these measures deal successfully only with the tip of the iceberg, but fail to provide a durable solution to the rising tide of political protest, now disseminated through networks of new technologies which cannot be efficiently controlled or regulated by the state.

The functional transformation of information technology from education and entertainment to embodying and facilitating political ends has been remarkable. A university student with access to computers may use them for his mathematical models, but can also receive messages and communicate with political groups in his spare time without even moving out of his department's computer room. In Saudi Arabia, this has given rise to a new brand of a *homo politicus,* who is capable of expressing his political views against central power and away from state control.[7] Access to these new technologies empowers individuals. The question at this juncture is whether this empowerment is illusory or real. While it is too early to give a definite answer based on empirical evidence, my guess is that the new *homo politicus,* by virtue of his command over new technologies can and will develop a consciousness of his real empowerment. Access to information, the ability to make news, influence public opinion and change attitudes are real outcomes of new technologies. How such changes will materialise in real power is not so self-evident. New technologies have become efficient vents for political protest; but its full materialisation and ability to trigger political change depend on other, non-technological variables. The major achievement of this political protest so far has been the politicisation of citizens, long slowed through oil prosperity, generous welfare benefits and efficient state control.

The use of technology for political protest has given rise to a dynamic political life, characterised by the coexistence of a multiplicity of political and religious discourses. Eickelman refers to this as the emergence of a culture of protest, reflecting in the Muslim world and elsewhere the fragmentation of authority, accompanied by the flourishing of multiple centres each with an agenda and a programme for change (Eickelman and Piscatori 1996). In his opinion, two scenarios may result: the intensification of dispute and contest leading to the polarisation of society; or a *modus vivendi* of accommodation and adjustment. It seems that Saudi society has recently moved in the direction of polarisation. Labels such as *islamiyyunn* (Islamists), *usuliuun* (fundamentalists), *ulmaniuun* (secularists), *ghulat* (radicals), *mutagharibuun* (westernised), *muhdithun* (modernists) have regularly made their appearance in everyday parlance and on the pages of both the official and opposition presses. These labels are new classifications gradually replacing conventional identities which in the past revolved around kin and tribe. They allow the categorisation of individuals on the basis of new criteria and discourses. They also capture the emerging new social identities and political orientations.

In the 1990s the Saudi state remains resilient to serious political change and resistant to widening real political participation and introducing legitimate mechanisms for the expression of political protest. The state has done all it can to suppress the development of civil society in its classical narrow definition. But in the 1990s, Saudi Arabia has also demonstrated some characteristics resembling those of the pre-state era of centralised tribal dynasties incapable of controlling their pastoral peripheries yet coexisting with other centres of authority. Today the state finds itself in a similar situation due to its inability to control information and communication.

While fission has not yet occurred, there are indicators pointing to the possibility of a return to the status quo ante, whereby the centralised power coexisted with alternative centres, capable at times of crisis of presenting real challenges to the state. It is hard to predict when this coexistence might erupt into major confrontations, but the proliferation of Islamist opposition groups indicates that this cannot be ruled out. Although these vary in their agendas and the number of their supporters, they agree on important principles: the need for political reform to limit corruption, to expand political participation and to provide for the legitimate expression of overt protest. Unless these issues are seriously considered by the state and its ruling group, the future of the country remains at stake, for new identities are forming and being given new meanings in the new context of mass education, competing discourses and new technologies.

The Saudi case demonstrates that if we continue to adhere to a rigid model which restricts signs of civil society to the formation of formal organisations and associations, then the country is obviously lagging behind. However, if we are prepared to widen our definition, there is a whole range of new mechanisms whereby civility is manifested. Today new technology has created a space beyond state control, which is appropriated by the new citizens. Technology has filled a gap in societies where absolute states continue to rule and where guilds, associations and other non-govermental organisations are banned. People evade state control by using new mechanisms, or transforming old ones to give them new meanings and functions, to guard their interests and bind them together. In this novel area we need more empirical investigation to assess the value of old concepts such as civil society.

NOTES

1. For a critique of Gellner's general theory of Muslim society, see Zubaida (1995). For an assessment of his theorising about the absence of civil society in the Muslim world, see Norton (1995, 1996).
2. Information on the Rashidi dynasty derives from my ethnohistorical research on this polity (Al-Rasheed 1991).

3. As a female researcher, I have no access to the princely *majlis* in Saudi Arabia, which remains a predominantly male arena. My ethnographic data is based on the accounts of those who have attended such meetings.
4. My research on the CDLR started in 1994. Most of the data here derive from the organisation in London.
5. In 1996, Britain rejected al-Massari's demand for asylum under pressure from the Saudi government. The court rejected the proposal to deport him to the Dominican Republic as requested by the Home Office. Instead, he was granted a temporary immigration status 'Leave to Remain in the UK', allowing him to continue his campaign from his north London office.
6. The CDLR publishes a number of Arabic and English communiqués, pamphlets and magazines to disseminate its ideas and political programme. These can be purchased in book shops in London and elsewhere or accessed through the fax machine and electronic mail.
7. *Homo politicus* described here remains male. Saudi women have not yet taken an active role in the political life of the country although during the Gulf War they succeeded in organising an unprecedented demonstration against the ban on women driving. Fifty Saudi women violated the ban and drove their cars to a shopping centre in Riyadh. The demonstration ended when the police arrested the women drivers. With the exception of this daring and couragous act of defiance, Saudi women are still politically inactive.

REFERENCES

Al-Rasheed, M. (1991) *Politics in an Arabian Oasis: The Rashidi Tribal Dynasty.* London: I.B.Tauris.
——(1996) Saudi Arabia's Islamic opposition. *Current History* 95, 597:16–22.
——(1997) Le Couronne et le turban: l'état Saoudien a la recherche d'une nouvelle légitimaté. In *Les États Arabes Face à la Contestations Islamiste* (eds) B.Qudmani-Darwish and M.Chartouni-Dubarry. Paris: Armand Colin.
Blunt, A. (1968 [1881]) *A Pilgrimage to Nejd, the Cradle of the Arab Race: A Visit to the Court of the Arab Emir and our Persian Campaign,* 2 vols. London: John Murray.
Committee for the Defense of Legitimate Rights in Saudi Arabia (CDLR) (1994) *Matha taqul lajnat al difa an al huquq al shariya fi al jazira al arabiyya.* London.
CDLR (1994) Al-huquq. *Communiques* 1–30.

Eickelman, D. (1992) Mass higher education and the religious imagination in contemporary Arab society. *American Ethnologist* 19, 4:1–13.

——(1996) Foreword. In *Civil Society in the Middle East,* vol. 2 (ed.) A.R.Norton. Leiden: Brill (pp. viii–xiv).

Eickelman, D. and Piscatori, J. (eds) (1996) *Muslim Politics.* Princeton: Princeton University Press.

Euting, J. (1983) Julius Euting, 1883–4. In *Hail: An Oasis City of Saudi Arabia* (ed.) P.Ward. Cambridge: Oleander Press (pp. 439–610).

Gellner, E. (1994) *Conditions of Liberty Civil Society and its Rivals.* Harmondsworth: Penguin.

Hann, C. and Dunn, E. (eds) (1996) *Civil Society: Challenging Western Models.* London: Routledge.

Kostiner, J. (1993) *The Making of Saudi Arabia 1916–1936: From Chieftancy to Monarchical State.* Oxford: Oxford University Press.

Norton, A.R. (ed.) (1995–6) *Civil Society in the Middle East,* 2 vols. Leiden: Brill.

Palgrave, W. (1865) *Personal Narrative of a Year's Journey through Central and Eastern Arabia (1862–1863),* 2 vols. London: Macmillan.

Wallin, G.A. (1854) Narrative of a Journey from Cairo to Medina and Mecca, by Suez, Araba, Tawila, al-Jauf, Jublae, Hail and Negd in 1854. *Journal of the Royal Geographical Society* 24:115–201.

Zubaida, S. (1995) Is there a Muslim society? Ernest Gellner's sociology of Islam. *Economy and Society* 24, 2:151–88.

The Fall of the Pharaoh
How Hosni Mubarak's Reign Came to an End

by DINA SHEHATA

FOR ALMOST 60 YEARS, EGYPTIANS HAVE CELEBRATED Revolution Day on July 23, to commemorate the day in 1952 when Gamal Abdel Nasser and the Free Officers overthrew the monarchy to establish a republic. Next year, the country will celebrate Revolution Day on January 25—the first day of the mass protests that forced Hosni Mubarak, the country's president for 30 years, from power.

For the 18 days from January 25 to February 11, when Mubarak finally stepped down, millions of Egyptians demonstrated in the streets to demand, as many chanted, "*isqat al-nizam*," "the fall of the regime." The Mubarak government first met these protests with violence, but its vast security apparatus soon crumbled in the face of an overwhelming numbers of protesters. Then, the state attempted to use propaganda and fear-mongering to scare the population back into its embrace, but this, too, failed. Finally, the Mubarak regime resorted to making concessions. However, these were too limited, and the death toll from the protests had already grown too high. Fearing that more violence would hurt the military's legitimacy and influence, the army broke with Mubarak and forced him to leave office.

The immediate trigger for the outbreak of protests in Egypt was the Jasmine Revolution in Tunisia in mid-January, which demonstrated that sustained and broad-based popular mobilization can lead to political change, even in a police state such as Tunisia. But other factors had long been at work in Egyptian politics and society. In particular, Mubarak's downfall was the result of three factors: increasing corruption and economic exclusion, the alienation of the youth, and the 2010 elections and divisions among the Egyptian elite over questions of succession. When these currents came together, they inspired a broad cross section of Egyptian society to achieve the unthinkable: removing Mubarak from power.

But the revolution did not lead to full regime change. Instead, it has achieved partial change: the military and the state bureaucracy remain in control and are likely to dictate the terms of the country's political transition over the coming months. What follows this transition will depend on whether the forces that staged the revolution can remain united and organized or whether some groups, such as the Muslim Brotherhood, strike a separate deal with the military. If this were to happen, the secular and youth movements that were the driving force behind the January 25 revolution would be effectively marginalized.

NASSER'S BARGAIN

In the 1950s and 1960s, the Nasser regime, which was at once authoritarian and populist, forged a ruling bargain with labor and the middle class. All political parties were banned and all civil-society organizations, including trade unions, came under the direct control of the regime. In return, the state provided social and welfare services in the form of government employment; subsidies for food, energy, housing, and transportation; and free education and health care.

In the early 1990s, a looming economic crisis caused by unsustainable levels of external debt forced Mubarak's government to sign an agreement on economic reform with the World Bank. Over the next two decades, the Egyptian government undertook a series of structural adjustments to the economy that reduced spending on social programs; liberalized trade, commodity prices, and interest rates; suspended the longtime guarantee of government employment for university graduates; privatized a number of public-sector companies; and suspended subsidies for many commodities. As state expenditures declined, public spending on social services—including education, health care, transportation, and housing—stagnated, and the quality of these services deteriorated.

Factory workers, landless peasants, government employees, and those who produce goods for the local market (as opposed to for export) suffered most. They depended on government services and subsidies, as well as on market protections, and many saw their fortunes fall as a result of the economic liberalization. At the same time, a new Egyptian business elite emerged: some people exploited the period of economic reform and openness to turn their contacts with the regime and international markets into vast fortunes. Just below this newly minted business aristocracy, a well-off middle class also began to develop. Thus, there soon emerged a two-tiered society: the majority of the Egyptian population was increasingly marginalized, while a small minority prospered like never before. Moreover, economic reform and liberalization led to the emergence of an unholy alliance between the ruling elite and the business elite. A select few—those closely aligned with the ruling National Democratic Party (NDP)—found themselves with special privileges to buy up public lands and public companies or put on a fast track to obtain state licenses and contracts.

Over the past five years, many workers—both blue-collar laborers and educated professionals—took to organizing strikes and other protests to show their anger at their economic disenfranchisement. These protests took place outside the control or leadership of the country's labor unions and professional syndicates, which were constrained by laws that limited their freedom to strike or carry out any protest. In 2008, property-tax collectors established Egypt's first independent trade union since 1959, the year that all such unions were brought under the control of the state. In 2010 alone, there were around 700 strikes and protest actions organized by workers across the country. However, these protests tended to focus exclusively on labor-specific demands and to shy away from political issues.

YOUNG MAN'S BURDEN

Egypt, like much of the Middle East, is in the middle of a dramatic and growing youth bulge. Today, more than half the total population of the Arab countries is under the age of 30; in Egypt, more than one-third of the population is between 15 and 29.

This demographic group faces a particularly frustrating paradox: according to the World Bank, the Middle East has both the fastest-rising levels of schooling and the highest level of youth unemployment in the world (25 percent, compared to a global average of 14.4 percent). Youth unemployment is highest among those with more education: in Egypt in 2006, young people with a secondary education or more represented 95 percent of the unemployed in their age group. Those who do find jobs often work for low pay and in poor conditions. This combination of high unemployment and low pay has kept many young Egyptian men from marrying and forming families. Approximately half of all Egyptian men between the ages of 25 and 29 are not married.

As a result of constraints on political life and civil society, youth in Egypt have been denied outlets for political and civic participation. Most cannot remember a time before the country's emergency law was last imposed, in 1981, which allowed the regime to freely persecute its challengers. Less than five percent of young people in Egypt belong to political parties, and less than 45 percent have ever participated in elections.

Partly because of such limitations, religious groups such as the Muslim Brotherhood were able to capitalize on widespread social grievances to recruit and mobilize young people in large numbers during the 1980s and 1990s. But after the state's harsh persecution of Islamists in the 1990s, youth activists began to express their grievances through a new generation of protest movements open to members of all ideological backgrounds and to those without any particular ideology at all.

One such movement is Kefaya, which has attracted legions of previously apolitical youth. In 2004 and 2005, it organized a series of high-profile protests calling for the end of Mubarak's presidency and the country's emergency law. In 2008, youth activists from Kefaya formed the April 6 Movement in solidarity with textile workers who were planning a strike for that date. The movement attracted 70,000 members on Facebook, making it the largest youth movement in Egypt at the time. Members of both the April 6 Movement and Kefaya were behind the creation of another popular Facebook group, one supporting Mohamed ElBaradei, the former head of the International Atomic Energy Agency, who returned to Egypt in February 2010.

Perhaps the most important Facebook group would arise some months later when, in June 2010, activists associated with the ElBaradei campaign created a Facebook page called "We are all Khaled Said" in memory of a young man who was beaten to death by police officers in Alexandria. Their page attracted more than one million supporters and became the focal point for a number of large protests against state abuses in the summer of 2010. By the end of 2010, Egypt's youth activists had succeeded in bypassing many of the long-standing constraints on political and civic life in the country. Although they may not have fully realized it at the time, all they needed to see their mission to the end was a final, triggering event—and that was gathering momentum some 1,300 miles away, in Tunisia.

THE EDIFICE CRACKS

As labor and youth unrest grew, another struggle was taking shape between Egypt's old guard, representing the military and the bureaucracy, and the new guard, representing Mubarak's son Gamal and his supporters in the business community and the ruling party.

Beginning in the mid-1970s, in an attempt to bolster his legitimacy both at home and abroad, then Egyptian President Anwar al-Sadat began to liberalize the political system. He allowed opposition parties and movements to gain some representation in the country's elected assemblies. As long as the ruling NDP maintained its two-thirds majority and its control over the real levers of power, the Egyptian opposition could contest elections and maintain a limited presence in parliament and in civil society. When Mubarak came to power, he continued to follow this same formula with few adjustments.

However, over the last five years, the Mubarak regime began to violate this implicit agreement, by imposing renewed constraints on the ability of political parties and movements to organize and to contest elections. Moreover, the state heavily manipulated the 2010 parliamentary elections in favor of the NDP, effectively denying all opposition groups any representation in parliament. (With opposition groups represented on the ballot but prevented from winning any races, the NDP won 97 percent of the seats.) For some in the opposition, the fraudulent elections of 2010 marked a departure from the limited political pluralism instituted by Sadat. The New Wafd party and the Muslim Brotherhood, among others, began to reconsider the utility of participating in elections under such conditions.

The regime's tactics in the 2010 elections were part of a broader plan to ensure a smooth succession from Mubarak to his son Gamal during the upcoming presidential election in 2011. This plan was the pet project of a group of businessmen closely associated with Gamal—such as Ahmed Ezz, a steel tycoon and a leading figure in the NDP—who had come to assume greater influence over the ruling party and the government in recent years. Not only did the country's opposition strongly oppose the succession plan, but many important factions within the state bureaucracy and the military were also skeptical. As 2010 came to a close, the country's ruling edifice was beginning to crack.

These underlying forces in turn spurred on the groups that participated in the mass protests in January and February: youth movements, labor groups, and the political parties that were excluded from joining parliament in 2010, including the Muslim Brotherhood. Youth activists agreed to hold protests against state brutality on Police Day, January 25. This demonstration begat others, and as the size and momentum of the protests grew, these activists formed the Coalition of January 25 Youth to present a series of demands to the regime: the resignation of Mubarak, the lifting of the state of emergency, the release of all political prisoners, the dissolution of parliament, the appointment of a government of independent technocrats, the drafting of a new constitution, and the punishment of those responsible for violence against the protesters. Egypt's youth activists refused to negotiate with Omar Suleiman, a Mubarak confidant who was appointed vice president on January 29 as a means of appeasing the protesters.

At the outset, Egypt's opposition was divided over whether to participate in the demonstrations. Some groups, such as Kefaya, the National Association for Change, the Democratic Front Party, the Tomorrow Party, and the New Wafd Party, endorsed and joined the January 25 protests, whereas other groups, such as the Muslim Brotherhood and the leftist Tagammu Party, did not officially join the protests until January 28 (although many of their younger members participated on January 25).

Many of the political groups taking part in the uprising disagreed over their demands and over how best to achieve them. Groups such as Kefaya, the National Association for Change, and the Democratic Front Party and individual leaders such as ElBaradei and Ayman Nour endorsed the demands of the youth coalition and refused to negotiate with the regime until after Mubarak stepped down. Others, however—the Muslim Brotherhood, the New Wafd Party, the Tagammu Party, and a number of independent public figures—agreed to enter into negotiations with Suleiman. These talks turned out to be short-lived: the regime refused to make any real concessions, and the protests on the street continued to escalate.

For its part, the Muslim Brotherhood threw its full weight behind the protests but purposefully kept a low profile. Its young members were an integral part of the coalition that had organized the protests, and according to some of the organizers, Brotherhood supporters constituted about one-third of the crowd occupying Tahrir

Square. Muslim Brothers made up a large share of the protesters in those cities where the group has long had a large following, such as Alexandria and El Mansura. However, throughout the protests, the Brotherhood was careful not to use religious slogans or to overshadow the secular, pro-democracy activists who were driving the demonstrations.

During the first two weeks of the revolution, labor movements and professional groups did not play a visible role, partly because the regime had shut down all economic activity during this time. However, during the final week, as economic activity resumed, workers and professionals began to organize strikes. In the two days preceding Mubarak's resignation, the country was approaching a state of total civil disobedience, with workers striking en masse in the transportation, communications, and industrial sectors. Judges, doctors, university professors, lawyers, journalists, and artists also organized protests. According to Shady El Ghazaly Harb, a leading Egyptian youth activist, it was this development that finally convinced the military to oust Mubarak and assume control.

LAST DAYS OF THE PHARAOH

During the three weeks of protests in January and February, groups that had previously competed with one another—Islamists and secularists, liberals and leftists—joined forces against the regime. There were fears that the opposition would fragment and that some factions would strike a separate deal with the regime, but such a turn of events never happened—although this had more to do with the Mubarak government's refusal to make any concessions and its apparent willingness to use violence. In the end, it was the unity of the opposition and broad-based popular mobilization that forced the military to oust Mubarak.

Unlike the opposition, the regime suffered from multiple divisions during the crisis. In the first week, the state tried to defuse the protests by sacking Gamal Mubarak as assistant secretary-general of the NDP and purging the businessmen closely associated with him from the ruling party and the cabinet. This effectively aborted the much-despised succession scenario and removed the new business elite from its privileged economic and political position.

Mubarak hoped that by removing Gamal and his business cronies, the protests would begin to lose steam. Indeed, these measures seemed to satisfy the majority of Egyptians; many observers in the media and even some opposition figures predicted that the revolution would come to a halt. However, the next day, after Mubarak announced that he would step down in September, security forces and hired vigilantes violently cracked down on the protesters—11 were shot and killed in Tahrir Square alone—turning the momentum back against the regime. Demands for Mubarak's immediate resignation intensified, and at that point, many new groups, mainly workers and professionals, joined the protests in large numbers.

The military, which until then had backed Mubarak while refraining from using force against the protesters, began to show signs of sedition. Throughout the crisis, the protesters had welcomed the presence of the military on the streets and urged it to side with them against Mubarak, as the military had done in Tunisia just weeks earlier. But until the last days of the crisis, the military seemed to back Mubarak's plan to remain in power until September and oversee an orderly transition to democracy. It took new groups joining the protests and the rising prospect of a confrontation between the protesters and the presidential guard for the military to finally break with Mubarak. On February 10, a spokesperson for the High Council of the Armed Forces delivered a communiqué that stated that the council supported the legitimate demands of the people. Mubarak was expected to resign that same night, but he did not. The next day, the military ousted him. The High Council of the Armed Forces assumed control of the country, and one week later, it announced the suspension of the constitution and the dissolution of both houses of parliament.

DEMOCRACY'S UNFINISHED BUSINESS

The revolution that pushed Mubarak from office has resulted in only a partial dissolution of his regime. The primary victims of this turn of events have been Mubarak's family, the business elites closely associated with it, leading figures in the state bureaucracy and the NDP, and members of the much-despised state security apparatus. The regime's basic structure remains largely intact, however: the military and the state bureaucracy are still in firm control of the country and in a position to dictate the course of the transition in the coming months. As of this writing, the High Council of the Armed Forces rules Egypt. The state bureaucracy, which comprises some six million people, remains in place, with state ministries and agencies largely unchanged and still responsible for managing day-to-day affairs.

Two scenarios seem possible. The first scenario involves speedy elections held over the summer, both parliamentary and presidential. This option appears to be favored by the military and the Muslim Brotherhood, but it is rejected by most of the groups that took part in the revolution. Such a schedule would benefit only those individuals and groups that are already positioned to achieve electoral success in the near future—namely, those associated with the NDP and the Muslim Brotherhood, the only two political organizations in Egypt with long-standing networks and bases of support that could be mobilized on short notice. Were such elections held, the outcome would probably be a power-sharing arrangement between the regime (or some new incarnation of it) and the Muslim Brotherhood, leaving little representation for the secular and youth groups that drove the revolution.

The second scenario would see the appointment of a three-member presidential council made up of two civilians and a military figure and the formation of a new cabinet composed of technocrats not affiliated with any one party. This option has been put forward by ElBaradei and is the apparent preference of the country's secular political parties and youth movements. The next step would be to hold presidential elections, followed by direct elections for an assembly that would then draft a new constitution. Until these elections were held, the presidential council would lift all constraints on political parties, the media, and civil-society organizations, which would allow secular forces the chance to organize themselves and attract voters. Parliamentary elections would follow the new constitution and the creation of new political parties, likely within one or two years. Such an arrangement would level the playing field and would allow secular parties and movements to compete more effectively with the NDP and the Muslim Brotherhood.

There are fears that if the first scenario prevails, the democratic revolution will be aborted and the old regime—under the guise of NDP loyalists in an alliance with the Muslim Brotherhood—will reassert itself. A new parliament, dominated by former NDP members and the Muslim Brotherhood would guide the drafting of the new constitution and would set the parameters of a new political system. Some important liberalization measures might be adopted to quell popular discontent, but full democratization would be unlikely.

If, however, Islamists and secularists remain united, the street stays mobilized, and international pressure is applied to the military, the second scenario may prevail. In this case, the various groups that drove the revolution would have the time to organize themselves into viable political parties—and only that can produce genuine democratic change.

CPSIA information can be obtained
at www.ICGtesting.com
Printed in the USA
LVHW050029010921
696483LV00002B/9